Moreton Morrell Site

Countryside Management

Countryside Management

Peter Bromley

E. & F.N. SPON

An imprint of Chapman and Hall

LONDON · NEW YORK · TOKYO · MELBOURNE · MADRAS

UK   Chapman and Hall, 2–6 Boundary Row, London SE1 8HN

USA   Van Nostrand Reinhold, 115 5th Avenue, New York NY10003

JAPAN   Chapman and Hall Japan, Thomson Publishing Japan, Hirakawacho
            Nemoto Building, 7F, 1-7-11 Hirakawa-cho, Chiyoda-ku, Tokyo 102

AUSTRALIA   Chapman and Hall Australia, Thomas Nelson Australia, 480 La Trobe
            Street, PO Box 4725, Melbourne 3000

INDIA   Chapman and Hall India, R. Seshadri, 32 Second Main Road, CIT East,
            Madras 600 035

First edition 1990

© 1990 P. Bromley

Typeset in 10/12pt Palatino by Best-set Typesetter Ltd
Printed in Great Britain at the University Press, Cambridge

ISBN 0 419 15140 0   (PB)   0 442 31290 3   (USA)

British Library Cataloguing in Publication Data

Bromley, P.
  Countryside management.
  1. Great Britain. Rural regions.
     Land use. Management
  I. Title
  333.760941
  ISBN 0-419-15140-0

Library of Congress Cataloging-in-Publication Data
available

*This book is for Gillian
and
for Jim and Ve*

Contents

Acknowledgements

Thanks are due to many people: Andy Rosen has for many years been an inspiration and a good friend; may this continue to be so. Thanks are also due to Amanda Savage (for the typing and being able to read my writing); Mark Ogden (for the photographs, and the fun we had taking them) and Mick Brabham (for the diagrams and, just as importantly, his scale of fees!).

Acknowledgement for use of original material and source ideas are due to many organizations and individuals. Wherever a diagram, table or idea is used in the text, its origin is always given. Particularly, though, I should like to thank the following organizations: The British Trust for Conservation Volunteers; the Countryside Commission for England and Wales; the Countryside Commission for Scotland; the Forestry Commission; the Centre of Environmental Interpretation; the Lake District National Park; Nottinghamshire County Council; and the Nature Conservancy Council.

Organizing, rearranging and juxtapositioning the many thoughts contained within this text has been rather like shuffling a pack of cards: that some may have been bent, dropped or lost altogether along the way is, of course, entirely my own fault.

· ONE ·

Introduction

Most people know what a doctor does. Similarly, most people know what an architect does. The level of understanding about the role of the countryside manager is a lot less developed. Indeed, it could be argued that even within professional and academic circles, the role of a countryside officer is poorly defined. The reasons for this are varied: existing professional groups such as planners and landscape architects have well-defined roles, which leads to confusion in the public's mind; the lack of clear legislative and policy guidelines for countryside work; the diverse nature of the British countryside; and the wide range of responsibilities with which a countryside officer could become involved. All of these factors play their part in bringing about confusion over what a countryside manager actually does.

This book seeks, primarily, to clarify the job of the manager, not just for the professional but also for the academic and the layperson. It also seeks to explore ways in which the countryside manager operates that set him or her apart from other environmental or landscape professionals. It is argued that countryside managers are sufficiently different – within the legislative framework in which they work and the skills that they must bring to bear – that their responsibilities can be clearly separated from other professional groups. These are detailed in later chapters where the issues of policy formulation, implementation, management, ranger services, interpretation and funding are discussed. What will become apparent is that no two countryside managers are likely to operate in exactly the same way. Some may be project based, others may concentrate upon interpretation. Others may focus their attention on publicly owned land, others on private land. Some may be site specific while others may deal with the wider countryside, however we choose to define that. This does not undermine the argument that there exists a range of core tasks for a countryside manager or that there exists, at least at a very broad level, a modus operandi. Indeed, it suggests the opposite and that within this variation in technique there is, and needs to be, a common thread.

This introductory chapter seeks to draw out some of this common thread by defining the scope of the book and by giving a brief background to the development of the work of the countryside manager.

1.1 SOME BACKGROUND

There are several key components to the background which has led to the development of countryside management. Firstly, it is necessary to take a broad look over the British psyche and its attitude towards the environment and the countryside. A further part of the picture is found in the growing concern for the countryside which is part of the growth of environmentalism that has been seen over the past twenty-five years. The final element is that of the social changes that have occurred in the countryside rather than outside it. These have brought pressure for change upon the physical environment as well as put a strain upon the social order within the countryside. Together these three form the backcloth against which we should view the role of a countryside manager.

1.1.1 Perception of the countryside

A historic perspective of the British concept of beauty and nature, and our attitudes towards access into that environment, is interesting in its own right. It has been reviewed by Lowenthal and Prince (1964) who explored the special relationship that has existed between man and the environment through time. One noteworthy trend was that of increasing empathy towards tamed, manicured environments such as those designed by the great landscape gardeners of the seventeenth and eighteenth centuries. Balanced against this was the distaste of the sophisticated people for the bleak wild places of upland England and Scotland. However, through the eighteenth century, and particularly through the nineteenth the work of the romantic poets and artists led to a new-found love for wild lovely places, thus reversing earlier trends. The lakeland poets, for example, first introduced the joys of what is now the Lake District National Park to a wider audience. Again, the relationship between literature, art and cultural perspectives on the countryside is a rich area of study but which here must interest us only in that it sets a context for the work of the countryside manager. This late nineteenth-century liking of wild moorland areas has manifested itself most noticeably in the areas designated as National Parks within England and Wales – almost exclusively upland areas. The British, then, have always had more than a passing interest in the countryside. Their taste for various aspects of it is a result of cultural, literary and personal influences which clearly vary over time.

The physical fabric of the countryside has also been subjected to many influences. The geological and geomorphological influences are beyond the scope of this discussion, but those brought about by man are clearly relevant. The land itself has its own cultural and social history. The way that these different elements have worked to create the physical countryside is well covered by a number of writers, but none, perhaps, more succinctly or evocatively than W. G. Hoskins in *The Making of the English Landscape*, the Scottish counterpart to which is, not surprisingly, *The Making of the Scottish Landscape* by R. N. Millman. Both stress the important influences that human activity has had on shaping the countryside, giving it many of the characteristics that we have come to accept as 'British'.

However, when it comes to managing or looking after that most valuable resource, the British have been particularly shy of tackling the issues. For example, the post-war Town and Country Planning framework is almost exclusively Town, not Country Planning. The cornerstone of the legislation, the 1947 Town and Country Planning Act explicitly excludes agriculture and forestry from most forms of planning control. The picture that emerges, therefore, is one of a nation drawn to the mysteries and beauty of the countryside yet officially prepared, at least in the immediate post-war years, to let the existing status quo prevail. This particular period is studied more closely in Chapter 3, where the relevant Acts of Parliament are discussed. However, it is clear that with the leisure boom of the 1960s and 1970s, as described and predicted in Michael Dower's report, *The Challenge of Leisure*, the countryside was ill equipped to take the new pressures placed upon it. This pressure came from a car-borne, mobile population seeking access to a countryside that was designed solely for the production of food or the growing of trees. Similarly, land pressure from developers for housing or industrial land and increasing alarm about the loss of habitats all brought extra strain on the countryside. However, outside urban areas there were few means available of protecting or managing the countryside to help to accommodate the new pressures. Over the years from 1945, therefore, there grew up a collection of Acts, parts of Acts, Government Circulars, reports and so on which collectively created a very loose toolbox enabling local authorities in particular to positively manage the countryside but only at the landowners consent. Thus, the issue of planning control in the countryside has been successfully avoided. This effectively fits in with the belief identified earlier that the British population equate the countryside with all that is wild and free, and the urban area as something that is ugly and in need of control. It is because of this early aversion to accept the need for some sort of 'control' in its broadest sense that such a varied collection of powers has been assembled to manage the countryside. For this reason, too, the countryside manager must have a working knowledge of a wide range of professional disciplines, including Town and Country Planning, landscape design, recreation, estate management, tourism and many more. Indeed, countryside managers are drawn from a wide spectrum of professional backgrounds reflecting this somewhat chequered history. All are, however, working to address the balance between the various pressures from agriculture, forestry, built developments, recreation, nature conservation and landscape conservation, be it on a site-by-site basis, in certain key or vulnerable areas or in the countryside as a whole.

This social, political and legislative background forms one part of the run-in to the development of the countryside manager. The other two strands identified earlier were those of the growth of environmentalism (as opposed to a 'love of the countryside') and a crisis which developed within the rural social and economic structures alongside the external pressures for change.

1.1.2   Environmentalism

Environmentalism can be seen as the popularized concern for 'the environment' which began to pick up its present momentum in the mid to late 1960s. The environment was and still is interpreted in the broadest sense, with some environmentalists particularly troubled (rightly) by global decimation of tropical rain forests and others (again rightly) concerned by local loss of community open space. All environmentalists are expressing a belief that good environmental practice need not be sacrificed because of the need for technological and social development. Indeed, it is necessary to respect and work with the environment to produce high-quality, long-lasting change. Two books in particular stand out at the advent of the environmentalist movement in Britain: Rachel Carson's *Silent Spring* and John Barr's *Derelict Britain*. Both of these drew attention to the waste of environmental resources due to over-exploitation of that same resource. Both also focused very sharply upon the problems as they related to Britain, something which until then had never been accomplished. The environmentalist concerns and the associated debate is now well documented (O'Riordan, 1976, for example) and the role of the countryside manager is part of the general movement towards good environmental practice.

1.1.3   Rural society

The third force identified as part of the background is that of rural change, which has happened within rural society itself. While no system is entirely independent of other systems, the rural socio-political scene has long been seen by the largely urban-based population of Britain as mysterious, unchanging and capable of self-maintenance for decades if not millennia. This partly explains why no major legislative powers operate over much of the rural environment. However, no system is static and change has been occurring since records began. During this century, the pace of change has quickened and has led to the rural fabric becoming strained from within as social order becomes disrupted, land-ownerships change and rural unemployment rises. This social and economic change within the rural environment is as equally well documented as environmental change. The period immediately after the First World War marked a watershed for many people. This war, from which the majority of young men from many rural areas returned either crippled or disillusioned, saw the beginning of the end of the rural existence given so much detail in *Lark Rise to Cardleford* by Flora Thompson. The changes themselves are recorded in *Akenfield* by Ronald Blyth, which plots this immediate post-war period. Since then a number of writers have traced the social and economic pressures within the countryside. A comprehensive summary is given in *Green and Pleasant Land?* by Howard Newby. The changes from landlord–tenant to owner–occupier systems are plotted, as too are the influences of the large financial institutions on land prices. One of the most striking trends is the increase in unemployment in rural areas. Where once the agricultural industry kept entire market-based communities active and viable, increased mechanization and increased reliance upon 'urban products' such as tractors, large machines and fertilizers have taken away large parts of the rural employment base. Successively, new rural employment opportunities have been sought in forestry, tourism and, more recently, farm-based recreation. None, however, will replace the labour-intensive agricultural practices that have been lost in the post-war years.

1.1.4 Summary

All of these trends were, therefore, developing in the years immediately after the Second World War, many coming to a head, like environmentalism, in the mid-1960s and early 1970s. It was exactly at this time that two of the formative bodies responsible for establishing the countryside management concept were created: the Countryside Commission for England and Wales and the Countryside Commission for Scotland. In 1968, the Countryside Commission was given its broad remit of exercising its functions 'for the conservation and enhancement of the natural beauty and amenity of the countryside, and encouraging the provision and improvement, for persons resorting to the countryside of facilities for the enjoyment of the countryside and of open-air recreation in the countryside'.

The threads came together and the opportunity for managing the countryside was taken up by a broad range of groups, independent bodies and local authorities.

1.2 PUBLIC, PRIVATE AND VOLUNTARY

The new opportunities and changes were taken and developed by a wide range of organizations, some carving new niches for themselves while others simply expanded upon existing bases and went from strength to strength. For ease of discussion, these groups and organizations are divided into three categories: public, private and voluntary. The lines between them are becoming more and more blurred, and the three sectors are no longer mutually exclusive. However, as a broad categorization, the three groups will act as a guide.

For a number of reasons, this book concentrates upon the countryside manager within the public sector, but there are many similarities between the work of such a manager in the public and private sectors. This suggestion would have been tantamount to heresy to many environmentalists not long ago. Witness for example the different reactions to the concept of 'marketing the countryside or the environment' at the Countryside Recreation and Research Advisory Group Conferences in 1984 and 1986 (notes on papers by Ken Robinson and Roger Vaughan respectively). In just two years the response turned from relative hostility towards private 'free market ideas' to an acceptance that the private and public sectors could learn readily from each other. While the countryside will never be a commodity in the same way as a can of beans, it *is* true that many countryside managers, particularly those involved with interpretation, earn their keep by actually 'selling' the appeal of the countryside through their publications and literature. Similarly, the problems associated with implementation, site wardening, and on-site education occur in both public and private sectors.

1.2.1 Public and private

The reason attention is focused upon the public sector is that, quite simply, most countryside managers are employed in the public sector, predominantly by local authorities at either county or district level. The countryside managers who are employed through the private sector are employed on recreation sites designed to realize a profit. One of the attributes of such a site is that it is situated in and has the look of the countryside. (Beaulieu and Longleat Safari Park are good examples.) There is only a very fine line between private and public sites; it could be argued, for example, that private operators protect the environment equally as well as public providers because if they did not, their profits would fall. This is not in question here. What is being suggested is that, within the legislative framework of successive Countryside Acts, the countryside manager works predominantly in the public sector. For this reason attention is concentrated on them.

Equally important is the actual responsibility laid upon local authorities by the legislation referred to above. This will be given in detail at a later stage, but it is the public sector that is responsible for the management of the countryside, and it has responded by developing the role of the countryside managers. For example, the 1968 Countryside Act, Section II, specifically states that:

> In the exercise of their functions relating to land under any enactment, every Minister, government department and public body shall have regard to the desirability of conserving the natural beauty and amenity of the countryside.

For this reason local authorities, along with some other public bodies, have expanded upon their general need to 'have regard' into a positive move to protect and develop the countryside resource. So local authorities are charged with the responsibility for the countryside and, as a result, employ most staff. These two reasons are why they are picked out for particular attention.

In all countryside circles, there no doubt remains an element of mistrust about the profit motive and environmental protection. It has already been indicated that this is not going to be debated at any length here, or that it is a reason for ignoring some of the valuable and innovative work taking place in the private sector. Like all good arguments there are two equally understandable view points at either end of a continuum somewhere along which lies the truth. Miles and Seabrooke (1977) in their early work on recreational land management stressed the comparative merits of private and public sector provision.

The equation of private and public provision does not, however, stop there. There is, of course, a third sector and one which, within the countryside and its management, is particularly strong. This, of course, is the voluntary sector. Within our field of concern the voluntary or charitable status sector runs from the multi-million pound operation of the National Trust, the nation's third largest landowner, to local, community-based wildlife trusts, which may control no more than a few pounds and a single street corner site. The whole range of organizations employ countryside management techniques in that they control people and, often, land. They try to balance competing demands for that land, namely: public access, its visual and aesthetic quality, its wildlife or natural history interest and any extraneous pressure such as that from developers or agriculture. Finally, these groups must interpret what they do and attempt to educate their members and others about the qualities of the land and resources they are trying to manage. Thus, the environmental message – the belief that the natural and semi-natural environment should be protected, not only for its own sake but also because it represents a finite resource all too easily destroyed by a range of human activities – is central to all of their philosophies. The message, along with associated information, is pitched at different levels depending upon the organization and the audience it seeks to address. The country garden, tweed suit image of the National Trust range of products is, on the surface, not connected to the hard, hand-written news sheets of the Leeds Wildlife Group for example. The similarity is, however, to be found with closer scrutiny and both are elements of interpretation and marketing.

1.2.2   Voluntary sector

The role of the voluntary sector is important in the countryside for two reasons. Firstly, the whole access and conservation movement is based upon early work and pressure from voluntary organizations and, secondly, rightly or wrongly, a lot of present political thinking sees the voluntary arrangement as being the best means of achieving environmental protection. This is witnessed by the growth in the number of Groundwork Trusts across the country and in the essence of the 1981 Wildlife and Countryside Act which lays a lot of emphasis on the voluntary protection of, in this case, Sites of Special Scientific Interest. The 1981 Act has received a lot of criticism for this approach but, in a wider context, it simply reflects present government thinking.

Early voluntary action fell into three distinct types of work; namely, nature conservation and species recording (by the still-very-prevalent-enthusiastic amateur naturalist who lies at the heart of many local wildlife trusts), the struggle for access onto private land (as exemplified by the earliest of amenity pressure groups, the Commons, Open Spaces and Footpaths Preservation Society, founded in 1865) and the out-and-out preservationists (such as the National Trust, formed in 1895 to preserve places of historic interest and natural beauty). Here then were the three main strands of countryside management, already *in situ* prior to the beginning of the twentieth century: nature conservation, access and recreation and landscape conservation. The countryside manager still deals with these central issues, but more strictly it is finding a balance between them that provides the headaches.

1.3 THE COUNTRYSIDE MANAGER

The three sectors – public, private and voluntary – all employ countryside managers in some form or another. That is, they all employ people who manage resources, one of which is the countryside or a single part of that countryside be it the landscape, the natural history or an even more specific part such as woodland. But what else does the countryside manager control or seek to influence and what sets him or her apart from other environmental professionals?

1.3.1 Resource conservation

In order to answer these questions we must sift through the historical precedents outlined in the foregoing discussion. There existed a 'gap' within the countryside which meant that few land operations in the rural environment were subject to control of any sort. Similarly, there were many concurrent pressures which were bringing about massive changes to the scale and techniques used in agricultural and forestry activities. Equal pressure was being brought to bear in the shape of the new leisured population looking for informal recreation opportunities within the countryside, and from an increasingly environmentally conscious population at that. As there were no existing mechanisms for reconciling all of these conflicting pressures, the role of the countryside manager was identified. It was, perhaps, Professor Gerald Wibberley who first identified the need for a Ministry of Rural Affairs based upon the Ministry of Agriculture, Fisheries and Food. Such a larger ministry would seek to address the recreational, social and environmental problems being faced in the countryside for which the existing planning legal framework did not allow.

Central to the manager's work is the requirement to resolve these many conflicting pressures for land use – agriculture, recreation, forestry, landscape and others. In this respect, the countryside manager is no different from, say, a town and country planner. Indeed, as we shall see later, many countryside management plans are based within local authority planning departments. However, much of the work of the manager is undertaken outside any statutory framework, so a whole host of techniques and methods are created to achieve the objective of balancing the various pressures. The need to work in harmony with the numerous agencies involved in the countryside is one of the key elements of the job of the countryside manager. It is not, however, the only one.

1.3.2 Public access

Three further key roles underlie the work of the manager. Firstly, the recreational environment of the late 1960s and 1970s ensured that any new methods and professions of environmental management had, almost by definition, to take the recreational element more seriously than had happened previously. Thus, central to any work of the countryside manager is the understanding that public access to the environment is a right and must form part of any successful scheme. This is one way in which the work of, say, the landscape architect differs from that of the countryside manager. The former might not necessarily include public access into landscape design; the latter should.

Increasingly over the years all government and quasi-government agencies have been charged with accommodating (if not encouraging) public access onto their operations where reasonable. Thus, the Forestry Commission has been empowered and charged with developing picnic sites and woodland walks/drives. To the private sector, on the other hand, this recreational element is the very life-blood of their enterprises. Without recreation, there are no members of the public 'going through the turnstiles'. Without that, there is clearly no money.

1.3.3 Interpretation

The third cornerstone to the work of the countryside manager is that of education. With the increasing concern for the environment has come an increased appetite for information about the countryside and its workings. In part, this is fed by the myriad coffee-table books or photograph collections of the British Isles. In part it is also fed by the information prepared and designed as part of the successful management of the countryside. Educative and interpretive material is discussed more fully later, but it is sufficient at this stage to acknowledge that the educative function is crucial to any countryside management programme.

1.3.4 Practical action

The final concern of the countryside manager must be to ensure that implementation takes place 'on the ground'. It is not sufficient to plan for changes or improvements to, say, the landscape or the natural history of an area; it must be the concern of the manager to develop means of achieving the desired ends. This can be through actually owning the land in question, through entering into management agreements with landowners or through any other means open to the manager. The reason that so many different types of management systems operate is because of the struggle to find a mechanism that can achieve things where it matters – within the natural and semi-natural environment. Again, the issue of implementation is covered in more detail later where the problems associated with making the jump from policy formulation to practical project implementation are addressed.

The four key roles identified above often merge to form a single element. The roles of education and implementation, for example, can both be covered by encouraging 'the community' to implement projects. With careful guidance and supervision the process of planting and nurturing a tree is probably one of the best means of learning about the environment.

This 'hands-on' education forms a central part of the work of many countryside managers. Similarly, the educative and recreational elements can be combined as part of an events programme where guided walks and nature days are provided. And again, farm open days help to overcome conflict between farmers and the public while at the same time providing an enjoyable recreational experience.

Therefore, while the four elements are isolated here, it is often not clear where one ends and another begins. That is the nature of countryside management.

1.4 WHAT IS THE COUNTRYSIDE?

Just as there is no clear definition of what constitutes the boundaries of management, as discussed above, the definition of countryside is equally vague. There is no absolute standard as to what is or is not countryside. Working definitions, on the other hand, abound. For example, one definition of countryside given in the dictionary is simply 'rural area', while both the Countryside Commission and the Nature Conservancy Council talk readily of urban countryside and urban wildlife. In geographical terms, therefore, there is, and always has been, a push-and-pull of the green line. No introduction to the subject of countryside, landscape or our changing attitudes to the environment would be complete without reference to Nan Fairbrother's work, *New Lives, New Landscapes*. Her book is particularly relevant here because she identifies the lack of a clear definition of what constitutes countryside and devotes a large part of her discussion to the green urban environment and what she terms the 'urban–rural countryside'.

Organizationally and officially the definition of countryside has also witnessed a shift away from the traditional rural idea to a wider rural–urban continuum. For example, the Countryside Commission for England and Wales took over a wider responsibility for countryside issues from the former National Parks Commission whose remit was restricted to the National Parks. (In Scotland, there was neither a National Parks Commission nor any National Parks, and therefore no comparable transitional crisis of definition.) Prior to the 1968 Act, which formed the Countryside Commissions, countryside had been virtually synonymous with wild, remote areas, many of which were eventually designated as National Parks or Areas of Outstanding Natural Beauty under the 1949 National Parks and Access to the Countryside Act. After the Countryside Commissions were formed, the definition of countryside broadened to accommodate the country park concept. Country parks were originally envisaged as 'honey pots' which were to be situated closer to the centres of population than National Parks and thus take away some of the recreational pressures from National Parks. The definition of countryside was, therefore, expanding to accommodate land closer to the built environment. This is clearly shown in rural studies' literature of the time, where the spatial arrangements of recreational and countryside resources around theoretical urban centres reflect this urbanization process (e.g. Clout, 1972)

It did not take the two Countryside Commissions long, however, to identify that the urban fringe countryside was also a valuable resource which was in danger of becoming devalued simply because it lacked a clear definition. Thus, it was prioritized as one of the key areas on which the Commissions should focus their attention. This manifested itself in the initiation of the Bollin Valley Project in 1972. This project, the forerunner of many subsequent management projects, was aimed at reconciling the conflicting interests within the Bollin Valley – a well-used river system running alongside the southern edge of the Manchester conurbation. The subsequent report (Countryside Commission, 1976) clearly identified the need to grasp the 'problems and opportunities of . . . the nearest "real" countryside'.

In planning terms, this area on the rural urban fringe is often designated as green belt, or agricultural policy area, which brings with it certain policy and planning implications and powers. However, it is now accepted that a policy designation is not sufficient in its own right and positive land management is needed to tackle the issues. Most major towns and cities now, therefore, have an urban fringe project, or an equivalent arrangement. How such a project works or operates is given in more detail later, but their existence reflects the increasing awareness that countryside can legitimately be defined as touching upon and existing alongside and within built environments.

The movement to take the countryside right into the heart of cities and towns has really been spearheaded by the wildlife or nature conservation movement, and popularized and articulated most successfully by

Chris Baines in *The Wildside of Town*. The concept of pockets of wild countryside surrounded by concrete and tarmac is an appealing one (if slightly over-stated) but for our purposes it supports the contention that countryside is not remote, not totally natural and is definitely not just rural. Simply, it is anywhere that people perceive as being countryside, natural or slightly wild and anywhere that the conflicting pressures exist.

The countryside manager can therefore operate in any of these geographical locations – anywhere along the rural–urban continuum.

1.5 SUMMARY

This introduction has done nothing more than raise some of the many issues surrounding the job of the countryside manager and offer a brief background to why the need for countryside management arose independently from the expertise available in already existing professional groups.

The important parts of this background are the social and political relationships that the British have always had with the environment, the increasing demand for access to the natural environment coupled with a legal framework ill equipped to deal with multi-landuse functions, and, more recently, the growing need for positive management which involves community and volunteer groups in the implementation of practical schemes.

It has been emphasized throughout that in order to bring all of these interests together, the countryside manager must bring a wide range of professional expertise to bear on individual projects or on wider policy decisions. The following chapters deal with each of these areas of expertise separately. The layout of the discussion is identical in each case: an analysis of the issues followed by a case study which reflects the advantages and disadvantages of one particular approach. In many respects, this is the optimal means of analysing the process of countryside management, given the many variables that surround the development and protection of the environment. In identifying the specific case studies, no implication is intended that these schemes represent the only examples available to illustrate a particular point; however, each is in its own way innovative and unique and represents a yardstick against which other projects and management methods can be measured.

The discussions devoted to each chapter vary in the amount of detail that can usefully be dealt with. Some areas, such as management theory and practice, are covered by a vast body of research and literature; to attempt to define the issues of relevance within that body of work would be time-consuming and, ultimately, unproductive. In this and similar cases, the subject is covered by discussion but with a relatively heavy reliance upon reference to alternative sources of information. Where the subject under discussion can be fully dealt with or is of key significance to the countryside manager (for example, the issues of wardening or rangers), full details are given.

Technical information, by way of relevant clauses of Acts of Parliament, contract details, specifications or design details are, by and large, included in the appendices in order not to break the main text.

BIBLIOGRAPHY

Baines, J.C. (1987) *The Wildside of Town*, Elm Tree Books, London.

Barr, J. (1969) *Derelict Britain*, Penguin Books, Harmondsworth.

Blyth, R. (1969) *Akenfield*, Penguin Books, Harmondsworth.

Carson, R. (1965) *Silent Spring*, Penguin Books, Harmondsworth.

Clout, H.D. (1972) *Rural Geography: an introductory study*, Pergamon Press, Oxford.

Countryside Commission (1976) *The Bollin Valley: a study of land management in the urban fringe*, CCP 97, Cheltenham.

CRRAG (1984, 1986) *Annual Conference: Conference Notes*, Countryside Recreation and Research Advisory Group, Bristol.

Davidson, J. and Wibberley, G. (1977) *Planning and the Rural Environment*, Pergamon Press, Oxford.

Dower, M. (1965) *The Challenge of Leisure: the fourth wave*, Civic Trust.

Fairbrother, N. (1972) *New Lives, New Landscapes*, Pelican Books, London.

Groundwork Trust (1986) *The Environmental Entrepreneurs*, Groundwork Foundation.

Hoskins, W.G. (1970) *The Making of the English Landscape*, Pelican Books, London.

Lowenthal, D. and Prince, H. (1964) The English Landscape, *Geographical Review*, pp. 309–346.

Miles, C.W.N. and Seabrooke, W. (1977) *Recreational Land Management*, E. & F.N. Spon, London.

Millman, R.N. (1975) *The Making of the Scottish Landscape*, Batsford Books, London.

Newby, H. (1979) *Green and Pleasant Land?* Hutchinson, London.

O'Riordan (ed.) (1976) *Environmentalism*, Pion Books, London.

Thompson, F. (1959) *Lark Rise to Candleford*, Penguin Books, Harmondsworth.

Town and Country Planning Act (1947), HMSO.

· TWO ·

Management

2.1 THE MANAGEMENT PROCESS

The need for management is perhaps too often overlooked but the purposes it fulfils in any organization have a direct relevance to work in the countryside.

One of the basic requirements of management is to come to terms with, and direct the constant flow of, interaction and change which occurs in the wider physical, cultural and economic environment. Drucker (1955) has suggested that 'The major concern of management . . . must be in the direction of systematically trying to understand the condition of the future so that it can decide upon the changes that can take (them) from today into tomorrow'. Management is therefore seen here as a process which both accommodates and initiates change. Given the constantly changing cultural, social and physical pressures which come to bear on the countryside, the management of change is obviously one reason to manage that environment.

A second requirement of management is that optimum use is made of resources. These resources include people, things and, more abstractly, ideas. McKenzie (1969) first identified these three types of resource available to managers. Notwithstanding the fact that 'the environment' is itself a finite resource, this model of management which brings together 'people, things and ideas' emphasizes the importance of making things happen. The link between policies, ideas or academic thinking and projects taking place on the ground is the arena within which the manager works. Often, it is this link which is most difficult to make but it is obviously crucial to the successful execution of 'good environmental practice'. Turning ideas into action is a function of management. This is particularly relevant in the countryside where, quite often in the past, the knowledge and information has been held by one group of people (the naturalists, ecologists or access groups) while implementation through the management of 'people and things' has been undertaken by other groups. Management, as defined here, brings together the three elements to ensure that the ideas flow directly into

action and the environmental lobby is not left, literally and metaphori-
cally, as a voice in the wilderness.

A third need fulfilled by management is that of providing a framework which allows different approaches to reaching objectives to be
explored. Torkildsen (1986) has suggested that 'management is malle-
able, amenable to change, flexible in organization'. Thus management
as a process allows the manager to determine his or her own way of
addressing problems or opportunities by drawing upon a series of
known and tested techniques and management tools, and indeed by
creating new techniques. By analysing management as a subject in its
own right, we gain a better grasp of the available information across
a wide range of disciplines which can then be related back to our
circumstances.

Finally, management provides a scientific basis for assessing situations. While arguably not an exact science, management does offer a
means of measuring how well objectives are being met and how best
conflicting information can be reconciled. Science is, almost by definition, objective, and within the context of a rapidly changing environment, management does offer a touchstone to which reference can be
made for some degree of objectivity. This does not mean to say that the
passion must necessarily go out of environmental debate (and there
is no issue that raises passionate debate as much as the diversion of
public rights of way, for example) but management provides a means of
drawing out of that debate work methods that lead directly to courses
of action which, in themselves, seek to bring about beneficial change.
Management, therefore, provides a relatively objective system of
working.

Management, then, is a process which must be used in order to bring
'ideas, people and things' together to meet aims and objectives and to
analyse the various means of achieving these objectives. In order to
manage, therefore, it is necessary to have a clear grasp not only of
these three groups of resources but also of the process of management
itself. By way of background, a historical perspective of the underlying
principles of management will provide an ideal introduction.

2.1.1   A historical perspective

The study of management is readily accepted as starting with Frederick
W. Taylor at the beginning of the twentieth century. 'Taylorism' was
concerned primarily with the study of management structures which
developed during the late stages of the process of industrialization.

With the apparently ever-increasing hierarchy of supervisors and
managers, two questions arose for Taylor: What special wisdom, skills or

technical knowledge was appropriate to this new kind of industrial man?; and, What basis was there for the authority that he exercised over other people? Out of Taylorism grew many early attitudes towards 'scientific management' such as bonus schemes, 'time and motion' and that the role of the manager is 'to find the best way of doing each defined task' and to present that to his or her subordinates. Thus, the work of every stage of a process should, according to Taylor, be fully planned by the manager. It is this technically minded approach to task implementation that gave rise to the 'scientific' label of Taylorism.

Partly as a reaction to the fully planned role for workers in Taylor's scenario, and partly as a result of wider sociological and psychological study, there arose a school of management loosely termed the 'human relations movement'. Based largely on work by E. Mayo (1933), the human relations ethos was that each worker would contribute to the overall progress of a project in direct proportion to his or her feelings of involvement or belonging. The social wellbeing of workers was equally as important as physical and environmental factors. It is from this school of management that much of our employer-based provision of recreational facilities arises. If the workers are happy, they will be more productive, and from here came the now accepted 'fringe benefit', the purpose of which is to improve the workers' sense of wellbeing and thus productivity. However, it is easy to identify the continuity with Taylor. The pre-occupation with both schools of study is that the efficiency of the workers can be improved although the means of achieving this differs greatly.

This brief analysis gives only scant regard for the two vast areas of study and empirical research. Wren (1972) has given more considered attention to the development of management thought from Taylor to the present day.

Running concurrently with the concern for worker efficiency was the study of the organizations within which managers operated. Within the organization, the manager has clearly defined functions, which were identified most succinctly by Fayol (1930) as: planning, organizing, commanding, co-ordinating and controlling. These areas were, as Fayol saw it, guidelines within which numerous other skills or 'principles' would be brought to bear. However, they ultimately become accepted not as guidelines but as absolute standards. From this grew 'classical management theory' concentrating on organizational systems and functions. From here many management systems, particularly in local government, have their roots; bureaucratic administration structures, departmentalization and that ubiquitous substance, red tape. As Stinchcombe (1965) has suggested, 'organizational types generally originate rapidly . . . but grow and change slowly after that period'.

The amount of work, study and empirical data collected on or about organizations is enormous. The benefits of exploring too deeply the outcome of this work is questionable, firstly, because of the sheer volume of work that would need to be condensed and, secondly, because from all the work one common thread is that 'industrial systems (are) an institutional apparatus with wide variations in appropriateness and effectiveness' (Burns, 1969). Thus, it is sufficient to know that organizational systems can and do vary, but if Stinchcombe is to be believed, they do not change much after their original inception. This clearly brings into question their effectiveness in addressing new and rapidly changing situations.

Recent management analysis has tended to move away from the single-minded desire for the efficient worker or the efficient organization. 'Behaviourists' have concentrated instead upon the individual and his or her basic requirements. From the individual building blocks, the organizational or industrial system can be built. The concern of the behaviourists, whose work can be associated with sociologists such as Illich, Fromm and Maslow, is that the individuals attain personal goals with their work and personal lives. Similarly with managers. Managers want to have control over their own decisions, want to be recognized as individuals and want to accomplish something that they consider to be worthwhile.

Maslow (1954) explored a hierarchy of human needs (Figure 2.1) which suggested that from the basic biological requirements of food and shelter, the human psyche requires, firstly, security then acceptance, then ultimately, self-esteem, and 'self-actualization'. This is required not only in the individual's personal life but also in the individual's work life. More correctly, the various elements of 'work, rest and play' actually intermesh into a wider 'lifestyle'.

Following Maslow, McGregor (1966) identified two ends of a management spectrum. His 'Theory X and Theory Y' analysis marks a turning point for modern management thinking. 'Theory X' states that people only work because they are made to or paid to: the carrot and the stick need to be used to get all individuals to work. McGregor felt that this is a totally inappropriate view of modern individuals. 'Theory Y' therefore states that people can and do choose to exercise individual control, set their own goals and can manage themselves. The role of the manager is therefore to support this individual motivation and provide the context of organization goals. Until Maslow had articulated his points, classical management theory had suggested that individuals needed rules, control and well-established institutional mechanisms to produce motivation at work. It is safe to say that many individuals seek to work in the countryside to escape these constraints. Likert (1967) elaborated upon

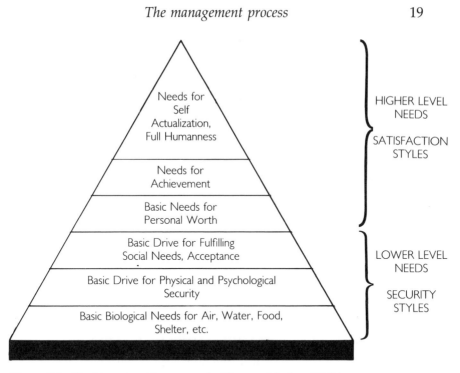

Figure 2.1 *The hierarchy of human needs.* (Source: *Maslow, 1954.*)

McGregor's work to suggest that along the 'Theory X and Theory Y' continuum, four management types exist: System 1 is authoritative–exploitive; System 2 is benevolent–authoritative; System 3 is consultative; System 4 is participative. This equates readily to the four styles of leadership identified later of 'tell, sell, participate and delegate'.

Large amounts of empirical data lie behind these generalizations, and the styles and techniques have been tested against real-life management structures. To summarize much of the recent study, it is evident that individuals within all management systems have self-set goals, objectives and requirements that relate to both their work and themselves as individuals – Maslow's 'self-actualization'. The role of the manager has therefore developed significantly from earlier models which had the manager as the only individual with responsibility, power and knowledge. The role of the manager, as identified by Fayol, is to plan, organize, command, co-ordinate and control (Fayol, op. cit.). This role has developed into a much more complex and sophisticated process, wherein the manager must balance the objectives of the organization with those of the individuals within it and with his own objectives. The manager is no longer directly responsible for all of the planning, commanding, controlling and so on, but is more likely to provide a suitable framework within which others can take these decisions. This framework is provided by helping the workforce establish its objectives, and within these criteria, work towards the objectives. Further support is given through developing a suitable management culture of open discussion and mutual trust.

Countryside management requires the bringing together of many skills, and the manager cannot be expected to be the master of all of these individual skills. Mutual respect and team work are therefore more appropriate than the Fayol-type plan–command–control system of management. The manager must also manage change and help the team to work through their problems. Again, this is a crucial component of management in the countryside where change is often rapid.

The manager is therefore no longer a commander but is part of a team. He or she is nonetheless ultimately responsible for the performance of that team, with a clearly defined role to play within it. Management is no easy task.

2.2   MANAGEMENT AND THE COUNTRYSIDE

There is no doubt that much of the above discussion will leave many environmentalists 'stone cold'. The world of management and organizational structures is a million miles away from the plight of the greater-horseshoe bat or the struggle for access to open land. Or is it? There is much to be gained from even a summary analysis of management thinking. Indeed, there has been a lack of desire on the part of many environmentalists or naturalists to enter into the world of 'management'. As has already been identified in the introductory chapter, the well-meaning amateur is one of the cornerstones of the modern countryside management system, but in a world where multinational decision making exploits the environment on a large scale, an increased managerial expertise of the countryside worker will only increase the impact that they have on this high-level decision making.

This, of course, has already been widely accepted. Many wildlife trusts, for example, are now firmly committed to professional management and many of the management techniques used by the British Trust for Conservation Volunteers, for example, are identical to those operated within industry or the Civil Service.

The management studies discussed in the previous section are of direct relevance to the countryside manager for three reasons. Firstly, they allow us to identify the basic skills needed by any managers which, by definition, are also needed by countryside managers. These skills include communications, decision making, personal management, and team building. Secondly, they allow us to explore organizational systems and types of management which may or may not suit different situations. Finally, they provide a comparison which can be used to assess the suitability of management systems.

2.3   ELEMENTS OF MANAGEMENT

Is management an art or a science? Can it be learned or is it something with which people are born? In truth, management is all of these things, and more. To quote Torkildsen (1986): 'Management is a continuous process. It is both human behaviour and a continual process. It is both flexible and changeable. It needs a framework, core elements, basic functions and logic to achieve its results, for management is a means towards ends.'' There are obviously parts of the management process which can only be learned through experience; but like all other processes there are many elements that can be taught. These are the tasks that all managers perform, either explicitly or implicitly, at which the manager must become adept in order to fulfil the roles expected of him or her. Thus, in order to plan, forecast objectives, motivate and monitor, managers must be able to make decisions, lead, communicate, develop organizational structures, build effective teams and, equally importantly, manage themselves, and coach and counsel work colleagues. The core elements of team building, decision making, communication, leadership styles, coaching and counselling and self-management are each, individually, important parts of a manager's make-up. Collectively, they set unique styles of management. It is therefore necessary for managers, firstly, to understand the individual elements and to know that each one can take many forms. (How many styles of leadership are there, for example?) Secondly, it is important for managers to be able to identify their own techniques and, finally, having understood their own techniques and measured them against the range of available techniques, it is necessary for managers to assess whether their individual styles are appropriate or fully developed in order to accomplish their own objectives.

This section examines the core elements of management and indicates how general management techniques can be applied to specific management situations.

2.3.1   Leadership

Until relatively recently, management has been synonymous with leadership. A good manager is a good leader: someone who tells subordinates what to do, someone who leads by example and makes most if

Management

not all of the necessary decisions. Traditionally, there have been leaders and followers, but, as we have seen, management is no longer as clear cut as this, if indeed it ever was. The work of the behaviourists has shown that all individuals, whether at work or in their leisure time, seek to establish their own objectives and take some part in controlling their own lives. Consequently, leadership styles are now seen as varying and, equally important, no single technique of leadership is 'right' for all situations. Managers must be able to adapt different styles of leadership for different situations. For example, in a 'crisis' situation the manager must take quick and often autonomous decisions and take control; for example, as leader when accidents occur on guided walks. This type of leadership would not, however, be appropriate in determining a five- or ten-year policy programme: in this situation leadership could be most effectively given by generating and sustaining discussion and innovative ideas. In short, therefore, the manager can no longer be expected to give 'leadership' in the traditional form.

(a) Leadership models

The range of leadership styles was studied by Tannenbaum and Schmidt (1958), who proposed a continuum of styles, as shown in Figure 2.2. The variables within their model are the amount of authority used by the leader and the amount of autonomy allowed to subordinates in reaching decisions. At one extreme, on the left of the model, is the manager who exercises tight direct control over all issues. At the other end of the continuum is the manager who releases all possible autonomy to his or her subordinates.

Tannenbaum and Schmidt identified six leadership behaviour points along the continuum, which are shown on the model. The 'short hand' for these behaviour points is summarized as 'tell, sell, participate and delegate'. It must be stressed that, with changing circumstances, each of these styles can be appropriate; a good manager will establish the optimal style to adopt in any given situation.

The concept of a continuum is important for several reasons. Firstly, it allows the manager to decide what style of leadership to adopt and gives an indication of the range of choices available. At all points on the continuum the manager is still ultimately responsible for the outcome of any decision made due to his or her leadership style and it cannot be over-stressed that delegation is not a means of abdicating responsibility. For this reason, many leaders choose the 'safest' option and keep a very tight control on all decisions.

The continuum of styles also helps all group members to identify how their manager operates and thus allows them some input into the

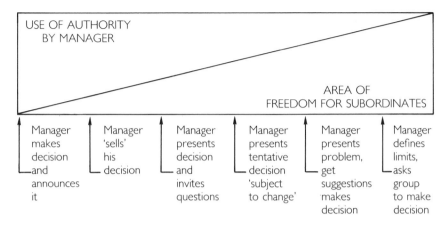

Figure 2.2 *Management and leadership styles.* (Source: *Tannenbaum and Schmidt, 1958.*)

management process. If, for example, decisions that subordinates feel should be made not by the manager but by the subordinates themselves are actually being given by the manager, the subordinates can question the leadership style of the manager in that specific situation, without personalizing or generalizing any disagreements.

Finally, the continuum allows the leader to determine what his or her preferred style of management is, and gives a mechanism for assessing the effectiveness of the manager. If a manager continually pushes decisions back to his or her subordinates, and refuses to take autonomous decisions even when pressed, the model allows the manager (and his or her superiors and subordinates) to identify this, question its effectiveness and, if necessary, explore alternatives for a better leadership style.

Several models exist which allow managers to assess their leadership styles. A good example can be found in Hersey and Blanchard (1972) which measures both leadership style and leadership effectiveness. Their argument is that managers may have a wide range of leadership styles, but if applied inappropriately this can be as ineffective as just using one style. Conversely, a manager can be more effective by improving upon a preferred style, and adapting that to suit circumstances.

Hersey and Blanchard identified four management behaviour styles, namely:

1. *High task–high relationship* in which the leader seeks to achieve tasks and to maintain good interpersonal relationships.

2. *High task–low relationship*   in which the leader seeks to achieve tasks but is not concerned about interpersonal relationships.

3. *Low task–high relationship*   in which the leader sees the maintenance or creation of good interpersonal relationships as more important than achieving tasks.

4. *Low task–low relationship*   in which the leader does not seem to know where his or her priorities lie. Not to be recommended.

(b)   Choosing a leadership style

The above model, and that of Tannenbaum and Schmidt, identify the range of leadership styles available to the manager and, in the case of Hersey and Blanchard, offers a means of assessing one's own style. Having obtained all this information, how does the manager assess the optimal leadership style in a given situation: what are the parameters which should determine how leadership is given? Leadership style depends upon three elements; namely, the task in hand, the organization and the people in it, and the behaviour pattern of the manager (see Figure 2.3). As each of these three parameters changes, so too will the style of leadership.

Figure 2.3 *Influences on the process of leadership.*

(a) *The task* The most important item in any leadership decision is the task or problem being addressed. For example, the leadership style to be adopted by a ranger on a leisurely tour of a lowland farm is different from that required of a ranger who is leading a 10-mile guided walk across moorland. In the former, the task is one of interpretation and education, so a reactive, discussive type of leadership is required. In the latter, a main consideration is getting from A to B safely, so a more authoritative leadership style would be appropriate. The task in hand, therefore, shapes the style of leadership to a great extent.

(b) *The organization* The individuals within an organization help to determine leadership styles. To take the above example, the leadership style of a ranger leading a farm tour will vary according to whether the group consists of school children or adults. In a more obvious work setting, inexperienced staff cannot be given delegated authority unless they are willing and able to accept delegation. Similarly, a farm project officer, with many years of experience in a certain area, may well want more delegation. There are several preconditions which must exist before subordinates can be given greater degrees of authority; these include a desire for independence, acceptance of the lack of clear orders, an understanding of the task in hand, sufficient knowledge of the importance of being delegated, authority and a willingness to generate mutual trust and respect.

(c) *The manager* The third important determinant of leadership style is clearly the behaviour pattern of the manager. He or she can develop management techniques, analyse his or her own particular style and assess the organizational requirements, but personality will always have an impact. This cannot be avoided, so it is necessary to acknowledge that it happens and at least be aware of the implications for effective leadership.

(c) Summary

The above discussion has shown that the manager is free to choose a leadership style from a range of options, depending upon external circumstances. These external circumstances depend upon three core elements – namely, the task, the organization and the manager. As these vary, so too should the manager's response to each situation. His or her leadership style should vary to meet set needs.

It is also suggested that all countryside staff, not just senior staff, can and do 'lead' in a variety of ways. Therefore, just as there is a responsibility on managers to involve subordinates in leadership, so

too must all staff accept the authority they hold, either within the organization or as 'leader' of members of the public on guided walks, farm open days or supervising staff.

2.3.2   Decision making

One of the key roles of the manger is decision making. Like the concept of management itself, decision making is a somewhat illusive concept yet all people, managers and non-managers alike, continually make decisions. A large part of the science of decision making is that of identifying which decisions need to be made and their likely outcomes. This infers that the process of decision making is as important as the actual decision itself. As with all elements of the management process, a number of alternatives are available to the manager in making decisions, all of which should be familiar to him or her.

(a)   Type of decision

There are a number of different types of decision which all managers face. Firstly, the crisis decision which needs to be made in an emergency. Although, ideally, these types of decision should be minimized through careful planning, it is inevitable that they will arise from time to time – if a storm leaves woodland in a dangerous condition, for example. The second is the organizational decision, e.g. where a set of guidelines or routines already exist and where decisions are made within limited predetermined criteria, or where work has to be allocated to one of a number of staff. Effectively, these types of decision maintain the existing organizations status quo. The third type is the planned decision where the manager anticipates decisions that need to be made and allocates time to manage the process of decision making effectively.

It will become evident that the actual process of decision making remains the same in all types of decision, although the amount of time available for making a decision and the number of 'free parameters' within which decisions are made will vary. With crisis decision, for example, the decision-making process needs to be contracted into a very short period of time – often only seconds. With organization decisions, many parameters are preset so much of the uncertainty of the decision is removed. Only with the planned decision can the full process be analysed with any accuracy.

Even a brief glance at the world around suggests that many decisions are only taken once a problem or, more accurately, its symptoms become obvious. This is often referred to as crisis management and as well as being very effective at creating headaches it is also a very responsive and thus negative way of reacting to situations! Further-more, decisions made in a crisis run the risk of finding cures for the symptoms of a problem rather than the underlying problem itself.

The organization decision also has its drawbacks. Most obviously this type of decision is important for the overall organization, but for the individual manager it is a very routine, unimaginative type of decision. It neither stretches nor develops the decision makers capabilities.

Once again, therefore, the planned decision is clearly the optimal one for both the individual and the organization, and it is the process involved in making planned decisions that must interest us.

(b) The decision-making process

Many writers have analysed the decision-making process from numerous different standpoints. The theorist (e.g. Edwards and Tuerskey, 1967), the statisticians (e.g. Moore and Thomas, 1976) and the pragmatists (e.g. Bunn *et al.*, 1976) have all analysed the decision-making process and identified a number of key steps. The actual number of key stages also varies according to author, but for our purposes they contain a number of common elements, most notably that they are all problem or objective orientated. Below is one assessment of the key stages in problem-orientated decision making.

(a) *Problem definition*   Clearly and accurately defining the problem to be solved is the most important step in the process. Often the problem will not be the first thing that is obviously 'wrong', but it will lie elsewhere. Similarly, the problem may not actually be identified as such. For example, a country park which attracts fewer visitors than the manager feels it could or should accommodate is not, in com-mon parlance, a 'problem', but for decision-making purposes it is. A very clear understanding of the issue that is being addressed is of crucial importance.

(b) *The alternatives*   Once a clear picture of the problem has been assembled, the search for alternative solutions can begin. Problems that have only one solution are few and far between. The more alternatives that are available, the stronger the options that are available for the manager. This part of the process also involves gathering all the necessary information surrounding both the problem and the alternative solutions. This information might be hard data (visitor numbers, plant surveys, etc.), opinion (the views or analyses of colleagues, for example) and an assessment of con-straints (legal boundaries or land ownership problems).

(c) *The consequences of alternatives* This stage is one of analysis, wherein the outcome of the alternative courses of action is assessed. 'If we do A what will happen and how will this differ from what happens when we do B?'

(d) *Choose from alternative* This is what most people would see as being decision making, but, as is being stressed here, it is only part of the overall process.

(e) *Implementing the decision* Managers are concerned with achieving results, so any decision must be implemented. This step involves many sub-stages, largely because those implementing the decision will often not be the same group of people who make the decision. One obvious way of overcoming this problem is to allow those people who will implement decisions to make or be party to the decisions – that is, keeping decision making as low as possible within the organization. In this way commitment to the decision can be generated, communication can be streamlined and motivation and job satisfaction will be maintained. A further consideration is that of determining who should be told of the decision, and how. For example, a decision to try a new footpath management technique to protect worn surfaces will be ineffective if the public are not at least told of the decision. If they are not, they are likely to keep using the old, worn route. Communication is itself a major element of management.

(f) *Monitoring* Monitoring the effectiveness of decisions is vital, but can only be realistically achieved if the problem is defined in the first instance. It is impossible to say if a problem has been solved if the problem was not identified in the first place. In this stage the opinion and evaluation of as many people as possible are needed, particularly people at the sharp end of an organization – rangers, receptionists or project managers.

These are the key stages within the decision-making process and the manager will become more effective in making decisions if each of the skills necessary in the process is developed. Each of the elements is discussed more fully later in the book. Implementation, for example, is discussed in Chapter 6, while problem definition is examined later in this chapter. The key skill which most directly follows that of decision making is 'communication'.

2.3.3 Communications

The game of Chinese Whispers depends upon people communicating badly. In the work situation too, poor communication results in many problems that could easily be avoided. There are, however, no secrets to effective communication.

Communication is a multi-purpose tool which can have a number of functions, such as passing on information, creating a reaction, persuading someone or transferring ideas. The aim of effective communication must therefore be to transfer a thought, idea or information to another person so that they have the same understanding of that thought, idea or information as the sender.

There are clearly a number of barriers to effective communication, and these can be summarized as follows:

(a) *Hearing what we want to hear*   Not actually listening to or absorbing what is being said to us.

(b) *Perception about the communicator*   If we do not have a high opinion about the sender of the message, we will tend not to attach any significance to the message itself.

(c) *Ambiguity*   The actual words or the content of the message might not be absolutely clear.

(d) *Jargon*   Use of unclear or vague words.

(e) *Emotional content*   Letting emotions or subjective opinion cloud statements or reception of messages.

(f) *Wrong medium*   Choosing a means of communication which is inappropriate to the message or the people involved.

Similarly, there are a number of means of overcoming these barriers which involve anticipating how the receiver will accept your message, choosing a suitable medium and using feedback. Communication is a two-way process, not a series of one-way orders. Kent (1981) described three common communication systems (Figure 2.4) which ironically suggests that the commonest system – the 'Chain' – is perhaps the least effective. He suggests, therefore, that a number of communication systems be used. He describes four – namely, 'hierarchical', 'technical', 'status' and 'friendship'. However, throughout all the communication systems the need for two-way working is emphasized.

2.3.4   Team development

The concept and practice of leadership, decision making and communication all imply the existence of a team. As elsewhere, the functioning of teams or work groups has been subjected to a large amount of research. It is agreed generally that teams function on two different levels. Technical team roles are those that a team member

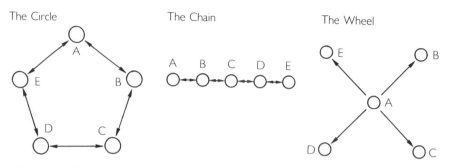

Figure 2.4 *Communication networks.* (Source: *Kent, 1981.*)

is employed to undertake. In our context these may be the roles of ranger, project officer, public-rights-of-way officer, planner or landscape designer. However, teams function and interact at a more personal level, and team roles can also be identified at this level too. Belbin (*The Observer*, 1980) has argued that a successful team has a good balance not only of technical skills but also for these 'team roles'. He also argues that a successful team is far more successful than any individual can hope to be.

The technical skills required of countryside managers are examined in later chapters, but the team role concept warrants further discussion. These team roles are based upon psychometric analyses of four principle traits: intelligence, dominance, introversion/extroversion and stability/anxiety. Eight different roles were identified, the traits of which are given below:

(a) *Chairman*   Not necessarily the team leader, but within the team he or she tends to co-ordinate effort to meet external goals. The chairman is stable, dominant and extrovert.

(b) *Shaper*   The shaper is full of nervous energy and is very much task orientated. The shaper wants to see projects pushed along, and is anxious, dominant and extrovert.

(c) *Plant*   This person is seen as the source of original ideas, without possibly having a grasp of application or implementation. The plant is dominant, intelligent and anxious.

(d) *Monitor*   The monitor tends to be dispassionate and analyses ideas and projects objectively. It is the role of a critic rather than a creator, and the monitor is intelligent, stable and introvert.

(e) *Company worker*   This role is one of a practical organizer. He or she turns ideas into manageable tasks that are feasible. The company worker is stable and controlled.

(f) *Resource investigator* This individual gathers information, ideas and resources from outside the team. Usually immediately likeable, the resource investigator explores and builds upon others ideas, and is stable, dominant and extrovert.

(g) *Team worker* The team worker is most aware of people's individual needs. He or she is loyal to the team and helps to cement it together. Stable, extrovert and low in dominance are normal characteristics.

(h) *Finisher* As the name implies, the finisher checks the finished programme and is never happy until all details are checked and all deadlines are met. Finishers are usually anxious and introvert.

In teams of less than eight, Belbin agrees that dual roles will be adopted by individuals, but in teams of over eight some conflict may arise, particularly between shapers or chairmen. However, the optimal balance of both technical ability and team roles, once achieved gives enormous benefit in increased performance. The importance of balanced team roles varies according to situations, but in areas of change and project implementation, all the team roles are needed.

Successful teams also develop their own dynamism. It is the manager's responsibility to nurture and encourage this dynamism. Argyris (1976) has identified ten components of a successful team.

(a) Contributions made within the team are additive.
(b) The group moves forward as a unit.
(c) Decisions are usually made by consensus.
(d) Commitment to decisions is strong.
(e) The group continually evaluates itself.
(f) The group is clear about goals.
(g) It generates alternative approaches to situations.
(h) It brings conflict into the open and deals with it.
(i) It deals openly with feelings.
(j) The group gives leadership to the person(s) most qualified in a given situation.

A team which is balanced and exhibits these attributes will clearly be more successful and productive than a disparate group of individuals.

2.3.5 Self-management

There is an infinite supply of management maxims which suggest that the first role for managers is to manage themselves:

'You can't manage others if you can't manage yourself.'

'A tidy desk means a tidy mind.'

'Every manager is responsible for his own development.'

and so on. As with other elements of management, there are no secrets to self-management. Personal skills such as time management, counselling skills and overcoming personal blockages can all be learned. The key to success in achieving any of these personal goals is, firstly, to be able to assess the existing situation; secondly, to be aware of how desired changes might be achieved; and, finally and most importantly, there must be a personal desire to bring about change. It is clear, therefore, that if managers want more control over their working levels, they must accept the responsibility that this brings by controlling or managing themselves. It is this that most individuals find difficult – even threatening. For this reason several sophisticated exercises have been developed for managers to objectively assess themselves to allow them to 'manage themselves'. Only by establishing where they are situated along the continuum of differing personality profiles can managers, firstly, assess whether that is where they want to be and, secondly, plan any changes they wish to make.

Most of the self-assessment techniques evaluate a wide range of personality traits such as self-esteem, aggressiveness, stress level, avoidance of issues and so on. Once this wide-ranging assessment has been made it is then up to qualified management counsellors to reflect the results back to the manager and then help to make any changes that are required by the manager.

The essence of this process is that while it might actually be uncomfortable for individuals to be faced with a 'true' reflection of their personality, in the long term the managers can actually choose how they wish not only to manage but also to live their life. This concept of absolute choice is almost diametrically opposed to the older concept that 'managers are born not made'. In this respect, the science of management has turned through 180 degrees.

2.4 SUMMARY

The science of management has moved progressively through several distinct phases. Present-day attitudes centre as much around the needs of the individual as those of the organization. This, at the same time, makes management more difficult and yet more rewarding. The essence of modern management techniques is that there is always a choice – how to lead, how to make decisions, how to create team spirit and, ultimately, how to manage oneself. Faced with this wide array of choices, the manager could easily become lost, or be forgiven for simply adopting one style and forgetting the concept of choice. However, a countryside manager is no different from any other manager as that person must have a grasp of the concepts of management as well as the concepts and issues of 'the countryside'.

All of these different elements, such as team building, decision making or leadership, need to be put together in countryside management. Increasingly, countryside management is being undertaken through teams of individuals rather than by single people so all the elements of management must also be brought to bear in a team situation.

The following extract shows eight management systems as identified by D'Arcy Cartwright (1968). They all refer to team situations, and even a swift analysis of the types suggest that the 'Executive Style' is most suited to modern countryside management. It is both concerned with achieving results (i.e. actually implementing schemes on the ground) while at the same time accepts that personal commitment and individuality of team members form an inevitable part of work. It is difficult to imagine a type of work more capable of generating commitment and individuality than countryside management!

> The Deserter is a manager who lacks interest in both the task and relationships and often shows it. He or she is ineffective, not only because of the lack of interest but also because of the effect of this on morale. Deserters shirk their own responsibilities and hinder the performance of others through intervention or by withholding information.
>
> The Bureaucrat shows only tacit interest in the task and relationships. However, this manager is partially effective in that he or she follows the rules, maintains an air of interest and gets less personally involved in problems. The Bureaucrat goes through the right channels and is a stickler for detail. His or her orientation is to the rules of the game; statutes are dogma.
>
> The Missionary is the kindly soul who puts happy relationships above all other considerations. Because of a low commitment to the task, a lack of responsibility in facing disagreements and an attitude to conflict which leads to poor management and low output, this manager is ineffective.
>
> The Developer is one who places implicit trust in people. He or she is the 'effective cousin of the Missionary'. The difference between them is that the developer works with and motivates people in a given situation and develops the talents of others.
>
> The Autocrat is one who puts the task above all other considerations, has no concern for relationships, he has no confidence in other people

and is therefore ineffective. People fear and dislike the Autocrat, working only when pressured. The Autocrat has a powerful effect on the organization and does not know it. He or she helps to produce cliques, trouble-makers and deserters. 'At best he gets blind obedience, at worst he gets desertion.'

The Benevolent Autocrat places implicit trust in his or her own sound procedures. This is an effective manager whose main skill is getting other people to do what he or she wants them to do without resentment. Although like the task-orientated Autocrat, the approach is 'smoother'. Knows the job and the people and by and large gets the job done.

The Compromiser is both task and relationships orientated in situations where only one or the other is appropriate. Ambivalence and compromise appear to be his trademark. All that perpetuates mediocrity perpetuates the Compromiser's style.

The Executive style is reflected in the behaviour of the manager who sees the job as effectively maximizing the effort of others in both the short and long run task. He or she sets high standards for production and performance but recognizes that because of individual differences it is necessary to treat everyone a little differently. The Executive is effective in that commitment to both task and relationship is evident to all, and this acts as a powerful motivation. His or her effectiveness in obtaining results in both these dimensions also leads naturally to high production.

'Executive' management is often team management. The manager encourages participation and obtains commitment. He or she handles disagreement and conflicts as natural phenomena and through these situations achieves commitment and results. All the team feels intimately involved in both failures and successes.

2.4.1 Management by objectives

Just as there are several types of management styles, there are several types of management systems. Some are technically orientated, such as the Critical Path Method which identifies flow systems and key points needed to accomplish given tasks. However, of most relevance to us here is MBO, or Management By Objectives. Management by objectives has several underlying principles. Firstly, that there is more than one way of achieving a goal or objective. Secondly, individuals within a team can decide for themselves what is the optimal route (*for them*) to reach a goal or objective. Finally, a major component of MBO is that, if all individuals within a team help to set the team's objectives, this in turn helps to generate commitment. Ordiorne (1965) defines it thus:

. . . a process whereby the superior and subordinate managers of an organization jointly identify its common goals, define each individual's major areas of responsibility in terms of the result expected and use these measures as guides for operating (the team) and assessing the contribution of each of its members.

The role of the manager is therefore one of helping the team to identify goals or objectives, identifying individual roles and objectives for individuals and monitoring the team and individual goals. It must also be recognized, of course, that individuals, and for that matter teams, will have not only organizational objectives but also personal, professional and team objectives.

This again appears to be most suited to countryside management, in that it accepts that individuals within an organization (such as public-rights-of-way officers, landscape planners or foresters) are not only capable of setting their own objectives but also have a desire and a right to do so. Clearly, once specific projects are identified which meet the stated objectives, a more rigorous system of planning, programming, budgeting and monitoring could be set up. In overall terms, however, the concept of management by objectives is a useful framework for operation. Having said this, it is surprising how many organizations, including countryside teams, operate in a vacuum, without ever stating team objectives, individual objectives or indeed wider organizational objectives.

2.5   CASE STUDIES

Throughout the book, actual working examples of countryside management will be used to illustrate specific points. There are three reasons for this: firstly, examples of good practice help to identify specific details not possible in a general discussion; secondly, as mentioned in the introductory chapter, there are so many methods and systems used in countryside management that only by giving examples can this wide range be described; and finally, actual examples help to tie in some of the theoretical discussion.

Within the general area of management it is worth raising two specific examples: the management plan and the management of countryside projects.

2.5.1   Management plan

If countryside management has a secret weapon it must be the management plan! The relevance here is clear because a management plan seeks to guide practical and physical developments towards clearly stated goals and objectives – MBO on a site-

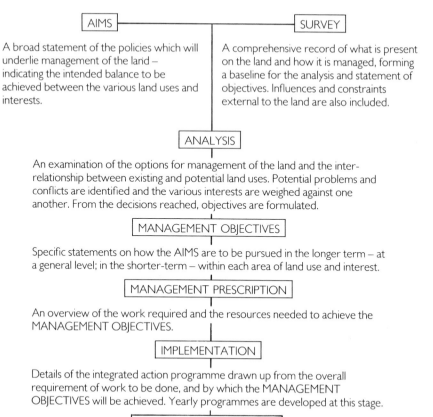

AIMS — SURVEY

A broad statement of the policies which will underlie management of the land – indicating the intended balance to be achieved between the various land uses and interests.

A comprehensive record of what is present on the land and how it is managed, forming a baseline for the analysis and statement of objectives. Influences and constraints external to the land are also included.

ANALYSIS

An examination of the options for management of the land and the inter-relationship between existing and potential land uses. Potential problems and conflicts are identified and the various interests are weighed against one another. From the decisions reached, objectives are formulated.

MANAGEMENT OBJECTIVES

Specific statements on how the AIMS are to be pursued in the longer term – at a general level; in the shorter-term – within each area of land use and interest.

MANAGEMENT PRESCRIPTION

An overview of the work required and the resources needed to achieve the MANAGEMENT OBJECTIVES.

IMPLEMENTATION

Details of the integrated action programme drawn up from the overall requirement of work to be done, and by which the MANAGEMENT OBJECTIVES will be achieved. Yearly programmes are developed at this stage.

MONITORING AND REVIEW

A record and assessment of management achievements together with proposals for periodic review.

Figure 2.5 *Management plans: a summary of the process by the Countryside Commission. (Source: Countryside Commission, 1986.)*

by-site basis. The Countryside Commission define a management plan as 'a site specific document prepared by the countrolling owner, occupier or manager of a piece of land and which guides the planning and management of that land' (Countryside Commission, 1986). The difficulties that arise in the production of management plans are as a result of the confusion over issues and objectives rather than any disagreement over format. For these reasons, the Countryside Commission and the Nature Conservancy Council offer different approaches to the production of management plans. Their outlines are given in Figures 2.5 and 2.6. The approach of the Nature Conservancy Council, particularly regarding data collection, is geared to natural history – for obvious reasons. Although of some

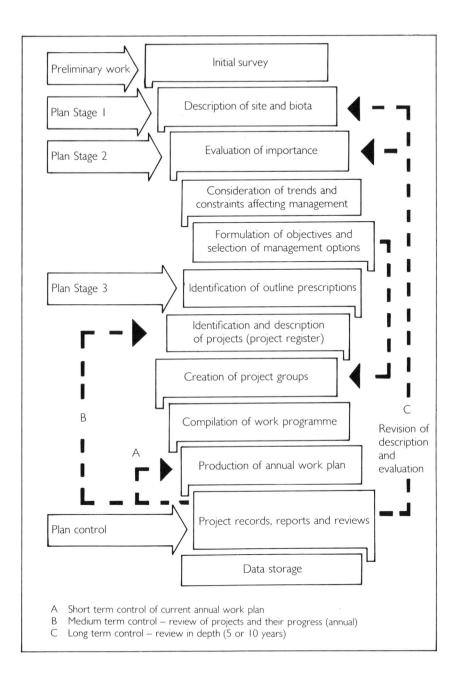

Figure 2.6 *Management plans: a summary of the process by the Nature Conservancy Council. (Source: Nature Conservancy Council, 1988.)*

interest, public access, archaeological sites and landscape consideration are all of secondary importance. The Countryside Commission's approach is somewhat different in that the overall aim of site management has to be determined before, or simultaneous with, site survey. For nature reserves or Sites of Special Scientific Interest, this overall aim is already predetermined, but for sites where the initial aims are not as clear cut, the balancing of sometimes conflicting aims is often a stumbling block. However, once the priorities the site must meet have been firmly established the construction of a management plan becomes easier

All management plans follow the same basic format: setting aims, survey, analysis, statement of objectives, a list of management prescriptions and a monitoring process. Within this format a wide variety of layouts and content can be accommodated – those suggested by the Countryside Commission and the Nature Conservancy Council are just two. The determinants of the contents of a management plan are not confined to its initial aims and objectives; the plan must not only be a policy statement for a single site, but must also be a working document. The information contained within it must therefore be sufficient to allow work programmes to be determined but not too cumbersome to bring interesting but nonetheless irrelevant facts into the discussion. The decision must therefore lie with the manager (and also with the potential grant aiding body if the management plan is being prepared as a means of securing financial support) as to the format the management plan will take and the level of information it will contain.

2.5.2   Countryside projects

Well over a hundred countryside management projects are implemented through a project officer whose appointment is made to address a particular problem in a particular area. This area might be any stretch of land from an Area of Outstanding Natural Beauty, or a misused part of the urban fringe. Indeed, one of the first project officers appointed worked along the Bollin Valley on the southern fringe of the Manchester/Stockport Conurbation.

One of the basic requirements of a project officer is to work with all interested parties within a project area. The problem of addressing conflicting aims, which was discussed in the context of management plans, is therefore met on the ground. Farmers, industrialists and recreationalists will all see a piece of land from entirely different viewpoints. It is the job of the project officer to work within this environment.

The Countryside Commission has suggested nine principal functions of a project officer within an area, including providing a focal point for all environmental concerns, taking quick action to resolve small conflicts, developing a plan to overcome longer term problems and stimulating local interest in the environment (Countryside Commission, 1978).

The management structure of countryside projects is designed to reflect the interested parties within the project area. Thus, a steering group is established which draws in membership from a wide range of groups and parties: the local authority, landowners, recreationalists, industrialists, the Nature Conservancy Council, the Countryside Commission and so on. It is usual for the steering group to meet about four times a year.

For more immediate and regular monitoring of the project officer's progress and work programme, it is also common for a much smaller group to meet monthly to assist and advise the project officer. This management structure is designed to allow clear policy information to reach the project officer and to allow monitoring to be regular but unrestricting. It is vital that the project officer has freedom to react to situations and respond to the needs of people living and working within the project area.

It is often the project officer who deals on a day-to-day basis with the conflicting problems of recreation, agriculture, nature conservation and other external pressures. Because project officers are at the sharp end of the countryside management process, in much the same way as rangers, it is vital that they are sympathetic to a wide range of viewpoints. As the Countryside Commission (op. cit.) stated:

> There is no single discipline that provides a suitable training for Project Officers ... The main requirements are an ability to communicate ideas and respond positively to the ideas of others; an ability to devise and implement practical solutions to problems and an interest and understanding of rural land management, conservation and recreation. Above all, he or she must be a good organizer.

A full analysis of the management of countryside projects is given in Chapter 11.

BIBLIOGRAPHY

Argyris, C. (1976) *Increasing Leadership Effectiveness*, John Wiley, New York.

Bunn, D.W., Hampton, Moore, P.G. and Thomas, H. (1976) *Case Studies in Decision Analysis*, Penguin Books, Harmondsworth.

Burns, T. (1969) *Industrial Man*, Penguin Books, Harmondsworth.

Countryside Commission (1978) *Local Authority Countryside Management Projects*, Advisory Book No. 10, Cheltenham.

Countryside Commission (1986) *Management Plans*, CCP206, Cheltenham.

Countryside Recreation Research Advisory Group (1984) *Training for Countryside Recreation Management*, Conference Proceedings, CRRAG, Bristol.

D'Arcy-Cartwright, J.A. (1968) *Situational Management*, W.J. Reddin, Canada.

Drucker, P.F. (1955) *The Practice of Management*, Pan Books, London.

Edwards, W. and Tuerskey, C. (1967) *Decision Making*, Penguin Books, Harmondsworth.

Fayol, H. (1930) *Industrial and General Administration* (translated by J.A. Coubrough), International Management Institute, Geneva.

Hersey, P. and Blanchard, K.H. (1972) *Management of Organisational Behaviour*,

Prentice-Hall, New York.

Kent, S. (1981) Good communications, *Parks and Recreation*, September, pp. 27–30.

Likert, R. (1967) *The Human Organization*, McGraw-Hill, New York.

Maslow, A.H. (1954) *Motivation and Personality*, Harper and Row, New York.

Mayo, E. (1933) *The Human Problems of an Industrial Civilization*, Macmillan Press, New York.

McGregor, D. (1966) *The Human Side of Enterprise*, McGraw-Hill, New York.

McKenzie, R. (1969) The management process in 3D, *Harvard Business Review*, **69**, September.

Moore, P.G. and Thomas, H. (1976) *The Anatomy of Decisions*, Penguin Books, Harmondsworth.

Nature Conservancy Council (1988) *Site Management Plans for Nature Conservation*, NCC, Peterborough.

Observer, The (1980) *Nobody's perfect, but a team can be*, April 1980.

Ordiorne, G. (1965) *Management by Objectives*, Pitman, New York.

Stinchcombe, A.L. (1965) *Social structure and the invention of organizational forms*, in *Industrial Man* (ed T. Burns), Penguin Books, Harmondsworth.

Tannenbaum, R. and Schmidt, W.H. (1958) How to choose a leadership pattern, *Harvard Business Review*, March–April, pp. 95–101.

Taylor, F.W. (1910) *Shop Management*, Harper, New York.

Torkildsen, G. (1986) *Leisure Management*, E. & F.N. Spon, London.

Wren, D. (1972) *The Evolution of Management Thought*, Ronald Press, New York.

Young, A. (1987) *The Manager's Handbook*, Sphere Books, London.

· THREE ·

The legal framework

Ignorantia juris non excusat.

Legal Maxim

The maxim that 'ignorance of the law is no excuse' is a sobering thought. If we examine all the operations that are undertaken in countryside management, we can begin to understand the enormous complexity of the legal framework. Development of land, the building of structures, the provision of safe recreation opportunities, protection of certain species and habitats and widespread legislative and common laws such as trespass, control of firearm, negligence or nuisance all come into effect at some stage in the career of countryside managers. It is impossible, other than in a specialized legal textbook, to cover all aspects of countryside and the law. This chapter is therefore concerned more with the legislative law – that which has been laid down through Acts of Parliament – which allows the countryside manager to positively develop the countryside rather than those common and legislative laws which restrict and control activities.

Fortunately, many excellent in-depth studies on the legal framework surrounding land and landuse have been written. Mostly, these books have been designed to service either the legal profession or the construction/architectural professions (see, for example, Harte, 1985; Heap, 1982; or Speaight and Stone, 1985).

3.1 COUNTRYSIDE LAW

In the period since 1949, there have been several very important pieces of legislation which have sought not only to protect the countryside but also to allow (but not force) local authorities, private landowners and other groups to use, interpret and otherwise manage the countryside. Underlying all of these pieces of legislation is the assumption – made in the Report of the Committee on Land Utilization in Rural Areas, otherwise known as the Scott Report, after its Chair (HMSO, 1942) – that agriculture and forestry were the true guardians of our countryside heritage and that, by and large, they should lie outside the planning machinery which controls and directs much of the built environment. All pieces of countryside legislation that have followed on from the 1942 Scott Report have therefore been attempting to allow some management over a resource which is basically outside legislative control. The result has been a tendency to designate areas of land, over which there are certain powers created which can often only be enacted on a voluntary basis. Throughout the discussion it will become evident that this lack of statutory power, while bringing some benefits, can also bring many problems.

The key processes of legislation that deserve further discussions are:

National Parks and Access to the Countryside Act (1949)
Countryside Act (1968)
Highways Act (1980)
Wildlife and Countryside Act (1981)
Wildlife and Countryside (Amendment) Act (1985)
Agriculture Act (1986)

At this stage it is worth noting that the law in Scotland is based on a different system, and most of these pieces of legislation do not directly apply to Scotland. The Countryside Act of 1968, for example, has a similar Scottish-based counterpart, Countryside (Scotland) Act of 1967, which established the Countryside Commission for Scotland. Some of the idiosyncrasies of Scottish Law are discussed in a separate section at the end of this chapter. Although this separate legal framework exists, it is useful to address the English/Welsh experience because many of the arguments and debates were paralleled in Scotland but because of the different legal system were addressed in different ways.

Further Acts and Government Circulars will be referred to as and when necessary, but initially the above Acts, assessed in chronological order, will provide a valuable insight into most of the relevant legislative background.

3.2 NATIONAL PARKS AND ACCESS TO THE COUNTRYSIDE ACT (1949)

With the end of the Second World War in 1945, Britain entered a period of rebuilding, both physically and legislatively. The planning process as we know it today is largely based upon legislation enacted in the immediate post-war years (as, too, are the agricultural system and regional development, which were all caught up in this desire to re-

The Howardian Hills Area of Outstanding Natural Beauty.

build). The attitudes of the day were included in much of the debate preceding the legislation, and this reflects itself in the resultant Acts. Thus the National Parks and Access to the Countryside Act of 1949 contained provision for the legal protection of landscape, natural history, public access and many positive provisions to encourage the sympathetic use of the countryside. It was and still is a wide-ranging and radical piece of legislation, owing much of its existence to pressure from lobby groups such as the Ramblers Association and the National Trust. However, the Act also contained the basic assumption that agriculture and forestry *per se* would protect and enhance the landscape and wildlife value of an area – an assumption that was hotly contested in later years, but one which at the time seemed reasonable.

The 1949 Act covered six major areas: the setting up of the National Parks Commission (which in the 1968 Countryside Act was to become the Countryside Commission); the creation of National Parks in England and Wales; Nature Conservation; public rights-of-way; access to open countryside and 'supplementary information' (which covered the designation of Areas of Outstanding Natural Beauty, general powers available to local authorities and a hotch-potch of provision to protect the rights of Crown land, the National Trust, Epping Foresters and the Burnham Beeches, for example).

3.2.1   National Parks Commission

The National Parks Commission was responsible for exercising the function laid down in the 1949 Act. It was placed under the control of the then Minister of Town and Country Planning (later the Department of the Environment) and effectively became part of the Civil Service, a situation which continued with the Countryside Commission until 1984 when the Commission became a quasi-independent body, still funded through the Department of the Environment.

3.2.2   National Parks

National Parks were to be designated to 'preserve and enhance the natural beauty of the areas specified, and for the purpose of promoting their enjoyment by the public' (Section 5). This was also tempered slightly by Section 84 which states that: 'In the exercise of their functions under this Act, it shall be the duty of the Commission, the Nature Conservancy and local authorities to have due regard to the needs of agriculture and forestry.' With the power to create National Parks, the Minister also had power to create or improve facilities such as parking places, camp sites and footpaths to encourage 'open-air recreation'.

The local planning authorities, in whose land the National Parks were to fall, also had responsibility to prepare development plans for the parks. The administration of the National Parks was envisaged as being through a Joint Board, with a high degree of autonomy from local authorities. Representatives on the Board were taken from the local authority and nominees of the Minister and his representatives. In effect, only the Peak District National Park and, to a lesser extent, the Lake District National Park actually established autonomous Joint Boards as originally envisaged in the 1949 Act and the preceding reports.

Eventually, by 1955, ten National Parks had been designated. Their choice was based largely on two reports which postdated the Scott Report but preceded the production of the 1949 Act. The Dower Report, produced by John Dower (HMSO, 1945), defined potential National Parks as:

An extensive area of beautiful are relatively wild country in which, for the nations benefit and by appropriate national decision and action:

(a) the characteristic landscape beauty is strictly preserved,
(b) access and facilities for public open air enjoyment are amply provided.
(c) wildlife and buildings and places of architectural and historic interest are suitably protected, while
(d) established farming use is effectively maintained.

Here we see the two strands of a love for wild places and a desire to protect the agricultural fabric of rural areas. This was followed up by the Hobhouse Report (HMSO, 1947a) which suggested twelve National Parks and an independent Parks Committee for each National Park. The two areas that did not make it to National Park status were the South Downs and the Norfolk Broads. Since 1955, no National Parks have been designated, although the Broads have since been given a unique status through their own Acts of Parliament in 1987. The National Parks created were a hybrid of the practicality of protecting private agricultural interests and protecting a truly national interest by public ownership and control through independent bodies. Since 1955 they have shown their weaknesses due largely to the many conflicting interests that they were designed to integrate. However, in scope and vision, the 1949 Act and the reports that preceded it have yet to be equalled.

3.2.3 Nature conservation

The Nature Conservancy, which was established in 1949 (but not through the 1949 Act) was charged with 'establishing, maintaining and manag-

Site of Special Scientific Interest: like most of the SSSIs, in private ownership, but it still requires management.

ing nature reserves in Great Britain'. The 1949 Act gave new powers to the Nature Conservancy and defined the purpose of the new nature reserves. Nature reserves can be established either through agreement with the landowners or through the purchase and management of the land by the Conservancy. In 1951 the first National Nature Reserve was established at Beinn Eighe in the Scottish Highlands. The 1949 Act gave the Nature Conservancy the power to create bye-laws to help protect the natural environment. Furthermore, the Act also empowered the Nature Conservancy to identify Sites of Special Scientific Interest, but which were not managed as Nature Reserves (Section 23). Two of the principal functions the Nature Conservancy still possesses, that of management of Nature Reserves and the identification and designation of Sites of Special Scientific Interest, were bestowed upon it in the 1949 Act.

Local authorities, too, were given the power to establish Local Nature Reserves on 'any land in their area' with the agreement of the land-owner and the Nature Conservancy.

3.2.4 Public rights-of-way

The creation of the National Parks Commission, the proposals for National Parks and the ideas of National Nature Reserves, Local Nature Reserves and Sites of Special Scientific Interest was covered in just 26 sections. It took a further 31 to begin to address the problem of putting order into the nation's public rights-of-way network. That process is still going on! The whole issue of public rights-of-way is complex and controversial. The practicalities of managing the public-rights-of-way network is discussed more fully later in the book, and the legal maze is explained excellently in Clayden and Trevelyan (1983).

The main basis for the legislation covering public rights-of-way within the 1949 Act was again from a report which preceded the Act by some two years (The Report of the Special Committee on Footpaths and Access to the Countryside, 1947). The thrust of the 1949 Act was that all local highways authorities were duty bound to prepare a draft map showing all public footpaths, bridleways and roads used as public paths (definitions were given in Section 27(6)). In order to produce this draft map the highway authority was to consult with the local parish councils. The draft map was to be published, together with a written statement for consultation by the public. Following consultation, objections were to be dealt with by the Minister, and new routes or closures made after which a provisional map and statement were to be produced and, finally, following further consultation, the definitive map was to be published. The definitive map was to be the complete map/statement identifying public rights-of-way in each county or borough.

This process appears logical on paper, but in practice it has proved to be a monumental task to which, some would agree, insufficient resources have been allocated by highway authorities. However, on the positive side the issue of public access and public rights-of-way was placed firmly on the countryside agenda through the 1949 Act, and has remained there ever since.

3.2.5   Access to open country

The issue of access to 'open country' was dealt with separately from public rights-of-way. 'Open country' is defined as 'predominantly mountain, moor, heath, down, cliff or foreshore' across which access agreements exist. In order to reach this open country the local authority can enter into access agreements with landowners to allow public access (Sections 59, 60 and 64). Each local authority was charged with preparing an access map which identified the land that could be considered as 'open country' within their area, and what, if anything they proposed to implement in terms of access agreements, access order or other measures. The Act allowed for compensation payments of monies to offset extra expense on the landowner and compulsory purchase.

This part of the Act was clearly aimed at land within National Parks and, for this reason, exemption clauses were included to cover woodland and danger areas (Ministry of Defence land). Again, conflicts appear to have been built into the legislation, but in 1949 it was clear that no such conflicts existed. The penultimate section of Part 5 of the Act (Section 82) gave local authorities power to contribute to work undertaken by other persons. A small enough and by present-day standards inconspicuous section but here it is possible to see the forerunner of so many local management programmes where work by farmers on private land is supported by the local authority because such work is to the general good of the population.

3.2.6   Additional powers

The final part of the Act raises many and various points. It contains, for example (Section 84) the proviso of having 'due regard for' agricultural and forestry interests – a phrase which keeps recurring in subsequent countryside legislation. Of more interest, however, is the issue of wardens and information. Section 86 states that it shall be the duty of the (National Park) Commission to secure that persons interested:

(a) will be informed of the situation and extent of long-distance routes and access land

(b) will be able to learn about the history, natural features flora and fauna of National Parks . . . and the opportunities for recreation therein.

As a continuation of this, Section 92 allows for the appointment of wardens. The wardens shall:

(a) secure compliance with any bye-laws . . .
(b) advise and assist the public . . .
(c) perform such other duties . . . as may be determined.

A further major achievement of the 1949 Act was to allow the National Parks Commission to designate Areas of Outstanding Natural Beauty (Section 87). These are areas outside National Parks but which none-theless the Commission feels are worthy of having 'the provisions of the (1949) Act relate to such areas'.

3.2.7 Summary

The only way to appreciate the enormity of the scope of the 1949 Act is to read it, for within it are held the seeds of everything with which a countryside manager must become familiar. The designation of areas of land to offer specific protection (in this case National Parks, Areas of Outstanding Natural Beauty, Nature Reserves, Local Nature Reserves, Sites of Special Scientific Interest and public rights-of-way), the provision of information and a wardening service, the ability to enter into agreement with and pay for work on private land and the need to 'have due regard for' agriculture, forestry, open-air recreation and access. In all respects it was an incredible piece of legislation.

3.3 COUNTRYSIDE ACT (1968)

Almost twenty years later, it had become apparent that there were flaws in the 1949 Act. Notwithstanding this, the 1968 Act could only add to the original Act, not alter it radically – the 1949 Act was still basically a well-accepted and sound piece of legislation. The 1968 Act sought as one of its main aims to extend the principles of the 1949 Act to a larger and wider area of countryside – the means of achieving this were, by and large, extensions of the powers available under the 1949 Act.

To this end the 1968 Act: widened the remit of the National Parks Commission by changing it to the Countryside Commission and extend-ing the powers; introduced several new designations of land, notably country parks; extended powers over Sites of Special Scientific Interest, open country, woodlands and water areas; increased the power of authorities to appoint wardens; charged all statutory undertakers and Ministers to have due regard for the environment; and made some amendments to the public rights-of-way legislation.

3.3.1   The Countryside Commission

The 1968 Act broadened the functions of the National Parks Commission to cover all the countryside, specifically the 'conservation and enhancement, of the natural beauty and amenity of the countryside, and encouraging the provision and improvement for persons resorting to the countryside of facilities for the enjoyment of the countryside and of open air recreation in the countryside' (Section 1). Its main responsibilities are therefore facilities for the enjoyment of the countryside, conservation of and enhancement of the natural beauty and amenity of the countryside and public access to the countryside, in addition to the responsibilities of the ex-National Parks Commission with regard to the 1949 Act (Section 2). The present-day establishment of the Countryside Commission still reflects this remit with separate parts of the Commission accepting responsibility for National Parks, access, landscape conservation, etc. The countryside manager, on the other hand, must accept responsibility for them all.

3.3.2   Country parks

Section 6 of the 1968 Act empowers local authorities to develop country parks, which had a twofold purpose: namely, to allow opportunities for enjoying the countryside (as with National Parks) but also have regard 'to the location of an urban or built-up area'. Thus the countryside was officially recognized as not just being wild or remote areas, as first suggested by Dower in 1945. The powers given to local authorities to establish country parks are wide-ranging, including purchase powers, powers to do works and provide facilities and enter into agreements with landowners.

This part of the 1968 Act also gives local authorities power to develop facilities on publicly accessible common land and to create picnic sites and camping sites. The outcome of this part of the 1968 Act was to introduce a new 'tier' of countryside site – the country park. The whole purpose of a country park was not to accommodate agriculture but to promote the recreational opportunities of the countryside. Recreational provision was on the ascendency. Until as late as 1988 (i.e. twenty years later) the country park concept was at the heart of the Countryside Commission's and local authorities' provision for countryside recrea-

National Land Designation: Yorkshire Dales National Park.

tion and it also offered the opportunity to extend many of the other managerial and interpretive functions of the countryside manager.

3.3.3   Nature conservation and access

The third part of the Act extended the concept of having 'due regard for' the countryside over a wider area. Thus, Section 11 states that: 'Every Minister, government department and public body shall have regard for the desirability of conserving the natural beauty and amenity of the countryside.'

The subsequent sections deal for a large part with amendments to earlier Acts and broaden the importance of the countryside. Section 16, for example, expands the definition of 'open country' given in Section 59 of the 1949 Act, and Sections 22 and 23 specifically empower statutory water undertakers and the Forestry Commission to 'provide or arrange for' recreational or sporting facilities, including picnic places, information centres and footpaths. The aim again is therefore to extend the concepts of the 1949 Act of access, information and natural beauty to a wider area in the countryside.

In a rather hotch-potch part of the 1969 Act, Section 15 leaps from 'natural beauty and amenity' to 'Areas of Special Scientific Interest' and empowers the Natural Environmental Research Council (of which the Nature Conservancy formed part) to enter into management agreements to protect 'flora, fauna or geological or physiographical features'. This links directly with Part 3 of the 1949 Act, as pointed out in Section 15(7) of the 1968 Act.

3.3.4   Public rights-of-way

Having dealt at some length with extending the original concepts held within the 1949 Act, the 1968 Countryside Act adds some further power to the local authorities over public rights-of-way. The main body of the Act (Sections 27 to 31) deals with powers and duties to signpost and maintain public rights-of-way. Furthermore, Schedule 3 at the end of the 1968 Act made some amendments to the process of producing the definitive map, which it was clear was too time-consuming and cumbersome to succeed. The 1968 Act sought to shorten this by, for example, allowing people to object to the draft definitive map directly to the Minister or Secretary of State. Furthermore, time limits were set for the various review and publication stages of the definitive map. The main process of reviewing and publishing the definitive map as a single unit was, however, left in tact.

3.3.5 Financial considerations and supplements

The 1969 Act allows the Minister, through the Countryside Commission, to make grants available for expenditure by local authorities in pursuance of many elements of the 1949 and 1968 Acts (Sections 33 and 34). Welcome news to most local authorities!

Other elements of this final catch-all part of the Act include the power to local authorities to extend the size of their wardening services to cover country parks, access areas and so on (Sections 41 and 42) and also the already familiar proviso that all agencies, should have due regard not only for the needs of 'agriculture and forestry' but also for the 'economic and social interests of rural areas' (Section 37). Here it is possible to see the beginnings of the conflicts, with the wider impacts of large-scale countryside recreation which many areas (particularly National Parks) were beginning to face and still do face.

3.3.6 Summary

The 1968 Act was not as radical or wide-ranging in its approach as the 1949 Act and in many respects simply sought to overcome problems that had arisen out of the original Act. However, several innovative and important issues were raised. Firstly, the concept of countryside was extended beyond the National Parks and Areas of Outstanding Natural Beauty and large-scale countryside recreation was encouraged through country parks. Secondly, powers to provide for countryside recreation – extended beyond local authorities to all statutory undertakers and public bodies, with specific mention being made of water authorities – was established and it is this body, together with its counterpart in Scotland, which has pushed the issues raised in the 1949 and 1968 Acts (and subsequent Acts) into the wider arena. The countryside manager, therefore, derives many of his or her powers from the 1968 Act.

3.4 HIGHWAYS ACT (1980)

The relevance of the 1980 Highways Act is the legislation it contains on the public rights-of-way systems. Being legally defined as highways, public rights-of-way (public footpaths, bridleways and byways) are subject to the same controls and statutory obligations as other highways. These are largely assembled within the 1980 Act. Specific issues which relate only to public rights-of-way are also covered. Thus, the legal process of creating a public right-of-way (Section 25 *et seq.*), the dedication of a highway (Section 30 *et seq.*) and the maintenance of public rights-of-way (Section 36 *et seq.*) are all within the Act.

The 1980 Act is very much a practical Act in that it lays down statutory obligations on landowners and local authorities to maintain public rights-of-way (in the broadest sense of 'maintain'). Clayden and Trevelyan (1983) deal with the intricacies of the 1980 Act at some length, discussing many of the court cases arising from the 1980 Act through claims such as obstruction, trespass and assumed rights-of-way.

3.5 WILDLIFE AND COUNTRYSIDE ACT (1981)

The Wildlife and Countryside Act of 1981 picked up the traditions of the two previous major pieces of legislation covering the countryside. It did not challenge the status quo regarding the status of agriculture and forestry; it covered a wide range of issues and relied very much on the notion of agreement as a means of overcoming possible conflicts.

The issues covered by the Act are: the protection of wildlife; nature conservation, countryside and National Parks; public rights-of-way; and lists of schedules of protected species.

3.5.1 Protection of wildlife

The first part of the Act covers the protection of specific species of birds, wild animals, plants and other wildlife. The protection is framed in several ways. General protection against 'intentionally killing or injuring any wild birds ... the nest of any wild bird ... or destroying the egg of any wild bird' comes through Section 1 of the Act, defining these as offences. Following sections deal with specific species of birds which attract 'special penalties'. Exemptions to the Act are given, and these include special licence holders, some landowners and game shooters in the allowed seasons. Trapping and the sale of birds also become offences for certain species. The aim of the first eight sections of the Act is to offer a general protection for all birds and specific, tighter protection for rarer species.

Sections 9, 10 and 11 cover protection of certain animals, the format being similar to that for birds. Certain wild animals are protected against being killed, having their 'shelter or protection' destroyed or being sold or bought. While not affording general protection, the Act does give specific protection for certain species of wild animals.

Section 13 offers protection to wild plants by giving protection against people 'picking, uprooting or destroying' specific species (again listed in the schedules within the Act) and offering general protection against 'uprooting any wild plant not included in the schedule'.

The remainder of the first part of the Act covers the introduction of wild animals 'not ordinarily resident in and not normally a regular visitor to Great Britain' and makes the release of these animals an offence.

Other sections deal with a miscellany of points including the interpretation of such terms as 'uproot', 'destroy' and 'wild animal'. Section 24 states that 'the Nature Conservancy Council shall regularly update the relevant schedules through the Secretary of State'.

3.5.2 Nature conservation, countryside and national parks

This part of the 1981 Act contains the elements which, since the Act received Royal Assent, have become some of the most controversial. Sections 28 and 29 lay upon the Nature Conservancy Council the obligation to notify local planning authorities, landowners and occupiers and the Secretary of State about their intention to designate a Site of Special Scientific Interest. This meant that the Nature Conservancy Council had to re-notify all such sites, giving the landowner 'not less than 3 months . . . within which . . . objections may be made'. These objections were to be heard at an inquiry. The process of re-notification was a lengthy one and, as was argued in the Nature Conservancy Council's Annual Report of 1984–85, the '3 month loophole' allowed landowners time to effectively destroy the proposed Site of Special Scientific Interest. Out of a total of 2835 re-notifications as of 31 March 1985, some 255 had been damaged prior to the re-notification being finalized (Nature Conservancy Council, 1985).

Section 30 of the Act states that 'The (Nature Conservancy) Council shall pay compensation' if as a result of notification or the restrictions on 'permitted operations' on the land, the value or income of that land is reduced. Thus, for the first time, the Nature Conservancy Council had to 'buy' land which was of national scientific importance. In many cases, particularly on potential agricultural land, this was prohibitively expensive.

Section 35 of the 1981 Act gave the Nature Conservancy Council power to declare National Nature Reserves on land that is of 'national importance' and owned, held or managed by the Nature Conservancy Council. It was accepted in 1985, however, that there was 'still some difference of opinion over the interpretation of "nationally important" between the NCC and the Government'. The contention of the Nature Conservancy Council was (and still is) that 'all Sites of Special Scientific Interest serve a national function' (Nature Conservancy Council, 1985).

Sections 36 and 37 introduced the concept of Marine Nature Reserves which the Nature Conservancy Council could nominate to the Secretary of State and, upon the latter's agreement, the Council could manage. Thus the protection afforded to nature reserves in land could, following the 1981 Act, be afforded to 'land covered continuously or intermittently by tidal water or parts of the sea'.

Section 38, which concludes the nature conservation element of the Act, allows the Nature Conservancy Council to award grants to any organization or person to do any work which is 'conducive to nature conservation of fostering the understanding of nature conservation'. Thus the interpretive element which was made central to the work of the Countryside Commission becomes an executive function of the Nature Conservancy Council.

Section 39 of the 1981 Act contains one of the most useful powers available to the countryside managers. Section 39 allows that

> A relevant authority may, for the purpose of conserving or enhancing the natural beauty of amenity of any land which is both in the countryside and within their area or promoting its enjoyment by the public, make an agreement (referred to as a management agreement) with any person having an interest in the land with respect to the management of the land during a specified term or without limitation of the duration of the agreement.

Section 39 agreements, therefore, allow local authorities to enter into agreement with landowners who agree to manage land in such a way to protect and enhance wildlife and landscape. Although arrangements have to be purely voluntary, Section 39 does allow public and private agencies to enter binding agreements for the benefit of the environment.

Section 40 gives powers to the Countryside Commission to undertake 'experimental schemes' in specific areas or on specific issues, but which the Commission feels are potentially of 'appropriateness for the countryside generally'. Section 41 places a duty on the Minister of Agriculture, Fisheries and Food and the Secretary of State for the Environment to offer advice to 'persons carrying on agricultural businesses' on the conservation and enhancement of the natural beauty and amenity for the countryside.

Sections 42 to 46 cover new initiatives for National Parks such as restrictions on ploughing, improvement to the mapping of certain areas, such as moor and heath, and the membership of National Park authorities.

Sections 47 to 52 are termed 'Miscellaneous and Supplemental', but Section 49 empowers local authorities to develop one of their most important functions, namely that of appointing wardens. Section 49 allows local authorities the power to appoint for 'any land in a National Park or in the countryside' as long as access is permitted. Thus, their use is no longer restricted to National Parks or country parks. It also states that 'the only purpose for which wardens may be appointed by virtue of Sub-section 2 is to advise and assist the public'. The 'old' concept of a warden being primarily an enforcer of bye-laws is replaced by a more interpretive role.

3.5.3   Public rights-of-way

Sections 51 to 66 cover a variety of issues about public rights-of-way. The body of the Act deals with the continual problem of the review of the definitive map. The 1981 Act changed the emphasis from a wholesale review to a 'continuous review'. Thus local authorities must bring the map up-to-date and continually keep it up-to-date using new procedures for modification order which are contained in the Act. Furthermore, many urban authorities formed prior to the 1974 Local Government Reorganization did not have to produce a definitive map. This was changed by the 1981 Act and all areas not previously covered by the definitive map were to be surveyed and a definitive map produced.

The result of the amendment gives local authorities power to review and amend the definitive map as events occur. It does not, however, do anything (if indeed anything is possible) to reduce the immense burden of the original review initiated as a result of the 1968 Act. This process is likely to continue for many years, with many authorities predicting work on the review going well into the twenty-first century.

3.5.4   Summary

The 1981 Wildlife and Countryside Act has been seen as a controversial Act since it was passed. The issues of payments to landowners, the definitions of 'national importance' and allowing landowners to keep bulls in fields crossed by public rights-of-way all remain hotly contested issues. On the positive side, the Act did try to come to terms with the perennial problem of the review of the definitive map and with the protection of certain species. Notwithstanding this, however, it was felt necessary only four years later to enact an amendment bill to the 1981 Act.

3.6 WILDLIFE AND COUNTRYSIDE (AMENDMENT) ACT 1985

The 1985 Act is very short, and was designed to close a number of loopholes in the 1981 Act. Section 1 sought, for example, specifically to make badger digging an offence.

Section 2, which ran to some eleven sub-sections dealt with the three-month loophole for the notification of Sites of Special Scientific Interest by stating that: 'As from any time when there is served on the owner . . . a notice . . . the notification shall have effect in its modified form.' In an enormously complex piece of writing, Section 2 seeks to allay some of the fears raised by the conservation lobby, including the Nature Conservancy Council, and yet keep the landowners content by giving way on some restrictions over 'specified operations'. It is still thought that the combination of the 1981 and 1985 Acts does not resolve the central issue of whether Sites of Special Scientific Interest should be firmly protected against destruction through tight legislation or voluntary agreements.

Section 3 deals with an extension of the definition of heaths and moors from the 1981 Act. Section 4 amends the 1967 Forestry Act by laying on the Forestry Commission a duty to strike a balance between timber production and 'conservation and enhancement of natural beauty'. This duty for balance was placed on the water authorities in the 1981 Act, but for some reason the Forestry Commission were omitted.

3.7   AGRICULTURE ACT (1986)

The 1986 Act is important for two reasons, above and beyond the fact that it deals with a subject at the very heart of the countryside. Firstly, the 'countryside' element of the Act (Part 5) was drafted as a result of a directive from the European Community Council – which points to the way that much of Britain's legislation could well be developed in the future. Secondly, the Act places on agriculture the duty to have due regard for the natural environment and proposes a mechanism for achieving this.

Section 17 states that: 'The Minister shall . . . have regard to and endeavour to achieve a reasonable balance between . . . the agricultural industry . . . economic and social interests in rural areas . . . conservation . . . and promotion of the enjoyment of the countryside.' This sets the scene for farm diversification, set-aside and a host of initiatives started in the late 1980s.

Section 18 follows the, by now, traditional route of designating special areas and empowering the relevant authorities to enact in these areas. The concept of Environmentally Sensitive Areas (ESAs) is developed. ESAs are designed to offer a mechanism to pay farmers to manage land in a way conducive to the protection of the environment. It was envisaged that ESAs were to provide a model for integrated farm management for all agricultural areas (cf. Haigh, 1988) but, initially, particularly historic or attractive landscapes were designated as ESAs such as the Somerset Levels and the Yorkshire Dales.

Swaledale Environmentally Sensitive Area, showing the several landscape/habitat zones including: valley floor, valley sides and upper slopes.

3.8   SUMMARY

Countryside legislation in England and Wales has, since 1949, been a very piecemeal process. (If Scotland is introduced into the equation, things become more complex. There was, for example, no equivalent to the 1949 Act in Scotland, but there was an equivalent to the 1968 Act which established the Countryside Commission for Scotland. Similarly, no public rights-of-way exist in Scotland, but general access is more widespread.) However, there are several strands within the successive Acts which can be drawn out.

The concept of designating specific areas is still central to the management of Britain's countryside. National Parks, Country Parks, Sites of Special Scientific Interest and, more recently, Environmentally Sensitive Areas are all cases in point. The need for this stems from the fact that both agriculture and forestry lie outside mainstream planning control; this is likely to continue in the foreseeable future. In 1987, the Norfolk and Suffolk Broads Act contrived this process by giving the Broads a special status, similar in some ways to a National Parks. Similarly, Heritage Coasts designated under the 1968 Act is another form of special status. The result of all of this legislation is a jigsaw of land designation which is more than confusing to 'the public' for whose benefit the designations are made.

A second strand is that of a developing role for rangers or wardens. Originally foreseen, primarily, as a group of countryside workers whose responsibility was to enforce bye-laws, the role identified in later legislation was that of 'aiding and informing the public'. Linked with this, the power given to local authorities to provide study centres and other educative services within the countryside places an increasing importance on an interpretive rather than a 'policing' role of the rangers.

A final trend worth highlighting is that of the onus which is increasingly being placed on all Government Ministers, statutory, undertakers and quasi-government bodies to have 'due regard for' the natural environment and the opportunities for recreation within it. Over the years, since 1949, the Forestry Commission, the water authorities, the local authorities and the farming industry as a whole have all been charged with some degree of protection towards the natural environment. Conversely, within all the 'countryside' legislation there has inevitably been a section which lays an obligation upon the implementers of the legislation to have due regard for the requirements of forestry and agriculture. The trend, therefore, is towards a meeting of all rural landusers, each having 'due regard' for others. The logical outcome of all of this is a rural landuse policy, which has been debated for over the last four decades. Indeed, with the pressure for reduced agricultural output (in

Western Europe at least) and the increasing pressure and awareness for access to and an understanding of the countryside, this process is set to continue. In the report of the Countryside Policy Review Panel (Countryside Commission, 1987), the arguments for this integrated approach is not only forcibly put, but is also costed and longer term implications are analysed.

Comprehensive legislation which enforces this integrated approach is unlikely, in the foreseeable future at least, to come from the British Government, so what remains is a piecemeal history of legislation with, on the one hand, trends towards land classification and, on the other, trends towards greater integration. Within this framework the countryside manager must work towards integration at a local and national level.

3.9 SCOTTISH LAW

Scotland has an entirely separate legal system from that of England and Wales (as, too, does Northern Ireland). For this reason separate legislation exists on all issues, including the countryside. It is clear, however, that many of the issues that English/Welsh legislation seeks to address are equally the focus of Scottish legislation. It will suffice here to look at some of the basic differences and how they manifest themselves.

At the root of English countryside legislation lies the 1949 Act. This Act is not part of Scottish law so, consequently, some land designations and mechanisms do not apply in Scotland. For this reason, National Parks do not exist, although the concept was suggested for Scotland (HMSO, 1945) and the debate still manifests itself periodically (Countryside Commission for Scotland, 1989). As no National Parks were designated in Scotland, no National Parks Commission was founded, and environmental issues were dealt with directly through the office of the Secretary of State for Scotland and through the Ministry for Home Affairs and Environment. In 1967, however, with the Countryside (Scotland) Act the Countryside Commission for Scotland was established with broadly the same remit as its English and Welsh counterpart.

In order to fill the recreational/landscape gap left by the 1949 'omission', the Countryside Commission for Scotland nominated and designated forty National Scenic Areas in 1978. These cover a wide spectrum of landscapes from that under intense visitor pressure (such as Loch Lomond or the Cairngorms) to that under very little visitor pressure, but nonetheless subject to landscape changes (such as Glen Affric/ Knoydart or the Shetland Isles and St Kilda). The concept of a National Park in its English context may therefore only be applicable in some of the forty sites.

While the Countryside Commissions have separate identities the Nature Conservancy Council, as defined under the Nature Conservancy Act of 1973, has a remit which covers all of England, Wales and Scotland. (Although this is in the process of changing; see section 3.12.1.)

Town and Country Planning legislation gives special powers to local authorities (again organized differently in Scotland) over five National Park direction areas and three reserve areas.

3.10 WIDER LEGAL ISSUES

The pieces of legislation described above provide the positive, legislative guidelines for the work of a countryside manager. There are clearly other pieces to the jigsaw. These include the Town and Country Planning process in Britain, Government guidelines (usually issued through Government Circulars) and the agricultural support system of Britain and, increasingly, Europe.

3.10.1 Town and country planning

The early work of the founding fathers of the planning profession was based upon an attempt to marry the beauty of the countryside with the necessary requirements of urban-based living. Ebenezer Howard (1946), in his work *Garden Cities of Tomorrow* created the concept of a social city where open space, natural landscape and all the necessary requisites of urban living were found together in one city. These concepts led directly to the creation of Letchworth and Welwyn Garden City and, ultimately, to the New Town concept. However, concurrent with these views was the idea that towns were somehow an 'evil necessity' and were to be contained (Hall *et al.*, 1973).

Thus, in the years after 1945, when the present planning machinery was being established, the powers given to planning authorities, by-and-large, related to the urban built environment, and were largely (although not exclusively by any means) geared towards the control of development. The 'country' was largely left outside the planning process, as envisaged by Howard and the early pioneers, and became, and still is, largely town planning (Hall, 1975).

In the late 1970s, however, there was a renewed interest in the problems of 'planning' in the rural environment, and the rural dimension of unemployment, public services and housing issues were discussed in their own right (Cherry, 1976). Within this rural planning framework, the countryside was seen as an identifiable element, and thus became part of the equation. For example, rural recreation, if managed properly, was foreseen as a means of easing, if not reducing, rural-based unemployment. On the other hand, designations of areas such as National Parks or Areas of Outstanding Natural Beauty was seen as one factor in pushing up house prices and leading to second home ownership.

As well as being an area of work in its own right, therefore, countryside management is part of the rural development equation. As shall be examined later, some agencies have begun to address the problems of rural development by promoting the countryside management as a major part of rural rejuvenation. The Integrated Rural Development Programme run by the Peak District National Park (Peak Park Joint Planning Board, 1984) is an example.

At a practical level, there are certain elements of the planning process that give powers to the countryside manager (tree preservation orders, local plans, subject plans, mineral working controls and restoration conditions for example). The countryside manager must also be aware of the position that 'countryside issues take in the wider socio-economic environment of rural areas' (Davidson and Wibberley, 1977). The practical powers gained through the various Town and Country Planning Acts are discussed in more detail, as means of implementation, in a later chapter. However, the importance of the planning process is that, firstly, it provides a statutory framework for policies (i.e. if countryside or environmental policies are embodied in a local or structure plan, they are, to all intents and purposes, given legal status), and secondly, certain specific powers are given.

3.10.2 Agriculture Acts

Having stayed outside the planning system, agriculture has been relatively well protected until the late 1980s through subsidies, grant aid and impact protection. The Agricultural Support System was established in 1947 through the Agriculture Act of that year and, even upon entry into the EEC, was afforded protection against competition and poor market performance. More recently, however, as was shown by the 1986 Agriculture Act, the position is changing. The overproduction of many products within Europe has led to calls for wholesale amendments to be made to the common agricultural policy. These widespread changes have yet to be made but the protective system is being altered slowly.

In this changing financial environment, the role of the countryside manager will become increasingly important as agriculturalists try to come to terms with not just managing food production but also incorporating other issues into their farm enterprise. Central to these 'other issues' are public access, nature and landscape conservation and interpretation/education. Slowly, therefore, the rural landuse patterns of

Britain will change and be more integrated. The countryside manager's ability to group all relevant issues and incorporate these into local situations should therefore continue to be the best means of achieving orderly change.

The agricultural system of Britain that has developed since 1947 is complex. The most important issue for countryside managers is that change is taking place and with it will come opportunities for implementing integrated countryside schemes, while having the necessary 'due regard' for the needs of agriculture and forestry.

3.11   OTHER LEGISLATION

The countryside, planning and agriculture framework described above gives the countryside manager the necessary authority to initiate and implement a wide range of schemes. The legislation can therefore be seen as a positive statutory support for the work in the countryside. However, countryside managers, like all managers, work in a more complicated legal world than this. Contracts need to be managed, visitor facilities need to be protected, ranger services are required to enact upon a wide range of laws and sites need to be safe for all employees and visitors.

The Health and Safety at Work Act (1974) brought together a varied collection of health and safety legislation in an attempt to protect all people at work (not just on specific sites, such as at factories, quarries or mines, for example). Not only were employees protected, but so too were persons affected by the work. This necessarily includes visitors to places controlled by others. From the point of view of the countryside manager, this places a great responsibility on protecting the 'health, safety and welfare' of visitors to sites, users of public footpaths and the general public at large. Jackson (1979) explains the detail of the 1974 Act for all managers, and all countryside managers must therefore, by definition, be concerned with its implications. Similarly, in the day-to-day workings of countryside staff, a host of criminal and civil crimes are encountered together with a welter of relevant Acts and case law precedents. These have been summarized in a handbook format by Parkes (1983). The text examines a number of site-based problems which are encountered regularly by countryside staff (particularly rangers and wardens) and explains the legal support that is available for such staff.

Where countryside managers use contractual arrangements to implement schemes, there needs to be some knowledge of contractual procedures (although, it is possible to 'buy in' this expertise). Particularly relevant are the contractual arrangements used by landscape architects and architects and, as with all the previous pieces of legislation, it is impossible here to do more than skim the surface, although Greenstreet (1981) and Clamp (1986) both give greater detail. Where a landscape or building contract is to be let, the complexities of the contracting process are such that, where the countryside manager does not possess the relevant expertise, the necessary skill should be brought in. As with all areas covered by civil or criminal law, the countryside manager cannot be expected to know all the details, but should, at the very least, 'know enough to realize when they don't know enough' and therefore seek extra information.

To summarize, the law of Britain is both complex and comprehensive. Rather than give a false impression here that all matters have been adequately covered it is only possible to raise the relevant issues and refer to more detailed analyses such as Walker (1981), for example. Ultimately, however, there will be a time in the career of all countryside managers when it is necessary to call in expert legal advice because, as we have seen, 'ignorance of the law is no excuse'.

3.12 CENTRAL GOVERNMENT GUIDELINES

The British legal system consists of legislation and precedents established by case work. The assumption is that all law is open to some debate and these debates can only be settled when the written laws are contested. Phrases such as 'reasonable', 'due regards for' and 'not normally' are all subjective and often need clarification. Successive governments have therefore issued guidelines on their interpretation of legislation, and these are produced as Government Circulars. These can be seen as the 'official' interpretation on how certain laws should be enacted. The Department of the Environment, or in Scotland the Secretary of State, (the most relevant department for countryside managers) issues many such circulars each year, in addition to which various discussion documents are also produced. There is, therefore, a steady flow of information with which the countryside manager must stay abreast. This is made somewhat easier by annual updates, such as the *Countryside Yearbook* published annually (Gilg (ed.)) which addresses all major initiatives in the legislation covering the countryside not only in Britain but also now in Europe. Environmental journals also analyse legislative changes and the implications of future changes.

Circular 32/81 published on 25 November 1981 gave details of the 1981 Wildlife and Countryside Act and how the Department of the Environment (and in Wales, the Welsh Office) saw the Act being interpreted. Each section is discussed with additional information being given; for example, on the issue of Section 39 Management Agreements, the circular indicates that 'Management Agreements made under this section will be legally binding upon successors in title'. It is for this reason that those Section 39 Agreements drawn up by Metropolitan County Councils fell to the Metropolitan Districts upon abolition of the Counties in 1986.

Circular 4/83 (Department of the Environment, 1983) followed up the contentious issue of payments made to landowners to protect and manage wildlife resources. The circular entitled *Financial Guidelines for Management Agreements* specifically deals with the financial implication of Sections 32, 39, 41 and 50 of the 1981 Act, covering such issues as grant availability, arbitration, rent review and liability.

Finally, in December 1987 Circular 27/87 was published (Department of the Environment, 1987b). This was entitled simply *Nature Conservation* and replaced the earlier document Department of the Environment Circular 108/77 (*Nature Conservation and Planning*). Circular 27/87 does not focus on a single Act or part of an Act but 'outlines relevant legislative changes which have taken place since the publication of the Department of the Environment's circular 108/77'. Circular 27/87 is lengthy by normal standards and covers a wide range of issues such as the Bern Convention, Development Control, Minerals Planning and Afforestation. The overall objective of the circular is to 'reaffirm the Government's commitment to protect and enhance the environment'.

Together, Circulars 32/81, 4/83 and 27/87 offer valuable background, insight and information to the 1981 Wildlife and Countryside Act.

The 'discussive' circulars cover many issues and, as often as the legislation itself, give clear indication of how Central Government will implement policies. To this end, Circular 16/87, *Development Involving Agricultural Land*, states the Government's attitude to the development control implications of agricultural surpluses. The message within the circular is much clearer than elsewhere. While all previous guidelines were written within the context of the need for greater agricultural production, 'the need now is to foster the diversification of the rural economy' and 'the continuing need to protect the countryside for its own sake, rather than primarily for the productive value of the land'. For countryside managers this indicates that the integrated management approach is valid not just on countryside sites such as National Parks or country parks, but also in the wider countryside. So although there is as yet no actual legislation to back up this assertion, the messages are quite clear.

A useful guide to existing legislation and background information such as Government Circulars and discussion or policy documents is given in Open University (1985). As new policies are brought in, however, the implications for countryside managers need to be assessed. This will take two forms: firstly, each new document will have direct implications (such as introducing new powers); and, secondly, each successive piece of policy or legislation will give a clearer picture of where the overall policy is progressing, and these wider implications will also need to be addressed either to assess whether they are desirable (if not, countryside managers should be free to question them as could any professional group) or to seize any opportunities that are presented or are likely to be presented.

3.12.1   The 1989 Environment Bill

Faced with the growing concern over a wide number of environmental issues, the Government of the day put together an equally wide ranging 'Green Bill'. This covered issues as varied as litter disposal, waste disposal, pollution control and, of great significance to the countryside manager, dramatic changes to the roles of and relationships between the Countryside Commission and the Nature Conservancy Council (HMSO, 1989).

The proposals are that, in Scotland and Wales, the Countryside Commission and the Nature Conservancy Council will merge, and in England they be kept separate. Furthermore, the Nature Conservancy Council will cease to be a national body and become a regionalized organization similar to the Countryside Commission. Thus the regional groups will be directly responsible to local boards of directors.

These proposals are, needless to say, highly contentious. Indeed, many within the Nature Conservancy Council see the moves as an attempt to reduce the efficiency of the NCC in opposing development proposals in or around valuable habitats – particularly in Scotland. The NCC Chief Scientists resigned in July 1989 in opposition to the proposals.

The former chief scientist felt that a major objective of the bill was to placate angered land owning and development interests in Scotland, who had been forced to concede to environmental interests on issues such as Duich Moss on Islay and the afforestation of the flow country in Caithness.

For the countryside manager the implications are many and varied. Grant regimes and constraints may change, information may be more difficult to obtain, national policies will become merely regional policies and, as the former chief scientist suggests 'any tinkering with conservation measures will be a bad sign, and backsliding on established gains a cause for real alarm' (*Observer*, 1989).

At best, the proposals within the Environment Bill appear to be another example of piecemeal legislation which 'tinkers' with fundamental problems. At worst, they are a regressive step, taken not in the interests of conservation, but in the interests of 'open-ended development and growth' (*Observer*, 1989).

3.13 WHAT OF THE FUTURE?

It is always difficult, if not completely foolhardy, to try to determine what will happen in the future in any area of work. It is even more fool-hardy than usual to try to predict where future countryside legislation will take us. The countryside is becoming a political issue, with all polit-ical parties trying to accommodate to the 'green vote'. Once an issue becomes so political it is difficult to determine how legislation will devel-op without knowing what political party will be in office, either centrally or locally. A short guide to the politics of nature conservation and the countryside can be found in Smyth (1987).

The only way to determine some broad policy directions for country-side legislation is to look at past legislation and see how subtly policy shifts are developing. (Much of the above discussion has been con-cerned with this.) We can also look at the discussions taking place among countryside officers and professionals. Although there is no guarantee that the advice of the professionals will be adhered to, there is some merit in looking briefly at the issues that are seen as forming the political agenda for countryside into the next century.

Much of the debate is focused upon the need to integrate the needs of agriculture and forestry with the other issues of recreation, conserva-tion and education. The report of the Countryside Policy Review Panel mentioned earlier (Countryside Commission, 1987) is, in part, a review of contemporary issues and serves as a useful synthesis of modern thinking. However, the report departs from a straightforward synthesis in its recommendations, which are classified under several headings, namely: agriculture, forestry and woodlands, recreation and access, pressure from the towns, integrating farming and environmental con-servation, encouraging rural enterprise and putting the pieces together. Within each of these categories a definite role is identified for central government and local government, and also general considerations are suggested. In order to achieve this co-ordinated approach it is estimated that some £320 million will need to be spent in the rural environment over the years until AD 2000. As the report suggests,

> this would be a small price to pay for the retention of a beautiful countryside and the revitalization of the rural community. Conversely, the changes that are being brought about through farm diversification and set-aside threaten to be the biggest changes in agriculture for many centuries. If not co-ordinated, these changes could be at best random and at worst damaging (Countryside Commission, 1987).

The Countryside Policy Review Panel's report (Countryside Commission, 1987) expressly avoided the issue of development and planning in the countryside as this, too, will see major changes over the next decades as the planning process comes under major review – a process initiated in the major metropolitan areas. This imbalance has been redressed by the Countryside Commission themselves through a discussion paper (Countryside Commission, 1988). Again, a co-ordinated approach is called for, with some ten policy areas being suggested. These are as follows.

1. The maintenance of a strong and effective system of town and country planning.
2. The conservation of natural beauty and regional diversity.
3. The creation of new countryside.
4. Environmental benefits from development.
5. An enhanced role for green belts.
6. New housing in the countryside.
7. Rural enterprise.
8. Large-scale developments in the countryside.
9. Better co-ordination between countryside agencies.
10. More countryside management.

The conclusion of this discussion paper, *Planning for Change*, will serve as a summary for both reports. However, it is unlikely that, in the foreseeable future, an all-embracing piece of legislation will pull all the elements together. It is more likely that the countryside manager will continue to operate in a legal environment which is not co-ordinated and lacks a central vision. However, the conclusion reads:

> In these 10 policies, the Commission sets out its views on how the quality of the countryside can be safeguarded – and often improved – as agricultural policies, population movements, social aspirations and a growing environmental concern mark a fundamental change in the countryside. Underpinning all of the Commission's policies is the conviction that we need a vision of the countryside we wish to leave for generation to come and the courage to use the tools of rural planning and management creatively to release that vision.

Courage and vision are two qualities that the early architects of the countryside movement had in abundance. It is up to all countryside managers to continue in that spirit.

3.14 EUROPEAN LEGISLATION

The British legal framework will increasingly be set within a European context. This is particularly relevant within the environment, as much of the European legislation concentrates on the environment: pollution, noise emission, agricultural production, rural society, etc. It is sufficient for the countryside manager to accept that this is the case and to identify the consequences. These practical consequences are most readily seen within the agriculture industry.

The Treaty of Rome (1957) states that the objectives of the Common Agricultural Policy is to:

1. increase agricultural productivity;
2. ensure a fair standard of living for the agricultural community;
3. stabilize markets;
4. assure the availability of supplies;
5. ensure that supplies reach consumers at reasonable prices.

The impact of this on British legislation has been to complement and enhance the agricultural support system. On the other hand, the Environmentally Sensitive Areas were first suggested as a direct result of European Directives.

An indication of the wide-ranging nature of legislation passed through the European Community is given by EC Directive 85/337. This enforces member states to ensure that Environmental Impact Assessments are undertaken to predict and reduce the impact of major developments. Considerations to be taken into account include landscape, nature conservation and communities/recreation. The British Guidelines for enacting the European Directive issued in 1985 were released in 1988 (Department of the Environment, 1988 Circular 19/88). Among other things, it is suggested that mineral applications in National Parks and AONBs should generally have Environmental Impact Assessments undertaken.

The ability of the European Parliament to generate environmental legislation will undoubtedly increase as the environment becomes a more important political issue. It is interesting to note the conflict between the inherently voluntary approach favoured in British legislation and the statutory approach taken in Europe.

3.15 CASE STUDIES

One of the overriding messages being given throughout the preceding discussion is that the countryside manager must work with all the available legislative tools which, as we have seen, are many and varied. Following from the previous call from the Countryside Commission for 'vision', the two examples of management explored here both show that once a clear vision has been created, the available legislation can be used in order to guide actions towards that objective. The Nature Conservation Strategy for Greater Manchester specifically mentions the legislation (including sections and sub-sections) which support policy statements laid out in the text. The Integrated Rural Development Programme of the Peak Park Joint Planning Board does not identify the underlying legal framework to any comparable degree, but it does show that, at the local level, integration across a number of areas can be achieved, and in a relatively cost-effective way.

3.15.1 Greater Manchester Nature Conservation Strategy

The Metropolitan Country Councils were formed in 1974 and abolished in 1986. In their brief life-span it is well accepted that they achieved a lot of environmental benefits. Each Metropolitan County Council had a different approach to its own area's countryside problems, and in Greater Manchester the Countryside Unit worked closely with the local districts. Perhaps, as a result of this, the local districts (ten in all) supported the retention of the Countryside Unit on a countywide basis after abolition in 1986. The Greater Manchester Countryside Unit, in its post-abolition form, was able to produce a non-site specific nature conservation strategy, based on the work undertaken prior to 1986. The strategy assembled a range of policy statements under the broad headings of, in Part 1, the reasons and justification for the strategy and, in Part 2, the policies themselves which cover: enjoying wildlife, protecting wildlife, improving wildlife, managing wildlife and information about wildlife.

The policy document shows that once the countryside managers are clear about what they want to achieve, the legislative framework can be assembled into a sound policy document. An extract from the statement illustrates this point. Policy 12 states that

> The Local Authority will encourage an increase in the number, size and quality of areas of nature conservation interest in the county, and the improvement of the general environment for nature conservation, so as to promote an integrated system of wildlife habitats throughout the county.

The supporting text emphasizes the importance of this particular policy for promoting not only nature conservation, but also recreation, education and amenity. In support of the policy, the document cites no less than five documents and Acts, namely: County Structure Plan; the 1968 Countryside Act (Section 7); the 1949 National Parks and Access to the Countryside Act (Section 21); the 1981 Wildlife and Countryside Act (Section 48); and the Town and Country Planning (Minerals) Act of 1981. The policy is then completed by indicating how schemes are to be implemented. These methods of implementation include derelict land reclamation schemes, management agreements and development control.

The Nature Conservation Strategy for Greater Manchester therefore follows the route from policy formulation and legislative background to a consideration of the methods of implementation. It was suggested in the introduction that this link between policy and implementation is vital to the work of a countryside manager, and within the Greater Manchester document we see the legislative framework being used to accomplish this.

3.15.2   Integrated rural development

The Peak Park Joint Planning Board project was aimed at achieving completely different objectives, but the Integrated Rural Development experiment has many similarities with the Greater Manchester initiative. Firstly, the policies and objectives were established as priority; secondly, the necessary legal framework was ensured; and, finally, a means of implementing the scheme was an integral part of the planning process. Three underlying issues lay at the heart of the project:

1. Different parts of the uplands have different characteristics, they should not all be treated as if they were the same.
2. Many elements of public support could be better harmonized. Individual public policies sometimes seem to be working against each other, often because they are so specialized.
3. 'For National Park purposes to be properly achieved, social and economic and environmental interests must combine in a single strategy' (Peak Park Joint Planning Board, 1984).

The final point made above follows directly from the directives and policy changes made within successive pieces of legislation, as discussed above. Similarly, the pre-requisite that all agencies must have 'due regard' for each other's workings is held within the second issue of 'harmonization'.

The project centred upon two villages (Parker, 1984) and aimed to support a wide range of initiatives within each of the two areas – Monyash and Longnor. These were not just environmental projects, but also social and economic. An important element of all of the projects was that the community itself, and individuals within that community, were responsible for developing schemes. Over sixty were undertaken within the study period, including the development of play areas, the establishment of a small folk museum, a small spinning-wheel manufacturing workshop and a landscape conservation project. Although apparently disparate, these projects all seek to achieve the cohesion of a number of rural initiatives, as inferred (if not stated explicitly) in the countryside legislation. In the words of the Peak Park Joint Planning Board, this approach 'starts from the customer's needs, not administrative separateness' – a necessary requirement of countryside management.

BIBLIOGRAPHY

Bowler, I. (1979) *Government and Agriculture; a spatial perspective*, Longman, London.

Cherry, G. (ed.) (1976) *Rural Planning Problems*, Leonard Hill, London.

Clamp, H. (1986) *Spon's Landscape Contract Manual*, E. & F. N. Spon, London.

Clayden, P. and Trevelyan, J. (1983) *Rights-of-Way: a guide to law and practice*, Pitman Press, London.

Clout, H. (1985) *A Rural Policy for the EEC*, Methuen, London.

Countryside Commission (1987) *New Opportunities for the Countryside*, CCP224, Cheltenham.

Countryside Commission (1988) *Planning for Change: Development in a Green Countryside*, CCP24, Cheltenham.

Countryside Commission for Scotland (1989) *The National Parks Debate*, CCS, Battleby.

Davidson, J. and Wibberley, G. (1977) *Planning and the Rural Environment*, Pergamon Press, Oxford.

Denyers-Green, B. (1983) *The 1981 Wildlife and Countryside Act: a practitioners guide*, Royal Institute of Chartered Surveyors,

Department of the Environment (1981) *The 1981 Wildlife and Countryside Act*, Circular 32/81.

Department of the Environment (1983) *Financial Guidelines for Management Agreements*, Circular 4/83.

Department of the Environment (1987a) *Development Involving Agricultural Land*, Circular 16/87.

Department of the Environment (1987b) *Nature Conservation*, Circular 27/87.

Department of the Environment (1988) *Environmental Impact Assessment*, Circular 19/88.

Gilg, A. (ed.) (Annual) *The Countryside Yearbook*, Geopublications, Norwich.

Greenstreet, R. (1981) *Legal and Contractual Procedures for Architects*, Architectural Press, London.

Haigh, V. (1988) Once in a landscape lifetime, *Landscape Design*, August.

Hall, P. *et al.* (1973) *The Containment of Urban England*, Allen and Unwin, London.

Hall, P. (1975) *Urban and Regional Planning*, Penguin Books, Harmondsworth.

Harte, J. D. C. (1985) *Landscape, Landuse and the Law*, E. & F.N. Spon, London.

Heap, D. (1982) *An Outline of Planning Law*, Sweet and Maxwell, London.

HMSO (1942) *The Scott Report* (Report of the Committee on Land Utilization in Rural Areas).

HMSO (1945) *The Dower Report – National Parks in England and Wales*, Cmnd 6628.

HMSO (1945) *National Parks – A Scottish Survey*, Cmnd 6631.

HMSO (1947a) *The Hobhouse Report*.

HMSO (1947b) *Agriculture Act*.

HMSO (1949) *National Parks and Access to the Countryside Act*.

HMSO (1968) *Countryside Act*.

HMSO (1971) *Town and Country Planning Act*.

HMSO (1980) *Highways Act*.

HMSO (1981) *Wildlife and Countryside Act*.

HMSO (1985) *Wildlife and Countryside (Amendment) Act*.

HMSO (1986) *Agriculture Act*.

HMSO (1989) The Environment Bill.

Howard, E. (1946) *Garden Cities of Tomorrow*, Faber, London (originally published in 1902).

Jackson, J. (1979) *Health and Safety: The Law*, Brehan Press.

Nature Conservancy Council (1985) *Annual Report*, NCC, Peterborough

Observer (1989) *All muck but little money*, 22 December, pp. 25–6.

Open University (1985) *The Countryside Handbook*, Croom Helm, London.
Parker, K. (1984) *A Tale of Two Villages*, PPJPB, Bakewell.
Parkes, C. (1983) *Law of the Countryside*, Association of Countryside Rangers Press, Suffok.
Peak and Park Joint Planning Board (1984) *Annual Report*, PPJPB, Bakewell.
Smyth, R. (1987) *City Wildspace*, Hilary Shipman, London.
Speaight, A. and Stone, G. (1985) *Architects Journal Legal Handbook*, Architectural Press, London.
Times, The (1988) *Push and Pull of Green Line*, June 1988.
Walker, R. J. (1981) *The English Legal System*, Butterworth, London.

FOUR

Supply and demand: the national picture

I thought it would last my time, –
The sense that beyond the town
There would always be fields and farms,
Where the village louts could climb
Such trees as were not cut down.

Philip Larkin, Going Going (1972)

While most countryside managers work within relatively fixed geographical areas, they still work within an international and a national context. Basic ecological training tells us that the environment does not regard administrative boundaries with anything but disdain. Similarly, the demand for access to that environment and the thirst for knowledge about it has an international perspective.

To place all of this in a manageable framework, all countryside managers need to be aware of the national trends in the resources that they manage locally. These resources are the landscape of the countryside, the natural history of the countryside, accessibility and recreational provision. Furthermore, each of these elements has a demand and a supply side to the equation. For example, the 'supply' of landscape is changing in that major pressures on the countryside are brought about by agricultural changes, development and recreational pressure. Conversely, the demand for landscape is also changing as more people seek 'attractive', 'quiet' or other similar places to either recreate or live.

A further reason for assessing national trends is that the forces influencing national change often work at a local level, albeit with local variations and differences. Thus, if we can understand national changes in the countryside, it leads to a better understanding of local changes.

Areas of land designation clearly follow geographical patterns, dictated to a large extent by conventional wisdom about what is attractive. Patterns of use of the countryside are largely related to socio-economic circumstances. It must be accepted, therefore, that to fully understand the reasons for change, we must address deeper psychological issues which underlie human needs, particularly in the area of leisure and recreation. Kraus (1978) and Nash (1960) provide useful appraisals. The human response to landscape and amenity is covered in Appleton (1975), Bracey (1970) and Shepheard (1967).

This chapter examines patterns of supply, of accessible countryside, recreation opportunities, the landscape and areas of natural history importance. The demand side of the discussion looks at similar areas. Finally, in order to pull the two parts of the discussion together, the concept of marketing is introduced as a method for balancing the demands made on the environment with the supply of available countryside.

4.1 LAND DESIGNATION

The plethora of land designation that cover the countryside have arisen, as we have seen, from the legislation that underpins the work of the countryside manager. With National Parks, statutory green belts and other designation some 50% of the rural environment of England and Wales is covered by at least one environmental designation. This led the then Secretary of State for the Environment to indicate that one of his 'nightmares' was that 'by the year 2000, all of Britain will be designated something or other' (*Observer*, 1988). However, as we have seen, the method of designation is one of the few mechanisms available to country-side managers to protect the environment. The lengthy public enquiry over designation of the North Pennines Area of Outstanding Natural Beauty suggests that the process of designation is getting more difficult (Countryside Commission, 1987b).

There are six major designations of land which specifically relate to the work of the countryside manager; namely, National Parks, Areas of Outstanding Natural Beauty, Heritage Coastlines, National Nature Reserves, Country Parks and Sites of Special Scientific Interest. Figure 4.1 shows the spread of National Parks, Areas of Outstanding Natural Beauty and Heritage Coastline in England and Wales. With the exception of coastlines and the Broads, the designations have an obvious correlation with upland areas. The reasons for this were explained earlier, but in the minds of many people, the countryside is still synonymous with the uplands. The history of the designation of the National Parks (and to a lesser extent the Areas of Outstanding Natural Beauty) is discussed in Bell (1979). In many cases the natural designations represent a major influence on local recreational patterns, policy formulation

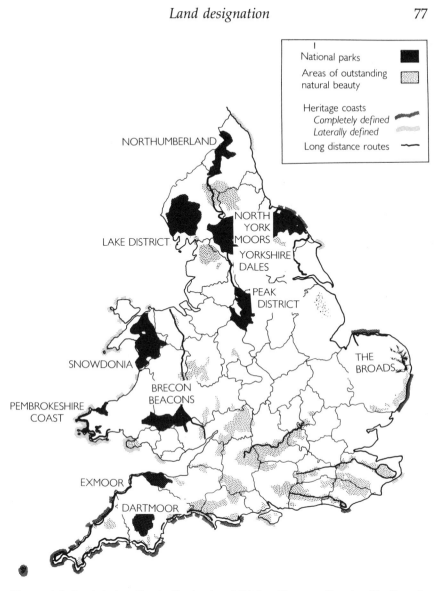

Figure 4.1 *Land designation in England and Wales.* (Source: *Countryside Commission, 1986.*)

and, hence, resource allocation. North Yorkshire County Council, for example, which contains two National Parks (North Yorkshire Moors and the Yorkshire Dales) and one Area of Outstanding Natural Beauty (the Howardian Hills) has its environmental resources stretched as most

Private Provision of Countryside: Most of Britain's countryside is in private ownership, but multi-land use is actually managed in many areas.

of the resources are, understandably, focused on these areas of national importance.

The Areas of Outstanding Natural Beauty are somewhat different and the reasons for their designation are different to those of National Parks (Countryside Commission, 1983a). However, whilst the designation is primarily to 'conserve natural beauty' and not to 'meet the demands of recreation' they do face many of the same problems as National Parks and, in reality, they are also important recreational and natural history resources. Many are managed by joint Advisory Committees (with representatives of local authorities, amenity groups and landowners) and some have project officers working within them to counteract any localized conflicts (Silverdale in Lancashire, for example).

Country parks are designated locally and there are over 200 country-wide; it is therefore impracticable to plot them all. Collectively, however, they also contribute to the national context in that they represent part of the overall provision of countryside that has been specifically designated to accommodate recreation and nature conservation.

Land designations also include land specifically allocated for nature conservation, principally Sites of Special Scientific Interest (SSSI) and National Nature Reserves. Some 8% of Britain is so designated, although all of these areas are not necessarily open for access by the public; indeed, many SSSIs are on private land, which in turn leads to problems of loss of ecological value (Bathe, 1987). There are some 4000 Sites of Special Scientific Interest scheduled in Britain and 200 National Nature Reserves. This number, however, fluctuates as land is lost, new sites are discovered and new designations are processed. From our point of view, the importance of such sites is that not only do they represent a national resource which in turn has local resource implications, but also the sites themselves are often managed by countryside managers (Nature Conservancy Council, 1987).

Other designations which have a bearing on the national provision of countryside are green belts and so-called agricultural policy areas, contained in Structure and Local Plans as prepared by local authorities. The original concept of a green belt was of a multi-functional area of land providing a landscape edge to the urban areas, a limit to development and a site where 'buffer' uses such as country parks could be provided. In reality, this multi-use function has become blurred and many countryside projects designed to alleviate conflict are now concentrated upon the urban fringe (Countryside Commission, 1983c, for example). Recent Government Guidelines suggest that this issue is likely to become even more blurred as green belts are identified as potential development areas to reduce pressure elsewhere in the country. The whole issue of the loss of land from agriculture and countryside to built development has long been of major concern in Britain, due to the size of the population and the relatively small size of the country (Best, 1981). The future of existing development plans, as produced by local authorities, is continually under review and pressure to release land for development, and thus reduce the supply of available countryside, will undoubtedly continue (HMSO, 1986).

While it is true that some 50% of the land surface of Britain has some environmental designation attached to it, it is not the case that such designation allows for or encourages all elements of an integrated management approach. Areas of Outstanding Natural Beauty, for example, are not designated to accommodate recreation although the designations do allow managers to prioritize their own objectives. Other issues, including public access and recreation, need to be addressed in more conventional ways. For this reason, the public-rights-of-way network is vital to allow and encourage public access into the 'wider countryside'. Underpinning all of these land designations, the public rights-of-way which cover the country are increasingly being seen as the key to access into the rural environment. For this reason, recent policy changes within the Countryside Commission have focused on public rights-of-way as a major issue for recreational provision in the twenty-first century (Countryside Commission, 1987b).

The above summary only represents part of the picture of the supply of countryside. Specific sites are designated to allow some degree of protection of recreational, landscape or ecological importance. Furthermore, to a greater or lesser extent, the whole of the countryside is accessible through the public-rights-of-way system. Countryside managers have an obligation not only to protect their own particular piece of this national jigsaw, but also to seek to protect the integrity of the whole national framework.

Before we assess the qualitative and quantitative changes that are taking place which affect the supply of accessible countryside we must also consider other elements of the countryside which are available for the public enjoyment of the natural environment.

4.1.2   Scottish land designations

In Chapter 3 we saw that the legislative framework of Scotland is different to that of England and Wales. As a result, the land classifications are slightly different, although the objectives of landscape and nature conservation and public enjoyment remain the same.

Sites of Special Scientific Interest and National Nature Reserves are designated within Scotland by the Nature Conservancy Council. The landscape/recreational designations do, however, differ. Prior to the 1949

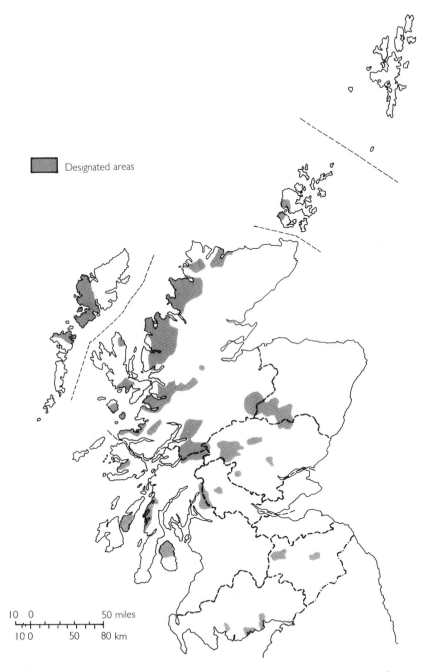

Figure 4.2 *National scenic areas of Scotland.* (Source: *Country Commission for Scotland, 1978a.*)

Act, there was also debate in Scotland about the benefits of National Parks, and while none was actually designated at the time, eight National Park Direction Areas were designated within which tighter planning controls were to be applied. These areas are: Loch Lomond/The Trossachs; Glen Affric; Ben Nevis/Glen Coe; The Cairngorms; Loch Torridon/ Loch Maree; Moidart/Knoydart; Glen Lyon/Ben Lawers; St Mary's Loch.

In order to provide a wider framework, particularly for landscape protection, the Countryside Commission for Scotland nominated in 1978 some forty National Scenic Areas. These were approved, special planning controls were initiated and forward planning proposals were generated. Responsibility for these plans falls to local planning authorities. More relevant is the suggestion that 'conservation . . . relates to land management, for instances by modifying planting, or . . . safeguarding public vantage points' (Countryside Commission, 1978a) (see Figure 4.2).

The third land designation unique to Scotland is the Regional Park. This is a loosely defined concept which, in terms of size and management, lies between a country park and a National Park. Regional Parks are managed by the regional planning authorities in Scotland.

4.2   VOLUNTARY AND PRIVATE PROVISION

The land designations discussed above are all statutory, and the Countryside Commission and other agencies have a duty to designate such land. Other government agencies and private/charitable organizations have no such duty, but choose to do so either because they have been instructed to have 'due regard for' the environment and public access (as with the Forestry Commission and the water authorities, for example) or because it is within their constitution to do so (the National Trust, for example) or because it is profitable (mainly private sector interest, such as theme parks or stately homes).

It is impossible here to list all the relevant sites or indeed even types of site. Some initiatives or organizations bear particular attention, principally statutory undertakers and several of the major charitable trusts. Many of the major statutory undertakers and quasi-government organizations have been specifically mentioned in countryside legislation, and now actively provide for amenity, recreation and protection of the environment – at least on specific sites, if not generally throughout their operations. The Forestry Commission's response to this call was initially through Forest Parks (which have developed into major tourist attractions and holiday centres) and picnic sites. Lately, however, a general policy move has been towards indigenous broadleaf woods, with a multi-functional management framework (Forestry Commission, 1985). Indeed, at a much lower level of priority, the Forestry Commission has provided for some levels of recreation for many years. More recently, however, it has become a major part of their policy.

Similarly, the various water authorities have begun to view the landscape, ecology and recreation as an integral part of their operations which are, essentially, engineering based. The North West Water Authority, for example, is a major sponsor of the West Pennine Moors project, while Thames Water are actively promoting access along the length of the River Thames. Similarly, access to reservoirs and balancing ponds is becoming more and more usual, rather than the exception to the rule (Countryside Commission, 1988b). Legislation to privatize the water industries has, however, affected this progress.

Among the charitable trusts, the National Trust and the National Trust for Scotland are by far the most important. Combined they form one of the three most important landowners in the country, surpassed in land-holding terms only by the Crown and the State. Their membership level is well over a million and a half, and in all senses they have a national impact on both site protection and public and government opinion. The original belief of the founders of the organization were principally for the preservation of buildings and places (Fedden, 1974); however, their remit has increasingly broadened to include landscape conservation, public access and nature conservation. The importance of the National Trusts is born out by the special relationships they hold with Government wherein land held by the Trusts is inalienable and cannot be removed from their ownership without a special Act of Parliament. In many respects, the Trust represents 'a peculiarly English (British?) insitution in that it fulfils a national need without being in anyway part of the state' (Fedden, op. cit.). We have already seen the reticence of Government to address the issues of conservation head-on and the National Trust does, therefore partly fulfil this role, at least on its own land.

Local conservation trusts (under the umbrella of the British Association of Nature Conservation) and other specific conservation groups such as the Royal Society for the Protection of Birds add to the supply of countryside by providing sites that they own and manage as local or private nature reserves. In 1989 it was estimated that there were some 1400 nature reserves managed by local wildlife trusts and 93 managed by the Royal Society for the Protection of Birds (Nature Conservancy Council, 1984). Table 4.1 shows the approximate area of land within Britain that is designated for nature conservation.

The only remaining significant blocks of land given special designations in England and Wales are commons. They cover some 4% of the

Table 4.1. *Categories of protected areas for nature conservation, 1984*

Category	Number	Area in hectares
National Nature Reserve	195	150 003
RSPB Reserve	93	43 728
Nature Conservation Trust Reserve	*c.*1400	44 090
Woodland Trust Reserve	102	1 214
Forest Nature Reserve	11	2 448
Local Nature Reserve	105	14 371
Wildfowl Refuges	44	11 180
(additional to those covered by other categories)		266 034
Bird sanctuaries	16	—
Biological SSSI	3166 } 4150*	
Geological SSSI	984 }	1 470 900

*including those covered by other listed categories.

Source: Nature Conservancy Council (1985).

land surface of England and Wales in around 8500 individual pieces of common. Commons have individual or groups of owners – commoners – who have certain rights over the land, such as the rights of herbage, estover, pannage, turbary or piscary (respectively the right to graze, take firewood, graze pigs on Beech or Oak mast, cut peat for fuel and fish). Some 20% of commons are also open to access for the public, and there are moves to make informal access a legal right rather than *de facto* (Countryside Commission, 1986). However, like all land, commons are under increasing pressure for agricultural intensification, development or recreation (Clayden, 1985). Status as a common, as with other designations, does not guarantee survival as open country. This usually comes with positive and active management.

4.2.1 Summary

The somewhat rapid role call of designations of land is intended as a guide to the more frequently encountered types of countryside. The overall impression is a confusing jigsaw of sites with any number of designations, not all of which are mutually exclusive. The Shropshire Hills Area of Outstanding Natural Beauty, for example, contains an area of common land (The Long Mynd), land owned by the National Trust (Cardingmill Valley), a number of Sites of Special Scientific Interest and an Environmentally Sensitive Area (Clun Forest), some nature reserves managed by the local wildlife trust, and a National Nature Reserve (The Stiperstones). And we wonder why the general public are confused?

Table 4.2. *Statutory land designations: a summary*

Designation	Act	By whom	Main purpose
National Parks	1949	Countryside Commission	Landscape, Recreation, Agriculture and Forestry
Country Parks	1967 (Scotland) 1968 (England and Wales)	Countryside Commission	Recreation and Landscape
National Nature Reserves	1949	Nature Conservancy Council	Natural History
Sites of Special Scientific Interest	1949 (1981)	Nature Conservancy Council	Natural History
Local Nature Reserves	1949	Local Authorities	Natural History and Education
Environmentally Sensitive Areas	1986	Ministry of Agriculture, Food, and Fisheries	Landscape, Natural Agriculture
Areas of Outstanding Natural Beauty	1949	Countryside Commission	Landscape
Regional Parks	1985	Regional Councils (Scotland)	Landscape and Recreation
Forest Parks	1968	Foresty Commission	Landscape and Access
National Scenic Areas	1967	Countryside Commission (Scotland)	Landscape

Notes: 1949 National Parks Act
1967 Countryside (Scotland) Act
1968 Countryside Act
1981 Wildlife and Countryside Act
1985 Local Govt. Act (Scotland)
1986 Agriculture Act

(All designations subject to ratification by appropriate Minister.)

The issue of designation is a matter of no small debate for countryside managers, but until such time as an integrated approach to land management in the countryside is taken, this plethora of designations will be an integral part of the scene. Table 4.2 summarizes the above information.

4.2.2 Changing patterns

The amount of designated countryside in Britain varies over time, although major designations are unlikely to change greatly. The most

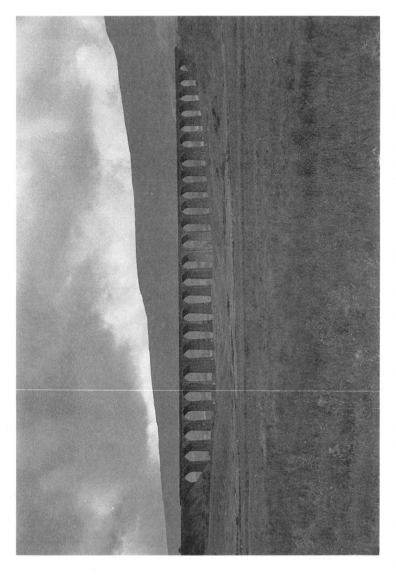

Ribblehead Viaduct: Synonymous with the national concern to keep beautiful areas accessible for the public.

recent cases (the North Pennines AONB and the Broads) have taken over ten years to reach the statute books. Arguably, the Broads, which now has its own special status under the Broads Acts of 1987 and which was finally granted National Park status in 1989, has taken forty years because it was originally suggested for National Park status in the Hobhouse Report of 1947. The amount of land lost to permanent development is similarly fluctuating but still relatively steady. Land loss to development is presently running at some 1% per decade. The major changes have not therefore occurred in the *amount* of countryside (although this trend may change in the latter part of this century) but in the *quality* of that countryside. The countryside manager must be aware of national changes to the quality of the countryside to both understand processes that occur at a local level and to put these local changes in context. This again helps the manager to prioritize issues on his or her own site or in the area for which he or she is responsible. The following discussion examines qualitative changes in the landscape and natural history of the countryside individually, although they are occasionally synonymous. The split comes as a result of the differing responsibilities of the two quasi-public bodies, the Countryside Commission and the Nature Conservancy Council, and the areas wherein their responsibilities lie.

4.2.3 Landscape changes

Although all development in the countryside brings about landscape change (built development, mineral extraction or statutory undertakings, for example), of most obvious concern to the countryside manager are changes to the landscape brought about by changes in agricultural and forestry practices. This is because these particular operations lie outside planning law and cannot be tackled through traditional means of development control or restoration conditions. Therefore, changes to the agricultural and forestry landscapes must be addressed by the countryside manager rather than the planner *per se*.

Soon after its formation in 1968 the Countryside Commission in England and Wales (and to a lesser extent the Countryside Commission for Scotland) identified the landscape changes occurring in lowland and upland Britain as matters of priority (Countryside Commission, 1974; 1983b). More recently, the issue of the loss of landscape (and wildlife habitat) has become one of national significance (Shoard, 1980), particularly with many people's growing concern about the devastation of the countryside brought about by agriculture, fuelled by national and integrated agricultural policies. While the legislative background to agricultural policy and this relationship to the wider environment is chang-

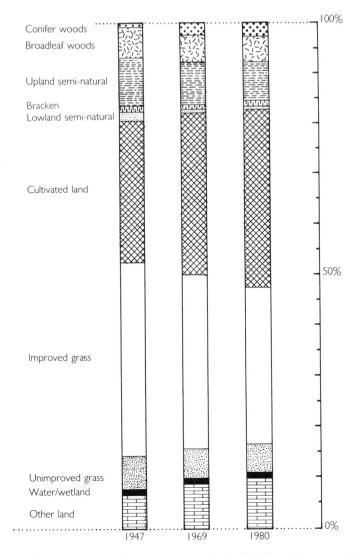

Figure 4.3 *Cover of major landscape types in England and Wales 1947–1980.* (Source: *Countryside Commission, 1987c.*)

ing, albeit slowly, the process of landscape change still continues. The Countryside Commission also undertook a national survey of landscape changes in 1987. For the first time this gave the nation a quantifiable measure of changes that, until the time of the survey, were known to exist but for which there was very little accurate evidence. The result,

Table 4.3. *Linear features: total lengths, England and Wales 1947–1985 ('000 km).*

	1947	1969	1980	1985
(i) Hedgerows				
England	662	578	534	507
Wales	134	125	118	114
England and Wales	**796**	**703**	**653**	**621**
(ii) Fences				
England	162	170	175	183
Wales	22	24	25	27
England and Wales	**185**	**193**	**199**	**210**
(iii) Walls				
England	101	98	96	94
Wales	16	16	15	15
England and Wales	**117**	**114**	**111**	**108**
(iv) Banks				
England	142	132	125	121
Wales	9	8	7	7
England and Wales	**151**	**140**	**132**	**128**
(v) Open ditches				
England	116	111	107	107
Wales	6	5	4	4
England and Wales	**122**	**116**	**111**	**112**
(vi) Woodland fringe				
England	201	201	201	202
Wales	40	40	42	41
England and Wales	**241**	**241**	**243**	**243**

Source: Countryside Commission (1987c).

Monitoring Landscape Changes (Countryside Commission, 1987c) gives percentage cover for thirty-one major categories of feature/rural land use for the years 1947, 1969 and 1980.

As a rough guide to the type of results obtained by the study, some features of note are that: semi-natural vegetation was reduced by more than 25% from 1947 to 1980; about 25% of all broadleaved woodlands were lost between 1947 and 1980; the amount of farmed land remained steady at 72% of land surface, but arable land rose from 27% in 1947 to 35% in 1980.

Figure 4.3 shows the relevant data for major landscape types over the study period, while Table 4.3 shows absolute changes in six important types of linear feature. The changes are clear – a move towards less semi-natural landscapes and less variation through hedges and ditches. There are also regional variations within this overall decline. For example, from comparable points in 1947, the south-east of England lost around 30 000 km of hedgerow, while the south-west of England lost 17 000 km.

Against this background there have been a number of measures to try to counteract the loss of landscape features not only through legislative means (Environmentally Sensitive Areas) but also work by countryside managers in a number of key areas. By and large, however, the positive management has been focused on the 'better landscapes of National Parks or Areas of Outstanding Natural Beauty', while its everyday land-scapes have declined most rapidly and are in equal need of balanced management.

There is little doubt, therefore, that the rural landscape of Britain is changing. Agriculture and forestry operations have changed rapidly since the original concept of the 1949 Act was drawn together. Then it was assumed that agriculture and forestry could somehow act as guardians to the rural environment. It is not so clear now.

But change is not necessarily a bad thing, and the Countryside Commission and others have been quick to spot the opportunities offered by moves to diversify farm enterprises. However, there is some concern that change will be random at best and harmful at worst. The result of this would be that the regional and local differences in landscape would be lost. Controlled change is required, at the centre of which must lie a landscape strategy for rural areas (Countryside Commission, 1988a).

4.2.4   Ecological changes

Parallel to, and sometimes synonymous with, landscape change is change to the ecological quality of the countryside. Each year the Nature Conservancy Council records trends and highlights specific examples of habitat loss and protection in the Annual Report. In 1984, many of these strands were brought together and the Council published a position statement within which several objectives were also restated (Nature Conservancy Council, 1984).

The changes that can be identified are, for the most part, for the worse. This is shown in the loss of not only rare habitats which have traditionally been seen as vulnerable but also in everyday habitats such as hedgerows, ponds and unimproved pasture. With these once common-place habitats, the numbers of formerly abundant species such as frogs, toads, butterflies and some 'agricultural weeds' are also decreasing.

The Nature Conservancy Council itself identifies seven 'failures' for conservation, the loss of habitats being 'the most serious failure of the conservation movement ... since 1949'. Many of the other failures, such as lack of integration, lack of resources and the misdirection of some research programmes, all link to the loss of habitats. It is impossible to identify fully all the trends or pursue the causes or consequences of any of them too vigorously. A short stocktake of some of the more striking examples will indicate the 'sheer scale of loss of damage to wildlife'.

As a guide, all semi-natural habitats have seen a reduction in area since the 1949 Act. Specific habitats show greater losses than others, as, too, do some regions. For example, in 1934 there were some 100 square kilometres of fenland in East Anglia; there are now less than 10 square kilometres. In 1933, there were some 142 000 hectares of semi-natural woodland in England and Wales; there are now less than 76 000. Over 60% of all lowland, raised mires have been lost since 1948 due to afforestation, peat-winning, reclamation for agriculture or repeated burning. In four National Parks (Dartmoor, Brecon Beacons, Snowdonia and North Yorkshire Moors) over 15 000 hectares of upland grassland, heath or blanket bog have been lost through landuse change. Four species of dragonfly have become extinct. Over 40% of all lowland, acid heaths have disappeared, and in some areas the loss is as high as 98%.

The catalogue could continue, indeed annually it does through the reports of the Nature Conservancy Council. Shoard (op. cit.) reserves space for her most forceful discussion for the people responsible for habitat loss. But it still continues. Recent legislation will eventually lead to some degree of stabilization of the intensification process but it will be too late to replace the habitats and pieces already lost.

A lot of the work of the Nature Conservancy Council and other groups is now geared towards protecting gene pools or wildlife reservoirs from which other areas – possibly set-aside from agriculture production or reclaimed from industrial dereliction – can colonize.

One reason for the loss of high-quality ecological habitats with concurrently only a slight loss of actual open countryside is that many of the changes in landuse are not from countryside to developed land but are within the general category of open space. Afforestation, agricultural intensification and mineral extraction all leave 'countryside', but it is a more sterile and less varied countryside. This need not be the care however, and countryside managers and others must seek to bring about environmentally stable change.

4.3   SUPPLY: A SUMMARY

Some of the most emotional debates about the countryside revolve around the loss of landscape and ecological quality. In purely quantitative terms, the loss of open countryside has been steady but relatively slow due largely to the planning machinery established in 1947. However, objective evidence shows how great has been the reduction in the quality of that countryside. This has come at a time when there has never been such a large demand for access to and recreational opportunities in the countryside. It is partly as a result of this demand

Pennine Way: Parts of a nationwide pattern of trails, long distance routes and paths, of which managers must always be aware, if not directly involved with.

that legislative changes have been made to accommodate wildlife and landscape within the remit of agriculture and forestry. Some of these legislative changes are beginning to be implemented now, through Environmentally Sensitive Areas for example. Central to the success of all of these varied initiatives is a co-ordination on rural policy at a national level. However, as the Nature Conservancy Council admit, while 'needs of nature conservation and scenic beauty do not invariably coincide, . . . the disparate development of the NCC and the Countryside Commission has continued to the present day' (Nature Conservancy Council, 1984, op. cit.).

The countryside manager who works at a county, district or subregional level therefore has a responsibility not only to provide for this recreational demand, but also to help to reverse the national trends of landscape and wildlife decline. This can be done by sympathetic and integrated management of key sites, and also by working with and influencing sympathetic work practices in others. If this is done we can avoid the following sad prediction.

I cannot say how shock'd I am to see
Such *variations* in our scenery . . .
All fields we'll turn to sports grounds, lit at night
From concrete standards by fluorescent light . . .
So don't encourage tourists. Stay you hand
Until we've *really* got the country planned.
Sir John Betjeman, *The Town Clerk's View*

4.4 DEMANDS

The demands upon our countryside are many. Developers, mineral extractors and statutory undertakers all require land to operate. However, while countryside managers must be aware of and seek to work with these pressures, it is the demands of the recreationalist that are of paramount importance here. The increase in this demand can be assessed in a number of ways: the rise in membership of conservation or recreation groups such as the National Trust or the Ramblers Association. It is estimated that around 20% of people in the country are members of one or more such groups. It can also be gauged from the number of visits to certain key sites. More generally, it has been estimated through survey work that on a summer Sunday upwards of 15 million people visit the countryside (Countryside Commission, 1985a).

Demand, for our purposes, takes two forms. Firstly, demand comes from the general public who use, visit, drive through the countryside either individually or in small often family units. Secondly, demand comes from a number of specific groups who have a membership motivated to protect either the landscape, or the natural history, or the public access, or often all of these. It is a peculiarity of countryside management that some of the groups that represent the 'demand' side are also evident on the 'supply' side of the equation. Local wildlife trusts, for example, are among the most active groups promoting the cause of nature conservation – demanding a great supply of good environmental work practices. Equally, they also supply, often for public access, sites of natural historical importance.

4.4.1 Public demand

There has long been in Britain a tradition of the public demanding, often forcibly, access to the countryside for informal and passive recreation. The conflict between the landowning interests and the would-be recreationalists is best exemplified by the series of confrontations around the Kinder Plateau in the Peak District. Events preceding the Kinder Trespass and following it are well documented in Hill (1980).

The largely urban-based demand for the opportunity for access to the countryside has increased greatly over the past two decades as a result of several factors. Awareness of the attractiveness of the countryside has undoubtedly increased, as too has the amount of leisure time available to the public. However, by far the most important single factor which has led to a massive increase in trips to the countryside is the growth in car ownership. Coppock and Duffield (1975) showed this most conclusively, and patterns of use and demand for sites and facilities are closely linked to levels of car ownership. Leisure travel is now as important a facet of countryside recreation as is walking or picnicking, and the issue of the ability of people to travel to the countryside is central to many policy decisions that have been made and will be made in the future.

The Countryside Commission's national survey of 1984 shows that 63% of all trips to the countryside are made by car – alternatively, someone with a car is three times more likely to visit the countryside than someone without a car.

The results of the 1984 household survey cover a wide range of issues, including the scale of use of the countryside. What sort of people use the countryside? What people actually do in the countryside? What are people's motivation and interests? In all, some 6302 questionnaires were completed with over thirty individual pieces of information gathered from each respondent. The complete data set is clearly a weighty document, but the trends that the study reveals and the implication that these have for countryside managers are of greatest interest (Figure 4.4).

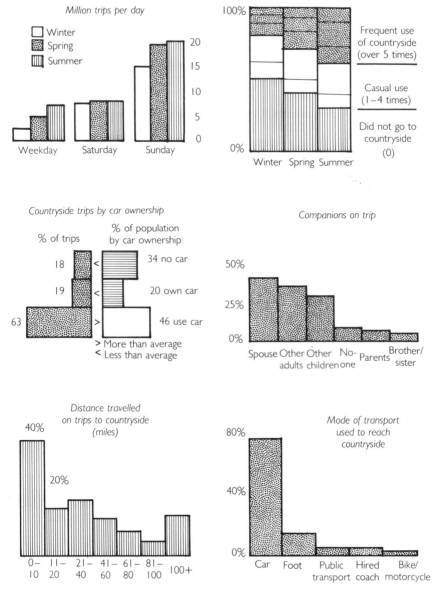

Figure 4.4 *Parameters of recreational use of the countryside.* (Source: *Countryside Commission, 1985a.*)

Since the first large recreational survey undertaken in recent years (Sports Council, 1967) the participation level in countryside recreation has increased. This increase is due, largely, to people who did not formerly visit the countryside now showing an interest – no participation dropped from 47% in 1977 to 32% in 1984. The demand for countryside recreation is therefore increasing. Furthermore, those groups who did visit the countryside in 1977 actually visited it more in 1984. Coupled with this overall increase in demand, there has also been a trend towards using 'local' countryside. An indicator of this is the fact that, in 1977, 39% of trips to the countryside were less than 20 miles in total. In 1984, this figure rose to 46%.

The reason that people visit the countryside is psychological to a large extent, but more practical reasons also underlie participation. Car ownership, as we have seen, has had a major influence; so too has the rise in disposable income, the increase in leisure time available and, in recent years, perhaps less fully understood, the steady rise in unemployment.

The implications of this information on the work of countryside managers are varied. Firstly, the scale and the varied types of participation make a 'standard response' to the demand impossible! Different types of groups, different types of activity and different geographical locations of facilities all require planning and managing. A second important implication is on the targeting of resources. The survey shows that most of the visits to the countryside are to what are termed 'areas unmanaged for recreation'; that is, the wider countryside. Instead of simply focusing resources on key sites such as country parks, therefore, countryside managers must now address the issue more generally. Thirdly, the importance of the countryside around major towns and cities is increasing as people now appear less willing to travel long distances simply to visit the countryside.

(Interestingly, if we compare the location of the National Parks with the major centres of population, the majority lie well outside the 20 miles round trip level.) Finally the Countryside Commission emphasize the limitations of 'traditional' countryside information, such as leaflets, guide books, etc., for general interest in the countryside. Most important of all is a 'welcoming high standard and pleasant countryside'. Once the public are aware that such a countryside exists, they will return to it and use it in a variety of ways, rather than have limitations or restrictions placed upon them through interpretive media. The countryside manager must therefore broaden people's experience of the countryside and offer them new ideas rather than channel their interests into traditional pursuits, all the while, however, being conscious of the other needs of the countryside, such as landscape conservation.

While most trips to the countryside are still by people who are not members of a countryside organization (such as the National Trust, Ramblers Association, Royal Society for the Protection of Birds or a Local Wildlife Trust), members of such organizations are more than twice as likely to visit the countryside than non-members. This suggests that for around 20% of the population who are members of countryside groups, the countryside represents more than a casual interest. The importance of these groups in maintaining a voice in the decision-making process both nationally and locally is therefore worthy of some extra attention.

4.5 COUNTRYSIDE ORGANIZATIONS

The countryside organizations fulfil many roles and have, apparently, an inexhaustible desire to multiply! Some, such as Friends of the Earth (formed in the United States in 1969) or the Council for the Protection of Rural England (formed in 1926) are purely pressure orientated, not being concerned with owning or managing land; notwithstanding this, they and other similar organizations have a vital role to play at the local and national level. Other organizations, such as the County Conservation Trusts (first one formed in Norfolk in 1926) and the Royal Society for the Protection of Birds (formed as the Society for the Protection of Birds in 1889, and receiving royal assent in 1904) play a dual role; not only do they 'supply' countryside through their land holdings but also actively demand better protection of the environment. The role of these organizations in the environmental and countryside movement cannot be overemphasized. Their impact has been threefold.

Firstly, these organizations have an impact on legislation. The most notable case is perhaps that of the National Trust which, in 1907, was the subject of the National Trust Act. Within this Act, the trust's land could not be removed from their ownership without an Act of Parliament. In effect, Trust land was safeguarded in perpetuity in England, Scotland and Wales. Other less obvious examples exist; the impact of the Ramblers Association on the access contest of the 1949 National Parks and Access to the Countryside Act, for example. Lowe and Goyder (1983) have plotted the links between environmental groups and the development of legislation in Britain which goes some way towards explaining the apparently haphazard way in which some of our legislation materializes.

The second reason for the importance of countryside organizations within the context of countryside management is their impact upon both the supply and the demand side of the equation. The Ramblers Association is one of the country's most vocal groups, which clearly demands certain rights and helps to protect the statutory rights-of-way systems. Furthermore, individuals within the Ramblers Association are often active in other countryside work. The Royal Society for the Protection of Birds and the British Association of Nature Conservation (formed 1979 as the umbrella organization for the County Conservation Trusts) both influence supply and demand: 'demand' by seeking to protect sites of natural history and social importance, and 'supply' by actually, owning, through a local/country network, sites which are managed as countryside sites, albeit usually only open for members. As organizations and individuals, many countryside groups both demand and supply good, well-managed pieces of countryside through their own sites and reserves.

Finally, countryside organizations often act as pressure groups seeking to change opinion in political, social and cultural ways. The lobbying activities of some organizations are often quiet and unobtrusive, but exist nonetheless. Other groups, such as the Council for the Protection of Rural England (founded in 1926) or Greenpeace (formed 1971), work in more high profile ways on a wide range of countryside/environmental issues. This, in turn, leads to changes in patterns of demand, which have an impact upon the management of the countryside. Often this change will be slow or apparently unconnected, but the links between environmentalism and countryside management ensure that wider changes in concern for environmental issues manifest themselves in changes in the management of the countryside.

In Britain there are scores of countryside organizations/environmental groups. Open University (1985) has listed some of the more important ones, but there exist many more, willing to oversee or follow developments in the countryside. Indeed, many of the landowning organizations employ countryside managers to handle their landowning obligations. Little wonder, therefore, that the roles of gamekeeper and poacher often become confused! Countryside organizations have a long history in British countryside management, with voluntary political concern for the countryside often being voiced decades if not centuries before political moves are made. The Society for the Promotion of Natural History was founded in 1782, for example – nearly 200 years before the Nature Conservancy was formed in 1949 (later to become the Nature Conservancy Council in 1973). Similarly, the Commons, Open Spaces and Footpaths Preservation Society was formed in 1865 and the 1949 Act only began the political concern for these issues over 80 years later. While the Scottish experience is less slow (with the first National Forest Park being formed in 1936 in Argyll and the first National Nature Reserve being formed in 1951, only two years after the 1949 Act) the voluntary organizations have led public opinion throughout Britain. As voices of demand, therefore, they have a long and distinguished history.

How do we value landscape? Many areas of Britain require some value put on their landscape or wildlife importance; this is a necessary pre-requisite of management, but is an illusive goal.

4.6 DEMAND – A SUMMARY

The demand for access to and quiet enjoyment of the countryside is increasing, and looks set to continue doing so as all the parameters governing countryside recreation continue to change. If this pressure is viewed in the context of pressures from other directions – new homes, holiday homes, mineral extraction, major developments such as roads, airports, etc. – the strain that will be placed on the countryside, particularly near to major centres of population, is self-evident. As this demand from *vox populi* for a pleasanter and more accessible countryside grows, it will increasingly have to be accommodated within the decision-making process. This is already happening; major sand and gravel extractors are now looking to restore workings not to agriculture as was usual before the advent of butter and wheat surpluses in the early 1980s, but to countryside recreation sites, often as private country clubs. There is clearly money to be made in countryside recreation.

This demand for access is a key feature in the work of the countryside manager and it is by providing for this demand that the manager is set apart from other environmental professionals such as horticulturalists, ecologists or landscape architects. Reconciling demand for recreation with the protection of the landscape and ecological quality of the countryside is not an easy task, but as the demand for access shows no signs of decreasing, it must clearly be addressed.

4.7 MARKETING

Marketing and the countryside may not, on first glance, appear to be compatible concepts. This is largely the result of popular conceptions about marketing. It is often viewed as being synonymous with high-pressure salesmanship or 'product-orientated selling': a company has a predetermined product or service which they then convince the public that they, as customers, need. To bring this example slightly closer to home, a local authority may provide a recreational facility which has been designated, built and opened without a single point of reference to the potential users. Opening times, programmes and charges are determined, again without reference to the actual customers (Torkildsen, 1985). This example probably highlights the problem more accurately.

The process of marketing, if undertaken well, reverses this trend. It is the customer's wants and needs which determine the service, product or experience that is being provided. Clearly, in this context there is no such thing as 'the general public'. There is a large body of potential users of a product, which can be separated into a large number of different markets. Some are well known to countryside managers, such as the disabled, young children, families, ethnic minorities, unemployed school leavers, etc.

The process of marketing gives the manager a means of identifying which groups or markets use existing services; whether this is acceptable; what to do if different markets or target groups are to be identified; and how to adapt the service to meet the needs of existing or new market groups.

The concept and implementation of marketing techniques is complex and there are many in-depth studies available including Kotler (1975), McIver (1968) and Martin and Mason (1980).

4.7.1 Marketing theory

The aim of marketing is to 'try to ensure that the requirements of people or organizations are continuously matched by opportunities and resources' (Clayden, 1985). Within this definition there are many terms which require further clarification. Firstly, 'people' needs to be defined. As we have seen, population falls into many separate markets, each with its own needs, requirements, desires and demands. The process of dividing the community into a number of markets is market segmentation. Each market segment can (and does) overlap with other segments. Commonly used bases for establishing market segmentation are such criteria as age, sex, socio-economic group, education, disabilities, family profile or cultural origins. The process of defining a target segment of the market is in itself a very complex process.

The second element of the above definition requiring some further explanation is 'opportunities and resources'. This is variably defined as the product, the service or the experience. Actually, defining 'the product' is again a very difficult process. For example, do people visit the countryside to walk? Or is it to enjoy the countryside experience and, if so, what is the countryside experience? The way that a product is advertised to different groups may well reflect the fact that different groups actually perceive a different product. A visit to a country park might provide unemployed persons with a means of increasing their self-esteem, while for parents it is somewhere for children to 'let off steam'. For the manager, this means that the product is not simply a country park, but a whole host of other products dependent upon the group or individual concerned.

The process of marketing is therefore a continual process of: (a) identifying existing markets (using questionnaires and surveys to establish who uses the product and why, and who does *not* use the product and *why not*), (b) setting or renewing marketing objectives (are existing markets all that are required?; does the manager want to increase the satisfaction of existing markets, or attract new markets – if so which groups?, (c) developing the product to meet the requirements of new or existing markets (either provide new or increased services developing innovative ideas and adapt existing product); (d) promoting and advertising the product (how do the markets find out about the product?; what media do they respond to?; what 'product' do they hope to find?); and (e) monitoring the success of the overall strategy.

It is impossible to explore fully the sophistication of this process within the confines of this discussion. It is important, however, that countryside managers are aware of the need to develop some marketing skills to help them meet wider objectives. In order to do this, it is easiest to look at what is called 'the marketing mix'.

4.7.2   The marketing mix

The marketing mix is the balance of a number of variables which, when successfully balanced, will provide the market with its requirements. There are four elements to the marketing mix, namely: product, place, price and promotion.

Product   The difficulty of defining the product has been discussed above. Physically, the product can be changed. In the case of the countryside manager this might be by providing a car park, by improving the visual quality of an area, by providing specialist events for children or by offering a different range of facilities. The amount of change that the product can actually accommodate will clearly depend upon wider objectives – namely, that the visual or ecological quality of the area cannot be destroyed or, alternatively, can only be changed within the constraints laid down by these wider objectives. Similarly, the product can be changed by redefining what is actually being provided – is it simply the countryside, is it an opportunity to fish or is it a chance to get away from the urban environment, however briefly? Defining the product, and changing it, requires a large amount of information about how the users and potential users of the countryside perceive it and actually use it.

Place   It used to be felt that countryside was a relatively fixed resource. However, it is now clear that countryside is wherever people perceive it as being. The opportunity to take a breath of fresh air can be provided within the urban fringe as well as in the National Parks. The countryside manager can therefore influence the place or location of the countryside either by promoting that which is already there or by creating and enhancing new sites.

Price This is a relatively straightforward concept but it, too, has its subtleties. The price charged to visit the countryside is often perceived as zero. This is not, true, however. Travel costs money; so does the purchase of food/snacks on site. The equipment needed to enjoy the countryside also costs money. A pricing policy must therefore take account of all of these factors. It is quite conceivable that, to an unemployed person, the cost of using public transport to visit the countryside is prohibitive and despite all the manager's attempts to provide a suitable product in a suitable place, the price of using that product may still be too high for a potential target group.

Promotion The promotion of a site is often perceived as being the sum total of marketing: advertising. However, as even this brief analysis indicates, it is in fact one of the last elements of the marketing process. Having established that the product provided meets the needs of the target groups in all respects, the potential markets need to be made aware of the product. This may be through something as simple as a sign on a roadside or a whole advertising/promotional launch, as used for the National Trusts Enterprise Neptune projects. In countryside work promotion does not simply mean advertising, it includes events, programmes, competitions, lectures, schools visits and published material, all of which contain an element of promotion within them.

The specific application of marketing techniques to countryside management is covered by Countryside Commission (1985a) at some length, where the full capabilities of the process are discussed. The two case studies examined here are both based upon marketing being used to match the objectives of an organization, the demands of a target group and the requirements of the countryside itself. Both studies have proved successful.

4.8   CASE STUDIES

4.8.1   Introduction

The Wayfarer Project and Operation Gateway were both concerned with the problems of meeting people's needs, but they were based on two different areas of countryside, the Peak Park and Yorkshire Dales National Parks in the case of the former, and the countryside around the urban centre of Nottingham in the case of the latter.

4.8.2   The Wayfarer Project

The Wayfarer Project (Countryside Commission, 1985b) took as its starting point the fact that while car ownership is a major influence on enjoying the countryside, there is still a large number of people who do not have access to private transport. In the large urban conurbations of Greater Manchester and West Yorkshire the car ownership levels are relatively low. However, less than 20 miles away the Peak Park offers an area ideal for outdoor recreation for those people who are interested in the countryside. The marketing dimension of the problem of matching opportunities for visiting the Peak Park with the potential demand of the non-car owning people of the areas around Manchester and Leeds is clearly stated in the study.

> Transport networks have generally evolved for needs . . . other than recreational access to the countryside. Moreover . . . potential passengers must be made aware of its (the service's) existence.

Here is reference to at least two components of the marketing mix.

Ultimately the aim of the project was to show to commercial transport operators that recreational use of the countryside is a potential market that they, the operators, could well supply.

The project had part of its history based in an earlier experiment with the Leeds–Carlisle railway line which provided a link to the heart of the Yorkshire Dales National Park (Countryside Commission, 1979). From this starting point the 'Wayfarer Concept' was developed. It looked at the problems people face when travelling by public transport: inconvenient times, booking a many-staged journey, lack of information or the sheer experience of taking several buses to reach a destination. The method of working was to appoint two full-time project officers, one for each conurbation. Both worked to a brief supplied by the Countryside Commission, but prepared in consultation with all interested groups, including local transport operators, local authority personnel, user groups and recreational providers. Collectively these groups formed the project Steering Committee.

The project officers' brief included items such as developing a transport service, promoting the new and existing services, liaison with other groups, etc. The main purpose of the project officers' job was to

> Investigate the suitability of existing bus and rail services . . . for access to the surrounding countryside and its facilities for informal recreation and to improve utilization of these facilities.

The method of working was initially that of identifying key existing routes or connections that could supply easy access to the Peak Park. The process of adjusting existing services (by supplying through tickets, giving simple timetables) and of advertising (boards, leaflets, posters and even giving existing bus services catchy titles such as Peak Wayfarer and Countrybus) was concentrated on these key services. The scheme was extended later to provide 'special/new services' to areas outside the Peak Park, and mixed mode travel.

The success of the scheme allowed all new services to more than cover the cost of the initial project. The success was not only confined to traditional, committed markets of ramblers, transport and outdoor enthusiasts but also to the wider cross-section at which the project was primarily aimed. The project was seen to succeed in several areas. Firstly, the through tickets not only cut the cost of travel, but also made booking and ticket purchase less complex; a further added impact was that of allowing residents of rural areas to have easier access to the urban centres for shopping, recreation or visits. Secondly, the special services gave a number of tangible benefits – for example, they provided a flagship for the greater possibilities available through public transport and gave a reduction in costs for not having to provide facilities for motorists. They also provided a good measure of success, which is less easy to establish on existing routes.

Thirdly, the benefit of liaison between operators was clear – an overall package was developed for the customers. Thus buses, trains and canal boats were all interlinked to provide not only access to the countryside but also an interesting trip in its own right. The concept of a network was seen as a major success; providers and users became more aware of the impact of their particular actions on a wider system, Finally, the promotion ceased to be sustained and demand for existing and new special services was reduced. In response to this, a variety of promotional techniques were used, including special clubs for children, ideas for new routes, specialist advertising or special fares.

The conclusion to this particular element of the project summarizes a central concept of marketing. 'Aiming at the general public is like firing expensive publicity material like grapeshot, with only a small percentage of the material reaching its ultimate targets.'

The work and findings of the Wayfarer Project have been reproduced or paralleled elsewhere – British Rail see 'Scenic Railways' as a central element of their marketing strategy, for example. Other examples include the London Underground (which has a long history of colourful, innovative advertisements for opportunities available through its service) and the Brighton and Hove Bus Company. The Countryside Commission have drawn together many of the results and implications of these studies and projects (Countryside Commission, 1987d).

4.8.3 Operation Gateway

Operation Gateway was launched by Nottinghamshire County Council in 1983. It was based on the awareness that 'certain sections of the population are not participating in countryside recreation or are under-represented in relation to their total numbers' (Nottinghamshire County Council, 1984).

The identification of the low participation groups in Nottinghamshire is a result of many years of market research into the use made of the countryside by the population of the county. The groups identified include low-income, car-less, one-parent families, Afro-Caribbean and Asian families and physically disabled. While it is accepted from national data that these and others form low-participation groups, the reasons for the low participation are not fully understood. In order to better understand the attitudes that lie behind non-participation, a series of discussion groups were arranged by the County Council in 1982/83 involving members of a certain number of groups. The purpose of these discussions was to identify barriers to participation.

Findings got further than simply identifying lack of a car or lack of money as root causes, since most people actually expressed a desire to visit the countryside. More fundamental reasons for non-participation included a lack of confidence about doing so, lack of a catalyst to help with organization, lack of awareness of opportunities and a lack of knowledge about what to expect from a visit to the countryside. In total, therefore, the reasons for a lack of participation were not obvious but more deep rooted.

The results of the discussion were used to develop Operation Gateway. Two project officers were appointed to work with local communities. The idea was that the project officers would act as 'animators' and help communities to help themselves to organize trips to the countryside. Information about sites, events and other details was given the community representatives and discussed. A further element of the project was the notion of a 'host ranger' at the sites visited. This ranger would deal exclusively with the special group and guide them through the opportunities and available facilities on the sites.

Many conclusions were drawn from the initial stages of the project which were later used to develop the scheme further. The success of 'self-help' initiatives, the need for personal help for groups, the labour-intensive nature of the project and the difficulties of organizing trips on public transport were all recognized at an early stage. The central conclusion was that special groups need to be connected with the countryside at a personal level. Once the confidence of that group has been developed, it can ultimately be left to organize itself. Furthermore, the wider implications of this process of 'connecting' was seen for the wider sphere of leisure interests.

In later stages, the project developed to include a wider range of sites, such as farms, and sites outside the county, and a wider range of special groups. Each time, however, the product offered was adjusted to fit in with the special needs of each group.

As the organizers of the project admit: 'estimating value for money' of a scheme such as Operation Gateway is a somewhat subjective exercise and to cater continually for all special groups is a costly and time-consuming process. However, if co-ordination can be achieved there is no doubt of the enjoyment experienced by the target groups – 'an aim which should not be overshadowed by the experimental nature of the probject'.

4.9 SUMMARY

This chapter draws together national patterns of supply and demand. The model of supply and demand, although essentially an economic one, does lend itself to environmental work because, in any analysis, the demand for various aspects of the countryside *is* increasing while, by and large, the supply of available countryside remains static. The argument that increasing demand for countryside recreation (and the closely related activity of tourism) is one reason for protecting and enhancing the rural environment is a strong one. However, protection of the countryside 'for its own sake' (to quote the 1986 Agricultural Act) is also accepted as justifiable. The countryside manager is therefore in the centre of the demand for the countryside and needs to protect those things for which there is demand – open air, attractive scenery, wildlife, historical sites and somewhere to get away from it all. The managers, therefore, need to balance the demand against the latitude that they have upon the land under their management. Encouraging and allowing unrestrained access to an ecologically delicate and attractive piece of landscape, for example, is not in the best interests of the countryside. Alternatively, unless something is done to accommodate recreational and sympathetic use, damage will result. This balance lies at the heart of countryside management. In order to strike this balance, the country-side manager must develop his or her strategies usually at the local level. This is the subject of the next chapter.

BIBLIOGRAPHY

Appleton, J. (1975) *The Experience of Landscape*, John Wiley, Chichester.
Bathe, G. (1987) The most obvious thing in the world, *ECOS*, 8(4), pp. 7–10.
Bell, M.D. (1979) *Britain's National Parks*, David and Charles, Newton Abbot.
Best, R.M. (1981) *Landuse and Living Space*, Methuen, London.
Bracey, M.C. (1970) *People and the Countryside*, Routledge and Kegan Paul, London.
Clay, R. (1984) *Marketing – The Introduction to a Concept*, Coventry Leisure Services, Seminar, February 1984.
Clayden, P. (1985) *Our Common Land*, Open Spaces Society, Henley.
Coppock, J.T. and Duffield, B. (1975) *Recreation in the Countryside*, Macmillan Press, Edinburgh.
Countryside Commission (1974) *New Agricultural Landscapes*, CCP76, Cheltenham.
Countryside Commission (1979) *The Dales Rail*, CCP120, Cheltenham.
Countryside Commission (1983a) *AONBs: Areas of Outstanding Natural Beauty: A Policy Statement*, CCP157, Cheltenham.
Countryside Commission (1983b) *The Changing Uplands*, CCP153, Cheltenham.
Countryside Commission (1983c) *An Experiment Continued: Countryside Management on the Urban Fringe of Barnet and South Hertfordshire*, CCP148, Cheltenham.
Countryside Commission (1985a) *National Countryside Recreation Survey: 1984*, CCP201, Cheltenham.

Countryside Commission (1985b) *The Wayfarer Project*, CCP193, Cheltenham.
Countryside Commission (1986) *Common Land: The Report of the Common Land Forum*, CCP215, Cheltenham.
Countryside Commission (1987a) *Agricultural Landscapes*, CCP176, Cheltenham.
Countryside Commission (1987b) *Policies for Enjoying the Countryside*, CCP234, Cheltenham.
Countryside Commission (1987c) *Monitoring Landscape Change*, Countryside Commission News, No. 27, Cheltenham.
Countryside Commission (1987d) *Public Transport to the Countryside*, CCP227, Cheltenham.
Countryside Commission (1988a) *Is Set-Aside Enough?*, Countryside Commission News, No. 30, Cheltenham.
Countryside Commission (1988b) *The Water Industry in the Countryside*, CCP239, Cheltenham.
Countryside Commission for Scotland (1974) *A Parks System for Scotland*, CCS, Perth.
Countryside Commission for Scotland (1978) *National Scenic Areas*, CCS, Perth.
Fedden, R. (1974) *The National Trust*, Jonathan Cape, London.
Forestry Commission (1985) *Guidelines for the management of broadleaf woodlands*, Forestry Commission, Edinburgh.
HMSO (1945) *National Parks: A Scottish Survey* (Ramsey Committee), Cmd 6631.
HMSO (1947) *Report of the National Parks Committee (England and Wales)* (Hobhouse Committee), Cmd 7121.
HMSO (1948) *Final Report of the Scottish National Parks Committee and the Scottish Wildlife Conservation Committee*, Cmd 7814.
HMSO (1986) *The Future of Development Plan*, DoE Green Paper.
Hill, H. (1980) *The Freedom to Road*, Moorland Publications, Derbyshire.
Kotler, P. (1975) *Marketing for a Non-Profit Organization*, Prentice Hall, New Jersey.
Kraus, R. (1978) *Recreation and Leisure in Modern Society*, Goodyear Press, California.
Lowe, P. and Goyder, J. (1983) *Environmental Groups in Politics*, Allen and Unwin, .
McIver, C. (1968) *Marketing*, Business Publications, London.
Martin, W.H. and Mason, S. (1980) *The UK Sports Market*, Leisure Consultants, Suffolk.
Nash, J.B. (1960) *Philosophy of Recreation and Leisure*, Williams Brown, Iowa.
Nature Conservancy Council (1968) *Nature Conservancy Handbook*, HMSO.
Nature Conservancy Council (1984) *Nature Conservation in Great Britain*, NCC, Peterborough.
Nature Conservancy Council (1987) *Annual Report*, NCC, Peterborough.
Nottinghamshire County Council (1984) *Operation Gateway*, Internal Report.
Observer, The (1988) *A Room of my Own: Nicholas Ridley*, July 1988.
Open University (1985) *The Countryside Handbook*, Croom Helm, London.
Samstag, A. (1989) *For the Love of Birds: The Story of the RSPB*, RSPB Publication.
Shepheard, P. (1967) *Man in the Landscape*, Ballantyne Books, Edinburgh.
Shoard, M. (1980) *Theft of the Countryside*, Temple Smith, London.
Sports Council (1967) *Household Recreation Survey: Pilot National Recreation Survey Report No. 1*, University of Keele.
Torkildsen, G. (1985) *Recreation Management*, E. & F.N. Spon, London.

· FIVE ·

Local provision

Britain, formerly known as Albion, is rich in timber . . . and has good
pasture for cattle . . . it has many land and sea birds of various
species . . . and is well known for its plentiful springs and rivers.

The Venerable Bede (AD 731)

*It is at the local level that most countryside managers operate. Although most of
their work must be firmly rooted in a national or international context, most
managers can only begin to affect and influence the allocation of necessary
resources on a more localized scale. The definition of 'local' will vary considerably; an amenity manager within a water authority or river authority may
have a river network as large as several counties within which to work, whereas a
countryside manager working within a small local authority may have a much
smaller remit – possibly only one site. However, many of the processes involved
with making the necessary decisions will be similar in all cases. The preceding
chapters have examined three major influencing factors which are common to all
countryside management. Similarly, this chapter explores the process of policy
and strategy formulation at the local level, focusing on the common elements.*

*The types of local strategies prepared by managers closely reflect the various
aspects of countryside that have already been identified, namely: recreation and
access; landscape; nature conservation; and interpretation. Each of these issues,
even at a relatively small scale, involves a large amount of analysis, survey and
implementation, which is why the various issues are more often than not dealt
with separately. Occasionally, however, it may best serve the manager and the
countryside to deal with all issues together, through an overall strategy or 'green
policy'. Whichever method the countryside manager feels is appropriate to
provide a framework for action (either through a series of strategy documents
or through a single strategy) the process will invariably contain a number of
key elements.*

5.1 PREPARING A STRATEGY

5.1.1 Introduction

The preparation of a strategy is, in many ways, similar to the preparation of a management plan, the only difference being that a management plan is usually (although not always exclusively) confined to a single site. The processes involved are identical and relate directly to the concepts of managing by objectives. The key stages are: the declaration of aims; the undertaking of survey work; the analysis of the survey information; decision making on the available management options; setting specific management objectives; devising a means of implementing the strategy; and developing a monitoring process.

The amount of detail within each of these stages will vary according to the area under consideration or the subject to which the strategy applies. For example, the management of private woodlands as part of a landscape strategy carries less direct implementation implications for the countryside manager than does management of land directly owned by the manager or his or her employers. However, notwithstanding the weighting that each section will carry, all strategies should contain some consideration of each of the issues. The overall development of a local strategy (and, ultimately, individual site-based management plans) is part of the process of focusing down on issues through national, regional and sub-regional levels to concentrate eventually upon specific issues.

5.1.2 Aims

The aims of any strategy are general statements of intent. They will clearly vary greatly depending upon the subject of the strategy. A landscape strategy, for example, may have as one of its aims 'the protection or enhancement of existing landscape features within the subject area' (the definition of 'landscape features' would be defined later within the strategy). An aim for a recreation strategy could be 'the provision of accessible countryside recreation opportunities for the population of an area' (again, the definition of terms would be tightened up later in the strategy). A broader 'green' strategy would clearly need to involve not only landscape and recreation, but also nature conservation, interpretation and a host of other issues. Within such a list of aims there would clearly need to be some prioritization, even more so at the stage of developing management objectives. The obvious reason for such prioritization is that it is almost inevitable that within the implementation stage of a strategy there will be an element of conflict and a clear guide to decision making will be needed by the manager. Simply, therefore, the aims do no more than set the broad framework for the strategy, but all subsequent decisions made in developing and implementing the strategy should concur with the aims.

5.1.3 Survey work

Any decisions require a sound base of well-documented research. The importance of market research was stressed in the previous chapter, and basic survey techniques come almost as second nature to ecologists, landscape architects or planners. For the development of a strategy it is vital that all aspects of the work are researched – and this will invariably include more than the obvious subject matter. For example, landscape strategies will have an impact on both ecological and recreational patterns, and so must contain some element of these issues in the survey. Similarly, a recreation strategy cannot ignore the implications of recreational use of the land, especially if the landscape strategy (or whatever) is to be considered as part of a wider countryside or green strategy.

Other elements of the survey include the wider implications of changes to the land and landuse. Consultation is, therefore, integral to the study. Agencies involved will include the Nature Conservancy Council, the Countryside Commissions, English Heritage, Farming and Wildlife Advisory Group, the Ministry of Agriculture, Fisheries and Food (or the equivalent in Scotland) and – depending upon the aims of the strategy – such others as the Forestry Commission, the water authorities or the local wildlife trusts. Similarly, planning restrictions on land have a bearing on any proposals, so the status of land being considered is important. Existing Structure or Local Plans often form a good starting point for surveys. Not only do they indicate broad land allocations, but they also have an analysis of local population trends, socio-economic statistics and transport problems. Where there is no Local Plan coverage, this information is needed to put elements in context, particularly the recreation potential.

The final context of any survey, particularly for recreational strategies, is a survey of the existing supply of similar facilities to those indicated in the aims. A recreational strategy designed to develop access to the countryside cannot disregard local or sub-regional attractions such as National Trust properties or private parks. In the very competitive area of leisure provision any organization, private, voluntary or public, ignores at its peril the existing competition. It has already been stressed that the countryside has both a supply and a demand part to its provision, so any survey must cover both of these aspects.

5.1.4   Analysis

The process of analysis involves assessing the 'interrelationships between existing and potential landuses and interests . . . in the light of the aims for the land and the results of the survey' (Leay *et al.*, 1986). The scale and range of the analysis will reflect the original aims, but will cover a variety of issues including farming, forestry, landscape, recreation/access, natural history and archaeology. Once an analysis of the available information has been undertaken the decision-making process must begin in earnest.

5.1.5   Available options

The analysis will undoubtedly reveal that a number of options will meet the original aims: a variety of locations for Country Parks could meet potential and actual patterns of demand, or any one of several measures could conserve and enhance local landscapes. The analysis will indicate which options are perhaps easiest to achieve (such as working on land already owned or managed by the countryside manager) or which are most pressing for one reason or another (a landscape in imminent danger of being altered irreversibly by agricultural or development pressures) but it falls to the countryside manager to identify the options that are available to implement the strategy. The actual decision over the options may or may not fall to the manager, for it may involve other individuals or agencies, but the assessment of the alternatives is the role of the countryside manager because that person should have the breadth of knowledge to effectively balance the various interests.

5.1.6   Setting objectives

Objectives begin to address the issue of implementation. In the light of the aims, survey results and decisions made about preferred options, objectives indicate how the strategy will be pursued. There is occasionally some confusion over the difference between aims, objectives and means of implementation. Leay *et al.* (op. cit.) defines objectives thus:

> The aim 'to conserve and enhance the quality of the landscape' might become the objective 'to minimize further hedgerow removal, to manage woodlands to retain a healthy broadleaved character' and so on.

Objectives, therefore, begin to identify priorities for action within the broader framework of the aims and other implications of the survey results.

5.1.7 Implementation

The inclusion of means of implementation within a strategy marks the departure of a countryside manager's work from the more traditional route of Local Plans, for example. Statutory documents such as Local Plans do not contain recognition of how the various landuse proposals are to be implemented (although most planners will clearly have more than a vested interest in seeing their proposals carried through). A means of implementing work is integral to the countryside manager's role whereas, again using Local Plans as a counterpoint, the responsibility for implementation often falls to groups other than those devising statutory plans. Where a break exists between policy formulation and implementation, problems of continuity, conflicting priorities and confusion over aims and objectives often occur. Management theory suggests that the individual is most likely to be committed to aims and objectives if he or she has been party to creating them.

Implementation is a subject in its own right, for it carries with it implications for the practical skills of managers and their knowledge of the countryside resources. To follow from the previous definition of objectives, the objective of 'minimizing further hedgerow removal' could be implemented in a number of ways: through a publicity and education programme with landowners, through discussions with representatives of landowners, by supplying grants to landowners, by implementing other financial incentives to landowners or by seeking wider national solutions to the problem. In practice, any process of implementation may well be a mixture of all of these, but for the purposes of the strategy some will have a greater short-term impact while others will be definitely long term. The countryside manager will identify these factors in the implementation section of the strategy.

5.1.8 Monitoring

The objectives and the means of implementation should be conceived in such a way that they can be easily monitored. This may involve no more than recording the number of trees planted, or the number of visitors to a site. Some objectives are, however, more difficult to monitor. Changes in public perception, for example, are usually imperceptible, at least in the short term. This does not mean that these issues should not be monitored, but suggests that in certain circumstances, subjective rather than objective data may be more appropriate.

Monitoring of objectives should take place at least annually, but this can be shortened as appropriate by the manager, depending upon the speed with which feedback is required.

Local Woodland Paths: A popular form of low-key, local countryside provision.

5.2 DEVELOPING SPECIFIC STRATEGIES

5.2.1 Introduction

Many types of strategy are within the remit of a countryside manager, and an integration of several strategies into an overview of the countryside is also central to the proper functioning of a countryside service. However, as planners, ecologists, recreationalists, environmental scientists and landscape architects, for example, may all potentially become countryside managers there is no possibility of actually becoming expert in all of the necessary disciplines, although the countryside manager must have at least a working knowledge of all of them. It is therefore the sign of responsible managers that they acknowledge their own shortcomings and those of the group within which they operate, and seek outside expertise when necessary. Often, this expertise already exists within a countryside team or group, but where it does not it must be bought in through outside consultancy or from the relevant government agencies. This information can usually be acquired freely through normal consultation processes (with the Nature Conservancy Council or English Heritage, for example) so it can easily and quickly be built into the strategic process.

A second point which cannot be overstressed is that while individual strategies are discussed separately here for the sake of clarity they are not separate in reality and the degree of overlap will be great. The emphasis for certain pieces of land will vary and one use will inevitably take precedence; possibly, on some occasions, one particular use might be excluded completely, as with public access onto sensitive conservation sites. However, the integration of the many implications of a series of local strategies is central to effective resource management.

The reasons that the four issues of recreation, landscape, nature conservation and interpretation have been separated here are, firstly, to simplify the issues themselves, secondly, to help to identify individual objectives more clearly and, thirdly, because most examples of local strategies have been devised to cover one aspect of the countryside rather than two or more.

5.2.2 Recreation and access

The role of the countryside in providing for recreational opportunities forms part of the continuum from urban sport and recreation to the less formal pursuits normally associated with National Parks. This is defined by Dower (1978) as 'Recreation for all, and the part of the spectrum of resources which shall serve it'. Recreational needs can be served in a number of ways and through a variety of means, and providing for countryside recreation is just one of many. This immediately raises a number of key issues in the preparation of any recreational strategy aimed specifically at countryside-based provision. Firstly, what is it about the countryside that make people turn to it for recreation; secondly, what is the market for countryside recreation; thirdly, what range of facilities should be provided to meet the demand and, finally, where should countryside recreation be provided? A strategy should aim to answer these basic questions at the local level, and begin to look at countryside recreation within the wider context of sport and recreation in both town and country. This reflects a shift from early recreational provision as directly resource-based (through country parks or National Parks, for example) to a more activity-based review. 'We have now arrived at a focus on activities from the opposite direction from that usually taken by providers' (Strelitz, 1978).

The question 'What is special about the countryside that makes people spend their recreational time within it?' is neither simple nor straightforward. Clearly, it appeals because of 'the peace and quiet', 'the fresh air', 'the wildlife' and any one of a host of responses associated with recreational survey work. But if we begin to define countryside at a broader level, and include urban fringe sites or even countryside sites within the urban area (such as the Lee Valley Regional Park) the issue becomes more complex, and other special features become important: 'somewhere to go', 'it's close to home' and 'water sports' are reasons to visit such urban sites. The conclusion is, therefore, that countryside, in its broadest sense, has many attractions both natural and man-made, which provide for a variety of desires. Some of these desires can, however, be met by providing other recreational facilities. The point at which the provision for recreation in the countryside merges with that of provision for formal sports is impossible to delineate. It is clear, though, that a recreational continuum exists. The countryside is, on the one hand, sufficiently attractive in its own right to make a large number of people turn to it for recreation. On the other hand, by providing additional facilities within the countryside, it can provide a context for a wider variety of recreational activities, some of which could be provided for in other ways.

The countryside as a resource, therefore, attracts for a variety of reasons. The patterns of recreational use of various pieces of countryside could be expected to vary according to the nature of the site. A study undertaken by the Tourism and Recreation Research Unit (1980) identifies that this is indeed the case. Four parks around Glasgow have some common patterns of usage with some elements of the parks appealing for common reasons (e.g. 'scenery', 'peace and quiet' and 'natural

Marketing Routes: Simply giving a network of Public-rights-of-way a name can be sufficient to give an area an identity.

features'). Each area also had its own local appeal for other reasons (e.g. 'fishing', 'bird watching', 'walking the dog' and 'accessibility').

The countryside manager must therefore be able to assess and make a decision as to what features within his or her area can provide the recreational experience that people desire. This implies that the countryside has its own character which, to a certain extent, can be amended by, for example, providing facilities or an interpretive service. Beyond a certain point, however, amending the basic resource too much would actually take away the original appeal that an area of countryside possesses. This is not 'expressing elitism' (Dower, op. cit.) but simply accepting that in a wider recreational context there are some desires which the countryside is best suited to meet, others which it can meet but only as well as other types of provision, and yet others which it cannot meet at all. As Elson (1975) has suggested, 'a demand dictated pattern of provision would find (countryside) recreation taking place in environments little better than those from which people had escaped'. Countryside managers must seek, if possible, to provide a variety of countryside in order to meet the various elements of demand that are expressed.

As well as assessing the potential of the countryside to accommodate recreational demand, the countryside manager must also have an accurate picture of local patterns of recreational demand in general and countryside recreation in particular. Some of the national data discussed in the previous chapter act as a valuable starting point for any local analysis. Much of the evidence about patterns of use and determinants of countryside recreation is so overwhelming that it applies almost universally. Car owners, for example, will always use the countryside more than non-car owners, the only variable that will change, in the short term at any rate, will be the relative proportions of owners and non-owners. However, the fact that some national data can be applied to local circumstances does not preclude the need for detailed local survey work.

A large amount of local data can be obtained from existing sources, such as census data, local plans and socio-economic statistics. These, coupled with a detailed knowledge of national patterns, will allow a picture to be assembled of local demand. There will inevitably be gaps in this information and it is then that local survey work requires a large amount of expertise in its own right, and a poorly thought out survey can at best provide meaningless results and, at worst, provide totally misleading data. Much pioneering work on recreational survey techniques was undertaken by the Tourism and Recreation Research Unit, and has been described in their publications (see, for example, Tourism and Recreation Research Unit 1970, 1972, 1973, 1975 and 1977). The

The Urban Fringe: Often run-down, but still the nearest area of countryside for much of our urban population.

techniques that should be applied should usually be bought in by the countryside manager unless a specialist post or section has been created to concentrate on research. The benefits of such a research post should be considered, because a continuous assessment of patterns of demand is a key element in provision.

Where such data are not readily available in-house, the countryside manager is faced with two options to obtain the information. Research can be undertaken by either a research organization which has some affinity with the environment and recreation or, alternatively, a market research organization which has no direct knowledge of the subject of the research but has possibly a greater knowledge of which research techniques to use. In either case, the countryside manager has to know exactly what information is required and what the information will be used for. A review of existing research methodologies helps to identify some of the methods previously used, and helps to concentrate upon some of the relevant issues. But unless the manager knows precisely what is required from the survey (be it a household survey, an on-site survey or simply a visitor and vehicle count) it is doomed to failure. Lengthy briefing discussions with the research organization are the only means of eliminating any potential pitfalls. In order to give the research organization some basis from which to work (and give a quotation for price if necessary) it is necessary to prepare a briefing note which contains a statement of broad content for the survey, approximate length, means of implementation, any specific analysis required, whether a full or half report should be written by the researchers and any other specific requirements. The actual content and methodology will need to be finalized later, but a briefing note not only helps the researcher but also concentrates the mind of the countryside manager on the issues in question.

The survey of the countryside and the survey of recreational demand give the countryside manager the basic information from which decisions can be made. We have seen that to supply everything within the countryside that was demanded would, in the long term, destroy the very uniqueness of the countryside itself. The countryside manager must therefore make the decision as to what facilities should be provided within the countryside and which demands should be catered for. There will clearly be value judgements in these decisions, but having a large amount of information available should enable these value judgements to be identified.

The provision of facilities provides a potential area for conflict, as was identified by the Sports Council (1987) when a range of countryside-based pursuits above and beyond the more traditional ones of 'walking, picnicking, and nature study' was reviewed. Cycling, sailing, horse-riding, hang-gliding, moto-cross and fishing are all in great demand, but most either conflict with each other or conflict with less active pursuits. The countryside manager must, in conjunction with other recreational professionals, identify which demands can be met without ruining the resource itself.

This analysis implies a continuum from the more remote, quieter areas of the National Parks and wilderness areas of Scotland through more high-pressure provision in country parks or project/access areas to the intense and semi-formal use of urban fringe countryside. This continuum was identified by Dower (1978) with the 'wilderness experience' being at one end of the continuum and the urban fringe and even leisure parks being at the other. To develop a strategy for all of these, the countryside manager must consider the resource, the demand and the geography of both. Within this analysis, pressure points will become evident and thus priorities for action will emerge.

One such prioritization was made in the Neath Access Project where the key priority was seen as developing the public rights-of-way system rather than any specific site-base facilities (Countryside Commission, 1988). This fits in closely with the Countryside Commssion's prioritization of the public-rights-of-way system. Such a decision takes the role of the rights-of-way network beyond that of a highway to that of a valuable recreational resource which of course it is. The work implied in upgrading, waymarking, clearing and designating the public-rights-of-way system is enormous, as we have seen previously, but in the long term the recreational potential is equally great.

A more urban-based authority, Doncaster, concentrates resources upon providing countryside opportunities close to all of the centres of population in the borough. 'Low key' sites are therefore spread about the borough so that a high proportion of non-car owners have easy access to areas of countryside for informal recreation. The access areas are either sites or footpath networks over private land: either way the opportunity for walking, cycling, picnicking and getting 'a breath of fresh air' is provided for (Doncaster Metropolitan Borough Council, 1988).

Meeting all the recreational demands in the countryside is clearly unrealistic, but the countryside manager must make the decision on what can be accommodated and where this should happen. Clearly, the manager must also keep the situation under review by monitoring both the countryside and patterns of recreational demand.

5.2.3 Landscape strategies

There is clearly a link between landscape and countryside recreation; one of the most obvious attractions of the countryside is its landscape and scenery. However, the protection and improvement of the landscape is an issue in its own right and must be approached, at least in part, separately from the issue of countryside recreation.

Broadly speaking, the aims of a landscape strategy can be either to protect existing landscape or to improve and amend landscapes. Although, at a first analysis, there does not appear to be a great difference between these two aims, each has its own implications for survey work, analysis and implementation.

The methodology employed to survey the landscape will depend upon the initial aims. Where the aim is to protect existing landscapes, it is important to identify some sort of hierarchy of landscapes, with the most attractive ones being afforded most protection through planning controls, for example. Exceptional landscapes might well be designated as special sites such as Areas of Outstanding Natural Beauty. The means of establishing a hierarchy is, however, a difficult and controversial issue.

Early attempts at defining landscape quality were founded in objective, quantitative techniques pioneered by Linton (1968) and Fines (1968). Although the validity of this method was questioned (Gilg, 1975), the qualitative methodology was adopted by a large number of agencies, particularly local authorities and many research institutes (Penning-Rowsell, 1981; University of Manchester, 1976). Simply, the quantitative approach to landscape evaluation was based on the balance of positive landscape features (presence of trees, water, varied topography, etc.) to negative landscape features (industrial sites, dereliction and built environments, for example) within a grid framework – usually kilometre squares. Each square would be allocated a value and, thus, a pattern of relative landscape quality could be established. At the time when many existing planning documents were being drawn up the quantitative technique was most in favour, hence the high representation in that methodology. Having established the 'best' landscapes within an area, protectionist legislation and policies can be concentrated upon these priority landscapes.

The advantages and disadvantages of this technique are both clear. In a world of finite resources, concentration of available money and manpower are needed to a certain extent, thus some form of hierarchy is needed. However, weighed against this is the obvious counter-argument that areas which are not prioritized do not receive any resource and therefore the landscape continues to decline. Arguably, areas of poor landscape quality require more attention than do areas of high landscape value.

Partly as a reaction to the quantitative approach to landscape assessment and partly as a reaction to the implication that non-priority landscapes must attract fewer resources, a number of studies in the mid to late 1980s began to accept that any appraisal of landscape is almost inevitably subjective and that landscape assessement should aim not at establishing a hierarchy but at establishing the elements that actually make up individual landscape, i.e. identify the positive aspects of all landscapes and work to improve those (Bromley, 1988; Countryside Commission, 1987b). For example, in certain agricultural landscapes the hedgerows, individual trees, small copses and 'intimacy' of the landscape are important. For other areas the openness, remoteness and absence of obvious tree-features may be the key to its appeal. Within the equation of determining the character of a landscape many elements are important; historical associations (old estate landscapes, sites of battles), literary associations (such as Hardy's Wessex or the Bronte's Pennine Moors) and perhaps most important of all, the views and opinions of the people who 'use' the landscape. All of these different ingredients play a part in determining a landscape character. Once the key elements have been identified they can be both protected and, more importantly, enhanced. This is the basis for landscape protection and improvement of Environmentally Sensitive Areas, wherein the unique elements within each landscape are identified, protected and enhanced (Haigh, 1988).

The difference between the two techniques is obvious, but the countryside manager must be able to establish the actual purpose of the analysis and assessment. Then, with confident handling of existing techniques, the manager can draw together a strategy.

The implementation of the landscape strategy again depends upon the overall aims. Protection of landscape through planning controls is a notoriously difficult process because, as we have seen, the agriculture and forestry industries are largely outside planning control. Most protection must therefore be through designation or through co-operation with landowners and developers. Indeed, any positive measures above and beyond the protection of existing landscape must also be through co-operation. Initiatives such as set-aside of agricultural land and landscape conservation grants administered by local authorities must be exercises in co-operation. Just as importantly, the various initiatives also need a framework within which to operate. It is the role of the countryside manager to establish this framework through a landscape strategy.

There is, of course, an entirely different means of examining and explaining the landscape which has an immense bearing on the work of a countryside manager, and that is through a historical perspective. All landscapes are not only products of underlying biological and geological processes but also of management by man. Thus, landscape can be seen as a record of time as well as of more physical and natural processes. Archaeology is of great relevance to the countryside manager, not only because history shapes the landscape but also because many features

Town and Country: Linear routes, such as cycleways, require different designs as they pass from urban to rural situation.

within the landscape form an integral part of it: Iron Age hill forts, ancient drove roads, parish boundary hedges, Celtic crosses, early drift mines, ancient quarries – the list is endless. The countryside manager must clearly be aware of any historical relevance of the landscape with which he or she is dealing. Specific sites of interest can usually be identified through local schedules of ancient monuments. More nationally important sites are often owned or managed by English Heritage or their corresponding organizations in Scotland, Wales and Northern Ireland, run directly from the Offices of the Scottish or Welsh or Northern Ireland Secretaries of State. Under certain conditions, or where exceptionally valuable sites are identified, the archaeological importance of a site will override the recreational or nature conservation importance of the area – such as Stonehenge or Culloden. However, in most circumstances the experience and expertise of qualified archaeologists will need to be added to the equation that eventually produces a management plan.

Through the landscape, therefore, the countryside manager often begins to draw in other important issues of the environment, such as archaeology, man-made elements, literary associations and others. Indeed, many of these heritage associations are so nationally important for the landscape that, for landowners, there exists at present an opportunity to avoid the payment of Capital Transfer Tax on 'Heritage Landscapes' (as defined in the Capital Transfer Tax Act 1984, Section 31 (lb)) for which management plans are drawn up and agreed by the Countryside Commission (Countryside Commission, 1986).

5.2.4 Nature conservation

Unlike landscape strategies, most nature conservation strategies possess an element of similarity. This similarity stems from a number of sources: firstly, only a relatively small number of nature conservation strategies have been developed, and most have been based on the innovative work of West Midlands County Council (1984); secondly, the methods employed in ecological surveys have been developed over a longer period of time than those used in landscape surveys and have therefore become standardized to a greater extent; and thirdly, the aims of conservation strategies tend to be more clear cut than those of recreation or landscape strategies for example, and this leads to a more common approach to the creation of strategies.

The West Midlands County Council (1984) identified six aims within their strategy. These were:

1. to ensure that all residents in the county have reasonable access to habitats with wildlife interest;

2. to protect and enhance a basic network of open space and wildlife corridors;
3. to improve the suitability of the County's undeveloped land for wildlife;
4. to protect rare habitats;
5. to protect the habitats of nationally rare species;
6. to promote the significance and encourage the consideration of the County's wildlife.

(An interesting point to note about these aims is that all the elements of concern for a countryside manager are represented – public use, interpretation, nature conservation and, albeit tangentially, landscape.)

The underlying requirement of all of the aims is that the natural habitats of an area (in this case the whole county, but it could just as easily be a protected area or a single site) need to be identified not just for their general importance but also in further detail to identify any rare species or habitats. The basis for this process of habitat identification is usually the standard classification developed by the Nature Conservancy Council, referred to as the Phase I survey. This is based upon a range of habitat types, defined by botanical information (such as broadleaved woodland, heathland or neutral grassland, for example). These habitat types are further sub-divided (into oak woods, beech plantations or birch/willow woodland and others in the case of broadleaved woodlands, for example). This information is usually recorded on a 1:10 000 map, with potentially interesting sites being identified as 'target areas'. These target areas then receive more detailed analysis through a Phase II survey, which collates information on flora and fauna, recorded on the relative abundance of different plant species, background information and notes on any rare species. These target areas usually represent the spread of 'areas of natural history interest'. This technique was used by St Helens Metropolitan Borough Council (1986) in *A Policy for Nature*.

It is often possible to short circuit this lengthy Phase I and II process by using existing data from both botanical records offices or local wildlife trusts. The only disadvantage to this is that information has often been collected over a long period of time and by a wide variety of groups, thus bringing into question the consistency of the information. However, as a means of identifying natural history areas that are locally important, it is relatively reliable and formed the basis of the *Tyne and Wear Nature Conservation Strategy* (Nature Conservancy Council, 1988).

Having identified key sites for natural history, the countryside manager can then build upon these individual blocks. It is usual to designate the key sites with a means of identification such as 'sites of scientific interest' or 'sites of nature conservation importance'. These designations serve to identify sites that are important primarily for their wildlife interest. In simplistic terms, the overall aim of most conservation strategies is then to safeguard these key sites and to form links between them. The links fulfil a number of functions, principally to avoid the key sites becoming islands, separated from each other. This is summarized in the Tyne and Wear Strategy (op. cit.) by suggesting 'it is possible to reduce the island effect, since wildlife will be able to move along these channels and perhaps colonize new sites'. This introduces the second strategic importance of the channels (corridors or links are other terms), which is their ecological importance *per se*. They might not represent sites of importance solely because of their ecological value, but they do represent more commonplace habitats such as woods, river banks or even roadside verges, for example. The concept of a series of key sites linked by less important but more expansive green corridors is an easy one to grasp, albeit slightly simplistic in ecological terms.

5.2.5 Interpretation

The development of a wider-ranging interpretation plan is a relatively unusual event, particulary in the context of countryside alone. Often, the interpretive implications for site management are included within specific site plans. Larger, specially designated areas such as National Parks do often have an overall interpretive plan (Robinson, 1978) but most areas at local government level lack such an overview. However, the interpretive potential of an area could form the starting point of any management process because it represents the potential of an area to educate, inform and entertain people, which, surely, forms much of what countryside management is about. This is the philosophy behind the recent moves by English Heritage in its attempts to review its visitor policy through interpretation (English Heritage, 1988).

A further confusion around interpretive strategies is their very close approximation to tourism promotion. Regional or sub-regional identities such as Robin Hood Country (Nottinghamshire), Catherine Cookson Country (South Tyneside) or Tarka Country (Devon) not only give inter-preters a theme that can be developed at country parks or other specific sites, but they also provide handy tourist promotion material. Further-more, the link that interpretation has with tourism is also strengthened by the link it makes between town and country (town trails and guided walks, for example) and between the present and the past (through history trails and archaeological interpretation). Thus, an interpretive overview is difficult to restrict to the countryside except in specific circumstances (such as National Parks). The example used in the case

Local Interpretation: Establishing countryside interpretation centres in urban locations is one way of taking the country into the towns.

study proves a good case in point because the interpretive strategy for Calderdale ranges through urban and rural issues, tourism and recreation, and ranger services and museums. There is obviously nothing wrong with this approach, and it simply serves to emphasize the work of countryside management within a wider group of education, recreational and environmental influences.

The interpretive process, like every other skill required by the countryside manager, has its own guidelines and rules. To a large extent these were developed in the United States of America within the National Parks network established there. Indeed, the first significant book on interpretation was written by the American, Freeman Tilden (1967), from which is taken this by now almost classic definition of interpretation:

> Interpretation is an educational activity which aims to reveal meanings and relationships through the use of original objects, by first-hand experience and by illustrative media, rather than simply to communicate factual information.

The British foundation for interpretive planning was laid by a two-volume publication, prepared jointly by the Countryside Commission for Scotland and the Countryside Commission for England and Wales. The first document deals with the interpretive planning process (Aldridge, 1975) and the second document deals with the media available to interpreters (Pennyfather, 1975). The former issue will be dealt with here and the means and methods of interpretation are dealt with in Chapter 8.

Interpretation can be defined as a cyclical process with the important questions being:

(a) Why provide interpretive facilities?
(b) What might be interpreted?
(c) For whom might it be interpreted?
(d) Where, when the how should it be interpreted?
(e) What subsequent management is necessary?

A summary of interpretation is given in Countryside Commission (1979); see also Figure 5.1.

The most obvious starting point is with the question, why? However simple this might seem, it is not always asked, yet interpretation that does not have a purpose is actually worse than no interpretation. Reasons for interpretation might include: enhancing visitor enjoyment, increasing public understanding, facilitating management by influencing visitor patterns, satisfying a known demand, making money, or putting over a particular point of view. As with all previously discussed strategies the aims of any interpretive programme should be defined

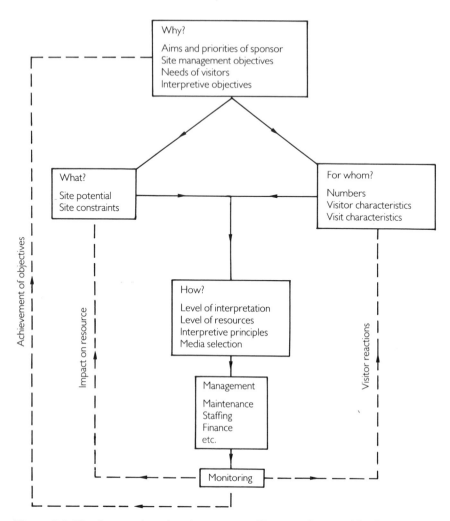

Figure 5.1 *The interpretive planning process.* (Source: *Countryside Commission, 1979.*)

clearly at the outset. Different objectives will have different implications of the media and techniques used to accomplish the objectives.

Interpretive opportunities – what might be interpreted – fall into several groups, including: geological/ecological/scientific features, archaeological features, landscape, socio-cultural characteristics or other special, identifying features. It is almost certain that all areas, particularly relatively large areas, have many characteristics that represent interpretive opportunities. Constraining factors therefore come into play.

These might be site constraints such as its accessibility, its character or any harm that interpretation might do. Alternatively, they might be management constraints such as inadequate staffing, lack of financial resources or potentially unacceptable levels of visitor use.

For whom should interpretation be provided? This is a question which is often not analysed sufficiently, and the lessons learned from marketing techniques are evidently applicable. The process of defining markets for the interpretation is a vital part of making the interpretation success. In order to identify target groups it may well be necessary to undertake site-based research about visitor groups and the elements of a site they find interesting, for example. Again, a further series of questions are needed, such as: What are existing patterns of use of the area? What is the profile of visitor groups? Are special groups such as schools, unemployed or non-English speaking people to be targeted? or Where do visitors come from? It is often the job of the countryside manager to identify specific target groups that are to be prioritized, and it is often here that the mixture of media and message differ subtly (or indeed, not so subtly) between interpretation designed for tourists in family groups or in specialist organizations interested in industrial archaeology and school groups of primary school age with little previous experience of the countryside. The identification of market segments is critical to the success of interpretation.

The where, when and how questions are dealt with in a later chapter, but all the varying options need to be weighed against some eighteen criteria:

(a) impact;
(b) flexibility;
(c) encouragement of participation;
(d) provocation;
(e) relationship to the visitor's pace;
(f) use by groups;
(g) visitor safety;
(h) links with surroundings;
(i) relationship to adjacent media;
(j) minimum visitor effort;
(k) simplicity;
(l) appearance;
(m) effect on the resource;
(n) durability;
(o) resistance to vandalism;
(p) reliability;
(q) cost;
(r) expendability.

Pennyfather (op. cit.) identifies some 63 interpretive techniques which are categorized into five groups: personal services, participatory media, live display, static display and 'gadgets'.

Finally, any interpretive plan has wider implications for the country-side manager and will clearly have repercussions on any one of a number of management issues, particularly visitor controls, site/area management of habitats and resources, the maintenance and repairs of interpretive media, emergency planning should some plans fail, staff recruitment and/or training, sales and purchases of books, signs or leaf-lets, financial policies for charging, payment of staff or concessionary/contract staff, publicity and promotion, relations with other organiza-tions/landowners/interest groups and, very importantly, the monitoring process – how efficiently is the interpretive plan meeting the objectives stated for the plan?

In many respects, interpretation is one of the roles of the countryside manager that sets him or her apart from other environmentally based professionals. Successful interpretive planning is critical to the develop-ment of a successful countryside service and should therefore be given the appropriate priority.

5.3 CO-ORDINATION

The above discussion separates the strategic role of the countryside manager into four elements: recreation, landscape, nature conservation and interpretation. It has also been stressed, however, that there are clearly links between these individual elements and that it can be argued that the divisions are false and of little use. The point that is being stressed is that only by clearly identifying the issue being analysed can a meaningful set of objectives be developed. Landscape and nature conservation issues are not the same, and to mix them without realiz-ing their potential conflict can lead to a lot of misplaced energy. The same applies to recreation and interpretation and the host of cross-relationships that exist between them.

The role of the countryside manager is to focus on the priorities that the analyses produce. Within a single strategy, specific sites will clearly be more important than others. Existing popular recreation areas will need more management in order to maintain their recreational and visual integrity. This could be overcome by improving facilities at the existing site, or perhaps developing alternative facilities to take some pressure off the existing site (as was originally one of the purposes for developing country parks *vis-à-vis* National Parks). The countryside manager must, from within single strategies, develop plans of action based on his or her priorities. The means of implementing strategies is

Cycleway: The many disused railways across the country form the basis of a wider network of recreational routes.

discussed in the next chapter, but within all strategies it is vital that the manger addresses the issue of actually carrying out the strategy. What is the single most important issue? By separating the task into the four separate elements of recreation, landscape, nature conservation and interpretation the process of crystallizing the important issues is made slightly simpler.

This does not mean to say, however, that these issues do not overlap. Indeed, the opposite is the case. If the area of land of which a country-side manager has responsibility can be envisaged as a base plan, the various strategies can be represented as a series of overlays. If four such overlays are produced, certain areas will be readily identifiable as pinch points of all four issues. It may thus be the contention of the manager that a single area warrants attention rather than a single issue or number of sites. This is the argument behind the call for more active management of Areas of Outstanding Natural Beauty, for example (Selgren, 1986), which suggests that, while the AONB network was established largely for the landscape value of the areas involved, they are, by their very nature, also important for a wide range of other reasons.

The role of the co-ordination of resources is central to the job of a manager, and the countryside manager is no exception to this rule. The process of setting priorities, and thus co-ordinating resources to meet these priorities, is made easier if clear objectives can be established at the outset. The process of developing a strategy is a method of establishing clear objectives and devising a means of implementing projects to meet these objectives.

5.4 PROFESSIONAL EXPERTISE

The best means of ensuring that the implementation steps taken to meet objectives are the right ones is to ensure that the information comes in a form that is readily usable and that it is professionally sound. To achieve this, the advice of people trained in the relevant professions is needed – recreation managers, landscape consultants, ecologists or interpreters. Ideally, the countryside manager will have at his or her disposal the necessary expertise, but where this is not the case the manager must identify when it is necessary to bring in professional guidance. Similarly, the countryside manager must be able to brief the relevant professionals on what is required of them. This is not always possible, for as Collis (1986) has suggested 'there is still a large gap in the understanding between the professions of planning and ecology'. For 'planning' and 'ecology' it is possible to substitute landscape consultant, interpreter, farmer, educationalist and so on. The manager in the centre of this 'understanding gap' must have sufficient breadth of knowledge in all areas to bring the disciplines together to meet clear objectives.

5.5 STANDARDIZATION OF TECHNIQUES

It was stated earlier that one of the hallmarks of the development of the role of countryside managers has been the 'horses for courses' approach, particularly in early developmental years. Because of the lack of legislative and central guidelines as to how countryside should be protected or developed, early work progressed on the lines of least resistance. To an extent this has continued, although training and standardized techniques developed in allied disciplines have led to some standardization. A cursory glance at the numerous strategies and plans that have been developed and continue to be developed, suggests that the standardization process has a long way to go. As in all debates there are two sides to the argument.

On the one hand, the variety of approaches taken to tackle localized issues means that each manager can assemble the variety of powers available to him or her and arrange them into a system which best suits the circumstances. On the other hand, standardization of techniques leads to more valid inter-area comparisons and a more readily assembled national bank of data and overall comparability. There is no clear outcome to the debate and in some respects it can be argued that while the analysis of relevant and valid survey techniques is important, too much attention to the methodology of building up information, particularly on the part of the implementers, will lead to 'an accurate, scientific and objective record of the complete decline of the British Countryside' (Nature Conservancy Council, 1988). Making the steps from setting aims and objectives, collecting information and, most importantly, doing something with the information – e.g. by way of practical projects to meet the objectives – is crucial.

5.6 CASE STUDIES

Because of the diversity of approaches to developing strategies for the four areas discussed in this chapter, three case studies are examined which tackle three separate issues – namely, recreation, nature conservation and interpretation. The range of authorities is similarly diverse, with a County Council, a District Council and the Civic Trust all being represented. The thread that the three case studies have in common is that they all address an issue over a relatively wide area.

5.6.1 Wakefield Metropolitan District Council

The report *Stepping out* (Wakefield Metropolitan District Council, 1988) examines the issue of pedestrian access across the entire district. In this sense the recreational uses made of public rights-of-way is within a wider context than that of simply countryside, or recreation. However, the document does examine the legal framework of the public-rights-of-way network and identifies the major issues surrounding its use. These issues are often comparable to those identified in urban areas, such as access, obstructions, poor facilities for the disabled and uncertainty about rights and responsibilities.

The policy is broken down into seven sections, covering the legislative background to public rights-of-way, the protection of public rights-of-way (and more specifically the role of the Council in this process), pedestrian facilities in urban areas, pedestrian facilities in rural areas, the definitive map, the legal process of creation, diversion and re-classification of public rights-of-way and, finally, an assessment of problems and complaints associated with public rights-of-way. Within the framework discussed at the beginning of the chapter, the strategy falls into the relevant stages, thus:

Aims The strategy states its aims as, firstly, being a factual document and, secondly, indicating what the District Council would like to achieve in relation to the development of facilities for pedestrians. Finally, the strategy will be updated through a continuous process of review.

Survey The survey work is through the existing and reviewed definitive map and through the survey of regularly occurring problems/comments about the public rights-of-way by members of the public.

Analysis Each issue is discussed separately under individual headings such as standards of maintenance, cycle tracks, bridleways, obstructions and nuisances and the rights and obligations of the public.

Objectives Although not explicitly stated, objectives relate to 'the development of the metalled footpath and footway network' and 'the enhancement of the network of public rights-of-way and permissive paths'.

Implementation The strategy is relatively strong on this section, and states precisely how the implementation is to be undertaken (through the Council's direct works organization and volunteers), how schemes are to be promoted (through the Council's countryside service) and some form of prioritization of work (through the 'enhancement' of routes by promotion, improvement to surfaces, stiles, gates and footbridges). Initially, work will concentrate on circular pedestrian routes, but in the longer term, routes will be provided for cyclists and horse riders.

The strategy is short and in a style that can easily be understood by the general public.

Public Transport in the Countryside: If the countryside is not to become the sole pre- serve of car-owners, a good public-transport network is needed.

The objective of any strategy must be to provide a statement of intent which allows the manager to readily identify a work programme. In this, the *Stepping Out* strategy succeeds in that it clearly identifies the resources that will be needed to implement the strategy and the skills the workforce will require. Rangers are needed to promote and help walkers use the routes; design skills are needed for publications; a workforce is needed with specialist skills in stile erection and footpath surface construction; and a co-ordinated approach is required to encourage voluntary wardens. Such a strategy allows the relevant manager to define means of implementing and co-ordinating resources, which is after all the role of a manager.

5.6.2   The nature conservation strategy for the county of West Midlands

The West Midlands Conservation Strategy (here referred to simply as the West Midlands Strategy, for the sake of brevity) was the first nature conservation strategy prepared in the country and, as such, gave a lead to the many subsequent strategies. Although new formulae have been adopted since the publication of the West Midlands Strategy, it still retains its importance because of the wide-ranging scope and influence that the report undertook.

More so than the Wakefield Strategy discussed above, the West Midlands Strategy moves carefully from one stage of strategy development to the next, with all the stages explicitly and carefully defined. Furthermore, unlike many strategies, the West Midlands document was produced and presented as a statutory planning document, receiving the approval of the Secretary of State for the Environment in 1984. It is thus not only an internal policy document, but also a statutory document to which all relevant organizations must adhere.

The West Midlands Strategy covers the five stages of preparation in the following way:

Aims   The aims are explicitly stated as 'to provide advice and information, to identify priorities, to put forward a programme of action and to provide a clear, strategic framework for planning decisions'. This last aim is identified as being the most important.

Survey   Again, the survey methodology is clearly stated as 'based on a list of thirty two possible habitat types, with a habitat survey team identifying over 20 000 habitat sites'.

Analysis   The analysis on each site and the overall juxtapositioning of the sites is based on several criteria, namely rarity, local/national importance, ownership, proximity to people/houses and status.

Objectives   Six objectives are given, in order of priority:

- To ensure that all residents in the county have reasonable access to habitats with wildlife interest.
- To protect and enhance a basic network of open space and wildlife corridors.
- To improve the suitability of the county's undeveloped land for wildlife.
- To protect rare habitats.
- To protect the habitats of nationally rare species.
- To promote the significance and encourage the consideration of the county's wildlife.

Implementation   The implementation of the strategy is described in great detail. Specific sites are identified with prescriptions for each site, and agencies to be involved are also identified. Some diagrammatic advice is given for some of the projects.

The West Midlands Strategy is a good example of a strategy leading to a clearly identifiable programme of work and a realistic consideration of how the work is to be done. The implementation of the strategy was continued through the work of an Urban Wildlife Trust which arose out of the interest and enthusiasm generated by the development of the strategy. In many ways, the West Midlands Strategy represented a turning point in the development of countryside policy-making.

5.6.3   Calderdale interpretive plan

The report *Caring for the Visitor: The Calderdale Interpretive Strategy Study* (Civic Trust, 1986) was prepared by consultants under the direction of the Civic Trust. The interest of the Civic Trust revolves predominantly around Calderdale's built and archaeological heritage. Lying in the heart of the Pennines, it was at the centre of the textile industry, and much of its history is based upon the buildings, canals and towns built up around this industry. However, like much of the Pennine belt, the towns soon give way to rural, upland scenery. As a result, the interpretive strategy covers both town and country, as well as a host of other issues.

A large part of the report concentrates upon analysis of the existing information – referred to as potential within the document, but it does follow the standard framework of the strategies previously analysed, albeit at a more discussive level.

Aims   The aims of the strategy are not explicitly stated, although in the foreword to the report, five reasons for having a strategy are proposed:

- To help develop a tourist industry.
- To help local people gain pride in their surroundings.
- To improve outdated and negative images of the area.
- To raise people's image of the area to help reduce vandalism and abuse of the environment.
- To act as a catalyst to other education and communciation.

Survey The survey work rests largely on a desk survey of tourist figures, existing use of interpretive facilities and existing interpretive provision. The survey work also bends into the analysis by identifying characteristics of the area that might benefit from interpretation. There are twelve such characteristics, including farming, the textile industry, natural environment, the built environment, religious non-conformity and local customs.

Analysis The analysis rests largely on an assessment of the 'potential' of each of the twelve local characteristics to benefit from interpretation. This is, of necessity, a subjective assessment because few objective criteria exist for such an analysis.

Objectives Again, objectives are not spelled out explicitly, but are presented in an implicit form. A short section summarizes 'the strategy' by examining the tourist potential of the area, selling Calderdale, and identifying key components of the strategy. Five components to provision are named:

- Finding your way about.
- Referral (face-to-face contact through information centres).
- Site-based facilities
- New facilities.
- People intensive facilities.

Implementation The strategy is very strong on identifying specific projects which arise from the strategy. Sign-posting programmes, the development of tourist information centres, the improvement of twelve site-based interpretation programmes and the development of ten new site-based resources are all given detail. The strategy also gives estimates of a five-year programme of works – something that most strategies do not.

A further part of the strategy is that it identifies a management structure that would be necessary to implement the strategy. Most of the work falls to various departments within the local authority but also it is recommended that a 'Calderdale Inheritance Trust' be established to provide a strategic overview to the development of the strategy.

The issue of a management structure which should implement the strategy is of direct relevance here, because it is the subject of the next chapter. Overall, the Calderdale Interpretive Strategy tends to follow the proposed framework of strategies implicitly rather than explicitly. This only serves to emphasize the multi-faceted nature of interpretation, as indeed the report reflects by referring to tourism, archaeology, culture, industry and religion as well as 'the countryside'.

5.7 VARIATIONS ON A THEME

The three case studies discussed here all relate to geographical areas corresponding to local authority boundaries. As we shall see later, management plans are most often prepared for specific sites and represent a very site specific strategy. The concept of a strategy can also be elaborated upon by exploring the options for a series of sites scattered over a large or small area; for example, National Parks at one level or a number of local wildlife trust sites within a small area at another level. The strategic approach to countryside management could and should be adapted to suit local or organizational needs, but throughout, the basic framework remains the same whether the strategy is being undertaken by a local trust, a residents' action committee or a county council. At a site specific level a management plan is needed, but where more than one site or a large area is involved, an overall strategy is required before individual sites are tackled.

BIBLIOGRAPHY

Aldridge, D. (1975) *Guide to Countryside Interpretation, Part One: Principles of Countryside Interpretation and Interpretive Planning*, HMSO, Edinburgh.

Bromley, P. (1988) After the coal rush, *Landscape Design*, No. 174, pp. 21–23.

Civic Trust (1986) *Caring for the Visitor: The Calderdale Interpretive Strategy Study*, Civic Trust, London.

Collis, I.R. (1986) Strategic planning for wildlife, in *Biological Survey and Evaluation in Urban Areas*, Nature Conservancy Council, Peterborough.

Countryside Commission (1979) *Interpretive Planning*, Advisory Series No. 2, Cheltenham.

Countryside Commission (1986) *Heritage Landscape Plans*, CCP205, Cheltenham.

Countryside Commission (1987a) *The New Forest Landscape*, CCP220, Cheltenham.

Countryside Commission (1987b) *Enjoying the Countryside: Recreation 2000*, CCP225, Cheltenham.

Countryside Commission (1988) *Neath Access Project*, CCP207, Cheltenham.

Davidson, J. (1970) *Outdoor Recreation Surveys*, Countryside Commission, Cheltenham.

Doncaster Metropolitan Borough Council (1988) *A Breath of Fresh Air: a policy statement for the countryside*, DMBC, Doncaster.

Dower, M. (1978) The promise – for whom have we aimed to provide, in CRRAG Conference Report: *Countryside for All?*, CRRAG, Bristol.

Elson, M. (1975) *Recreation Demand Forecasting: a misleading tradition*, Occasional Paper in Town Planning, Oxford Polytechnic.

English Heritage (1988) *Visitors Welcome*, HMSO, London.

Fines, K.D. (1968) Landscape Evaluation: a project in East Sussex, *Regional Studies*, **2**, pp. 31–42.

Gilg, A. (1975) The objectivity of Linton-type methods of assessing scenery as a natural resource, *Regional Studies*, **9**, pp.

Haigh, V. (1988) Once in a lifetime landscape, *Landscape Design*, No. 174, pp. 31–34

Leay, M.J., Rowe, J. and Young, J.D. (1986) *Management Plans: a guide to their preparation and use*, CCP206, Cheltenham.

Linton, D.L. (1968) The assessment of scenery as a national resource, *Scottish*

Geographical Magazine, **84**, pp. 28–36.

Nature Conservancy Council (1988) *Tyne and Wear Nature Conservation Strategy*, NCC, Peterborough.

Penning-Rowsell, E.C. (1981) Fluctuating fortunes in gauging landscape value, *Progress in Human Geography*, **6**, pp. 20–31.

Pennyfather, K. (1975) *Guide to Countryside Interpretation, Part Two: Interpretive Media and Facilities*, HMSO, Edinburgh.

Robinson, T.W. (1978) *Exmoor National Park Interpretive Plan Study*, Countryside Commission, Cheltenham.

St Helens Metropolitan Borough Council (1986) *A Policy for Nature*, St Helens MBC.

Selgren, J. (1986) More active management for AONBs, *ECOS*, **7**, pp. 29–34.

Sports Council (1987) *Access to the Countryside for Recreation and Sport*, Sports Council and Countryside Commission, Seminar Report, Countryside Commission, Cheltenham.

Strelitz, Z. (1978) The countryside and the city dwellers: people's needs and leisure, in CRRAG Conference Report, *Countryside for All?*, CRRAG, Bristol.

Tilden, F. (1967) *Interpreting our heritage*, University of North Carolina Press, Chapel Hill.

Tourism and Recreation Research Unit (1970) *The Pentland Hills: some aspects of outdoor recreation. A Research Study*, TRRU, Edinburgh.

Tourism and Recreation Research Unit (1972) *A Survey of Summer Visitors to Edinburgh*, TRRU, Edinburgh.

Tourism and Recreation Research Unit (1973) *Outdoor Recreation Traffic Patterns in the Edinburgh Area*, TRRU, Edinburgh.

Tourism and Recreation Research Unit (1975) *STARS Series, No 1: Survey Description*, TRRU, Edinburgh.

Tourism and Recreation Research Unit (1977) *Patterns of Outdoor Recreation in Scotland*, TRRU, Edinburgh.

Tourism and Recreation Research Unit (1980) *A Study of Four Parks in and around Glasgow*, TRRU, Edinburgh.

University of Manchester (1976) *Landscape Evaluation: Report of the Landscape Evaluation Project 1970–75*, Centre for Urban and Regional Research, Manchester.

Wakefield Metropolitan District Council (1988) *Stepping Out*, Wakefield MDC, Wakefield.

West Midlands County Council (1984) *The Nature Conservation Strategy for the County of West Midlands*, Birmingham.

SIX

Implementation

You can never do merely one thing – hence the first rule of
intelligent tinkering is to save all the parts.

Paul Ehrlich (1971)

*Implementation of well-thought-out strategies is, in practical terms, the
equivalent of managing by objectives. Integral to the work of the countryside
manager is the ability to plan for, initiate and monitor the implementation of the
strategies. Indeed, there is inevitably a degree of overlap between implementation
and policy formulation, with one colouring the other – a completely unworkable
policy is of no use at all, neither is a work programme which lacks a clear
objective. A balance between the policy-making process and scheme implementation is therefore required. Figure 6.1 shows a model which identifies the options
available to most managers. They (and their sections) can become involved with
policy making across a wide range of environmental issues, or become involved
specifically with the countryside as defined here and spend time on policy
formulation, the development of strategies and the actual implementation of
schemes. It is the latter which is the key work pattern of most countryside
managers.*

*The term 'implementation' covers a wide variety of implications. Broadly,
these can be split into two areas. Firstly, certain practical skills are needed to
work in the countryside. These include habitat management, forestry techniques,
dry stone walling, fencing and much more – skills that cover a range of
situations. These practical skills are covered separately in the next chapter. The
second broad issue covered is that of means of implementaion, which is covered by
this chapter.*

*The 'means of implementation' include the structure of the countryside
manager's organization, the method of appointing a workforce and the option
available to the manager from where a workforce can be drawn.*

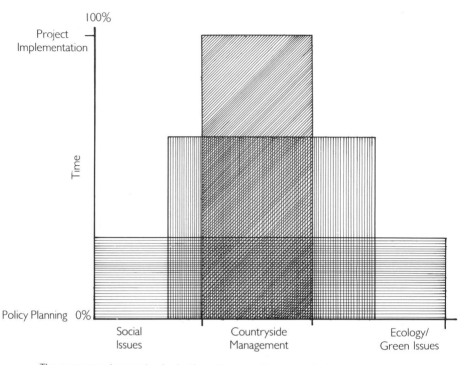

The manager can become involved with a wide range of issues at policy level, or more effectively, restrict the scope of attention and plan, implement and manage countryside projects.

Figure 6.1 *Options for the countryside manager.*

6.1   STAFFING

The first step in implementing policies and strategies is to establish a staffing level which reflects the proposed work. Furthermore, the method of working and aims and objectives will also influence the type of organization which is established to implement schemes. Thus, countryside units, countryside projects, trusts, voluntary organizations and private companies can all manage the implementation of countryside works. The common feature of all of these types of managerial structure is that they reflect the objectives of the parent organization – each managerial structure has its advantages and these should be identified as part of the process of building up staffing levels. There are, however, some basic underlying principles to the process of staffing.

The first principle of establishing a staffing framework is that it should reflect the aims and objectives of the strategy that the organization is to implement. Furthermore, strategies should also identify priorities that allow staff to concentrate on certain areas of work. However, staffing levels and resources rarely match overall strategy requirements and, furthermore, staff are usually already in post and are often involved in the creation of new strategies or the re-affirmation of old policies. Indeed, they should be closely involved in the process, as was discussed in Chapter 2. The implementation of a strategy in these circumstances will involve the re-allocation of existing staff resources and priorities. Understanding and sympathetically managing this situation – managing change – is a skill in itself, the essence of which lies at the heart of *In Pursuit of Excellence* (Peterson, 1985). Staffing is therefore seldom as simple as appointing new staff to new posts.

Staffing, and the process of establishing an organization to deal with countryside strategies, can be seen as having twelve key elements (Torkildsen, 1985):

(a) *Train and deploy* Recognize the way that staff are trained and deployed affects results.

(b) *Study legislation, principles and structures* Understand unity of command, logical assignment and span of control. Recognize the limitation of a span of control.

(c) *Create formal structures* Provide for clear lines of authority and chains of command – a formal structure.

(d) *Permit informal structures* Recognize informal structures and their importance to essential cross communications. In doing so, accept levels of bypassing chains of command.

(e) *Present sound proposals* Sound staffing proposals, which identify essential levels, responsibilities and roles, are needed.

(f) *Create team management* Recognize the benefits of working as a well co-ordinated team rather than a group of individuals.

(g) *Avoid rigid line structures* Consider appropriate hybrids to meet particular situations. Structures must be tailor-made to suit the services to be provided.

(h) *Make conditions flexible* The complexity, hours and patterns of provision of a countryside service call for flexible attitudes.

(i) *Construct departments and decentralize* Divide work out into logical units of sections and identify their functions. Identify the tasks and responsibilities attached to each position.

(j) *Start with essential staff* When providing a new service or new post to an existing function, start only with essential staff.

(k) *Consider alternative structural elements* Consider the values of different staffing structures – volunteers or trusts, for example. Discussions with trades unions will be necessary to explain the need for community involvement.

(l) *Use structures as means, not ends*   Remember that a staffing structure is only a means to an end. It must be used and, if necessary, it must be changed.

6.1.1   Countryside staffing

Four broad types of structure are relevant for countryside management, namely: voluntary, public sector, project based and private sector. The advantages, disadvantages and characteristics of each type of structure are discussed below.

(a)   Voluntary

Much of the early foundation for modern professional countryside management was based on voluntary organizations. The voluntary sector itself has also developed from the early days of the National Trust and the amateur naturalist. Many voluntary organizations now benefit from charitable status and many have also formed into trusts which brings many of the advantages associated with this form of arrangement.

The main advantage of a trust system is that a small core of full-time and/or part-time employees can be appointed to work directly to a group of trustees who, in turn, have a wide range of responsibilities, wide terms of reference and direct control of day-to-day management. It is obviously possible for a local authority, a private company or any other body to take an element of their work away from the mainstream management structure and place it under the management of a trust. Key facilities, such as major country parks or heritage sites might, for example, have so many divergent interests within a single enterprise that a trust system that bypasses normal procedures is the best means of organizing a workforce.

The voluntary sector, however, often gains charitable trust status simply to allow financial management and commercial survival. The advantages associated with such a status include: direct access from executive control, through management to implementation; a wide representational basis for the governing body; a partnership between statutory, voluntary and private organizations if required; and the trust mechanism actually promotes a feeling of ownership which a limited or public liability company might not. A further major advantage is the relative freedom of a trust arrangement which, always providing sufficient funds are available, allows for exploration and experimentation with management techniques. Perhaps the best environmental example of this, which is explored in more detail in the case studies at the end of this chapter, is the Groundwork Trust network.

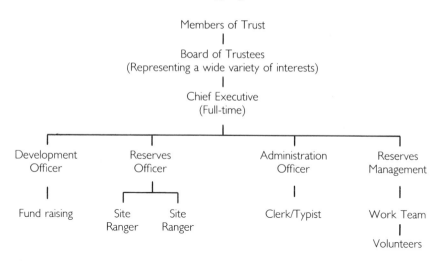

Figure 6.2 *Possible staff structure for County Wildlife Trust.*

Clearly, there are disadvantages to the trust system. The most obvious one is the lack of clearly identifiable capital and revenue resources. Often the trust will be established to help raise and manage finances. This necessarily implies that a hand-to-mouth existence is needed for survival. In the past, this has meant a relatively heavy reliance upon Central Government sponsored employment schemes, except perhaps in a few exceptional cases such as the National Trust.

Within the voluntary sector, however, the trust system of management remains the most common format. Within this system staffing depends upon available resources and the role of the organization/trust involved. Figure 6.2 shows a general trust structure based upon a county wildlife trust. The point at which staff become volunteers or part time depends very much upon the available resources. In the case of many wildlife trusts, this is often at the level of the reserves warden/ranger. The key posts within a wildlife trust are those of the chief executive (who is responsible for overall policy/management), the development officer (responsible, usually, for generating income, business planning, some policy work), reserves officer (in charge of co-ordinating wardening management plans and other site-based issues), administration officer (processing membership, clerical work, financial control) and the management officer (responsible for the physical management of sites and land, often through voluntary workers). Increasingly, the work of generating membership – and thus a through-flow of money – is vital.

For many trusts, the development of a business plan, geared towards fund raising, is an integral part of countryside management. The

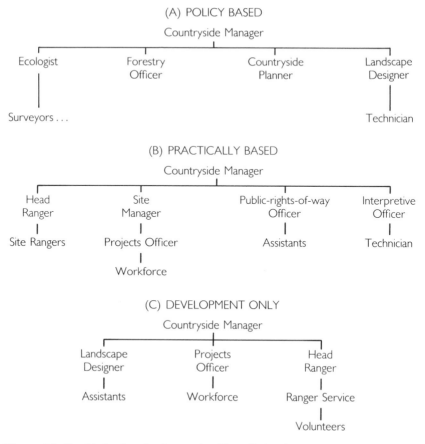

Figure 6.3 *Possible local authority countryside-unit structures.*

important work, particularly of a site-based nature, that many trusts undertake make them a vital component of the overall environmental protection movement, yet, paradoxically their main concern is increasingly in the area of maintaining financial solvency.

The trust system is by no means the only one used by the voluntary sector. Often no actual structure is agreed, but 'informal' committees develop policy. The politics and development of the voluntary movement and their potential for bringing about change at a local level is described in some detail in Clifford (1986). Whatever system is adopted, however, many elements of the work of voluntary organizations can be readily defined as countryside management and, to a greater or lesser extent, the skills needed will be similar to those of a professional countryside manager.

(b)   Public sector

It has already been suggested that most professional countryside managers work within the public sector, largely because the legislative framework allows for and lays a duty upon the Local Authorities for such provision. Not surprisingly, therefore, the staffing process is relatively well defined within the public sector. Notwithstanding this, there are many variations upon the theme of a 'countryside section' or 'countryside team'. The form and staff structure depends upon the objectives and remit of the sections concerned.

Figure 6.3 gives three examples of a countryside section that might be found within a local authority. The first example is for a countryside section which is concerned primarily with the development of policy at a county level.

The second example is for a countryside section which is concerned not only with policy but also with implementation through an established ranger service. In this second model it is also assumed that the responsibility for public rights-of-way also lies with the countryside section.

The final model is one which assumes an emphasis on the development process. This is perhaps most appropriate where a large amount of development of new facilities is needed and where, perhaps, the development of an 'aftercare' or interpretive service is a second phase.

It must be stressed that each of these models represents a theoretical situation and the staffing structure of any organization, which clearly includes the specialist countryside section, is in part the responsibility of the manager. Often, the countryside manager is faced with an existing structure which may or may not be suitable for tackling existing problems. A review of existing policy compared to staffing is central to a continuously adapting section. There is no set answer to any problems or opportunities that arise in the countryside. The countryside manager must therefore be responsible for reviewing the staffing structure and re-assessing whether the structure meets the needs and objectives of the section. In certain cases it might not only be appropriate to alter staffing structures, but it might also be necessary to alter staffing systems and, for example, establish a trust as opposed to a countryside section within the main local authority framework.

(c)   Countryside project

Numerous countryside projects have been established across the country, usually as joint ventures between one or more local authorities and the Countryside Commission who have taken responsibility for monitoring and financing the projects. Central to all of the projects has been the countryside project officer whose role it is to act as a focus for all the interested groups and individuals within the poject area. (The proJect area is often on the urban fringe, but others include Areas of Outstanding Natural Beauty or areas within National Parks.)

Other than the appointment of a countryside project officer, staffing as such is flexible and variable. A large part of the work of the project officer is to use local resources to overcome local problems, and to this end a large amount of work is undertaken through the use of community groups, volunteers, government-sponsored job creation/ training programmes and local landowners. For example, one country-side project (Newcastle Countryside Project, 1986) is defined as:

> . . . an environmental improvement scheme working with voluntary and community groups on the western and northern edges of Newcastle-under-Lyme and the Potteries.

Another (Operation South Cannock, 1985) is defined as:

> . . . a community based project aimed at tackling the many small scale environmental improvements that are necessary to complement the major restoration schemes . . . on the urban fringe.

Most countryside projects define themselves in similar terms, with community-based, small-scale environmental improvements being the main components. The use and reliance upon volunteers brings with it some disadvantages, which are discussed in the next section. However, the use of volunteers to implement work does bring with it many advantages. Most important is the greater understanding that com-munities have towards environmental problems if they are involved, at a local level, with their solution.

In staffing terms, the countryside project revolves around one or possibly two project officers, tackling issues that arise from within the community using available resources and, usually, a very limited budget for implementation costs.

(d) Private sector

The private sector staffing structures are almost as varied as those found in the public sector. For single-site centres, the staffing structure will bear more than a passing resemblance to single-site structures in the public sector. The greatest difference lies in the forms of association adopted by private practices. Consultancy practices specializing in countryside or environmental issues can be engaged by local authorities (who, for example, want information or management expertise but do

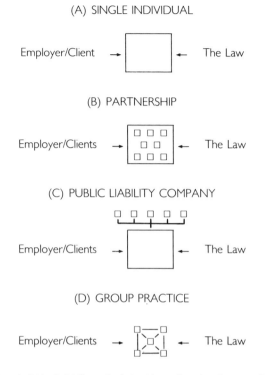

(A) SINGLE INDIVIDUAL

Employer/Client → ▢ ← The Law

(B) PARTNERSHIP

Employer/Clients → ▢ ← The Law

(C) PUBLIC LIABILITY COMPANY

Employer/Clients → ▢ ← The Law

(D) GROUP PRACTICE

Employer/Clients → ▢ ← The Law

Small squares show individual's liability and relationship to clients/employers and the legal system

Figure 6.4 *Forms of private practice appropriate for countryside management consultancy.* (Source: *Greenstreet, 1981.*)

not want to make a long-term commitment to certain issues), private companies (who perhaps want to develop countryside-based facilities) or by government agencies (such as the Countryside Commission or the Nature Conservancy Council, for example, which regularly uses outside consultancy groups to monitor or establish experimental or new projects).

Association within the private sector can take many forms. Figure 6.4 shows, diagrammatically, a number of forms of association often encountered in private practice. These forms (taken from Greenstreet, 1981) represent the commoner types of association which might be adopted by any private practice, including architects, landscape architects, planners or chartered surveyors, all of whom could offer countryside management expertise as part of their service.

The single individual model (A) in Figure 6.4 represents the simplest form of association, within which the responsibilities and liabilities in law are clearly identified as attaching to one individual.

A more common business association is the partnership (Figure 6.4(B)). To quote Greenstreet: 'A partnership exists where two or more individuals carry on a business in common with a view to making a profit to be shared in proportions agreed by the partners'. A partnership therefore allows individuals to pool their resources and expertise in an agreed way. Partnerships are largely governed by the Partnership Act of 1890. In terms of responsibility under law and to the client, the partnership differs from the individually based model described above because the partnership may sue or be sued in the name of the partnership, rather than the individuals. This clearly offers the individuals some protection, although the individuals still remain personally liable for the negligent actions of the firm.

A partnership allows various levels and types of expertise to be assembled (in much the same way as a local authority countryside team) which reflect both the interests of the partnership, and the requirements of the people or organizations seeking work through the consultants – the clients. This relationship between client and consultancy is usually formalized through a contract wherein the brief of the client is enacted upon by the consultancy. The necessary expertise within a partnership will vary over time as the client's requirements vary – the conservation of heritage landscapes is, for example, a relatively new area of work. The partnership must thus be flexible enough to respond to the client's changing requirements. In this respect, the work of the private consultancy is slightly more reactive than that of, say, the countryside policy makers within a local authority.

Within a partnership, there are several types of partner, namely;

Equity partners   Full partners, enjoying all the benefits and responsibilities of the firm.

Salaried partner   An individual who is employed by the partnership, so in effect is not a partner in the 'true' sense of the word. He or she may, however, carry some of the responsibilities of partner status.

Limited partner   A partner whose liability is limited by the extent of his or her investment in the partnership.

Associate   A salaried position which carries a limited status, usually a small share in the profits of the partnership. As with a limited partner, there is no fixed framework for fixing responsibilities or liabilities for associates.

It is clear that, within private practices, much more emphasis is placed on the responsibilities and liabilities of the staff (Figure 6.4(c)). The possibilities of mis-practice (say, the failure to meet contractual require-ments) or professional negligence (say, in designing a pond which subsequently so affects the water table as to flood someone's land) are guarded against securely.

In a group practice (Figure 6.4(D)) the individuals maintain their individual identities while pooling resources, capital or expertise at certain points in time. Often, group associations come together for specific projects where one partnership or individual does not want to buy in expertise simply to undertake one task and so enters into a project-based group association to fulfil one contract.

(e) Summary

The analysis of various forms of staffing arrangements above is de-signed to explore the possibilities that are available to certain organiza-tions. In practice, some systems work better in some circumstances than others, and symbiosis exists within countryside management between the public, private and voluntary sectors. Public bodies often call in outside consultants to undertake country park visitor surveys, for example, or to monitor specific projects. Alternatively, project officers may be appointed to undertake specific schemes. Another example of the symbiosis might be where a local authority part funds a voluntary trust to undertake a special project: Groundwork Trusts, for example.

In short, many staffing systems are available to the countryside manager and each has its merits. The right staffing system to meet individual objectives is critical to the success or otherwise of countryside management.

6.2 WORKFORCES

6.2.1 Introduction

As there are several management systems that can be used to undertake research, practical, managerial and monitoring work so, too, are there a number of ways of appointing a workforce to undertake the work. Typically, the types used by countryside managers are: volunteers, con-tractors, direct labour and government sponsored training/employment initiatives. Each has its advantages and disadvantages, and these are discussed below.

6.2.2 Volunteers

Before volunteers work on countryside projects, either on practical work or as volunteer rangers, it must be clear in the mind of the manager why the volunteers are being involved. Unless these objectives are clear, volunteers and voluntary work are doomed to failure. 'We regret the tendency of some volunteer users, especially some of those delegated to supervise the tasks, to regard volunteers as cheap labour, often accompanied by the tendency to overestimate the skills or capacity of the volunteers' (Countryside Commission, 1980). Rather than cheap labour, voluntary involvement presents the community and keen amateurs with the opportunity to become involved in managing their own environment and to gain personal satisfaction from doing so. Even within the body of 'volunteers' there is a wide range of skill, depending upon the source of volunteers. Primary school children will clearly be less able, and have a much lower threshold of boredom, than, say, a group from the British Trust for Conservation Volunteers. At one level, the educational rewards for school children may far outweigh the amount of practical work achieved. At the other level, a balance will be struck between the work output, the enjoyment of becoming involved and the social, community and educational benefits. Furthermore, volunteers are, after all, just that – volunteers. They are not paid professionals and, while it is acceptable to expect reasonable objectives to be met, it must be clear what these expectations are to be. The enthusiasm of volunteers is fragile, and their involvement in a partnership must be planned with the volunteer group being carefully matched to the task and the expected level of achievement.

There are several key stages when involving volunteers in a project:

(a) *Identifying the tasks* These will necessarily be small-scale or alternatively larger tasks that can be broken down into small, identifiable units so as to allow volunteers the sense of having achieved or completed something. A never-ending litter pick or a large-scale scrub clearance is guaranteed to destroy volunteers' enthusiasm. Suitable tasks, provided that they are planned properly with appropriate elements of education, fun and supervision, include tree planting, woodland restoration, public footpath maintenance, waymarking, fencing, ditch/pond creation or rangering (Shell, 1986).

(b) *Planning the task* This depends largely upon the source of volunteers, their ages, experience and so on. Apart from a specified project, planning involves securing access to correct tools (possibly lent by the British Trust for Conservation Volunteers, or a local authority), necessary transport, food and/or accommodation if required, and insurance. (Under the Health and Safety at Work (1974) Act volunteers are contracted to employment and are therefore not covered by the employing organization's insurance. However, the organization to which the volunteer is associated does have an obligation – again the British Trust for Conservation Volunteers can arrange necessary insurance.) In some circumstances it might also be important to train volunteers if they are to be involved in difficult or new tasks or if they are to be relied upon over a long period of time as, for example, voluntary rangers or working in visitor centres.

(c) *Organization of the task*   The organization of the task is designed to bring the volunteers closer to the task thereby giving them a greater sense of involvement and a greater degree of satisfaction from the work. The preliminaries will include a series of site visits by representatives from both the volunteers and the user body. Lines of communication, responsibility for ordering necessary materials and arrangements for transport, food, insurance, first aid and other details should be agreed. Before the task starts the volunteers will need to be briefed – although they are volunteers they will still want to know what they are doing, why they are doing it, and where it fits into the greater scheme of things. Volunteers will also want to know the more mundane information, such as start times, location of toilets and where they are to be fed. A work programme is vital to the successful use of volunteers. This should cover not only the work to be achieved, but also rotation of the workforce (so that volunteers do not get bored with working on one task for a long period of time), full use of the workforce (so that no one is left standing around) and contingencies to cover a lack of enthusiasm from some volunteers (flagging energy, or the fact that it is raining, and fewer volunteers than expected may turn out). To this end, a series of goals for the day's/week's work is better than a fixed goal so that whatever the circumstances a tangible result can be seen at the end of the task.

(d) *Training and supervision*   Some degree of training should always be given to volunteers because it can never be assumed that they will know the details. Young school children, for example, may never have used a spade properly. The level of training will depend upon both the complexity of the task and the volunteers. Often, a short period of time taken at the beginning of a task will suffice as long as it is backed up with adequate supervision. Supervision should not only aim to ensure correct use of tools and to pass on technical skills, but also to ensure safe working and instil enthusiasm into the team of volunteers.

(e) *Additional points*   Unless a large degree of fun is injected into voluntary work, volunteers are likely to 'vote with their feet' and either leave a task early or not turn up in the future. Thus other elements must be introduced such as visits, slide shows, or social meetings of volunteer groups. For the user group, even a note of thanks to the voluntary group or badges for younger volunteers all help.

All of these issues may well raise the question as to whether it is worth using voluntary workers. The answer must be 'yes'. The public have a right to be involved in the protection and improvement of their own environment, and managers who have a responsibility to that environment have a duty to include that right in their plans. Volunteers are not just cheap labour, and must never be seen as such, and as long as it is accepted that the educative element of volunteer involvement is as important as the actual work produced, the manager must include volunteers in his or her assessment of potential workforces.

6.2.3   Direct labour

Direct labour falls into two categories: rangers, 'who have a role to play in practical management', and estate workers. The practical role of rangers is discussed in Chapter 9 where the overall contribution of rangers to the countryside management process is discussed. This section deals with the practical estate or environmental workers under the direct control of the manager.

In practical terms such an arrangement might best be envisaged as that of an estate team, the workload of which is the responsibility of the manager. Thus, a work programme for a week, a month, or possibly even a year needs to be pre-planned – according to set objectives – obviously with some time allowed for unforeseen work or for responding to new situations.

The advantages of working with a direct labour team can be summarized as follows:

(a) The manager has ready access to a team of workers which is, more often than not, actually on site all the time.
(b) A full year's work programme can be determined which, while allowing for some degree of certainty, can be changed if necessary.
(c) An on-site team can often be a confidence boost for members of the public. If they see a country park being continually managed, they feel that they too should respect the site.
(d) A regular team can develop the skills necessary for estate management and develop a feel for countryside work.
(e) The manager has direct line control over the workings of the team.
(f) Once the salaries of the team have been established within budgets, the cost of implementing schemes is identified as 'materials only'.

A direct labour team will therefore develop a 'feeling' for a site and the skills necessary to manage it practically. For example, a particular site or project area might have a large number of dry stone walls as one of its characteristic features. A team which regularly works in such an area will build up excellent skills in dry-stone-walling techniques.

There are obviously some disadvantages to working with a direct labour team. These are:

(a) It is difficult to control start and finish dates for specific projects.
(b) There is a lack of financial or other controls on the work of the teams to ensure a desired standard of work.
(c) Actually managing a team of workers can detract from the time allowed for planning, designing or monitoring projects.
(d) A team of workers can, occasionally, become an 'institution' which ceases to become involved with development.

Many private estates and voluntary sector sites have direct labour teams with outside contractors brought in to undertake specific, identifiable duties. In situations where the public are regularly on site, therefore, a small team of 'estate type' workers is able to keep on top of the regular small-scale development work that is necessary due to visitor pressures. Such potential for a rapid response to physical damage (such as worn footpaths or broken fences) stops the site from looking neglected and therefore not only gives visitors a more accessible environment, but also deters additional damage. Clearly, this is not necessary for all sites but on more popular, highly pressured areas, the countryside manager should explore the need for such a direct labour team.

6.2.4 Contract labour

The management of contracts is a profession in itself – indeed, much of the professional training of architects, engineers, landscape architects and quantity surveyors is geared towards the correct means of managing contracts. Consequently, the management of projects by these various professions centres around contractual arrangements. However, for various reasons the countryside manager may wish to involve other groups in the implementation process. Notwithstanding this, there are many occasions that implementation of schemes through the contract mechanism is the optimal arrangement.

Given the scope of contract law, accepted forms of contractual arrangements, standard specifications and standard forms of agreement, this section can do no more than identify the main issues in managing a contract.

Almost all work involved in countryside management can be undertaken by contractors working to contractual instructions issued either by the countryside manager or by the countryside manager for his or her client. It is often suggested that some countryside work requires a 'feel' for the countryside, and dry stone walling, for example, cannot be quantified or qualified sufficiently well to merit a contract. It is up to the countryside manager to determine the best means of working in any given situation, but few if any operations undertaken by or for country-side managers could not be undertaken by contractors.

Clamp (1986) identifies four main components of a contract, which are:

(a) *Specification*   Giving details of the quality of workmanship, materials and performance of the work to be provided.
(b) *Schedule of quantity*   Giving details of how much of each material is to be provided. In some circumstances this is referred to as the Bill of Quantites.
(c) *Drawings* Showing details of the location of materials and works to be carried out.
(d) *Conditions of contract*   Bringing together all the different elements, and also adding the obligations of the various parties and other details of contract operation.

(a)   Specification

The specification gives a precise written description of all of the elements of the work to be carried out. In countryside management this may include the quality of tree stock to be used, the quality and wearing potential of stone for path surfaces, the quality of soil or the quality and life expectancy of timber used for fencing. Clearly, each piece of work will be different, so specifications will vary from project to project. However, there are standard specifications which can be used off-the-peg so to speak, although care must clearly be taken for some jobs where specifications will need to be written individually – say, for a pond which requires restocking with plants from a certain location or neigh-bouring pond. Standard clauses have been drawn up by a number of organizations, including the Property Services Agency, the Greater London Council and the National Building Specification. Further detail of quality is available through the British Standards Institute or is available in an abridged form (Lovejoy and Partners, 1986).

(b)   Schedule of quantity

The schedule of quantity fulfils two main purposes. Firstly, it ensures that all the materials needed to undertake a particular project are contained and itemized within the contract and, secondly, it ensures that all the organizations that tender for the work are applying for and giving rates for the same work. In short, it cannot be assumed that all the information can be taken from contract drawings except in the simplest and most straightforward of projects (even in these cases, a schedule of quantity is included within the drawings). For most projects, particularly landscaping works, the schedule of quantity is sub-divided into seven sections, namely:

(a) Introduction
(b) Preamble
(c) Cultivation and preparation
(d) Seeding and turfing
(e) Planting, including shrub and tree planting
(f) Thinning and pruning, tree surgery, grass improvement
(g) Protection of existing artifacts

This schedule was agreed by the Joint Council for Landscape Industries (1978) which seeks to standardize the letting and management of landscape contracts. For contracts which contain 'hard' works (foot-paths, stone walls, car parking or steps, for example) a different system of sub-division is needed which allows for the hard elements to be billed separately.

(c) Drawings

The drawings which form part of any contract contain all the necessary information for works to be carried out at the correct location both in absolute terms (i.e. on-site) and in relative terms (i.e. each element of the project is correctly located in relation to all the others). British Standard BS 1192: Part 4, 1984 relates specifically to contract drawings.

As with all other elements, standard procedures exist for drawings which helps to avoid different parties mis-interpreting details within a contract. Accepted practice at drawing is a profession within its own right. For soft or landscaping work, the landscape architect is the professional exponent, and for building work the architect is the expert. (Both are served by existing professional institutes, the Landscape Institute and the Royal Institute of British Architects, respectively.) There are, however, some areas of overlap in countryside work – small bridges, external detail or hard elements to a project could both, arguably, be designed by either profession. However, it is increasingly being accepted that the treatment of many elements of hard landscape work should be designed by landscape architects. It is for the manager to determine the optimal approach.

The designer must aim to 'communicate with accuracy, clarity, economy and consistency of presentation between all concerned with the construction industry'. Familiarity with all commonly accepted forms of presentation is likely to result in greater efficiency with the preparation and interpretation of landscape drawings and minimize the risk of confusion on site (BS 1192).

(d)   Contract conditions

Contracts can be conveyed in a number of ways: verbally, by letter, or by an exchange of agreements. The essence of contractual law, however, is that an offer of contract be made and accepted by the parties involved. In order to avoid any confusion over conditions of contractual arrangements, standard forms of agreement also exist for most contractual situations which have been agreed by all interested parties within the relevant industries – landscape, architectural or engineering, for example. For countryside managers, the two most important standard forms are those drawn up by the Joint Council for the Landscape Industry (1978) and the Joint Contracts Tribunal (1980). The former deals with landscape contracts where only soft/planting works are involved; the latter deals with contracts where both soft and hard works are involved. Other forms of contract do exist, although these are usually for major engineering or building works.

The conditions of the Joint Council for Landscape Industry aim to establish the intentions of the various parties, work practices, commencement and completion dates, penalties for non-completion, payment procedures and other obligations on both parties. As suggested, however, the expertise required in managing contracts requires specialist training in its own right, and if a countryside manager determines that this particular skill is needed, he or she can either acquire the expertise or pay for the services of a consultant. In any events, the conditions of contracts and methods of measurements change rapidly, so care must be taken in contract situations.

The proximity of landscape design and landscape contract management of countryside management is described in Brooker and Corder (1986). Their text explores methods of monitoring and developing open space, particularly in the urban environment, which not only maximizes its wildlife potential but also provides recreational open space while seeking to reduce maintenance costs.

6.2.5   Government-sponsored schemes

Since government-sponsored schemes began to appear on the employment scene in the mid-1970s they have been called many things – both officially and unofficially. However, the various schemes have had a number of similar characteristics, namely:

(a) they have been geared towards helping unemployed people re-enter work;
(b) placements on the schemes have been, except in exceptional circumstances, reserved for unemployed people;
(c) the wages of the people on the schemes have been paid directly by Central Government;
(d) the placements on the schemes have been temporary – usually one or two years; and
(e) some additional funding for training and supporting the project work of the people on the schemes has been provided by Central Government.

The two main target groups for existing Government Sponsored Employment Schemes (GSES) have been young school leavers who have been unable to enter full-time employment or further education (the Youth Training Scheme) and the older long-term unemployed (out of work for over six months).

The benefits of working with the GSES are clearly financial – the wages of the employees do not fall to the manager, so effectively all projects become 'materials only' costs. This has resulted in many environmental groups, particularly in the voluntary sector, becoming heavily involved with GSES, and indeed much work was undertaken using Community Programme labour in the early to mid-1980s. However, this often became dependent upon the 'free labour' and when the scheme changed in 1988 to become 'Employment Training' rather than 'Community Programme' many voluntary sector organizations saw their workforces reduce drastically as the people holding government-funded posts lost their financial support. One such group of organizations were the Groundwork Trusts which, from the outset, were heavily reliant upon GSES. Indeed, the rules for these temporary employment measures will constantly change and it is therefore always going to be dangerous to become too heavily involved in, or over-reliant on, such measures.

A further shortcoming of the workforce provided through such schemes is the fact that most of the workers are almost by definition untrained either because they have just left the educational system or because they are moving from one type of work to another in an effort to broaden their future employment possibilities (Department of Employment, 1988). Thus, a lot of time needs to be spent training the workers and, given the fact that most posts are temporary in the first place, a relatively inexperienced workforce will be the norm. In short, GSES cannot be seen as simply a source of cheap labour.

Table 6.1. *Relative success of tree-planting schemes undertaken by different workforces*

			Quartiles	
Trees planted by	*Number of schemes*	*Median survival, %*	*Q1, lower*	*Q3, upper*
Local authority staff	29	90	70	100
Voluntary labour	20	81	46	96
Landowner or staff	93	76	43	96
Professional contractor	105	76	54	95
Unspecified	41	71	41	94

Source: Countryside Commission (1986).

If sufficient attention is given by the countryside manager to the important elements of supervision, training and delegating the correct type of tasks to the individuals on the schemes, good results can be expected. The Countryside Commission (1986) suggests that the type of labour used to plant trees, for example, does not have great significance on the success of tree-planting schemes – of far greater importance are the quality of the tree stock, the after care, the size of the trees, the location of the planting scheme, and so on (Table 6.1). Indeed, the survey shows that, in the study areas, survival rate of trees planted by volunteers and Government Sponsored Employment Schemes is greater than that of trees planted by landowners or their staff. Actual rates of planting were clearly much lower for volunteers and GSES, but quality was maintained.

As long as countryside and environmental work are underfunded some reliance upon a government-funded workforce will be inevitable within a countryside manager's work – particularly in the voluntary sector, in local conservation trust for example, who might not otherwise be able to afford the upkeep on nature reserves. However, it is up to each individual countryside manager to determine the relative advantages and disadvantages of GSES because the schemes bring with them both problems and opportunities.

6.3   CASE STUDIES

Two case studies are presented here which reflect two different approaches to establishing organizations and workforces to implement different countryside schemes. The CARE Project (Community Action in the Rural Environment) adopts a community led approach to tackle community problems, while Groundwork Trusts are established to tackle a wide range of problems in a variety of ways. Both, however, provide models that may be appropriate in other situations.

6.3.1 CARE Project

The CARE Project was established in 1986 by Barnsley Metropolitan Borough Council to address environmental and community problems in the western fringes of the borough, which includes part of the Peak District National Park. Many of the communities in this part of the borough are small, isolated, rural communities – not what might immediately be anticipated within a metropolitan borough. The scheme is intended to 'promote the involvement of rural communities in the management and use of their local environment' (Roome, 1988). This involvement can be through any means of activity that encourages and fires the imagination of the community. On the one hand, therefore, pocket parks are created and landscape enhancement schemes are undertaken; at another level, communities are encouraged to 'celebrate place through the production of oral histories, parish maps and village appraisals, footpath maps, the recording of historic and present-day landscapes and ecological surveys' (Roome, op. cit.).

The part of the CARE Project that sets it apart from other projects or countryside schemes which appear to meet similar objectives is the way in which they are achieved. The CARE Project is as much concerned with *how* the practical results are achieved and *who* does the work as it is with the tangible outcome. The project aims to develop the community's self-awareness and confidence in such a way that not only does the community undertake the schemes, but also plans, co-ordinates and maintains the impetus of the schemes.

The back up comes in the form of a CARE project officer and a working budget. The funding of the overall costs comes from the Countryside Commission, Barnsley Metropolitan Borough Council, local parishes and the Peak Park Joint Planning Board. (In this respect, it is one of a series of community action 'experiments' which are run by the Countryside Commission and the Countryside Commission for Scotland, the aims of which are broadly similar to those of the CARE Project.) Funding in 1988 stood at only £21 000.

In addition to the project officer (called in this case an advisory officer to emphasize that he or she does not get actively involved in work on the ground, but works as a facilitator) the Steering Group offer administrative support, but little else. The communities, therefore, are really on their own. Unless they do something, nothing will happen, and this includes raising additional funds.

In a strict sense, therefore, the CARE Project has a very limited organization – in effect, one full-time officer. But in another way, the size of the organization is only limited by the number of people living in the area.

It is difficult to monitor the success of community action schemes, because success may not lie in the number of trees planted but in the fact that the community even thought about wanting to plant trees. Notwithstanding this, the success of the CARE Project can be seen on the ground, and in the communities; the natural and social landscapes are both changing. The true test of its success may, however, come when the advisory officer leaves the scene – as with all community-based schemes.

6.3.2   Groundwork

The Groundwork movement in England and Wales, and more recently in Scotland, arose out of the Countryside Commission's interest in land management on the urban fringe, as exemplified in the Bollin Valley Project. In 1981, this interest was coupled with the then Secretary of State for the Environment's belief that inner-city social problems could, in part, be alleviated through having a better managed environment. This was felt, in turn, to be best provided by a partnership of private, public and voluntary groups. From this was born the first Groundwork Trust – Operation Groundwork in St Helens and Knowsley.

Because of this early political support, Groundwork has developed until many more areas of urban fringe have Groundwork Trusts. The formation of a trust allows public and private funding to be brought together to undertake Ground-work projects. Knightsbridge (1985) states that these projects must have as their aims one or several of the following:

> . . . clear dereliction and eyesores; find productive use for wasted assets; conserve and enhance good environments for wildlife, leisure recreation and agriculture; assist farmers in realising the full potential of their land . . . ; improve the management of footpaths and public open spaces; and provide small-scale parking, picnicking and recreational facilities.

These objectives do not differ greatly from those of many local authority country-side managers, but the Groundwork Trusts are set apart from their local authority counterparts through their organizational elements. 'The novelty is not necessarily in the aims, but in the way that they are achieved' (Knightsbridge, op. cit.).

A trust framework allows complex financial deals to be arranged, and private sponsorship to be channelled into environmental schemes. Again, this is not dissimilar to many local authorities or indeed urban wildlife groups (Smyth, 1986) but the high profile nature of the Groundwork Trusts ensures that the partnership and entrepreneurial image are projected.

The initial aim of the Groundwork Trusts (of which there were twelve in 1987, with three or four planned for each of the next four years) was to make each one financially self-supporting after three or five years. This has not been the case and core funding tends to come from local or central government sources with private companies buying in the professional landscape services of the Groundwork Trust staff or sponsoring individual projects.

The staff within Groundwork Trusts vary, but a chief executive reports to a Board of Trustees comprising individuals from the sponsoring organizations. The chief executive is responsible for a number of staff who have design, implementational or interpretive skills. In the past, great use was made of Government Sponsored Employment Schemes, but this has reduced over recent years. The core teams, therefore, revolve around a small team of professionals who operate in a way that lies somewhere between a local government countryside team and a group of private consultants, and as their work has taken Groundworks into urban centres, the Countryside Commissions have found it increasingly difficult to sponsor their work, so in 1987 the source of funding switched from the Commissions directly to the Department of the Environment or the Scottish Office (Countryside Commission, 1987a).

The Groundwork Trusts have a staffing structure which is tightly defined by their objectives, with landscape architects, project officers/supervisors and community rangers being employed through most trusts. Practical implementation is achieved through a variety of workforces, including volunteers, contract labour and GSES.

BIBLIOGRAPHY

British Standards Institute (Various Years) *List of British Standards*, BSI, Milton Keynes.

Brooker, R. and Corder, M. (1986) *Environmental Economy*, E. & F.N. Spon, London.

Clamp, M. (1986) *Spon's Landscape Contract Manual*, E. & F.N. Spon, London.

Clifford, S. (1986) *Holding your Ground*, Common Ground, London.

Countryside Commission (1980) *Volunteers in the Countryside*, Advisory Series No. 11, Cheltenham.

Countryside Commission (1986) *An Assessment of Amenity Tree Planting Schemes*, Cheltenham

Countryside Commission (1987a) *Annual Report*, Cheltenham.

Countryside Commission (1987b) *Enjoying the Countryside*, CCP225, Cheltenham

Department of Employment (1988) *Employment Training*, HMSO.

Greater Manchester Countryside Unit (1988) *Annual Report*, GMCU, Tameside

Greenstreet, R. (1981) *Legal and Contractual Procedures for Architects*, Architectural Press, London.

Groundwork Foundation (1986) *Groundwork – The Environmental Entrepreneurs*, Macclesfield Groundwork/Shell UK.

Joint Council for Landscape Industry (1978) *Method of Measurement of Soft Landscape Works*, JCLI (available through Royal Institute of British Architects, London).

Knightsbridge, R. (1985) Groundwork and nature conservation, *ECOS*, **6**, No. 3, pp. 25–29.

Lovejoy and Partners (1986) *Spon's Landscape Handbook*, E. & F.N. Spon, London.

Newcastle Countryside Project (1986) *Annual Report*, Staffordshire County Council.

· SEVEN ·

Practical skills

Fortunate, too, is the man who has come to know the gods of the
countryside.

Virgil, Georgics (30 BC)

*The range of practical skills needed to design and undertake countryside project
work is enormous. Without including the more academic skills of survey
technique, monetary planning and personnel management, the term 'practical
skills' covers many items: habitat management, habitat creation, drawing and
design skills, construction techniques, estate work (including dry stone walling,
fencing, stile erection, hedge laying and ditching) and practical knowledge of
grassland, woodland, wetland, moorland and coastal management techniques.*

*Any introduction can only hope to scratch the surface of the topic. Of great
importance, therefore, are the many existing publications, which give great detail
of individual parts of the complex array of 'practical skills'. The need to have a
personal command of all the practical skills very much depends upon the
countryside manager's overall level of responsibility. Figure 7.1 shows a model of
the skills needed by various levels of countryside manager.*

*The areas of knowledge broadly divide into three categories. Firstly, the
habitats within the British Isles can be categorized into five general types:
grassland, woodlands, heath and moor, wetlands and ponds, coasts. The
countryside manager, at whatever level, must have at least a working knowledge
of these habitats and know how to manage them. The second area of knowledge
might be termed 'estate skills', such as dry stone walling, hedging, fencing and
ditching. This list might also include such items as the use of machinery and
hand-tools and maintenance techniques. The manager must therefore be able to
identify areas of responsibility and allocate these areas, thus cutting out the need
for any individual to have a detailed knowledge of all areas of work.*

*The third area of knowledge with which the manager must be concerned is the
specialist information, which will become important in specific circumstances.
Certain work situations will require knowledge of farming techniques for*

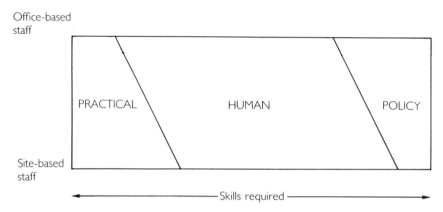

Figure 7.1 *Levels of management skill.*

example, or archaeological survey techniques or the potential problems associated with working in areas of archaeological importance. Where use is being made of historically important buildings, the manager might also feel it appropriate that a member of staff has some knowledge of vernacular architecture. These items, it must be emphasized, will only be of marginal importance in all but a handful of cases and will thus only warrant marginal interest from the manager. However, if only in a brief way, it is important to raise them as issues in order to identify the broad range of considerations that are part of the countryside management process.

7.1   HABITAT MANAGEMENT

7.1.1   Introduction

Managing natural habitats and the natural environment is, in many respects, similar to managing more formal, horticultural situations. The methods of planting trees, sowing seed, using hand-tools and using machinery are all identical in most circumstances. What are different about natural habitats are the underlying principles that guide their development and hence their management. It is these general principles with which we are concerned here.

The term 'natural habitat' is somewhat misleading because many of the habitats with which a countryside manager becomes involved are not natural, but man-made and man-managed. Many woodlands, for example, have been actively managed for several centuries and have reached a balance between wildlife and what might be best termed 'traditional management techniques'.

The term 'natural habitats' is therefore used to cover a wide range of habitats, from ancient woodland to totally man-made hedgerows. What must concern us are the techniques and principles needed by the countryside manager to ensure that these habitats meet set objectives – be they recreational, ecological, landscape or educational, or a mixture of all of these in varying quantities. However, if we destroy the habitats we destroy the very basis for the recreational, ecological or other objectives for which we strive. For these reasons the principles of habitat management are a necessary prerequisite for countryside managers.

The following analysis looks at only three types of habitat – namely, (a) grasslands, woodlands, heaths and moors, (b) wetlands and ponds and (c) coasts. The discussion does not consider the ecology of these habitats except where it is of direct relevance to the management process. However, it is evident that for countryside managers the link between ecology and management should always be considered. For this reason, some references are made in the bibliography to texts which discuss the ecology of the common habitats with which this chapter deals.

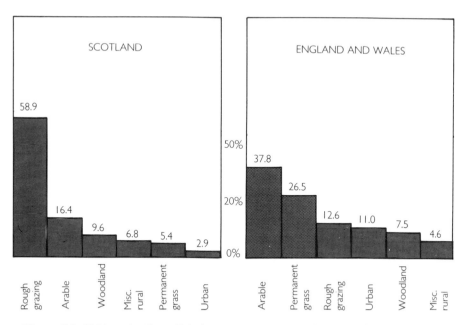

Figure 7.2 *Habitats in Great Britain – percentage cover in 1985.* (Source: *Nature Conservancy Council, 1984.*)

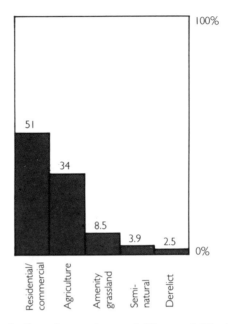

Figure 7.3 *Habitats in the urban environment (Tyne and Wear).* (Source: *Nature Conservancy Council, 1988.*)

7.1.2   Grassland

The Nature Conservancy Council (1984) have estimated that around 26.5% of England and Wales and 5.4% of Scotland are down to permanent grassland. In addition to this, 12.6% of England and Wales and 58.9% of Scotland are down to rough grazing. A large proportion of this rough grazing will be grassland of one sort or another. In short, therefore, a large proportion of Great Britain is covered by grassland. Furthermore, the Nature Conservancy Council (1988) identified that in the built up areas of the Tyne and Wear conurbation 8.5% is amenity grassland, while even in such an urban setting some 34% of land is agricultural (Figures 7.2 and 7.3).

As there is such a large amount of grass around, it is inevitable that the countryside manager should have some working knowledge of grassland management. There are three principal stages to grassland management (which will be repeated for all of the habitats discussed in this chapter):

(a) *Setting objectives*   What sort of grassland is required and why?
(b) *Establishing the grassland*   'Getting the grass to grow' and establishing a management regime.

(c) *Maintenance* Keeping the grass in the necessary condition and with the necessary species diversity to meet known objectives.

(a) Objectives

It may appear to be a strange notion that managers can set objectives for grassland. However, in the context of management plans for Country Parks, the manager may wish to identify those areas that will receive heavy wear and those areas that will be expected to support a wide variety of plant and insect or animal species. In project areas, on the other hand, which are based on predominantly private and agricultural land, the decision over objectives may be pre-empted by other factors and the countryside manager may be responsible for implementing existing objectives, such as maintaining a valuable flower-rich meadow. In most situations, however, the manager will be seeking to meet a number of objectives, either by establishing different sorts of grassland in various locations across his or her area or through establishing grassland which, because of its characteristics, can actually meet various objectives. Because of the obvious concern of countryside management for the natural environment, the preference for indigenous, natural grassland will be usual.

(b) Establishing grassland

Often the manager will be faced with an existing grassland which either needs to be diversified or needs to be maintained in its existing condition. (Indeed, an ancient wildflower meadow cannot be created or established, which is why it must be protected wherever possible.) The process of establishing a grassland therefore involves one of two processes for countryside managers, namely creating new grassland and adapting existing grassland.

Establishing a grassland (either grassland *per se* or a wildflower grassland mix) from seed is relatively simple. For anything but the most monotonous, amenity sward, the key to establishing diversity is to keep the soil nutrient level as low as possible. This encourages delicate, native species rather than the hybrid cultivars of rye-grass, bents, and fescues which thrive on soils with a high nutrient value, and are usually associated with short mown urban grasslands.

The simplest way of establishing a flower/grassland mix is to leave the area of low-quality soil open and, in time, wild grasses and plants will colonize the area. This process does not take a long time, but the process of colonization is somewhat random and unwanted species may take over sites. A much quicker and more controlled method of establishing a

Grassland Management: Deer form an attractive and efficient form of management. The llamas are less common!

new grassland is to sow onto the low nutrient soil. The choice of species will depend very much upon the qualities of the soil – the acidity, the soil texture, water table and so on. Duffey *et al.* (1976) have identified the characteristics inherent in the semi-natural grassland of Britain. These types of grassland – as with other habitats, represent a balance between soil, location, water table, climate and management, and each factor is difficult to analyse separately. The grasslands fall into three broad categories, depending upon soil type.

Calcareous grasslands usually occur on limestone or chalk which give rise to basic soils with a high calcium carbonate content.

Acidic grasslands occur on a variety of soils with the common factor of a low pH.

Neutral grasslands occur in the intermediate range on soils that are neither acid nor basic, such as clays or loams.

Having established the appropriate seed mix (which can often be taken from an analysis of adjacent grassland species), this is sown according to basic horticultural techniques (e.g. Baines, 1984). The aim is clearly to establish a grassland sward which provides visual and wildlife interest and meets the management objectives.

The process of diversifying or altering existing grassland is somewhat more difficult, particularly where the grassland in question is of a high nutrient content. In these conditions the sward is dominated by alien cultures of rye-grass, bent or fescues. Leaving such areas to their own devices will simply produce long, alien cultivars, and not a more diverse sward. Similarly, scattering seed and/or individual plants within such a sward will have little or no impact upon the vigorous, tight growth of cultivars. Thus, two processes must be introduced if a regularly mown, amenity area of grass is to be altered to produce a more attractive or diverse sward. Firstly, the nutritional level of the soil must be reduced and, secondly, the sward must be broken up to allow competition between existing plants and newly introduced, probably less vigorous, plants.

Clearly, once new grasses and flowers have become established maintenance regimes must take account of the ecological requirements of the plants within the grassland. Each of these plants will have requirements for growth, flowering, fertilization and seed setting. This introduces the final area of concern for the countryside manager, that of maintenance.

(c) Grassland maintenance
It is exceedingly difficult to separate grassland maintenance from other issues, such as species diversity or the use to which the grassland can be

put. For example, ancient meadows in agricultural areas are the product of many seasons of hay cropping and/or grazing. By hay cropping the nutrient levels are kept relatively low allowing competition, thus helping to establish a site of wildlife importance. In turn, this also means that the grassland increases in its natural value for hay – a fine balance is struck between the grassland, its management and the use to which it is put. Baines (op. cit.) explores the basic principles behind the management of spring and summer meadows – the names reflecting when the flowers and grasses are allowed to set seed and, hence, the types of species present. However, in our context even the two types of meadow have wider implications. Spring meadows, for example, provide attractive and relatively low growing areas of grassland which are ideal for country parks, picnic sites or well used sites. Summer meadows are characterized by relatively tall growing species and thus tend to deter regular use by visitors.

Duffey *et al.* (op. cit.) and Countryside Commission (1977) deal with the maintenance of grassland and the impact that this maintenance has upon the grassland's wider potential. In short, the manager has four broad options for maintenance: grazing by animals; cutting by horticultural machines; cutting by agricultural machines; and burning. The advantages, disadvantages and optimal circumstances for each member are given in Table 7.1. Most countryside managers will not be called upon to use or manage all of these techniques, so intimate knowledge of them is not critical. However, it is clear that they all have knock-on effects, and these in turn influence the manager's overall responsibility. Some techniques are not suitable for areas to be used for general, informal activities; some do not maintain the resident bird populations; and some, such as burning, are, at least temporarily, decidedly dangerous to the public. Conversely some, such as grazing by deer or sheep, are in themselves attractive to visitors.

Other than the objectives behind maintaining the grassland in the first place, one of the main determinants of a maintenance regime is cost. Indeed, close mowing grass with a tractor-drawn gang mower is one of the cheapest ways of maintaining a sward. Much time and effort has therefore gone into trying to reduce and/or justify the cost of not only establishing natural and semi-natural grasslands, but also of maintaining them. Corder and Brooker (1981) gave details of the cost and relative efficiency of different maintenance techniques, similar to those involved in creating spring or summer meadows. It is clear that while maintaining areas of semi-natural grassland is neither cheaper nor more expensive than more austere maintenance regimes, the best method of maintenance is to reproduce traditional and often well-tested techniques through grazing or hay cropping. The multi-dimensional importance of

Table 7.1. Techniques of grassland management

Type of management	Advantages	Disadvantages	Situation when appropriate
1. Grazing	i Attractive feature in country parks. ii Potential source of income. iii Saves costs of cutting. iv Can be used on steep slopes were cutting is impossible.	i Requires experienced labour, fencing, additional machinery, etc. ii Potential risk of stock fatalities (litter and dogs). iii Livestock might create unpleasant mud, smell, flies, etc.	i Grassland with water and fencing and where visitor pressure is not too great nor is there a dog problem.
(a) Sheep	i Maintain floristic diversity. ii Safe with people. iii Traditional animal on certain grassland types. iv Saleable products – animals, carcase, wool. v Attractive feature of interest for visitor, especially lambs.	i Susceptible to dog worrying. ii High level of husbandry required, especially when breeding. iii Disease prone on wet poorly drained areas. iv Unsuitable on very productive grass swards over 10 cm.	i Chalk, limestone grassland especially steep slopes. ii As component of mixed grazing on meadow, parkland, rough grazing. iii Low-medium public use, or intermittently on high public use areas when alternative grazing is available. iv Ancient earthworks and hill forts etc.

Table 7.1. (cont)

Type of management	Advantages	Disadvantages	Situation when appropriate
(b) Cattle	i Maintain floristic diversity. ii Safe with people. iii Not susceptible to dog worrying (excluding calves). iv Saleable products – animals, carcase, hides. v Attractive, moving feature in landscape. vi Attract subsidy in certain cases. vii Certain breeds are ideal for reclaiming rough pasture.	i Calves susceptible to dog worrying. ii Minority of public may be scared by their 'inquisitive' behaviour. iii Can cause erosion on steep slopes. iv Can poach grass in wet weather. v Can damage cars. vi Cow pats most offensive type of dung.	i Chalk/limestone grassland not steep slopes. ii Meadow land. iii Parkland. iv Control of long coarse grass. v Reclamation management.
(c) Deer	i Exceptionally attractive feature in country parks. ii Very hardy requiring minimum maintenance. iii Saleable products – venison, hides, antlers. iv Docile and harmless to public. v Less susceptible to dog worrying.	i Very high costs involved in erecting and maintaining deer fence. ii Requires specialized labour with knowledge of deer husbandry. iii Tends to reduce floristic diversity. iv Occasional rogue stag may be potentially dangerous in latter stages of rut.	i Established parkland with deer fence.

(d) Horse

i Attractive feature in parks.
ii May be used for rides for public which can bring in revenue.

i Temperamental behaviour, especially if annoyed – may kick or bite.
ii Very selective grazer can spoil the floristic composition of sward – behavioural habits associated with dunging.
iii High initial expense.

i Confined to paddock with public/horse interface at fence.
ii Larger open areas where they can retire away from public.

2. Cutting

i Eliminates cost of fencing.
ii Potential saleable product/rent from cutting rights.
iii Can be used at all intensities of public use.
iv No dog worrying problem.
v No dung, smell, flies.
vi Management has control over the type of finish on the grass, time and frequency of cut.

i Costs money to purchase, run, maintain and repair machinery. This has increased considerably in recent months.
ii Can create a rather uniform and uninteresting landscape, more typical of recreation grounds.
iii Can't be used on steep slopes.
iv Advantages of livestock foregone.
v Labour on cutting could be more profitably employed elsewhere.

i Situations when livestock requirements cannot be provided, or public pressure is too high for livestock.
ii Games and certain picnic areas.
iii Formal areas.

Table 7.1. (cont)

Type of management	Advantages	Disadvantages	Situation when appropriate
(a) Gang mowing	i Can cover large areas quickly. ii Leaves ideal finish for sports areas etc.	i No income can be generated, only costs incurred. ii Creates uniform and uninteresting sward. iii Needs to be cut regularly – gang mowers cannot cope with long grass. iv May produce undesired 'town park' appearance in country parks. v Clippings left on ground. vi Ground must be fairly level.	i Games areas and certain picnic areas. ii Areas of high public pressure.
(b) Flail, rear mounted and rotary cutter	i Maintain large areas of grass in once/twice year cuts. ii Can cope with long coarse grass or scrub. iii Versatile – can be readily adjusted.	i No income generated. ii Clippings left on ground. iii Can leave uniform and uninteresting appearance to park.	i Topping grass swards. ii Forestry rides. iii Light-medium scrub control. iv Sports grounds.
(c) Hand operated machines	i Can be used in places where tractor powered machinery is unsuitable.	i Small rates of cut. ii High labour requirement.	i On slopes – small areas. ii Surrounding trees, car parks, etc. iii Formal areas.

i Cylinder mowers			Formal gardens, flower beds, bowling greens, etc.
ii Rotary mowers			Areas surrounding trees, car parks, small picnic areas, etc.
iii Flymo			Grass banks. Areas around trees, car parks, etc.
iv Portable Bush Saw			Clearing scrub off steep slopes.
3. **Agricultural Cutting Machinery** – operated by farmers or as part of country park's own management programme.	i Reduce costs of grassland maintenance. ii May provide income – sale/rent. iii Feed value of grass can be utilized instead of wasted.	i Lack of precise management control. ii Litter may be incorporated into livestock feed. iii May have to leave grass longer than otherwise e.g. if using maintenance equipment.	i Large areas of grassland at present cut by maintenance machinery. ii Management can utilize/sell the product. iii Suitable farmers willing to operate his own machinery.
(a) Hay making equipment, cutter bar, tedder baler – plus carting bales.	i Traditional technique may be vital for maintaining floristic interest of sward.	i Bales may be knifed by visitors if left around too long.	i Fairly highly productive grass – low intensity of public use.

Table 7.1. (cont)

Type of management	Advantages	Disadvantages	Situation when appropriate
(b) Forage harvester	i Can be used more regularly e.g. every 6 weeks in growing season.		i All types of grassland on a terrain suitable for the machinery.
4. Burning	i Cheap. ii Used when grazing and cutting are both unfeasible. iii Traditional method for maintaining heathland, and certain grassland areas. iv Controlled burning may reduce risk of accidental burning e.g. bracken.	i Potentially dangerous if out of control. ii Temporarily unattractive feature on landscape. iii Regeneration after fire may favour potentially undesirable species e.g. bracken, purple moor-grass. iv Limited period of year when safe or useful (February–March).	i Steep, unfenced grassland where grazing/cutting impractical. ii Regenerate old stands of heathland. iii Control of bracken litter.

Source: Countryside Commission (1977).

these techniques (providing attractiveness, efficiency, wildlife interest and an interpretive resource) make them particularly important to countryside managers.

Maintenance, therefore, lies at the heart of creating good, semi-natural grassland. This central importance of maintenance is a recurring theme as we look at other habitat types – indeed, many of our habitats as we have seen are the result of hundreds of years of a true balance being struck between the natural environment and traditional management techniques. It is the role of the countryside manager, as far as possible within the framework of his or her objectives, to pursue these traditional techniques.

7.1.3 Woodland

Woodland occupies some 7–8% of the land in Great Britain. For purposes of definition, woodland is often defined as having an area of half a hectare or more. This broad definition, therefore, covers as wide a range of woodlands as is possible to imagine in Britain: from the monocultured, softwood plantation to the ancient hardwood woodlands; from small game coverts to the massive blocks of coniferous planting predominantly found in upland Britain; and from continuous tracts of woodland to the more open, less easily defined woodlands such as the New Forest or Cannock Chase.

The importance of woodlands to the countryside manager (and to the wider public) cannot be overemphasized (Rackham, 1976). Woodlands are visually imposing; they number some of our most valuable habitats and natural history resources; they are attractive to the public; they are mostly relatively tough habitats that can accommodate some visitor pressure; and they offer almost endless scope for education and interpretation. It is therefore ironic (to say the least!) that many British semi-natural woodlands have disappeared over the years since the Second World War, mostly in the name of agricultural progress (Shoard, 1987).

There are some twelve main types of semi-natural woodland in Britain, which are detailed in Table 7.2. These twelve groups are further sub-divided in thirty-nine sub-groups depending on location, soil type, sub-dominant species and rainfall. The picture is further complicated by not only the virtual disappearance of many trees through disease (e.g. Dutch Elm) or natural disasters (e.g. the hurricane that struck south-east England in 1987) but also by the introduction and subsequent success of some alien species such as sycamore (*Acer pseudoplatanus*) or sweet chestnut (*Castanea sativa*). Notwithstanding these complications, it is the aim of the countryside manager to recreate or manage these woodland mixes through various silvicultural and traditional management techniques and to optimize the benefit derived from the woodlands

Table 7.2. *Types of semi-natural woodland found in Britain*

1. ASH-WYCH ELM WOODLAND
1A. Calcareous ash-wych elm woods
1B. Wet ash-wych elm woods
1C. Calcareous ash-wych elm woods on dry and/or heavy soils
1D. Western valley ash-wych elm woods

2. ASH-MAPLE WOODLAND
2A. Wet ash-maple woods
2B. Ash-maple woods on light soils
2C. Dry ash-maple woods

3. HAZEL-ASH WOODLAND
3A. Acid pedunculate oak-hazel-ash woods
3B. Southern calcareous hazel-ash woods
3C. Northern calcareous hazel-ash woods
3D. Acid sessile oak-hazel-ash woods

4. ASH-LIME WOODLAND
4A. Acid birch-ash-lime woods
4B. Maple-ash-lime woods
4C. Sessile oak-ash-lime woods

5. OAK-LIME WOODLAND
5A. Acid pendunculate oak-lime woods
5B. Acid sessile oak-lime woods

6. BIRCH-OAK WOODLAND
6A. Upland sessile oakwoods
6B. Upland pedunculate oakwoods
6C. Lowland sessile oakwoods
6D. Lowland pedunculate oakwoods

7. ALDER WOODLAND
7A. Valley alderwoods on mineral soils
7B. Wet valley alderwoods
7C. Plateau alderwoods
7D. Slope alderwoods
7E. Bird cherry-alderwoods

8. BEECH WOODLAND
8A. Acid sessile oak-beechwoods
8B. Acid pedunculate oak-beechwoods
8C. Calcareous pedunculate oak-ash-beechwoods
8D. Acid pedunculate oak-ash-beechwoods
8E. Sessile oak-ash-beechwoods

9. HORNBEAM WOODLAND
9A. Pedunculate oak-hornbeam woods
9B. Sessile oak-hornbeam woods

10. SUCKERING ELM WOODLAND
10A. Invasive elm woods
10B. Valley elm woods

11. PINE WOODLAND
11A. Acid birch-pinewoods
11B. Acid oak-pinewoods
11C. Calcareous pinewoods

12. BIRCH WOODLAND
12A. Rowan-birch woods
12B. Hazel-birch woods

Source: Evans (1984).

for access, wildlife and visual amenity. Clearly, the balance will vary from woodland to woodland, depending, for example, upon location *vis-à-vis* centres of population, the existing condition of the wood and the objectives for its management.

> Defining the objective of planting or management of broadleaved woodland involves difficult decisions . . . . In spite of such difficulties, the clarification of objectives and the decision of priorities is the single-most helpful step . . . . There are few situations where two or more objectives are wholly incompatible.

More simply, if a woodland is 'wrong' in year 1, it is 'wrong' in year 51 or 101. And the best way of getting it wrong is to be unclear about why a woodland is being created or managed at all.

(a)   Creating woodland

The creation of woodland is dependent upon several factors, which include the site conditions, the species to be used and the technique to be adopted to create the woodland.

One of the simplest methods for 'creating' woodland is simply to leave well alone. Many open areas will eventually be colonized by trees and in the fullness of time develop into woodland. This is one of the simplest and cheapest methods of creating woodland. There are, however, constraints on this method: clearly, a supply of seed needs to be naturally available and sites that are isolated from existing woodlands are much less likely to self-set with native tree species. Furthermore, where existing landuse is in some-way prohibitive to new seeds taking root, the arrival of a naturally germinating woodland may be delayed for a long period. Densely growing amenity grassland, for example, is unlikely to develop quickly into a young potential woodland. It is much more appropriate therefore that the process of creating woodland is controlled, directed and helped by the manager.

The method used depends very much upon the site to be afforested. (Within this discussion the terms 'woodland' and 'forest' are used synonymously, although both terms raise different perceptions as to the size of plantation being referred to, and the types of trees within the plantation.) Woodland can be created by planting into bare ground, or converting grassland by planting into it; or by properly managing derelict or vestigial woodland. In each case, however, the aim is not simply to plant trees, but to create a balance between species types, the different layers of the woodland and to create a use of the woodland. As Baines (op. cit.) suggests: 'A wood is much more than a few trees.'

Creating woodland from existing grassland can be seen as an extension to the 'letting nature take its course' approach and revolves around allowing the trees to develop in competition with the existing vegetation. This can be done by killing off the grassland and either seeding or planting the area. A less drastic alternative is to strip areas of grass and seed or plant these areas with trees. This, combined with the longer term aim of leaving the grassland to its own devices, will speed up the natural process. The main difficulty in creating woodland from grassland is that in the establishment period the area looks relatively 'untidy'. This is clearly a relative concept, and areas of scrub are, to many people more attractive than areas of closely mown grass. However, careful management of the new woodland, particularly at the margins, is needed to assure users of the area that the developing woodland is actually part of a development process and not just an example of a forgotten piece of land. In this context, information or interpretation of the process serves a useful purpose in keeping members of the public informed of the purpose and nature of the work.

Planting into new areas is, in some ways, similar to planting into grassland and seeks to create a balanced woodland and reduce competition from weeds and unwanted species. Any unwanted competition should be eradicated before planting; this makes it much easier to control as the woodland develops. In planting new areas, a further major determinant is the site condition. To a certain extent, site conditions are also important when planting into grassland or existing woodland. However, localized conditions have a greater impact on open, bare sites. Evans (1984), for example, lists the two main determinants as climate and soil conditions. This information becomes more critical in certain conditions which are extreme or certain factors become overriding. Wilson (1986), for example, explores the process of creating woodland on reclaimed mineral workings, and Table 7.3 gives an example of the type of information that is crucial on any site where woodland is to be developed.

The final 'method' of establishing new woodland is to develop or improve existing woodland. The unmanaged, neglected woodland resource in Britain is great. The Countryside Commission report (1983), *Small Woods on Farms*, identified the scale of the resource which presently lies unmanaged. In many cases, the original purpose of the farm woodlands has disappeared – farms and farmers no longer need or want to grow their own fence posts, wattle hurdles or firewood. Consequently, the woods themselves have become unmanaged because of the lack of clear definition of why they are there in the first place. The countryside manager must therefore be concerned not only with the improvement of the woodland fabric (in consultation with professional

Table 7.3. *Details of tree analysis chart (should include all trees for managed area)*

Name	Size & growth	Tolerance	Preferred conditions	Management notes	Comments
Conifers					
Juniper	20' (6m)	O	Chalk, limestone, brown earths, acid or dry soils	(C, Pcs, U) Bird, insect food (fruit), nest cover, deer browse	Mainly SE, N Eng + Scot birch & pine woods. Poor regeneration. Berries flavour gin.
Pine, Scots	80' (24m) (−)	EFIV	(LW) Light or sandy soil or acid peat if drained, low rain; tolerant	(A1, B, Ps, S, T, U) Best conifer for wildlife	Useful nurse. Often regenerates naturally where protected from grazing, but susceptible to exposure to sea wind.
Yew	45' (14m) (−)	EPSV	Mainly chalk, limestone but tolerates all but very acid soil	(C, Pcs, S, U, W) Bird food (fruit), nest sites, deer browse	Good windbreak or clipped hedge, but poisonous to stock. Best planted small. Casts dense shade.
Broadleaved					
Alder, common	73' (22m) (+)	CDEPSV	Hardy. Any damp soil (best if flushed) except very acid	(A1, E, I, Ps, S, t, U) . Bird food (seed), nests, insect habitat	Often coppiced. Stands flooding, helps stabilize banks. Fixes nitrogen, improves soil. Voles eat bark.

Table 7.3. (cont)

Name	Size & growth	Tolerance	Preferred conditions	Management notes	Comments
Alder buckthorn	20' (6m)	CD	Damp peats to acid sands in lowland fens & woods	(Ps, t) Bird and small mammal food (fruit)	Brimstone butterfly food. Once widely coppiced for fuse charcoal.
Ash	90' (28m) (+)	CDEOPSV	(LTW) Best in deep calcareous loams	(A1, E, Ps, T, U, W) Bird & small mammal food (seeds)	Profitable but difficult as timber tree. Good coppice. Avoid in gardens, cultivated areas because surface rooting and freely naturally regenerating. Good deadwood.
Aspen	80' (24m) (+)	DEOPS	(L) Hardy. Heavy clay, damp fertile soils	(A3, I, Pcx, S, t, U, W) Good gen wildlife value, deer browse	Pioneer or nurse for upland shelterbelts but timber seldom good in Britain. Bushy on poor soil. Suckers freely.
Beech	90' (28m)	CEPS	(TW) Any soil but peat, heavy clay	(A15, C, E, f, H, Ps, S, T, U, W) Bird and small mammal food (seeds)	Good for underplanting. Needs nurse on exposed sites. Bark disease and grey squirrel damage serious in some areas. Good park tree.

| Birch, hairy | 60' (18m) (+) | CEDPV | Tolerant but especially on poorly drained peat and heath soils | (A1, Ps) Invertebrate habitat, bird food (seeds) | Good nurse. Best in groups. Major fen, heath, felled-wood invader but sometimes hard to establish on sites which have not carried trees. |

NOTES FOR TABLE HEADINGS

Size and growth Size = normal maximum height in Britain (+) = fast grower in good conditions, (–) = slow grower.

Tolerance C = tolerates cutting, D = tolerates or prefers damp soil (usually with some flow of soil water), E = tolerates exposure, F = tolerates spring frosts, O = tolerates sea wind, P = tolerates smoke or air pollution, S = tolerates or prefers shade, V = grows in a wide variety of soils, I = infertile dry soil.

Preferred conditions L = light demanding, T = frost tender (damaged by late spring frosts), W = wind firm.

Management notes A = availability, A1 – freely in a range of size, A2 – in a restricted range of sizes, A3 – from some nurseries, A4 – from specialist growers only, A5 – may be in short supply; B = attractive bark; C = varieties, cultivars or related species available in columnar (fastigiate) form; E = suitable for elm replacement; F = showy flowers or fruit; f = showy autumn foliage; H = suitable for use in livestock hedges; I = invasive; P = easily propagated, c – by cuttings, l – layering, s – seeds, x – by suckers or stooling; S = suitable for use in shelterbelts or amenity hedges; T = major timber use in Britain; t = limited or specialized timber use in Britain; U = suitable for urban use (e.g. in confined spaces, near buildings, along streets or in polluted conditions); W = varieties, cultivars or related species available in weeping (pendulous) form.

Comments The abbreviations 'N', 'S' etc refer to general regions of Britain, but distributions cannot be indicated precisely in the limited space. See Perring and Walters (1962) for details.

Source: BTCV (1980).

Table 7.4. *Analysis of multi-use potential of woodland.*

Secondary objective	Designated primary objective						Conservation	
	Commercial timber production	Minor products/estate needs	Landscape	Recreation	Sporting	Farm woods/shelter	general	specific
Commercial timber production	—	*	**	***	**	*	**	***
Minor products/estate needs	*	—	*	**	*	*	*	**
Landscape	*	*	—	*	*	**	*	*
Recreation	*	**	*	—	**	**	**	***
Sporting	**	**	*	***	—	*	*	**
Farm woods/shelter	**	*	**	***	*	—	**	***
Conservation: general	**	*	*	*	*	*	—	—
Conservation: specific	**	**	*	***	**	***	—	—

Legend Effect on main objective of integrating secondary one:
* little effect, easily reconcilable;
** may locally restrict carrying out of main objective;
*** greatly affect main objective, substantial compromise and considerable care needed to achieve both objectives.
Note: Conservation: general – encouragement of habitats favourable to wildlife;
      specific – conservation of rare species or woodland ecotype.

Source: Evans (1984).

foresters) but also, and perhaps more critically for the wide-based approach inherent in countryside management, with the setting of new objectives of woodland. In keeping with the overall approach of the countryside manager, these objectives will need to cover a wide range of issues, including nature conservation, recreation and landscape conservation. The revitalization of existing woodlands is constrained by existing site conditions, the competition imposed by existing trees and the condition of the individual trees; if, for example, the trees in a woodland are all of a similar, over-mature age, then the woodland may require extensive work. However, a woodland which shows signs of natural regeneration may only need some thinning. Greater changes to the woodland will clearly come if footpaths, visitor centres, interpretive panels or other features have to be accommodated. This multi-dimensional approach to woodland is discussed in Countryside Commission (1987a) and Forestry Commission (1985) (Table 7.4). In this context, single use, monocultural woodlands are not part of the countryside manager's remit, for it is the balance between uses with which the manager is concerned.

In all these examples of creating woodland, several key practical skills are necessary for the successful establishment of trees. These are discussed in the second part of this chapter with other skills and techniques used in the management of the countryside.

7.1.4 Woodland management

The management of woodlands, particularly broadleaved woodlands, is based upon traditional techniques. It is only recently that the techniques associated with softwood production have begun to shape the woodlands of Britain. The management of ancient and semi-natural woodlands is based upon the purpose of the wood. The objectives of woodland management have traditionally been multi-faceted; it is only relatively recently that monocultural/single objective woodland has become important, and this appears to be changing again, particularly through the work of the Forestry Commission which is now legally obliged, through the 1985 Wildlife and Countryside (Amendment) Act, to achieve a 'reasonable balance between afforestation and enhancement and conservation of natural beauty, flora, fauna, geological or physiographical features'.

Traditional forms of management have, therefore, struck a balance between practical techniques of timber production and management techniques designed to meet a range of objectives. Countryside managers could do well to follow these traditional management methodologies. Peterken (1981) has identified several types of woodland, based not on species content but, by way of a cross reference, on their management regime. Briefly, these are:

(a) *Wood pasture*   Woodland where the herb layer is available for grazing.
(b) *Wood pasture on commons*   As above, but where grazing is restricted through commoners rights.
(c) *Forests and chases*   Formal woodland, usually grazed but also used for hunting and other 'recreational' pursuits. Designed to support some wildlife.
(d) *Coppice management*   The most important traditional management technique, designed to supply all local timber needs, from large standards to small poles and brush.
(e) *Primary woodlands*   Arguably, unmanaged; tends to be restricted to native pine woods in Scotland and other 'remote areas'.

The coppice management regime is arguably the single most important traditional technique, for, as Peterken (op. cit.) suggests, 'Most ancient woods have been managed as coppice for most of the last thousand years.' The skills of coppicing are discussed in section 7.2.2, but the result of coppice management is usually a species rich, variable stand of timber which has a wide range of ages for the individual trees. Furthermore, a variety of visual and potential recreational features are developed through coppice cycles – glades, open rides, attractive flora and fauna and educationally valuable features, for example. Recently, particularly since 1945, the amount of traditional management of woodland – particularly coppice – has reduced, but with the advent of multi-use woodland the traditional means of management could increasingly form part of a wider management regime; they should certainly be part of the countryside manager's repertoire.

Countryside management is both an approach that is taken to a wide range of problems and opportunities and a collection of management techniques. Therefore, as there are several demands and objectives for woodlands, it is appropriate to have a series of underlying principles to management. Peterken (1981) lists some fifteen such principles. These can be amended and added to accommodate the countryside manager's wider remit. These principles are:

(a) *Site grading*   Distinguish between (1) individual woods of high conservation value, (2) woodland areas of high conservation value, (3) other woodlands.
(b) *Management priorities*   Afford special treatment to special sites and areas. Establish clear objectives for the woodland.
(c) *Clearance*   Minimize clearance in accordance with objectives. Ne-

cessary clearance should avoid sites and areas of high conservation value.

(d) *Afforestation* Accept afforestation, except on sites of high nature conservation value, but not so much that non-woodland habitats are reduced to small islands.

(e) *Woodland patterns* Develop (or retain) large blocks of connected woodland, while maintaining a scatter of small woods between large blocks.

(f) *Change* Minimize rates of change within woods.

(g) *Stand maturity* Encourage maturity by maintaining long rotations. If this is not possible, leave a scatter of old trees after restocking.

(h) *Native species* Encourage native species and use non-native species only where necessary.

(i) *Diversity* Encourage diversity of (1) structure, (2) tree and shrub species, (3) habitat and (4) use of the woodland in so far as these are compatible with priorities.

(j) *Regeneration* Encourage restocking by natural regeneration or coppice growth.

(k) *Rare species* Take special measures where they are necessary to maintain populations of rare and local species.

(l) *Records* Plan and keep records of management for future consultation.

(m) *Natural woodland* Manage a proportion of the woodland on non-intervention lines in order to restore natural woodland in so far as this is possible.

(n) *Traditional management* Maintain or restore traditional management where this is possible and appropriate, including the multifunctional approach to management.

(o) *Modern management* Accept the multifarious demands made upon woodland and accommodate these into planning and procedures.

Management of woodland for a single reason is not synonymous with countryside management. Conversely, countryside management is not synonymous with the management of woodland, even for a wide range of objectives. However, given the biological, visual and recreational importance of woodlands, it is clear that there is a great degree of overlap between woodland management and countryside management.

7.1.5 Ponds and wetlands

The British love water; so too, probably, do most people, but for whatever reasons the British love of water is famous. This is epitomized by Philip Larkin's poem entitled *Water*, the first stanza of which is:

If I were called in
To construct a religion
I should make use of water.

In ecological terms, too, water is invaluable. Not only does it provide one of the basic requirements of survival, but it also provides variety to any ecosystem of which it forms a part. Ponds, bogs, streams, lakes, reservoirs, dew hollows and, not least, the sea and estuaries, are all magnets to wildlife and people alike.

This chapter examines just a few of the many and varied aquatic habitats in Britain, principally ponds and waterways. Other aquatic habitats such as blanket bogs, estuaries, fens, coastal zones and lakes require a different scale of management. Roberts and Roberts (1984) examine some of the larger scale issues which connect ecology with habitat management engineering.

The issues discussed in this chapter are those of the creation, improvement and management of ponds and waterways as a means of increasing their ecological, visual and amenity importance. Semi-natural aquatic habitats are becoming scarcer, as we saw earlier in Chapter 4, so the sympathetic creation and management of the resource is vital.

(a)　Ponds

The reasons that ponds exist at all vary considerably – a point which must clearly be borne in mind when embarking upon a creation or management process. The pond has a unique ecological and historical place in the British landscape; settlements grow up around natural and/or newly created ponds. Landowners created them, estate owners formalized them, early industrialists harassed them and now, in recent years, we have begun to fill them in at an alarming rate.

(b)　Pond creation

In the process of pond creation, the objectives behind the need for the pond must be clearly established. A pond that is created as a visual amenity and for education purposes should be designed differently from a pond created for purely natural history purposes, although all semi-natural ponds will need to contain similar elements.

The British Trust for Conservation Volunteers (1976) identify four reasons for creating a naturalistic pond, namely:

(a) to diversify habitats generally;
(b) to provide for particular types of wildlife;

(c) to provide an educational resource;
(d) to improve visual amenity.

There are a number of factors to consider when creating a pond, such as the destruction of existing habitats (usually wetlands or damp areas, because it makes most sense to create ponds in already wet areas), local drainage patterns which may or may not give a steady supply of water, and the problems associated with siltation. Specific considerations also arise when the different objectives mentioned above have differing importance.

(a) In ponds being created for wildlife purposes a varied shoreline is important, with steep and shallow banks. A pond depth of up to 3 metres is necessary to avoid total freezing, and access may need to be restricted.
(b) A specific habitat needs to be understood before it can be recreated. Thus deep ponds may be required by some species, whereas shallow scrapes may be preferred by others, such as amphibians. Area of surface water is also important with wildfowl clearly needing a greater landing area than smaller animals.
(c) An educational resource requires easy access for schools (to allow observation, pond dipping or monitoring) and safety features. Locations for notice boards or panels need to be designed into the pond and a nearby footpath to allow casual visitors to see the area may also be required.
(d) A pond designed to raise amenity will also involve specific design considerations such as a slightly tidier feel to the overall area, more safety features if the pond is to be accessible, and an overall shallower pond, except for an area in the middle. This does not, however, dictate that an amenity pond needs to be a sterile habitat. Some compromise is inevitable, but not a complete abandonment of natural principles.

Pond creation entails three major elements: creating a hollow, maintaining water levels and designing features.

Quite simply a 'hollow' can be created by either digging a new one, using the excavated material to make banks, thus making the pond larger or by flooding existing areas. If areas are flooded the resultant waterbody will tend to be relatively shallow unless existing vegetation is removed, silting is prevented or encroaching vegetation such as reedmace or reedgrass are prevented. A deeper flood pond can be created by importing suitable material to build up banks and by damming outlets at a higher level.

Maintaining water levels in the pond involves a number of processes.

Firstly, the pond needs to have an impermeable base. Traditionally, this has been puddled clay (puddling involves compressing water and clay together in thin layers to create an impermeable barrier). Puddled clay needs to be at least 150 mm deep; it is a long process, but is great fun for children. Alternatively, artificial linings can be used. These range from concrete to flexible 'plastic' linings such as bentonite, butyl or polythene. As with puddling, the pond profile needs to be established before the lining is organized. Occasionally, naturally impermeable layers of clay or rock may be present, and in these circumstances no artificially created lining will be necessary.

The second element of maintaining a water level is the water supply. Existing water levels should be monitored over a year in a test pit before any ponds are dug. A high water table will help in the process of pond creation, and water must be present all year round. A dam will help to raise water tables, providing of course a suitable water supply is available. Once a suitable supply is identified, the pond can then be created either on or off stream. On-stream ponds, created as part of the water course, tend to bring more problems than off-stream ponds, e.g. silting, turbidity and the necessary strength of dams. Finally, having ensured that water can get into a pond, it is also necessary to ensure that water can get out of a pond, so an outlet and overflow are necessary. This maintains a slow through flow of water which helps to keep the water oxygenated.

The design features of a pond are the elements which meet objectives other than simply collecting and retaining water. Thus islands, banking, pond profile, stocking with plants and surrounding vegetation and habitats and provision for access are all features that need to be thought about during the design phase. The British Trust for Conservation Volunteers (op. cit.) deal with all of these issues, and the training of most landscape architects will contain some elements of dealing with natural features, including ponds. Baines (1984) gives a summary of the techniques used to create natural and semi-natural ponds.

Finally, ponds require a large amount of aftercare if they are not to silt up, become over-populated with dominant species of reed or become too eutrophic due to a contaminated water supply or leaf fall. Ponds and inflows/outflows need to be cleared or dredged regularly – dew ponds every three years or so, for example – but not at a time when the silt is likely to contain all of the pond's habitants. Banks need to be protected from the water action of the pond and the treading action of people or animals; linings need to be repaired if necessary and checked for leaks; and board walks, fences and islands need to be checked. However, this investment of time is well worth the effort, for the result is an area of open water which will become part of the fabric of the British landscape.

7.1.6 Waterways

Waterways – rivers, streams, drains and canals – form an integral part of the British landscape. In absolute terms the number of *linear* waterways is decreasing as canals become derelict and ditches fall into disrepair. In England and Wales, for example, some 35000 km of open ditch disappeared each year between 1947 and 1980, although more recent trends (from 1980 to 1985) suggest that new ditches are being dug at the rate of 200 km per year. Overall, therefore, the linear *amount* of waterways is relatively static. Of greater concern, however, is the quality of these waterways, with an increasing tendency towards sterile, engineered watercourses. The main thrust of the work of the countryside manager must therefore be to work with landowners, river engineers and water authorities to develop drainage schemes which meet the engineering requirements but also include features of natural history and landscape value. We have seen (in Chapter 3) that water authorities are specifically charged with exercising their functions 'as to further the conservation and enhancement of natural beauty and the conservation of flora, fauna and geological and physiographical features of special interest' (Wildlife and Countryside Act 1981). In Scotland, under Section 66 of the Countryside (Scotland) Act 1967, the relevant authorities are charged with having 'regard to the desirability of conserving the natural beauty' although it is felt by the Secretary of State for Scotland that water authorities should 'act in accordance with the spirit of the section' (in the 1981 Act, which only applies to English/Welsh water authorities). These legal requirements are therefore relatively strong and the work of the countryside manager is made slightly easier because of them.

It is rare that completely new watercourses are created, except on newly drained farmland. More often, existing watercourses are deepened, widened, canalized or re-vetted. Major engineering schemes cost many millions of pounds, so it is a relatively small addition to build into that process an element to cover landscape/ecological work. Newbold *et al.* (1983) estimated that, at prices for that year, a generous landscaping programme would cost £1500 per kilometre. By contrast, a scheme in that year to improve a river in Worcestershire cost £200000 per kilometre.

At the other end of the scale, small works associated with existing drains or streams can have a major effect on the wildlife value of the watercourse and the budgets are not nearly as daunting. Furthermore, much of the work can be undertaken by volunteers, small estate teams or rangers if necessary. This chapter therefore looks at the two issues of conservation in association with river engineering and small-scale works.

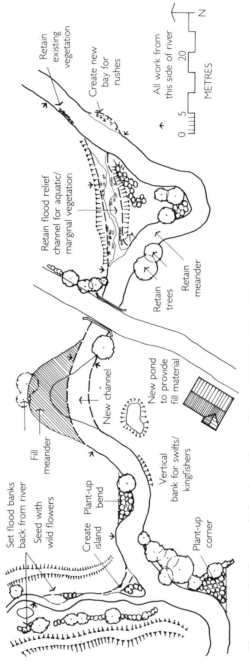

Figure 7.4 *Draft proposals for river scheme.* (Source: Newbould *et al.*, 1983.)

Retain existing vegetation

Create new bay for rushes

All work from this side of river

Retain flood relief channel for aquatic/ marginal vegetation

Retain trees

Retain meander

New channel

New pond to provide fill material

Set flood banks back from river

Seed with wild flowers

Fill meander

Create island

Plant-up bend

Vertical bank for swifts/ kingfishers

Plant-up corner

N

METRES

0   5   20

(a) Conservation and engineering

Once it is known that an engineering scheme is to take place on a river, the countryside manager could become involved in the project, either in a watching capacity or as an advisor. In the cases of the larger water authorities, a landscape architect and/or ecologist may well be appointed to the project, but in cases where this is not so, and the proposed scheme has an impact on the area of the countryside manager, advice and assistance could be given.

Newbold *et al.* (1983) outline the procedure for accommodating conservation within engineering schemes. Firstly, an ecological and visual survey of the area is undertaken, and the relative value of each is assessed. Much larger schemes may require an Environmental Impact Assessment, under European Guidelines. Following the survey, a draft project should be prepared, with the ecologist and visual proposals presented, along with a rough estimate of cost. The draft scheme should include: tree planting and fencing; the creation of bays and berms; the protection of hollows and old meanders; any necessary compensation; working around landscape features; varied bank angles; extra features.

Figure 7.4 shows a draft scheme, identifying the main points that should be incorporated into a proposed scheme. At this stage it is important to include all recommendations – the discussion and compromise can be undertaken later.

The final stage of the process is the implementation, and it is here that a working knowledge of engineering principles is a vital part of the countryside manager's toolbox. Within the constraints of efficient land drainage or flood relief many techniques are available to allow watercourses to be developed to improve not only drainage but also wildlife and visual attraction. Some fifteen techniques for combining river engineering with conservation are given below (Newbold *et al.*, 1983) with bank and berm treatment being explained more fully in Figures 7.5 and 7.6:

- *Working from one bank* Where rivers are narrow enough, one bank working is vital to protect existing sites so that re-colonization can occur.
- *Treatment of banks* Vary bank profiles as in Figure 7.5.
- *Create berms* Where bank angles cannot be created, instal berms to compensate for habitat loss.
- *Create riffles* The bed of a river should also be uneven, with shallows, shoals and pools encouraged where possible.
- *Sympathetic dredging* Time, degree and site for dumping of dredging are all important and should be timetabled accordingly.
- *Saving meanders* In river-straightening schemes, meanders can be

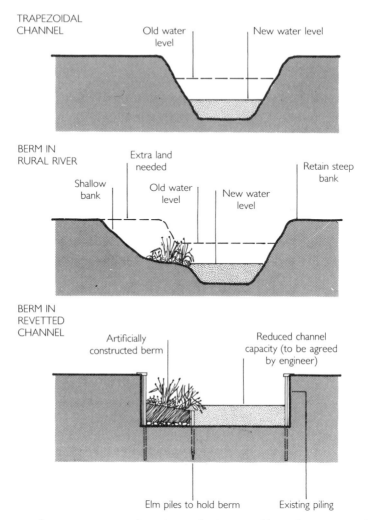

Figure 7.5 Common types of engineered river profiles. (Source: Newbould *et al.*, 1983.)

retained as pools, through flows or relief channels, providing water can be kept in them

- *Flood relief channels* Flood channels only fill up in times of flood. If some water can be kept in them all year round, a good damp habitat can be created.
- *Two-stage channels* Instead of deepening and widening existing

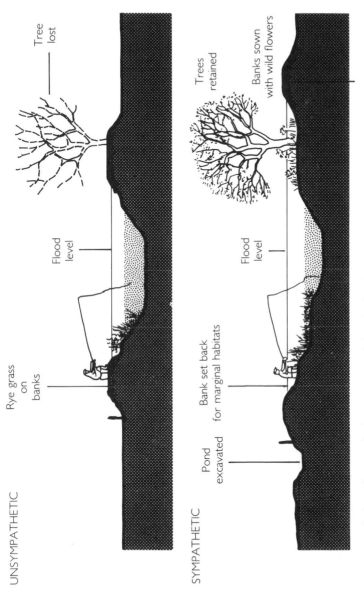

Figure 7.6 *Unsympathetic and sympathetic treatments of river banks.* (Source: Newbould et al., 1983.)

drains, it may be possible to create a two-stage channel which will come into operation only at time of flood.

- *Pools* Ponds or pools can be created next to rivers, which take advantage of the water table.
- *Bays* As well as varying the banks vertically, indents and bays should be created.
- *Flood banks* The location of flood banks is critical. Figure 7.6 shows sympathetic and unsympathetic treatment of banks.
- *Islands* Islands should be retained or only slightly modified.
- *Bank reinforcement* Natural techniques exist for strengthening banks, such as planting strubs, using local stone, woven willow wands or using reeds.
- *Otter holts* Given the delicate state of Britains otter populations, artificial otter holts could be created.
- *Buildings* All buildings should be landscaped
- *Trees* Protect existing trees, and design schemes to accommodate new planting.

(b)   Smaller projects

Drainage schemes undertaken under the direction of the countryside manager or his or her representative are clearly of a different order of magnitude to those administered through a drainage engineer. Obviously, the countryside manager must seek advice on the drainage implications of any proposed work, but small schemes will usually be part of a wider project, such as landscape conservation, or habitat creation.

The work that might be involved may range from bank stabilization to dam creation or from planting to watercourse creation. The skills necessary to undertake these tasks are covered in detail by British Trust for Conservation Volunteers (1976). It is important, however, when undertaking any practical works in the countryside to keep the project in its wider context. This is particularly true of works that influence and affect the water table and the quality of water. Forestry Commission (1988b), for example, examines the relationship between forestry and the aquatic environment of upland Britain. Figure 7.7 shows how activities associated with the production of timber might be undertaken to accommodate water and wetland conservation.

The Countryside Commission (1988a) takes a broader look at the water industry in the countryside and how changes in the water system or the countryside affects the other components of the jigsaw. The implications of changes to the practical management of watercourses has knock-on effects for landscape, wildlife conservation, public access

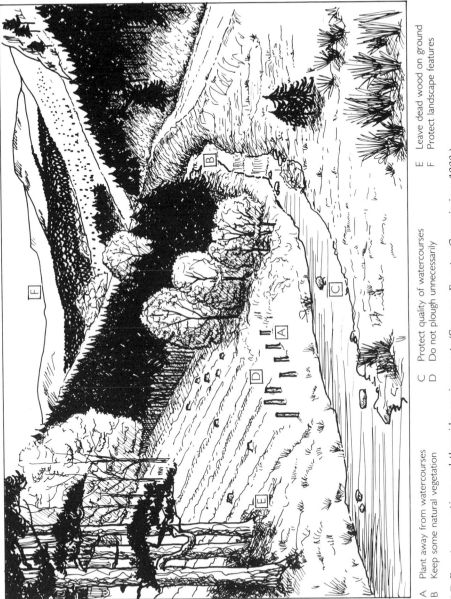

Figure 7.7 *Forestry operations and the wider environment.* (Source: *Forestry Commission, 1988.*)

A   Plant away from watercourses
B   Keep some natural vegetation
C   Protect quality of watercourses
D   Do not plough unnecessarily
E   Leave dead wood on ground
F   Protect landscape features

and local amenity (Countryside Commission, 1987b). Indeed, the often inextricable interlinking of issues lies at the very heart of countryside management, and all the practical skills discussed here have much wider recreational, educational and landscape implications. For these reasons, the privatization process which involves the statutory undertakers such as the water authorities is being viewed with some concern by many countryside managers.

7.1.7 Other areas

It is impossible to assess in detail the practical management of Britain's diversity of habitats. So many different factors influence the natural and semi-natural habitats of this country that, in each situation in which a countryside manager might be called upon to manage, a natural resource might be considered unique. Thus coastal habitats, fen land, raised mires, geological outcrops and heathland, for example, all require specialist knowledge and skills. And so do what might be considered historic landscapes. While all habitats and landscapes are to some extent 'historic', some landscapes, because of the features they contain, are more important for their archaeological remains than for their ecological or landscape significance. Included within this might be old field patterns, ancient barrows, stone circles, settlement patterns or old estate land. Understanding historic landscapes is a specialism in its own right, co-ordinated nationally by English Heritage whose own assessment of the issues (English Heritage, 1988) identifies the importance of a historic perspective when managing any land.

The processes in managing any piece of land have common threads, based on the principles of aims, survey, analyses, objectives, prescriptions, implementation and monitoring. The countryside manager co-ordinates all of these different elements and, depending upon local circumstances, becomes actively involved in specific parts of the process.

7.2 PRACTICAL SKILLS

Habitat management, landscape management and estate management depend partly upon large-scale, conceptual issues, or practical management knowledge as outlined in the first part of this chapter. Management, at grass roots level also, depends upon practical skills, coupled with an empathy for the countryside developed through a combination of training and experience. The range of habitats and landscapes that require management is large, and only three have been dealt with here.

Stone Walling: Clear details of a 'standard' stone wall, including through-stones, coping and staggared rows.

Similarly, the practical skills involved in countryside management are varied, and only a few of these skills can be dealt with. A list of these skills – which can be seen as estate skills, traditional skills or practical skills – would include path construction, dry stone walling, fencing, stile erection, gate hanging, hedge laying, tree planting, ditching and tree felling. The amount of time that a manager will have to devote to these skills will again depend upon local circumstances: a project officer who often works alone, would clearly need a good knowledge of most of these skills; the leader of a countryside team or a private firm of consultants would only require a working awareness of the skills to ensure that the work on the ground was carried out satisfactorily. The following analysis presents a brief description and assessment of some of the practical skills associated with the countryside.

7.2.1 Dry stone walling

Dry stone walls are a common feature of many of Britain's landscapes and, because they are constructed out of local materials, are ecologically and visually sympathetic to the countryside. The Yorkshire Dales Environmentally Sensitive Area, for example, identified the dry stone walls as being one of the most important elements of the Warfedale landscape (Haigh, 1988). The ability to construct or, more usually, reconstruct dry stone walls is therefore a crucial part of any manager's toolbox.

Dry stone walling serves the dual purpose of using loose stones from potential pasture or arable land and of delineating field systems. Dry stone walls tend, therefore, to be a feature of upland landscapes where there is a ready supply of local materials. This introduces two common elements to the skills being discussed here. Firstly, the use of local material is vital if local integrity within landscapes and habitats is to be maintained. Secondly, it is equally important to use local/traditional techniques. Dry stone walls vary across the country. This is partly as a result of local or individual idiosyncrasies in the waller, but is mainly as a result of the characteristics of the local stone. The slate of the Skiddaw area, the Lake District, has different characteristics to that of the limestone of the Peak District or the gritstone of West Yorkshire, or the older igneous rocks of Dartmoor. Consequently, dry stone walls have regional characteristics which reflect these differences.

Figure 7.8 shows the profile of a dry stone wall which contains many common elements of walls across the country. The basic rules of walling are really common sense: place the biggest stones at the bottom; cross the joints; keep the middle full ('keep your heart up'); taper the wall; and

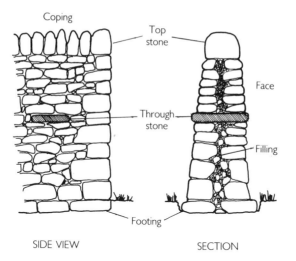

Figure 7.8 *Dry stone wall construction.*

follow the correct batter. The procedure for constructing a dry stone wall is a follows:

(a) Dig out the entire foundation trench.
(b) Set out a supply of stones alongside the trench.
(c) Position large foundation stones along the entire trench.
(d) Set up the batter frame (to give shape of wall).
(e) Build wall to about 0.3 m.
(f) Put horizontal guidelines at height of first throughstone (Figure 7.8).
(g) Build to first throughstone (about 0.6 m).
(h) Lay first layer of throughstone.
(i) Repeat to second layer of throughstones (about 1.1 m).
(j) Repeat to third layer of throughstones if there is one.
(k) Build final courses of the wall, and flatten to take top stones.
(l) Position top stones.
(m) Tidy up.

British Trust for Conservation Volunteers (1977) gives information about the history of dry stone walling and the many pieces of detail that are needed for successful dry stone walling. Furthermore, the publication also gives a useful bibliography on the subject of walling.

Dry stone walls, therefore, represent a cultural, practical and visual element to the landscape, but their principal purpose – that of containing stock – must not be overlooked!

Hedge laying: West Midlands style, showing stakes, binding and pleachers.

7.2.2 Hedging

The lowland equivalent of the dry stone wall is the hedge. The parliamentary enclosures of 1750 to 1850 are accredited with producing the hedgerow landscape of much of Britain. However, the planting of hedges to contain stock, rather than let them graze on common land, started well before 1750 (Hoskins, 1970). Hedges also therefore represent a historic as well as a practical and visual part of any landscape. The art of hedging contains several constituent points, including planting, trimming, laying and maintaining. Tree planting is discussed below, but the various methods of maintaining a hedge are skills within themselves. The use of local materials and regional variations in style and technique are as important in hedging as they are in dry stone walling. Local materials here represent the correct species mix for hedges with local pattern best determined from existing hedges. Regional variations are apparent in planting styles (double or single row planting, for example, or the spacing of the plants) and in the method of maintaining (coppicing, for example, where the plants are cut to ground level every twelve to fifteen years, which was traditional in much of the south-east and south-west. Conversely, the English Midlands has a distinctive style of hedge laying as, too, does the north-west of England and the numerous counties of Wales).

The standard style of laying tends to be regarded as the 'Midlands style' and Figure 7.9 shows the various elements of a laid hedge. The procedure is as follows:

(a) Set out stakes (pieces of wood to place within the hedge to help maintain its shape when laid) and binders (thin pieces of wood to control newly laid pieces of hedge – usually hazel).
(b) Remove rubbish from hedge, including unwanted trees/shrubs.
(c) Give a preliminary trim to cut or reduce side growth.
(d) Cut and lay pleachers (strong vertical stems of living wood that brought over to an angle of 30 degrees by almost cutting through the stem)
(e) Stake the laid pleachers.
(f) Bind the hedge along the top.
(g) Trim stakes and hedge for an even, level finish.
(h) Collect rubbish and cuttings.
(i) Protect any stock in adjacent fields and make sure hedge has no gaps.
(j) Clear any adjacent ditches.

The British Trust for Conservation Volunteers (1975) has produced a thorough book of the art of hedging, which includes information on

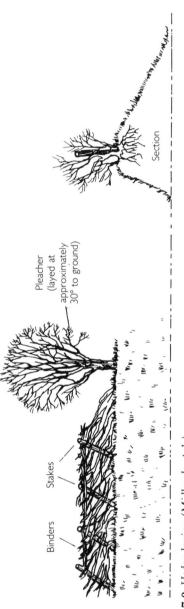

Figure 7.9 *Hedge laying (Midlands style).*

laying, coppicing and other details. The above very brief list of procedural points is taken from that publication. As with dry stone walling, hedging (and all other skills) must be learned, so this description cannot be taken as anything but a brief look at the key points to hedging and, particularly, hedge laying.

7.2.3 Fencing

Fencing in the countryside fulfils a number of roles. Firstly, it acts as a stock proof barrier, either between fields so that grazing patterns can be established or between fields and woodlands in order to keep stock out of young plantations thus giving woodlands a chance to regenerate naturally. In these cases, fences serve the same function as hedges or dry stone walls.

Fencing can also be a temporary measure to protect young planting from stock grazing, trampling or, indeed, human pressure. Furthermore, fencing can also act as a deterrent to trespass – the physical existence of a fence will make most people think twice about climbing over it. Finally, in many cases fencing forms an integral part of the landscape. Formal estate lands, for example, are often identifiable as much by their fences as by the layout of the grounds. On the urban fringe, new solid-looking fencing helps to define the edge of the urban area thus protecting the countryside.

As in all cases of countryside management it is necessary first to identify the purpose of the fencing. This, in turn, will determine the type of fence that is necessary. This section does not deal with the mechanics of fence erection but with the types of fencing that countryside managers might be required to consider. There are numerous organizations which deal with fence erection, including the British Trust for Conservation Volunteers and the Forestry Commission.

For most situations that will confront a countryside manager the types of fencing that are needed can be simplistically divided into all timber fences (post and rail) and timber and wire fences (post and wire). Other types do exist, such as concrete and wire, weldmesh, close board and so on, but these satisfy specialist needs and are best dealt with by fencing contractors.

The post-and-wire fence is comparatively cheap compared to post-and-rail but is much less sturdy and has much less of an impact on the landscape than a post-and-rail fence. For these reasons, it is most often used to provide a stock proof barrier in fields around woods or other areas. A post-and-wire fence can also be used as a psychological barrier for people – it will not provide a secure boundary but can provide a means of directing visitor movement because most people will not climb over a fence.

Having said that post-and-wire fencing is cheaper than post-and rail, it is nonetheless, expensive. A simple post and tensioned wire fence (with three, four or five strands of spring steel wire between intervening posts) is made more expensive if the fence must not only keep out or control large stock such as cows and horses but also control smaller mammals such as rabbits. In these latter circumstances, it is necessary to affixed mesh fencing to the lower strands or wire to stop movement by the rabbits. (See Forestry Commission, 1988a, for example, on fencing of farm woodlands.) Post-and-wire fencing is often used on farms to provide temporary (or not-so-temporary) field boundaries. Many farms, having lost their hedgerows, still require some methods of delineating field spaces. A post-and-wire fence provides the easiest alternative.

Post-and-rail fencing is a much sturdier and visually intrusive product and is correspondingly more expensive. It does, however, give an air of permanence to a landscape or feature. Other than on formal estate landscapes, the countryside manager may wish to fence a country park boundary with post and rail in order to emphasize the area available for free access. Where gates and stiles are needed in fences, a post-and-rail fence provides a much more visually appealing surround. As with all practical techniques the manager is advised to observe other techniques and styles of fencing and, if necessary, to keep abreast of modern developments. Where the manager is able to delegate the practical work to other people within his or her team, these developments can be more accurately addressed.

The countryside manager must, however, be aware that alternatives to fencing do exist. For field boundaries, for example, a better alternative will almost inevitably be a hedgerow, and for visitor control, a thickly planted belt of shrubs or trees will act as a more secure boundary, once the planting has become established. An understanding of the relative value of the alternatives to land management is central to the work of any countryside manager, whether engaged in practical work or office-based policy development.

7.2.4 Footpaths

Footpaths, and the surfacing of footpaths, lie at the heart of access to the countryside. For most of the countryside in Britain, access is only possible through the public-rights-of-way system. The maintenance and upkeep of this system is therefore crucial to the whole issue of a multi-use, balanced countryside. Furthermore, a safe footpath system through a woodland or around a country park immediately opens up an area for a whole host of informal recreation pursuits. Clearly, many paths do not require surfacing or step building, but for over-used paths, routes that

Footpath Control: Over use of certain routes needs management, but brings new problems of over use if not thought through.

are to be promoted for use, or surfaces used by horses or bicycles, some work will be necessary.

Footpaths (and other routes) are a historic part of Britain's landscape, and often have cultural or social backgrounds. All of these issues need to be acknowledged when preparing to work on a footpath. A thorough survey is therefore needed which assesses the status of the path, its history, obstructions and so on. Only when these issues have been determined can the manager decide how the path or recreational route should be developed.

The British Trust for Conservation Volunteers (1983) has identified the following programme for developing footpaths, which is designed to incorporate all the necessary works, beginning with survey and ending with waymarking; all of the intervening steps need not be necessary.

(a) *Survey* Establish the history and context of the route. This will help to determine whether or not it should be surfaced for example, or whether it will form an interesting route for the public.
(b) *Path plan* Look at the physical details of the path – its slope, its topography, underlying rocks, whether it is water logged in parts and the feasibility of the proposed works.
(c) *Path clearance* Remove unwanted obstructions, old fences or gates and so on.
(d) *Drainage* Establish which areas need drainage and what sort of drains are needed – french, field, run-off, cut-off or whatever.
(e) *Surfacing* What sort of surface is acceptable or will survive the anticipated wear and tear? The mechanics of laying a surface and the necessary diameter for construction. Common surfacing includes ash, limestone, flagstones, rough stone, compacted earth, ballast and wood chippings.
(f) *Bridges and broadwalks* Are they needed; if so where? What span is required and how should they best be constructed?
(g) *Steps* The slope may be so great as to require steps (or a ramp, if disabled access is needed) or in extreme circumstances timber ladders. (Step construction is a skill in its own right.)
(h) *Erosion control* The path needs to be protected against erosion and from surrounding earth, rocks or vegetation damaging the surface or making it irreparable. This may require revetments, vegetation control, or seeding.
(i) *Stiles and gates* If the route crosses fences or stone walls, pedestrian or horse gates will be needed; alternatively, stiles will be needed, built to acceptable dimensions. If vehicle access is needed for maintenance for example, a larger gate will be required.
(j) *Waymarking* If the path may form part of a special route or may

be along difficult terrain, where appropriate, waymarking will be needed (Brown, 1974).

All of these stages may or may not be required, but each step requires a large degree of practical knowledge for specialist techniques. These techniques may not be needed in detail by the countryside manager but will be required by someone within the organization, be it the ranger, countryside project officer or the landscape architect.

7.2.5 Summary

There are an almost infinite number of skills required to manage the countryside. The foregoing section has dealt with only four of the commoner ones, and these only in brief detail. It is not necessary for the countryside manager to become acquainted with all of the techniques, unless the manager is directly responsible for the actual implementation. However, some knowledge about practical techniques is needed at all levels of management. Often this knowledge can only be gained through experience; many stone wallers have or had their own techniques, for example, and these can only be learned through observing the results of their work. Much of the knowledge can be gained through written work, and the texts quoted within this chapter form excellent starting points for the relevant techniques and skills. The British Trust for Conservation Volunteers has been particularly active in recording details of practical conservation skills, and many organizations and individuals owe them a debt for their work.

7.3 OTHER SKILLS

There are many more skills which may, in some circumstances, be required by either a countryside manager or, more usually, by one of his or her staff. It is only possible here to identify very briefly some of these skills.

(a) *Knowledge of machinery* Rangers will need some form of transport, whilst estate workers will require some machinery for maintenance or management. Some knowledge of these machines will be needed.

(b) *First aid* In any situation where staff and visitors are in close contact with the natural environment, it is almost inevitable that some accidents will occur (although it is the responsibility of the manager to try to remove these risks altogether). It is therefore necessary for someone to have first aid experience. Where a manager's responsibility covers several sites, a first aider will be needed on each site.

(c) *Specialist outdoor skill* In some situations a knowledge of outdoor pursuit skills may be either vital or advantageous. Where rangers are involved in more mountainous areas, for example, knowledge of mountain crafts will be vital. In other areas part of the interpretive programme may involve outdoor pursuits such as canoeing or abseiling.

7.4 SUMMARY

This chapter seeks to introduce the practical skills needed by countryside managers or their staff in dealing with the many issues within the countryside. It is only possible within this context to offer very brief guidelines, and thus give some indication of the scope of the knowledge that is required. It is clear that it goes well beyond the technical expertise required by, say, a planner, or a landscape architect. The ecological, historical and social importance of all features needs to be acknowledged, as too does the recreational importance of the countryside.

The manager must decide the issues that are of most importance. Where the manager is not directly responsible for practical work, but only needs to provide instructions for staff or to produce working briefs for external contractors, a relatively undetailed but nonetheless comprehensive understanding of the issues is required. Where the manager is practically based, however, a much more detailed and technical knowledge is required.

7.5 CASE STUDIES

It is difficult to present a case study of practical management techniques without simply going over all the issues raised in the foregoing discussions. It is of more value, therefore, to examine a management plan and establish where, within the implementation of a management plan, the practical skills will be needed.

Figure 7.10 gives detail of a hypothetical zoning plan prepared by the Forestry Commission (1986). Within it there are several features which could easily be designed into any recreational or nature conservation site: car parks, interpretive areas, picnic sites, footpaths, landscape viewing areas, amenity woodland areas and a Site of Special Scientific Interest. Each of these will require a different specialist skill to be used in its implementation.

(a) *Car parks* What sort of surface/area is required? Similar processes to footpath construction will be required to determine content, scale, surface, drainage requirements and so on.

Well designed car-park: Most people arrive at the countryside by car, therefore their parking requirements are always a major consideration.

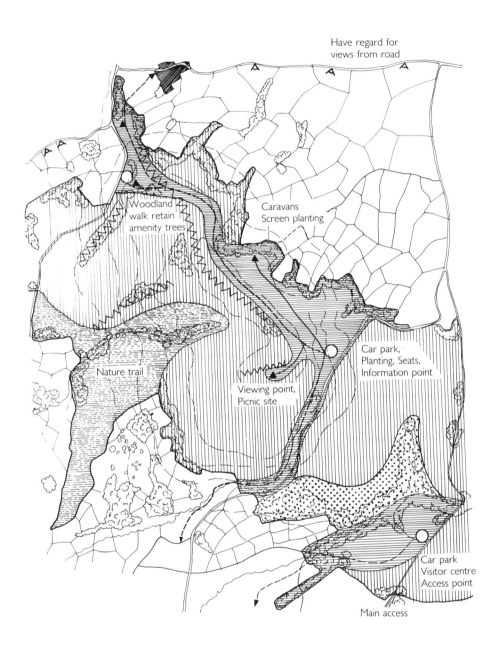

Have regard for
views from road

Woodland
walk retain
amenity trees

Caravans
Screen planting

Nature trail

Viewing point,
Picnic site

Car park,
Planting, Seats,
Information point

Car park
Visitor centre
Access point

Main access

Figure 7.10 *Woodland management plan identifying practical works.* (Source: *Forestry Commission, 1986.*)

Kissing-gate: Details of countryside design and management need careful thought; kissing-gates stop illegal vehicle access, but also pose problems for wheel-chair users.

(b) *Footpaths* What surface, where and for what purpose? Will it allow for disabled access in wheelchairs or should it provide a tapping board for blind people? Will it damage or disturb any valuable habitat?

(c) *Amenity planting* Native species will be needed. What sort of management is best? What sized areas? Will rabbits attack new stock? or deer?

(d) *Site of Special Scientific Interest* What management, if any, is allowed by the Nature Conservancy Council? What are the special features of the area, and how should it be managed?

(e) *Picnic areas* Where should they be located, what construction should the site use, and should play provision for young children be made?

It is evident that the management of a countryside site requires a wide range of practical knowledge, from habitat maintenance to estate skills. At the very least, the countryside manager requires an *understanding* of these skills.

BIBLIOGRAPHY

Agricultural Development Advisory Service (1976) *Agriculture in the Urban Fringe: A Survey of the Metropolitan County of Tyne and Wear*, MAFF, London.
Baines, C. (1984) *A Guide to Habitat Creation*, Greater London Council.
Baines, C. (1985) *How to make a Wildlife Garden*, Elm Tree Books, London.
British Trust for Conservation Volunteers (1975) *Hedging*, BTCV, Wallingford.
British Trust for Conservation Volunteers (1976) *Waterways and Wetlands*, BTCV, Wallingford.
British Trust for Conservation Volunteers (1977) *Dry Stone Walling*, BTCV, Wallingford.
British Trust for Conservation Volunteers (1980) *Woodlands*, BTCV, Wallingford.
British Trust for Conservation Volunteers (1983) *Footpaths*, BTCV, Wallingford.
Brown, A.H. (1974) *The Construction and Design of Signs in the Countryside*, Countryside Commission for Scotland, Battleby.
Corder, M. and Brooker, R. (1981) *Natural Economy: An Ecological Approach to Planting and Management Techniques in Urban Areas*, E. & F.N. Spon, London.
Countryside Commission (1977) *The Management of Grassland and Healthland in Country Parks*, Cheltenham.
Countryside Commission (1983) *Small Woods on Farms*, CCP143, Cheltenham.
Countryside Commission (1987a) *Forestry in the Countryside*, CCP245, Cheltenham.
Countryside Commission (1987b) *Changing River Landscapes*, CCP238, Cheltenham.
Countryside Commision (1988a) *The Water Industry in the Countryside*, CCP239, Cheltenham.
Countryside Commission (1988b) *Broadleaved Woodlands: A Bibliography*, CCP212, Cheltenham.
Duffey, E. *et al.* (1976) *Grassland Ecology and Wildlife Management*, Chapman and Hall, London.

English Heritage (1988) *Visitors Welcome*, HMSO, London.

Evans, J. (1984) *Silviculture of Broadleaved Woodlands*, Forestry Commission Bulletin 64, HMSO, London.

Forestry Commission (1976) *Rabbit Management in Woodlands*, Forestry Commission, Edinburgh.

Forestry Commission (1985) *Guidelines for the Management of Broadleaved Woodlands*, Forestry Commission, Edinburgh.

Forestry Commission (1986) *Forestry Practice*, Forestry Commission, Edinburgh.

Forestry Commission (1988a) *Farm Woodland Practice* (ed. Hibberd), Forestry Commission, Edinburgh.

Forestry Commission (1988b) *Forests and Water*, Forestry Commission, Edinburgh.

Gorer, R. (1978) *Growing Plants from Seeds*, Faber and Faber, London.

Haigh, V. (1988) Once in a lifetime landscapes, *Landscape Design*, August 1988.

Hoskins, W.G. (1970) *The Making of the Scottish Landscape*, Pelican Books, Harmondsworth.

Nature Conservancy Council (1984) *Nature Conservation in Great Britain*, NCC, Peterborough.

Nature Conservancy Council (1988) *Tyne and Wear Nature Conservation Strategy*, NCC, Peterborough.

Newbold, C. *et al.* (1983) *Nature Conservation and River Engineering*, NCC, Peterborough.

Peterken, G. (1981) *Woodland Conservation and Management*, Chapman and Hall, London.

Rackham, O. (1976) *Trees and Woodlands in the British Landscape*, J M Dent & Co., London.

Roberts, R.D. and Roberts, T.M. (1984) *Planning and Ecology*, Chapman and Hall, London.

Shoard, M. (1987) *This Land is our Land*, Palladin, London.

Water Space Amenity Commission (1980) *Conservation and Land Drainage Guidelines*, WSAC, London.

Wells, T. *et al.* (1981) *Creating Attractive Grassland using Native Plant Species*, NCC, Peterborough.

Wilson, K. (1986) *A Guide to the Reclamation of Mineral Workings for Forestry*, Forestry Commission Research Paper 141, Edinburgh.

EIGHT

Rangers and rangering

12 for the 12 Apostles
11 for the 11 who went to heaven
10 for the 10 Commandments
9 for the 9 Bright Shiners
8 for the 8 Bold Rangers

I'll Sing You One-O, *Traditional*

The 1949 National Parks and Access to the Countryside Act gave local authorities and National Park authorities the power to appoint rangers, initially to enforce bye-laws and assist the public. The role of rangers and the professionalism of rangers has, however, developed enormously since the first rangers were appointed within National Parks. Furthermore, many organizations other than National Parks and local authorities now employ rangers.

This chapter examines the history of the ranger service in Britain and looks at the future of the service as perceived from within the ranger movement. More practically, the development of a ranger service and the scope of its involvement and its role are also explored. This offers guidelines for the formation of a ranger service and how an effective ranger service provides a firm base for countryside management in general.

8.1 RANGERS IN BRITAIN

The history of the ranger movement in Britain is closely allied to the legislative framework described in Chapter 3. The 1949 National Parks and Access to the Countryside Act gave National Park authorities the power to employ rangers (then called wardens) predominantly to 'enforce bye-laws. Under Section 92 of the Act, the authority may appoint such numbers of persons . . . to act as wardens . . . to secure compliance with bye-laws, to advise and assist the public and to perform other duties'.

Following on from the establishment of the National Parks, it took until 1966 for the inaugural meeting of the Association of National Park Wardens to be arranged in the Peak District National Park. The title of the organization changed in 1969, following the inclusion into the Association of Rangers from country parks, which were beginning to appear as a result of the 1968 Countryside Act. Indeed, the Countryside Commission, which also arose out of the 1968 Countryside Act and early National Park legislation, has kept close contact with the Association of Countryside Rangers (ACR). The Commission, for example, still support the Annual ACR Conference, and the ACR link the work of their organization closely with that of the Commission (Association of Countryside Rangers, 1987).

The issues identified by the nine men who met to form the Association of National Parks wardens have remained topical ever since 1966. The two most important points have remained central to the development of a 'professional' ranger service. Firstly, it was identified very early in the development of the countryside ranger service that employing authorities or organizations did not tend to value the work done by rangers and, secondly, in order to further the cause of rangers, a truly representative body was needed which took a major role in the training and development of its members (White, 1987). Within the ranger movement, these are still seen as major issues.

Much of the concentration of the ACR upon the issue of developing a more professional service stems from the early problem of employers apparently not listening to or discussing issues with the people 'on the ground'. A letter from one of the founders of the ACR to the National Parks Commission states that ' . . . we are the ones with practical matters relating to the countryside and its uses: . . . and yet our voices are rarely heard . . . I feel that wardens as a body have a contribution to make towards the solution (of basic countryside problems)'. Apparently the letter went unanswered and less than a year later the Association of National Park Wardens held its first meeting.

For the future, the ACR see their role as very firmly linked to the countryside management process (Association of Countryside Rangers, 1988):

> Rangers are therefore part of the countryside management process and not a separate service. This implies that the future of one is inextricably linked to the future of the others. The ACR's National Committee does not therefore accept the sharp distinction drawn between countryside management and the ranger service.

The ranger service sees itself at the sharp end of the countryside management process and therefore the training and career needs of rangers are identical to those of countryside managers – differences between rangers and managers are ones of degree and not of work content and objectives. Indeed, many rangers do take the step from rangering to management. Again, as the ACR point out, 'Countryside services should be run by staff who are properly qualified and experienced in countryside work. What better way to achieve this than by recruiting from among the ranks of countryside rangers?'

On the one hand, rangers view their role as an integral building block in the countryside management process; while, on the other, the rangers also perceive an unwillingness by managers to accept this viewpoint. It is clear, however, that any analysis of the management process will identify that rangers do indeed form part of the continuum of countryside management. It would also appear to be clear that the countryside ranger represents one element of the countryside management process that is relatively unique to countryside work, as opposed to estate management, landscape design or rural planning, for example. In bringing together a mix of recreation, interpretation, landscape and nature conservation, the role of the ranger is critical and for the future, the ACR wishes to strengthen this role.

In a wider context, it can be argued that 'service delivery' is critical to the success of any organization. In the countryside, it is the ranger who delivers the service and countryside managers should, like all managers, develop an organization where 'people who deliver the service predominate' (Fretwell, 1988). Thus, an effective ranger service is absolutely vital to successful countryside management, and this cannot be overstressed!

8.2 THE RANGER SERVICE

The ACR is very clear on what role the ranger service should provide in the future, but what are the present characteristics of the work that rangers undertake? It will hardly be surprising that these vary from one situation to another, but notwithstanding this variation there do exist core tasks which the ranger performs. These tasks can be defined (cf. Countryside Commission, 1979) as:

(a) enhancement of the visitors' enjoyment of the site by information and interpretive duties;
(b) protection – or better conservation – of the site through management practices;
(c) protection of the visitor from known hazards, and possibly from the activities of others, by good management and information;
(d) surveillance – ensuring that visitors behave in a way sympathetic to the site and to other people's enjoyment of it; and to see that bye-

laws are observed.

The original duties of a ranger were defined in the 1949 Act primarily 'to secure compliance with bye-laws'. In this context, the interpretive, educative and positive roles of the ranger are now more important than the surveillance role.

The Countryside Commission for Scotland (1987) gives the same core tasks, but affords them slightly different emphasis, namely:

(a) to provide information, help and advice;
(b) to encourage good behaviour;
(c) to provide assistance in emergencies;
(d) to conserve the areas in their (the rangers) care.

The Countryside Commission for Scotland has also defined where a ranger might operate (Countryside Commission for Scotland, 1988). These include areas owned by a local authority or others and used for informal recreation, a country park, the urban fringe, a public path, long-distance route or public rights-of-way and land adjacent to or extending for a reasonable distance from the boundary of any of the foregoing. In effect,the ranger can operate in a very wide range of areas. So here, too, the work of the ranger has developed from the National Parks, which were the original work base of the ranger service.

In truth, the work of rangers will vary according to site and situation. A ranger in the rough terrain of the Lake District National Park or the West Highland Way will need different skills to those of a ranger in the Lee Valley in North London. But regardless of the actual priorities given to, say, mountain rescue skills as opposed to, say, skills in interpretation, the core elements remain the same and warrant further discussion.

8.2.1   Countryside interpretation

Many interpretive techniques succeed only if there is a enthusiastic and informed exponent leading the interpretation. This is one of the roles of the ranger. Early attempts at interpretation were centred around 'fastening a hand written note to a gate inviting visitors to the National Park to accompany him (the ranger) on a walk' (White, op. cit.). This has now developed to the extent that rangers not only lead guided walks, but also lead activities for children, adults and organized groups, give lectures and talks to various groups and generally adopt a range of media to allow and encourage people to become involved in the countryside. Indeed, the range of interpretive skills now used by rangers tends to mean that the traditional guided walk is only a small part of the overall picture. In order to keep abreast of the developing techniques (such as acclimatization, urban safaris and dance and

Guided Walks: Despite many advances in interpretive techniques, guided walks still remain popular.

theatre, which will be detailed in the next chapter) rangers must continally undergo in-service training to help develop these techniques.

The ranger's role is to develop the interpretive service to the general public, so the personal qualities of the individual are as important as the environmental expertise. Furthermore, it is clear that the skills and knowledge required of a ranger whose main responsibility is managing a visitor centre are different from those of a ranger in, say, an urban fringe project area. Indeed, the range of skills required by rangers are very similar to those required by countryside managers. In most cases, it will be the role of the ranger to develop the necessary techniques to allow him or her to communicate most effectively with, and interpret for, the visitors and to have a say in the development of overall policies which guide the interpretive process.

8.2.2   Site management

The ranger is often called upon to undertake practical work to maintain the fabric of the site or area for which he or she is responsible. The types of work involved are described in the previous chapter, from which it is clear that an enormous amount of knowledge is required to manage habitats and the countryside successfully. To expect a ranger to accommodate the interpretive and the practical skills is really to expect too much of one individual and, increasingly, rangers are being required to concentrate upon the personal skills rather than the practical skills. However, it is still necessary for rangers to have knowledge of the practical elements of countryside management; indeed, in some cases the role of the ranger may well need to be biased towards the practical work. In the Countryside Commission's view, however, 'rangers are not primarily manual staff . . . and where appropriate a separate estate gang should be employed for heavy tasks' (Countryside Commission, 1979, op. cit.).

The responsibility for the site management will usually be part of the remit of a ranger, while its practical implementation will be undertaken by others. This line management responsibility in itself implies that the ranger needs direct experience of the relevant skills. Furthermore, some small-scale, routine or emergency work will necessarily involve the ranger in direct work. In order to keep on top of the damage that a site suffers through deliberate or accidental misuse, it is necessary to respond quickly to broken fences, bent waymarks or rutted paths, and the ranger is most often best placed for these types of work.

Finally, as part of the interpretive process that most rangers now see as the main part of their work, visitors and specialist groups often wish to become involved with practical work. This is again part of the responsibility of the ranger, so here, too, a knowledge of practical conservation and management techniques is required. More often than not, the level of pactical expertise will not be great and will involve tree planting, pond clearance, step construction and so on. However, the ranger requires a wider knowledge of the techniques involved in management and, just as importantly, why certain tasks need to be undertaken in the first place. Only by fully explaining to volunteers and the community why certain task are being performed (why some areas are fenced off; why certain surfaces are used for footpaths; why a hedge is laid in a particular way) can the information be passed on successfully. This interface between practical work and interpretation is again the domain of the countryside ranger.

8.2.3 Protection of the visitor

The protection of the visitor, as was outlined in Chapter 3, is the responsibility of the countryside manager. By inviting or allowing the public onto land, the manager is responsible for their safety and wellbeing under the Health and Safety legislation. Clearly, many potential problems can be overcome through good design and management, but the countryside is a notoriously dangerous place, and often the manager needs on-site help in affording the necessary protection. The nature of this protection will vary from site to site with urban fringe community sites offering different dangers to that of, say, the Lake District National Park. All sites will therefore require a different set of skills, all of which may not necessarily be transferable from one site to another. The dangers presented by farmers' electric fences, quarrying operations or stubble burning are clearly different from those of rock falls, blizzards at 2000 feet or a lost compass bearing. The ranger, therefore, has to decide, in conjunction with the manager, which particular skills are relevant to a given situation. As the Countryside Commission has noted, however, 'In most cases, a high degree of physical fitness is essential.'

The assumption that the protection must be directed simply towards the visitor is, in many cases, now outdated, and the ranger is not only a source of information and protection for the visitor but also for the community and, in a wider context, the people who live and work in the countryside. For example, the farmer will often see the ranger as the point of contact if his crops are being damaged by trespass or if he wants to dedicate a public right-of-way. Thus, the ranger must protect (if 'protect' is the right word) the landowners and local residents from the visitors. This might result in simply speaking to both parties or in putting the landowner in touch with the correct organization. Being a point of contact, the ranger assumes a very important role within the countryside manager's organization, because he or she is the person who delivers the service to all members of the community, and is the front-line worker of the whole countryside management process. It cannot be stressed enough that to back up the provision of practical countryside works, it is vital that a sufficiently well-funded and well-trained ranger service is provided to interpret, liaise and become involved in the process.

8.2.4 Surveillance

Rangers have a responsibility to ensure that visitors act in responsible ways when in the countryside. Given the importance of the two-way relationship that exists between landowners and visitors the ranger also has a responsibility to give advice on 'responsible' behaviour to all interested parties, but perhaps not to the same extent as, say, a country-side project officer.

The type of surveillance for which a ranger must be prepared ranges from pointing out unconsciously irresponsible behaviour from visitors (say, wandering into a particular delicate habitat or wandering off a public right-of-way) to enforcing bye-laws (such as those that forbid the riding of motorcycles or fishing). Finally, there are some activities for which the ranger must be vigilant which are illegal (trapping animals or damage to property) and may require some sort of action, if only that of calling the police. This range of activity, which may all be defined to a certain extent as surveillance, requires a range of approaches to the task from the ranger. On the one hand, the unintentional act of a person unused to being in the countryside can usually be set right by a quiet word – almost an extension of the interpretive process. Similarly, most people transgress bye-laws and laws of the land simply because they are unaware of them. Again, a quiet word is usually all that is required. It is comforting to know that most 'unacceptable' behaviour is as a result of simply not knowing – a situation that can easily be rectified.

Whether or not the ranger becomes involved in a more active policing role is a case for some debate. However, the Countryside Commission point out, 'Experience shows that where a ranger becomes preoccupied with a police role, understaffing, inexperience or inadequate information and interpretive services are generally the cause' (Countryside Commission, 1979). The enforcement of the law is the role of the police, and rangers cannot be expected to deal with the range of problems identified above. Rangers are not security staff, any more than police-men or women are rangers. Both roles are markedly different and should be identified as such.

This does not deny, however, that rangers are often witness to or the first on the scene of more serious transgressions of the law, and must therefore have a working knowledge of the relevant laws of the countryside. These are analysed in the next section. Implicit in this is, of course, a skill that the ranger must develop: that of distinguishing between the youthful excesses of a group of teenagers on BMX bikes whose most dangerous objective is to try to annoy the ranger, and the more difficult problem of a group of potential poachers. A ranger treads a fine line between the necessary elements of visitor supervision and the essentially negative and/or dangerous elements of the work. It is safe to say, however, that a ranger's work is interpretive, educational and positive before it is negative and restrictive.

8.3   RANGERS AND THE LAW

Notwithstanding the foregoing discussion, the ranger has an important role to play in helping to uphold the law within the countryside, primarily as an accomplice to the police force. The single most useful text for identifying the role of the ranger in this respect is Parkes (1983), which stresses the symbiosis that a policeman tries to develop 'with his local farmers, residents, rangers, landowners and gamekeepers'.

Parkes identifies the three categories of offenders as indicated in the previous section, and terms them:

(a) *genuine* – is ignorant of the law or breaks it unwillingly;
(b) *chancer* – probably realizes what he or she is doing but takes the risk anyway;
(c) *obstructive* – is possibly hostile.

It is upon dealing with the last type of offender that the book concentrates. It is unlikely that a ranger will operate for any length of time without encountering the problems associated with such offenders, and possible approaches to these problems are needed. Sir Derek Barker, the Chairman of the Countryside Commission in 1987, emphasized the positive role of rangers 'putting a new stress on the outward looking element of the job . . . working much more closely with the community . . . this implies new skills to be added to the old ones which remain important'. These 'old skills' include the ability to react to potentially obstructive behaviour.

The first important point is that of taking notes: a notebook is essential, not just for recording details of the park for management records but also for recording details of offences and other potentially important situations. These include the location of the event, the date and time, a description of the offender and, if possible, the name (usually Mickey Mouse or Donald Duck!). The ranger must also record what happened, what he or she actually saw and what was said in response. Other obvious evidence could be the registration number of cars or other identifying behaviour.

Quite often, the ranger may not have the opportunity to record certain details before the would-be offender is approached. 'The initial approach to an offender often determines the reception you will get and subsequently the outcome' (Parkes, 1983).

Again, concentrating upon the potentially obstructive offender, the ranger should:

(a) adopt a friendly attitude;
(b) stop a reasonable distance away;
(c) identify himself or herself and show some authority (a badge if applicable);
(d) point out what the offender is doing is wrong;
(e) if possible, establish whether the person knew that what was being done was illegal;
(f) produce a copy of the law/bye-law if possible;
(g) point out the ranger's responsibility for identifying misbehaviour and why it is necessary on the park or reserve;
(h) give an appropriate warning if there is a good response;
(i) report more serious offences to the police.

The foregoing may be academic in some circumstances in which it may be too dangerous or impossible to approach offenders – say, with a group of armed poachers, if the offender refuses to leave or becomes hostile, the ranger should not become further involved. 'Any loss of dignity at beating a hasty retreat is often made up by calling the police and having an offender dealt with properly. He who laughs last, and all that' (after Parkes, 1983).

8.3.1 Relevant legislation

It is impossible to list all the pieces of legislation of which a ranger could possibly have need to refer in the course of his or her work. Parkes (op. cit.), for example, discusses some twenty-five areas of involvement for the ranger, including theft, trespass, assault, firearms, game preservation, access to land, litter, offences on highways and the protection of birds and plants. There is also the legislative framework given in Chapter 3 of this book which forms the basis of the ranger's work and with which the ranger must also be familiar. Furthermore, many other, more general, pieces of legislation have sections or clauses which relate specifically to the countryside. Lane (1988) discussed six such areas of interest, namely landscape protection, habitat protection, wildlife protection, planning law, access and pollution. Each area in turn is covered by upwards of a dozen single pieces of legislation. This clearly identifies a number of points: firstly, in order to cover countryside issues professionally a multidisciplinary team is required; secondly, the protection of the countryside is based upon assembling a plethora of individual pieces of legislation; and, thirdly, and of most relevance here, certain pieces of legislation will be best monitored and, if necessary, upheld by the ranger than by the countryside manager. As the person inevitably nearest to the problem, the ranger has the capacity to react most immediately to situations as they arrive.

The most common laws to which the ranger refers are those connected with trespass/access, criminal damage, highways offences, litter and bye-laws. It is safe to say that most offences are minor, as has been stressed previously.

(a) *Trespass* is a civil offence, which means that it is usually an issue decided in civil courts. Where trespass is aggravated (as in the case of burglary or an intention to cause criminal damage) it may become a criminal offence. The usual form of trespass – where someone is on land, water or buildings for which no permission has been granted – is civil trespass. Action can be taken against trespassers in civil courts but it is usually prohibitively expensive. (So what, one might ask, is the use of a 'Trespassers will be prosecuted' sign?) The ranger is ideally placed to point out the inadvertent (or otherwise) trespass and act, on behalf of the landowner, by asking the trespasser to leave, return to the path or whatever. Police are empowered to act only in criminal law, and can only help the ranger to encourage the trespasser to leave.

(b) *Access*, which is closely related to trespass, is either through the ownership of the land, through agreement with the owner (be it a private individual, a local authority or a charitable trust) or through public rights-of-way. In cases where access is allowed or a right, the ranger might be involved in helping to uphold these rights. Where access is not allowed, the ranger might be involved in deterring trespass either through management works (fencing, signs or footpath design) or by other means as discussed in the previous section.

(c) *Criminal damage* can be summarized as the act or intention to damage/destroy another person's property without a lawful excuse. Thus vandals, unsanctioned tree fellers, and people who damage wild plants are all guilty of criminal damage. The damage done in most countryside areas can be reduced if not eliminated totally by simply having a ranger's presence which not only deters would-be offenders in a physical way, but also lets it be known that simply because an area looks wild – like a country park or a nature reserve – it is still cared for and managed. Thus most 'genuine or chancer' offenders will be deterred. The hostile offenders may not, but if damage occurs, the police can be called to deal with the criminal offence.

(d) *Highways offences* form a common and often apparently intractable problem for many countryside managers, and once again it is often the ranger who is best placed to try to overcome the problem. Driving a motor vehicle without lawful authority on land not designated as a road on open land, moorland, or other land or on a public bridleway/footpath is a criminal offence under the 1972 Road Traffic Act. The crime of riding cars, dune buggies and most often motorbikes on land or public footpaths is a common problem particularly on urban fringe sites. A regular presence from a ranger occasionally backed up by police support usually removes the problems to allow the land to be enjoyed by those seeking to use it legitimately. Having said this, motocross riders do need somewhere to practice and simply removing them from one site often makes the riders go elsewhere. The solution to this wider problem is, however, beyond the scope of most rangers.

(e) *Litter* and associated problems, again form a common problem which ranges from the small-scale dropping of a cigarette packet to the much more serious problem of large-scale dumping either by private individuals too lazy to drive to a council refuse site or by builders or other businesses who do not want to pay for waste disposal. The litter laws are quite extensive but really only need to be brought to bear upon serious offenders. Most litter or rubbish problems can be solved by regularly clearing away any litter that is dumped. People soon realize that they are not supposed to do it. A further help is to identify dumpers (it is astounding how many people dump old envelopes or other material which makes them traceable) and send letters spelling out the law, be it the 1983 Litter Act or the 1978 Refuse Disposal (Amenity) Act. The ranger is again the most ideally placed person to identify problems as they begin to arise. As with most similar problems, a regular ranger presence and swift action (in this case by removing the litter) have a major impact.

(f) *Bye-laws* can be created by most public authorities such as local councils, water boards, the Forestry Commission or the Nature Conservancy Council. The bye-law must be agreed by the Department of the Environment. All bye-laws are minor offences, which do not carry powers of arrest, and are designed to solve local problems.

For example, bye-laws can require all dogs to be kept on a lead or can require that the public keep to set routes in a nature reserve.

Bye-laws must be displayed in a prominent position where they can be seen by the public. Contravention of the bye-laws can be followed up by reporting the offender through the local magistrates court. This is most often undertaken by the ranger, although as with all previous cases, only persistent offenders need be dealt with in such a way.

The legal or policing role of the rangers depends very much on the situation in which rangers find themselves. Some well established sites need no more than the occasional quiet word to potentially high-spirited people. Other sites, where landuse conflicts and/or misuse have not been fully resolved, may require a firmer control. It is the skill of the ranger that is most important in determining whether offenders are simply ignorant of the law, whether they are trying to 'wind up' the ranger or whether they are intending to commit a premediated criminal act.

8.4 PART-TIME AND VOLUNTEER RANGERS

The above section serves, among other things, to emphasize the professionalism of rangers and the wide level of training needed to understand and implement just one role of the ranger. There are, as we saw, four such roles, all of which require equal professionalism and training.

Given this long-term development of skills it is clear that within a ranger service – that is, the service given by a co-ordinated group of rangers, usually under the line management of a senior ranger or countryside manager – the scope of part-time or volunteer rangers developing the necessary skills is limited. This raises the question 'why bother?'. There are, however, a number of reasons why part-time or voluntary help is valuable to full-time rangers. This is reflected by the fact that most organizations that run a ranger service also support that service with part-time or voluntary help.

The difference between 'part time' and 'volunteer' is somewhat hazy, but here part time implies paid, relatively regular work, while volunteer represents unpaid, irregular working in which the volunteer has as much say in work patterns as the employing organization. However, volunteers can be paid some expenses and in some cases, such as National Parks, are expected to turn out regularly to a set rota and perform specific tasks for which they receive training. There is no doubt that people respond to such a rigorous workload on a voluntary basis largely because, like most rangers, volunteers are devoted to their job, and also because working within a National Park even on a voluntary basis is an enjoyable experience.

There are four reasons why the manager might consider encouraging part-time or voluntary rangers.

8.4.1 Irregular workload

In country parks or on other sites, major attractions such as shows, events, or guided walks bring more visitors than usual to the site. This brings with it problems of visitor management, car parking, overcrowding, and ultimately, litter collection. As this level of on-site management is not usually required it is not wise to build up staffing levels to cope with events which only arise once or twice a year. In this case, part-time help is the easiest and best solution, because most of the tasks associated with events can be taught relatively easily.

In cases where the peaks of use are relatively predictable, such as summer weekends, a regular part-time ranger presence may be viable. This must, however, be supported with a higher degree of training because regular use of part-timers implies a heavier reliance upon their work. This in turn means that the part-timers will be required to deal with the situations normally dealt with by full-time professional rangers. These include interpretation, leading guided walks, talking to the public or staffing visitor centres. All of these clearly require an element of training which must be taken into acount when making estimates for the provisional costs of a ranger service.

8.4.2 Specific tasks

There are some tasks that can most optimally be undertaken by either part-time or volunteer staff for a number of reasons. The first reason is identified in the previous section, namely the seasonal or irregularity of the work. The second is the nature of the work itself. The ranger, as we have seen, should represent a large investment of time and training on the part of the countryside manager and employer. Therefore, as any manager would appreciate, each member of staff is best employed to do the tasks for which he or she has been trained. It is therefore a waste of the ranger's energy and expertise to undertake tasks that can be done by part-time or voluntary rangers. Nor need these tasks be too boring for the volunteers or part-time staff. Staffing visitor centres, for example, is one such job that a part-time ranger could do, leaving the full-time staff to follow their usual function. Similarly, acting as sources of information for visitors either at an information point or by being available on site is a task that could, and perhaps should, be undertaken by part-time staff.

There is clearly a compromise between letting full-time staff have all the most interesting jobs and allowing part-time and voluntary staff to become completely disheartened because all they ever seem to do is clean out toilets. The manager must strike the correct balance to allow some development of the part-time and voluntary staff, but also to optimize the support and hence efficiency of full-time staff.

8.4.3 Community involvement

The importance of allowing members of the public, particuly local people, to become involved in managing their own environment was stressed in Chapter 6. The emphasis is not upon substituting unpaid for paid labour (this should never be foremost in a countryside manager's mind) but upon allowing active involvement. This is particularly relevant when people volunteer to become unpaid rangers. Just as some individuals want to become involved on practical projects, others want to become involved with interpretive, educative or simple patrolling duties. The community benefits of voluntary involvement have been identified previously, but can be stressed again: a better feeling of belonging; a greater understanding of the countryside; a broader public support; greater respect for the countryside; and a sense of pride from active voluntary involvement. For these reasons alone, there should be a role for voluntary rangers. However, it must be said that a few voluntary rangers can take their sense of belonging too far and begin to impose their own views on how a site should be managed and how offenders should be dealt with. It is, therefore, vital that volunteers be made aware that while they are volunteers, they are still 'employed' as representatives of the employer and must respond to common management policies. This is best achieved by starting from the outset the basis of the volunteers' involvement: a trial period followed by a review after which an identity card is issued only if satisfactory progress has been made. A further annual review is also a common feature. These may seem rather harsh steps which might remove the spontaneity of volunteer rangers, but unless the volunteers are involved in anything but simply watching and reporting back to full-time staff, there is a risk of untrained staff allowing personal views to predominate.

The opposite side of this rigorous vetting procedure is that volunteers also need training if they are to be allowed regular work on site. The level of training will clearly reflect the degree to which the volunteers become involved in the more professional duties of the ranger service. In the Peak District National Park, for example, the volunteers must undertake at least a set number of work days, including weekend, and must perform specific duties. Furthermore, only after an initial lead-in period will ranger identification be issued. However, in return the volunteers receive a thorough training that would match that of many full-time rangers. It may be clear that the Peak Park, among other authorities, relies heavily on its volunteer network, particularly for weekend work in the very popular areas of the National Park.

In this case the line between professionalism and voluntary involvement is a fine one, which introduces the final reason for developing volunteer and part-time ranger services.

8.4.4   Career development

Notwithstanding the irregular hours, hard physical work and, often, low starting wages, there is no shortage of people trying to become countryside rangers, especially in National Parks. Indeed, in any circumstances the vocation of a countryside ranger is popular. As we have seen, however, the role of the countryside ranger is still developing and, in its earliest form, only started in Britain in 1966 as a recognizable organized body. As such, the mechanisms for becoming a countryside ranger is as yet poorly defined. Whereas other professional groups have easily identifiable training and career structures (entrance examinations, professional placements, and career examinations) the career development of the ranger is not as clearly defined. This is inevitable to a certain extent as the backgrounds from which countryside rangers come is in itself varied. For this reason, there needs to be some mechanism for allowing people from these diverse backgrounds to develop some experience before they decide upon a career as a countryside ranger or to learn some of the elements of the job before becoming a full-time ranger or before embarking upon a training programme, often at postgraduate level, to complete the necessary qualifications. The role of volunteer or part-time ranger therefore fills this gap – as near as the countryside ranger can have to an apprenticeship. Clearly, not all volunteers or part-time rangers aim to progress to a full-time post, but for those who do wish to move into rangering, the volunteer part-time/full-time path offers a means of gaining the necessary experience.

8.5   EMPLOYING A RANGER

The previous discussion identifies common threads which link most rangers and the roles that they fulfil. However, the countryside manager must be concerned with how, in his or her organization, the ranger or rangers must operate. The preceding chapters have focused upon the many concerns of the countryside manager – recreation, landscape conservation, nature conservation and interpretation. Having identified objectives within these broad concerns, the manager must also identify how the ranger fits into fulfilling these objectives.

8.5.1 Role identification

The number of situations within which a ranger is called to operate has increased over the years. The role of the original rangers employed through National Parks in 1949 has changed markedly until the present day when the ranger's core tasks have changed and the techniques employed by the ranger have also developed. The basic task of the countryside manager is therefore to identify what role the ranger will play in the operations of the management. The role of a ranger within a nature reserve, for example, may be primarily concerned with site supervision and, on a lesser basis, with the practical management of the site. A ranger on the urban fringe, however, might not have any practical management within his or her job and the primary concern may well be with education and interpretation, given the pressure that comes from urban centres upon the metropolitan countryside. These roles do, however, represent examples of the 'traditional' role of rangers. Increasingly, the ranger is being called upon to fulfil other roles including site manager, controller of budgets, visitor centre manager, receptionist or lecturer. These roles are increasingly important because of the development of capital intensive facilities, including visitor centres and major interpretive sites. These bring with them clear revenue implications for the maintenance, running and operation costs. A clarification of definitions is needed, because some rangers may feel that being responsible for a visitor centre may not be comparable with the status of a ranger. The countryside manager must, therefore, determine whether a ranger can best operate the modern countryside facilities or whether a specialist manager, or perhaps catering manager, might be more appropriate.

The initial concern of the countryside manager must therefore be to identify clearly the role of the ranger either before the ranger is appointed or, if this is not possible, during any review of policy or operations which the countryside manager undertakes.

8.5.2 Job description

The manager, having determined the work and priorities of the ranger, must define these roles within a job description. It is worth identifying the importance of the job description for several reasons. Firstly, a clear job description in any circumstance is a valuable tool for a manager, because it gives structure to the work of the individual. This is important for both sides of the process, namely the ranger and his or her manager. All employees welcome a clear statement of exactly what is expected of them.

The second reason for the importance of a precise job description is that it gives the manager and the ranger an opportunity to state several policies which might otherwise go unstated. The emphasis placed on various functions of the ranger will, for example, give an indication of the way that the manager and the ranger seek to address the relevant issues. Appendix 1 gives a job description for rangers, with different emphasis on the community, education, practical work and specialist skills.

Finally, a precise job description makes the management of a ranger and/or a ranger service an easier process. A job description identifies the areas of work that each ranger must cover. This in turn allows the manager to identify how to monitor the work of the ranger, and allows the ranger to identify how to gear his or her workload. Having agreed these issues, the ranger should be relatively free to pursue these areas of work with the necessary autonomy which, as we shall see, is a fundamental principle of the management of a ranger service.

8.5.3 Training

The training that a ranger must undergo depends upon the role identified for the ranger and the experience and training that the individual has already received. So much is obvious. What each manager and ranger must establish together is where the ranger's major weaknesses are to be found and, just as crucially, how the ranger's role is likely to develop in the future. A review of how the ranger service in general has developed gives some indication as to how the ranger service is developing now and how it is likely to progress in the future. This in turn gives us a clear indication of how, in broad terms, the individual ranger's workloads are likely to develop.

Recently the emphasis has been with human skills. These might include dealing with school children, with the public, with ethnic minorities or with other target groups (see, for example, the details of the Operation Gateway in Chapter 4) or may entail developing the skill necessary to operate and staff a visitor centre.

Once these changes in emphasis have been identified (if indeed they are deemed necessary), training is vital to secure the implementation of what is, in effect, a change of policy. Some organizations may not feel it necessary to adopt a user-based approach – rangers who operate on closed nature reserves may spend most of their time working on site supervision and some practical projects.

Training can be undertaken within the organization or outside it either by bringing in trainers or by sending rangers on training courses. Because of the increasing diversity in the ranger's workload, it is becoming important to seek out the optimal source of training, and what might be considered as traditional sources of training have to be expanded upon to accommodate changes that the manager and the ranger wish to make.

The new directions that the ranger movement takes is determined by many pressures and demands. The Association of Countryside Rangers clearly has a role in determining its own professional direction. The Countryside Commission also has a role in determining how it should like to see the ranger movement develop. This interest is based on the policy guidelines that the Countryside Commission develops (Countryside Commission, 1988) and is reflected in the amount of grant aid that the Commission devotes to ranger services across the country (e.g. Table 8.1).

8.5.4 Procedures

Establishing procedures and management systems within which the ranger can operate is, in many ways, synonymous with establishing an integrated ranger service. The ranger, almost by definition, spends much of his or her time outside the direct supervision of the countryside manager. In this case, it is essential that the manager and the ranger or rangers develop procedures which keep the lines of communication working freely. The most usual and simplest form is through a written report. This can be submitted on any suitable time basis, which usually depends upon the reason for the reports being produced. If the manager feels the need to keep in direct touch with the work of the ranger, a daily or weekly report might be suitable. However, if the manager is satisfied that the ranger need only report on major issues, a bi-monthly report may be all that is required. However, such a report should be accompanied by a managerial assessment and, at least on a monthly basis, a discussion about the report between the manager and the ranger. This discussion should concentrate upon issues that both people see as important, and also upon discussing the ranger's progress in the major work areas defined in the job description.

The written reports can usefully be collated into an annual report, written for the ranger service as a whole. This should not simply be a distillation of the individual reports, but should form part of a review and projection for the policies of the ranger service – in much the same

Table 8.1. *Relative amount of grants paid by Countryside Commission for England and Wales for rangers*

	(A) Non-public £'000	(B) Public £'000	Total £'000	Previous year £'000
Acquisition and development of				
(a) country parks	18	524	542	640
(b) picnic sites	12	45	57	59
(c) informal recreation facilities	235	439	674	739
Amenity tree planting, woodland management and other conservation work	1 678[a]	3 183[a]	4 861	1 977
Coast and countryside management services	159	1 178	1 337	887
Countryside advisory services	222	97	319	202
Information and visitor services	332	344	676	602
Provision of youth hostels	48	—	48	107
Ranger and warden services	**491**	**2 279**	**2 770**	**1 707**
Long distance routes	—	674	674	641
Recreational footpaths and bridleways	77	300	377	376
Voluntary work in the countryside	392	—	392	369
Access/management agreements	—	203[b]	203	211
Land acquisition	464	249	713	1 033
Countryside initiative grants	200	—	200	205
Special metropolitan county abolition posts	—	240	240	429
Removal of eyesores	46	—	46	—
Countryside information and training	57	—	57	18
Other approved categories	—	203[c]	203	260
	4 431	9 958	14 389	10 462

[a] This includes grant aid of £103 609 (non-public) and £2 464 655 (public) in respect of Task Force Trees.

[b] This includes grant aid of £200 000 in respect of management agreements in national parks.

[c] This includes grant aid of £182 487 to the Broads Authority.

As at 31 March 1988 there were outstanding commitments to £872 569 in respect of grant assistance to be provided under Section 9 of the Local Government Act 1974.

Source: Countryside Commission (1988).

way that most annual reports contain elements of policy review. The work of rangers is, in many ways, a responsive role and because of this is likely to need reviews more regularly than another part of a countryside service, such as landscape policies or recreational policies, although all are clearly connected.

8.5.5 Autonomy

As part of the procedural considerations that the manager must address is the degree of autonomy that the rangers need to enjoy. As a guide, the ranger is, more than anyone else, at the sharp end of the countryside service and for this reason must be allowed to develop the necessary rapport with the visitors, farmers, schools and so on that are, ultimately, to benefit from the physical and interpretive work that the countryside service provides. This, in part, will mean that the ranger will have a major role in creating his or her own agenda and/or priorities. To this end, the autonomy of the ranger, in certain circumstances, must be an integral part of his or her work. Autonomy does not, however, mean that the ranger is unmanaged, but what it does mean is that the ranger can reach the objectives of the manager and organization in ways that he or she determines.

In other circumstances, where the ranger works within closely defined parameters such as in a site-based shop, the autonomy is clearly much more difficult, but the ability to communicate with all sectors of the public to a great extent depends upon the ranger being allowed to develop a personal style in service delivery.

This autonomy may well also stretch to the responsibility for some budgetary provision. Wherever the ranger needs access to a ready supply of petty cash and/or materials for exhibitions or interpretation, it is vital that the individual ranger or the ranger service has easy access to the necessary resources. This again is important when dealing with the public – farmers, visitors, recreationalists or others – who are not necessarily interested in the financial procedures of any particular organization, but are interested in getting or seeing results. As it is usually the ranger who delivers these results to the public, the manager must be confident enough to see that the necessary responsibility, be it financial or otherwise, is pushed as far down the organization as possible in order to ensure an efficient service.

8.6   THE RANGER SERVICE

The manager has a responsibility not only to the public and the individual rangers (and, obviously, the countryside) but also to the collective role of all the rangers under his or her management – in short, the ranger service.

There are no hard and fast rules about the organization of a ranger service, and the manager must use the ranger service in order to best meet any number of objectives. Furthermore, throughout the year the ranger service may be called upon to perform a variety of functions, and the collective way in which the rangers are organized may vary. Notwithstanding these reservations, it is possible to identify three broad systems that are used to manage a ranger service. In all three systems, which are discussed individually below, it is useful to picture the hierarchy of voluntary ranger/part-time ranger/full-time ranger/head ranger/countryside manager (Figure 8.1). This does not imply that each of these levels has identical roles; far from it. But it does help to establish how each of the tiers interacts within a ranger service. The three systems that are common within countryside manager are: site based; area based; role based. These are discussed below.

8.6.1   Site based

The site-based ranger service, as the name suggests, revolves around individual sites that, together, form the area for which the countryside manager is responsible. This might be a series of country parks, several nature reserves or any combination of any designated sites. The characteristics of a site-based service is that the rangers operate within a single site, usually under the line management of a head ranger who might, in turn, be responsible to a site manager. The presence of a site manager is determined by the range of facilities on site. A country park with a large visitor centre, with a shop and restaurant, and perhaps formal sports facilities such as sailing or windsurfing will usually have a site manager to co-ordinate all of the operations. A smaller site, with only limited facilities, may not require the co-ordinating role of a site manager and the most senior person will then be the head ranger. In turn, the head ranger or site manager will be responsible to the countryside manager.

There are several advantages of a site-based service. Firstly, it allows the manager to develop a thorough interpretive and educational service

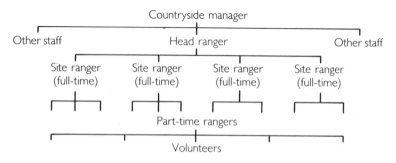

Figure 8.1 *Hierarchy of ranger service.*

on a specific site. Furthermore, the survey and research work necessary to provide an interpretive service is also a useful and valuable end in itself. To have a thorough knowledge of a single area allows the rangers to fully understand the site's cultural, historic, ecological, archaeological and recreational context. This is particularly rewarding when the site is based around an old estate which will have many angles to its importance. In the case of a nature reserve or a site run by the voluntary sector, the research and the ecological or site information may, of course, be the most important objective, but in most cases the information will be gathered in order to pass on some of it through interpretive media.

A second advantage to developing a site-based service is that the rangers themselves can develop a strong feeling for and relationship with the site. The relationship is important not only for full-time staff but also for part-time and volunteer rangers who, in normal circumstances, will be local people who may welcome the opportunity to seek for themselves some details about the area in which they live.

A further reason for having an on-site ranger service is based purely upon the resource allocation necessary to develop a countryside site. Where major expenditure has been incurred in the development of a countryside site, the manager may decide that the best means of 'protecting' this expenditure is to have a ranger service permanently on site. A variation of this is that a major countryside site is likely to attract a large number of visitors. (Some country parks attract upwards of a million visitors per year.) In order to manage a large visitor population it is clearly necessary to have a site-based ranger service which not only provides the interpretive, directional and wardening roles that are needed, but also provides the workforce necessary to direct cars, pick up litter, talk to visitors, etc.

Finally, a site-based ranger service is occasionally the only option that is available to a countryside manager. Where the only land resources managed are sites, the rangers themselves can clearly only operate on the sites. This will be the case for county-based wildlife or conservation trusts where the trust manages a number of reserves spread across the county in question. In these situations, some of the smaller sites may require no more than a single ranger, or even a part-time presence. However, these situations can still be considered as a site-based ranger service.

8.6.2 Area based

The area-based ranger service has been common in the National Parks since the role of the rangers developed. The reasoning behind the area-based rather than site-based approach is that, within National Parks, the ranger – and, by inference, the management process – is concerned not just with specific sites, but with the countryside as a whole. Indeed, the National Parks Act of 1949 gives the National Park authorities the responsibility of protecting the landscape and recreational opportunities of the Parks. Furthermore, the interests of the local agricultural and forestry industries must also be borne in mind when decisions are made, as too should the local natural history; the remit is therefore very wide and this is reflected in the remit of the ranger service.

The wider, non-site specific role of the ranger is becoming more commonplace, particularly among local authorities which now see their countryside functions as extending beyond the management of country-side recreation sites. As these authorities extend their concern for the countryside beyond the 'honeypot' sites (often country parks) so, too, do the ranger services extend their role. Therefore, rangers are be-coming involved in landscape projects as schools liaisons officers or as the first point of contact for many people living and working in the countryside, as well as those using it for recreation.

This concept of rangers extending their role, and acting as a link between town and country, and country parks and the wider country-side, is one that the Countryside Commission (1987) is keen to promote, as they have identified this developing role for rangers in their own policy statement for the beginning of the twenty-first century. Under the issue of 'making things happen', the Countryside Commission suggests several major redirections for ranger services.

Ranger services to take on management responsibilities in the wider countryside beyond recreation sites;

Ranger or visitor services taking on new responsibilities for informa-tion provision in towns and forging links with urban communities;

The work of rights-of-way staff to be seen within the wider context of other countryside recreation opportunities.

This approach should, suggests the Countryside Commission, be adopted in a limited number of areas, in order to develop the new function. Furthermore, in order to introduce the changes in a managed way, training and special funding should be made available to train existing rangers and new rangers. These will be in addition to the more traditional, practical role that rangers had in their early years of professional development.

In essence, the area-based ranger may not require too many skills that are different to those of the site-based ranger. This, however, depends upon the priorities set by the countryside manager. In any given situation, the priorities may vary. For example, in a rural area, the ranger may require some skill in dealing with farmers and landowners as well as the public.

8.6.3 Role based

A role-based ranger service is something of a hybrid, in that it represents a mixture of a site-based and an area-based approach. The role-based service seeks to match the requirements of the manager with the flexibility of the ranger service. The types of role that might be allocated to rangers are those already identified – schools liaison, contact with farmers, working with the disabled or other target groups or preparing guided walks programmes. Having determined the roles that are important in any particular management situation, the physical location for meeting those objectives will vary. Schools work, for example, may be best concentrated on well-known, accessible sites, such as country parks. Guided walks, however, might be most appropriate in a variety of locations in order to maintain variety and originality. Should the ranger service be responsible for producing management plans, these will clearly be site specific, whereas interpretive plans or integrated countryside plans will be more general in the geographical area to which they relate.

The converse of a role-based ranger service is an extension to either a site-based or an area-based service. A ranger who works from a country park or a nature reserve can also be allocated a wider remit, such as a specialism in disabled access, which runs alongside his or her site-based role. Equally, an area-based ranger can be allocated some specific duties, dependent upon the requirements of the ranger service and the countryside management service as a whole.

8.7 CONCLUSIONS

The ranger service that operates within England, Wales and Scotland has developed from the earlier wardening service that was initiated within the National Parks network, which was established following the 1949 Act. The emphasis since the 1949 Act has been away from the policing role (although this remains an important element of the work of a ranger) to a more positive, educative, helping role. This is further developing into a much broader role, acting as a link between town and country and the people who live, work and recreate in the countryside. The Countryside Commission (1987) stated that this was 'an integrated approach to the work of countryside rangers'.

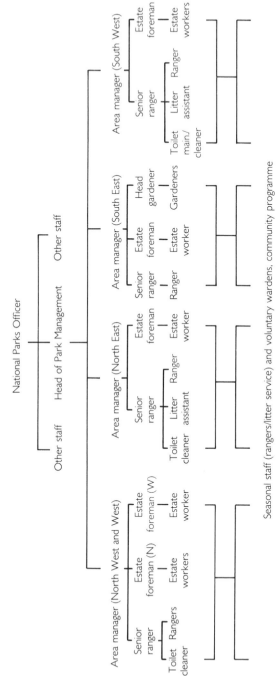

Figure 8.2 *Ranger service in Lake District National Park (1988).* (**Source:** *National Parks Officer, Lake District National Park.*)

Seasonal staff (rangers/litter service) and voluntary wardens, community programme

National Parks Officer

Other staff   Head of Park Management   Other staff

Area manager (North West and West)

Senior ranger   Estate foreman (N)   Estate foreman (W)

Toilet cleaner   Rangers   Estate workers   Estate worker

Area manager (North East)

Senior ranger   Estate foreman

Toilet cleaner   Litter assistant   Ranger   Estate worker

Area manager (South East)

Senior ranger   Estate foreman   Head gardener

Ranger   Estate worker   Gardeners

Area manager (South West)

Senior ranger   Estate foreman

Toilet main./ cleaner   Litter assistant   Ranger   Estate workers

A central link to this ever-changing service is the absolute importance of the ranger in the management of the countryside. Alongside any physical or promotional work that takes place in the countryside, there is a basic need for the ranger service to work with these changes. Rangers are the people who, more than anyone, deliver the service and make sure that the development proposals actually work. The rangers are the staff who set countryside management apart from any other land-based professions; no other group of developers of land, as part of their professional practice, work with staff who deal so closely with the public, landowners, recreationalists and other groups and individuals who have an interest in the countryside. An innovative, enthusiastic and aware ranger service is almost synonymous with a countryside management service, and must therefore remain at the heart of countryside work.

8.8 CASE STUDY

If all ranger services within England, Wales and Scotland were described, it is likely that each one would have sufficient individual characteristics to be truthfully defined as unique. For this reason, only one case study is presented here. The example of a ranger service is taken from the Lake District National Park because it represents three of the elements that are characteristic of a ranger service. Firstly, the service is split upon a purely area basis. Secondly, the work of the rangers is separated from that of the more practically based estate teams. Finally, the full-time service is augmented by part-time and volunteer workers.

Figure 8.2 shows the relevant chains of command and the various splits within the overall management service and, within that, the ranger service forms an integral part.

The reason for the area-based service lies in the *raison d'être* of the National Park. The attention is to an integrated management of the whole resource, under the control of the National Park authority. This authority is made up of representatives of the local authorities and a smaller number of representatives elected directly by the Secretary of State for the Environment. The National Park Authority is responsible not just for a number of sites, but for the whole National Park system – specifically its landscape and recreational importance. The only way of achieving this is through an overall service, concentrating upon priorities rather than sites. For this reason, an area-based management service has been developed. In this way, landscape projects on private land or access problems on common land can be addressed, whereas with a site-based management service, such initiatives would be impossible.

In order to reflect the area-based management, and to act as the deliverers of the service, the ranger service is also area based, with four areas being covered by separate teams. Furthermore, the work of the rangers is distinct from that of the estate teams, which are responsible for practical management projects. The collective responsibility for the area-based ranger service and the area-based estate team falls to the area manager, who refers directly to the head of Park Management.

The full-time rangers are helped by volunteers and part-time/seasonal staff. This reflects both the desire by the public to become involved with the management of a National Park and also the seasonality of demand upon the resources of the management/ranger service. The summer months and Bank Holiday/Half Term peaks in the usage of the National Park need to be matched with a corresponding peak in the service provided by the rangers. Therefore, the volunteers and part-time staff meet this need.

The work of the individual rangers will inevitably match the physical characteristics of the Lake District National Park. Being a mountainous and often hostile environment, individual skills in mountain craft and outdoor pursuits will form the basis of the ranger's personal role. Conversely, the sheer popularity of the Lake District also means that rangers also require skill in dealing with people, many of whom may not be used to being in the mountains or in potentially dangerous situations.

The Lake District has also a large number of National Trust properties, many of which are land holdings. These land holdings clearly need managing and, as a result, many have rangers operating within the site. In effect, therefore, while the National Park Authority operates an area-based ranger service, the National Trust for example operates a site-based service within the National Park as, too, does the local county conservation trust.

BIBLIOGRAPHY

Association of Countryside Rangers (1987) *Ranger 2000*, Conference Proceedings ACR, London.

Association of Countryside Rangers (1988) *Coming of Age: A Strategy Document for the ACR*, ACR, London.

Barker, Sir D. (1987) The Countryside Commission and the Ranger Service, *The Ranger*, Spring 1987, Volume 8.

Countryside Commission (various years) *Annual Report*, Cheltenham.

Countryside Commission (1979) *Countryside Rangers and Related Staff*, Advisory Series No, 7 Cheltenham.

Countryside Commission (1980) *Explore your Local Countryside*, CCP135, Cheltenham.

Countryside Commission (1987) *Enjoying the Countryside: Priorities for Action*, CCP235, Cheltenham.

Countryside Commission (1988) *Enjoying the Countryside*, CCP234, Cheltenham.

Countryside Commission for Scotland (1987) *Countryside Rangers in Scotland*, Battleby, Perth.

Countryside Commission for Scotland (1988) *Grants for Countryside Rangers*, Battleby, Perth.

Fretwell, L. (1988) Right shape for the future, *Local Government Chronicle*, September 1988.

HMSO (1949) *National Parks and Access to the Countryside Act*, HMSO, London.

Lane, A. (1988) *Practical Conservation: Legislation and Regulation*, Open University/ Hodder and Stoughton, London.

Parkes, C. (1983) *Law of the Countryside*, Association of Countryside Rangers, London.

White, F. (1987) The earlier years of the ACR, *The Ranger*, Spring 1987, Volume 8.

NINE

Interpretation

When we left the street and were in the country, Father became instructive:

'This is a thistle,' he would cry into the wind pointing a pale finger, and we looked. Then further along 'There is another thistle' again pointing. There were a lot of thistles in Scotland. We were soon well acquainted with them. Mother was also informative:

'Look, a patch of grass!' And we dutifully twisted our heads.

Ivor Cutler, Life in a Scotch Sitting Room, *Vol. 2*

Interpretation is one of the most important processes that helps to distinguish the work of the countryside manager from that of other land-based and design professionals. It is important, therefore that the manager has a full grasp of not only the underlying theory of interpretation, but also of the practicalities of interpretive work. Furthermore, as it is one of the most progressive and dynamic parts of the countryside manager's work, it is also important that the manager (or one or more members of a countryside team) keeps fully abreast of developments in interpretation. Interpretation is a skill and a discipline in its own right, which forms a part of the manager's portfolio of skills. It would be helpful initially to look at some of the things that interpretation is not.

Firstly, it is not advertising. The production of a leaflet which simply informs people of the existence of certain sites is not interpretation. Admittedly, a leaflet or video that is a well-designed interpretive product does, in part, advertise a project or a site. However, interpretation does far more than advertise, yet we must ask ourselves how many so-called interpretive exercises do no more than advertise?

Secondly, interpretation is not education. The father in the quotation at the beginning of this chapter may well have been attempting to educate his children but he was definitely not interpreting. Again, it is clear that interpretation contains many educative elements. As Miles and Seabrooke (1977) suggest: 'Countryside interpretation seeks to expand the meaning or to communicate the significance of some aspects of an area.' Furthermore, Tilden (1967), in what was perhaps the pioneer work on interpretation, started his definition of the process as 'an educational activity'; however, as if to pre-empt any narrow definitions of interpretation he went on to say that interpretation is a much wider process 'rather than simply a communication of factual information'.

Finally, interpretation is not purely recreational. While activity days, guided walks, and film shows may be enjoyable experiences, 'it is widely accepted that interpretation is concerned with changing the attitudes and opinions of visitors' (Countryside Commission, 1979). Interpretation does not fit snugly into any single existing definition. In this context interpretation as a process crosses many traditional boundaries. The complete definition originally given by Tilden (op. cit.) identifies this: 'Interpretation is an educational activity which aims to reveal meanings and relationships through the use of original objectives by first-hand experience and by illustrative media rather than simply to communicate factual information.'

Having defined what interpretation is not, we must now see what it is. This chapter firstly identifies the philosophy of interpretation by looking briefly at its historic development. Following this introduction to the theory of interpretation, the practicalities of interpretive planning are explained and the many media available to the countryside manager are discussed. Finally, some modern trends in interpretation are analysed to attempt to foresee where techniques will develop in the future.

9.1   THE INTERPRETIVE PROCESS

Freeman Tilden (op. cit.) was the first writer to attempt to define interpretation in 1967. He also explored the reasons for interpreting anything. His approach to the subject laid the foundations for almost all subsequent studies, and most developments in the field of interpretation follow his rules and guidelines.

The interpretive process is another concept which, along with National Parks and ranger/wardening services, originated in the United States of America but over the years has been adapted and changed to suit British requirements, not only in National Parks but now increasingly in most areas and aspects of the countryside. At the heart of the interpretation of American National Parks is the Interpretive Prospectus. The Prospectus gives an indication of what is to be interpreted and precise details of how the features are to be interpreted. The concept of the interpretive prospectus was used by several British authorities, including, in the early years, some National Park Authorities (Robinson, 1979). It was only in the mid to late 1970s that the interpretive process began to be analysed in Britain. The formative work was produced in 1975 in two volumes. Aldridge (1975) produced a guide to the interpretive process while the second volume of the work (Pennyfather, 1975) examined in detail the various media that are available to the countryside manager. The Countryside Commission (1979) summarizes the interpretive process. This can be represented diagrammatically, as in Figure 5.1 and in brief can be analysed as seeking the answers to four basic questions namely:

1. Why provide interpretive facilities?
2. What might be interpreted?
3. For whom is the interpretation provided?
4. How is the interpretation to be carried out?

We can see that the question 'why' is the first to be listed, which reiterates the common thread that links all elements of countryside management; the setting of objectives.

9.1.1 Why provide interpretive facilities?

The interpretation of a site or an area is only one part of the overall service that the countryside manager must provide. It is clear, therefore, that the need for any interpretation must be established in order to prioritize the resources that have to be put into the interpretive process. It is important to accept that not all sites require interpretation and the decision as to whether or not interpretation is needed can only be made with a thorough assessment of the area. This assessment must include such issues as the potential of the site for interpretation, the requirements of the visitors and methods, other than interpretation of meeting management objectives.

Having established the need for interpretation within a countryside management programme, the objectives for this interpretation must be established. The aims of the interpretation can be any one of a number of things. Bearing in mind the definition that is given in the opening section of this chapter, the aims of interpretation can cover a range of issues, including: increasing the visitor's understanding of the countryside; increasing understanding about specific issues; encouraging visitors to concentrate their attention in one or two areas of a site and hence relieve pressure on other areas of the site.

As the Countryside Commission states: 'The precise aims of any interpretive programme should be stated at the outset. Throughout planning, construction and use, all proposals should be realistically assessed to ensure that they are accomplishing their aims.'

9.1.2   What might be interpreted?

The simple answer to this question is 'Anything!'. Any facet of the countryside or a countryside site warrants interpretation. The important issue for the countryside manager is, therefore, what in each particular circumstance is the most important thing to interpret? In physical terms, the geology, geomorphology, land forms or ecology of an area can all be interpreted, as too can the human dimensions, such as landuse, archaeology, social/historical features or cultural heritage. At a more specific level, individual features can also be interpreted – buildings, plants, archaeological remains or, indeed, anything that is either unique to the site or is of greater importance than any other feature or collection of features.

A clue to what might best be interpreted will be obtained through the objectives that are set when the manager establishes why he or she wants to interpret a site or feature. If the principal objective is to entertain the general public, a subject such as glacial geomorphology may be slightly tedious for most people. However, if the objective is to increase a particular target group's knowledge and understanding of a site, glacial geomorphology might well provide a suitable topic. In short, while the site itself might provide a number of items that could be interpreted, there are many constraints which will also determine what can be interpreted.

These constraints can be split into two categories (Countryside Commission, 1979), namely: site constraints and management constraints. Site constraints are imposed by the physical limitation of the site and by the location, accessibility and popularity of the site. A physically limiting site is one where large-scale use of notice boards or self-guide trails will clearly impose some constraints on what might be interpreted (and indeed how it might be interpreted). Similarly, an inaccessible area may not attract a broad cross-section of the public, thereby reducing the types of features that might be interpreted to those that would appeal to a limited sector or market of the population. Similarly, an inaccessible area which has an element of wilderness appeal to it may not require interpretation, despite having a plethora of potentially interesting features. A further site constraint that has to be taken into consideration is the potential competition from nearby or adjacent sites. A feature may be worthy of interpretation in one area, but if a better, more accessible example of the same feature is to be found in a nearby area, which can also be interpreted, this obviously dictates what should be the subject for interpretation in each case. This phenomenon often leads to a 'theme' being developed within or indeed between sites which adds an element of uniqueness to an area and also links the interpretation on each site. Hence, many local authorities have adopted 'themes' such as 'Robin Hood Country' or '1066 Country' or 'Land of the Prince Bishops'; and, similarly, many privately or voluntarily run sites have adopted themes not only to help with interpretation but also to help develop an identity to an area or site.

Management constraints are imposed when the possible interpretation of a site comes into conflict with other management issues or objectives. Thus, if the interpretation of a site would lead to greater visitor numbers it is conceivable that this side effect would be unacceptable to the manager and would result in a rethinking of the interpretive programme. A more usual constraint is the knock-on financial implications of a thorough interpretive programme. The implementation of the programme clearly has financial implications, but so too do the continuing items, such as extra staffing, maintenance and running costs. Should the interpretive programme conflict with the finances for the site, it is clear that the subject of the interpretation may well have to be amended from, say, the whole site to just a small part of it.

9.1.3 For whom is the interpretation provided?

'For whom?' is a simplistic way of determining the market segment for which interpretation is to be provided. Where the countryside manager is responsible for a consumer led service (as opposed to a service which is more concerned with protecting natural history sites) this is the most important question of all. The market for which the manager provides the interpretation determines what should be interpreted and how it should be interpreted. The market response to the interpretive programme also determines the success of the programme. For example, if part of the interpretive strategy is to provide a leaflet to interpret a site but the leaflet is not read, understood or even picked up by the target market, the interpretive programme is not a success. No matter how attractive, how prestigious or how well planned the distribution, if the leaflet does not reach its target, it is a failure. Without overstating a case, managers must ask themselves whether interpretive displays or events are created for the public or for the managers themselves. If the answer is 'the public' (or, more correctly, a market segment within 'the public') the results and success of the interpretive programme should be monitored, like every other item within a management plan or strategy.

Chapter 4 examined some of the basic principles of marketing, but for the purposes of interpretation, some of the fundamental questions that need to be asked about 'for whom is the interpretation provided?' are: how many people are anticipated?; what socio-economic groups are to be targeted?; what age groups?; are they repeat visitors?; how will they get to the site?; are there any language barriers for, say, ethnic groups?; how do the target groups communicate – verbally, through writing, using pictures or are they comfortable using all three; with which interpretive media is the target group familiar?; what is the party size and structure of the target group? . . . and so on.

Interpretation is not simply about producing leaflets, videos or guided walks but is about people. Consequently, the people themselves must have a major role in determining how they obtain the information, guidance and education provided through interpretation.

9.1.4   How is the interpretation to be carried out?

The next section of the chapter is devoted to a discussion on the various media that are available to the countryside manager. However, to complete the assessment of the four basic questions of interpretation – why, what, for whom and how – we can examine the principles (from Countryside Commission, 1979) that will help to determine how countryside interpretation should be carried out.

1. Interpretation provides more than information. It should explain and invoke a response.
2. Interpretation should provide a complete picture.
3. Most people absorb information more easily if contained within a story or theme.
4. Interpretation should relate what is being displayed or described to something within the personality or experience of the visitor.
5. Visitors take part in interpretation from choice, so it must be enjoyable.
6. Interpretive programmes must be geared to specific target groups.
7. Visitors are likely to appreciate a story more if it is expressed in a variety of media, appealing to a variety of senses.
8. Each part of the interpretive programme should be undertaken through the medium best suited to that part.
9. Subject specialists – such as ecologists or landscape architects – are not necessarily good communicators. Interpretation is a skill in itself, but interpretation as a process involves many skills.
10. Some sites do not need interpretation.

All of these principles will lead the manager to a decision about how – if at all – a site should be interpreted. The following section deals with methods of interpretation.

Visitor Centres: Provide a focus for many of the countryside manager's work, including interpretation, rangers, visitor management and recreational provision.

9.2 TECHNIQUES OF INTERPRETATION

The definitive guide to techniques of interpretation for Great Britain is without doubt Pennyfather. The guide forms the second part of the two-part guide developed by the Countryside Commission and the Countryside Commission for Scotland in 1975. Pennyfather (1975) seeks to evaluate 63 interpretive media against a set of criteria. The list of criteria against which media are evaluated is as follows:

1. *Impact*   The overall impact and degree of stimulation provided by the medium.

2. *Flexibility*   How far the medium is adaptable to changes in emphasis, design or layout (e.g. to make it possible to cater for a range of interests of visitors or for those of varying ages).

3. *Encouragement of participation*   The extent to which the medium enables the visitor to become actively involved in some way, or encourages him (or her) to do so.

4. *Provocation*   How far curiosity is aroused, and how far the visitor is provoked to discover more for him (or her) self.

5. *Relationship to visitor pace*   How far is it possible to cope with visitors of varying comprehension or physical pace and capability.

6. *Use by groups*   The extent to which the medium is suitable for simultaneous use by large groups of visitors.

7. *Visitor safety*   How far the visitor is protected from any significant risks.

8. *Links with surroundings*   How far the visitor is encouraged to explore his immediate surroundings (e.g. to seek out, in the locality, actual examples of objects that are described in a visitor centre).

9. *Relationship to adjacent media*   The degree to which the medium may intrude, or require to be isolated from other media (e.g. rear projection slides with sound commentary could interfere with the visitors' concentration on an adjacent display board).

10. *Minimum visitor effort*   The degree of effort required: it should not be implied that a visitor should be able to see and hear everything without exerting some effort, but until his (or her) attention has been captured, the visitor will be more likely to respond favourably if the effort required is kept to a minimum.

11. *Simplicity*   The ease of installing or introducing the medium without excessive preliminary research or design.

12. *Appearance* The degree of visual intrusion caused by the medium.

13. *Effect on resource* The extent to which the medium may cause damage to the habitat (e.g. by erosion of surfaces, noise, or other effects on wildlife).

14. *Durability* How resistant the medium is likely to be to normal weathering or normal wear and tear.

15. *Resistance to vandalism* The degree to which the medium is vulnerable to wilful damage.

16. *Reliability* How far the medium is prone to failure or breakdown.

17. *Cost* Relative indication of low capital and operating costs.

18. *Expendability* The ease of maintenance, repair or replacement.

This list of criteria for evaluation is somewhat dated in that the criteria themselves are objective. It is clear that the monitoring process needs to pick up the effectiveness of the interpretive medium in meeting financial constraints or visitor safety. However, it is equally if not more important to assess the actual effectiveness of the medium in meeting the demands of the public. Indeed, the best method of motivating some groups is not through traditional or more commonly accepted methods of interpretation, but through more innovative or unusual methods. Playing table tennis with a group of unemployed school leavers might not be considered as interpretation; if, however, this is what is necessary to gain the interest of some groups prior to their visiting a country park, it could legitimately be thought of as part of the interpretive process. Recent thinking (Countryside Commission, 1987 for example) indicates that the success of interpretive programmes should, in the future, be gauged by the degree to which the public are encouraged to visit the countryside. This implies a need to reassess the effectiveness of interpretive media. These new developments and projections are discussed later, but notwithstanding these, Pennyfather's original assessment of the criteria of effectiveness remains a valid tool for examining interpretive media.

9.2.1 Types of interpretive media

The media types assessed by Pennyfather can be grouped into five categories.

1. *Personal service* Interpretation by a guide or expert in person by means of talking, demonstrating, illustrating, explaining and answering questions, e.g. lectures, guided walks.

2. *Participating media*   Media which assist the visitor who is prepared to make some effort in seeing or identifying natural features, living organisms or processes or which include some other elements of visitor participation and encourage use of the other senses as well as sight, e.g. courses on country crafts, nature rambles.

3. *Live display media*   Media, including gadgets, which facilitate the display of live objectives or processes with minimum effort, but which do not include any appreciable element of visitor participation, e.g. aquaria, dramatized tableaux.

4. *Static display media*   Media which facilitate the display of inanimate and silent objects or inanimate representations of live objects or processes, and which do not include any appreciable element of visitor participation, e.g. publications, exhibitions.

5. *Gadgets*   Mechanical, optical or electrical devices which introduce sound, light or movement for added realism or illustration, or to improve communications with the visitor, e.g. films, *son et lumière*.

Cross tabulating media with the criteria for effectiveness could give an objective assessment of various media. The point that must be borne in mind when looking at media options is expressed by the Countryside Commission (1979). 'There are rarely occasions where the choice of medium is a foregone conclusion. The interpretive planner should analyse the message he wishes to get across and what there is about it that suggests a particular means of presentation.' Added to this are the recurring questions of 'who is the interpretive medium meant to influence?' and 'what is the objective behind wanting to interpret a site in the first place?'.

9.3   DETAILS OF COMMON TECHNIQUES

Notwithstanding the wide range of interpretive media available to the countryside manager, one of a relatively small number of media usually forms the cornerstone of the interpretive process on most sites or situations. Clearly each site or situation will use the interpretive media in different ways, but there does exist a core of common techniques for interpretation that are used frequently by countryside managers to interpret the countryside, their work or other aspects of the manager's remit. This section deals with four specific techniques, each of which, it could be argued, is a series of techniques. However, for the sake of simplicity the basic details of each technique are given; and variations need to be explored by individual managers for each situation. The four techniques are: interpretive panels; leaflets; audio visual displays; and live acts.

9.3.1 Interpretive panels

Throughout this discussion on interpretive media, it is essential that the original definition of 'interpretation' is borne in mind, because in each individual medium the concept of interpretation is clearly pre-understood. This is suggested by Lindesay and Dagnall (1985) who indicate that: 'An interpretive panel is not an amenity instructional or directional sign. It usually contains a combination of explanatory text, drawing photograph or map imaginatively presented to tell a story about an object or place.' This is a narrower but similar statement to Tilden's original definition of interpretation. The interpretive panel must therefore adhere to the basic principles of interpretation, as too must all other media.

There are a number of basic points that need to be accommodated when preparing a single panel or a series of panels. These basic points go someway towards influencing design and determining the best method of constructing a panel. The points mainly indicate the fundamental pitfalls which await the countryside manager who wishes to consider using interpretive panels.

1. Is a panel acceptable at all? Some historically important sites, for example, may be totally spoiled by an interpretive panel.
2. Is a panel the best medium? This re-emphasizes the need for objectives and a means of evaluating interpretive media.
3. Locate any panels tactfully. Panels can be located on plinths, walls, be freestanding or on columns, for example.
4. Design the panel with its location in mind. Colour, size, shape, images and other considerations need to be acknowledged relative to the site.
5. How close to the panel can prospective readers get? This will have an influence on panel size, text size and overall design.
6. What form will illustrations take? Illustrations can, if used well, almost totally obviate the need for text, on the other hand technical drawings can leave most visitors puzzled or confused.
7. Maps are difficult to memorize. A map on an interpretive panel cannot be carried around by the visitor, and maps are also sometimes difficult to read.
8. The content of the panel must be relevant and obviously so; furthermore, this relevance is not simply in the mind of the panel designer but more importantly in the mind of the visitor.

Interpretive Panels: Almost standard at most countryside sites, and like everything else require careful planning.

9. It is not possible to say all that could be said on one or even a series of panels. It is often better to try to make only one or two points rather than a whole series of points.
10. Text should be simple and clear. It is surprising how complex interpretive text can become. Text should relate to the visitor, not the academic or researcher.

A fuller discussion of these points is given by Piersenne (1985) and Parfit (1985).

The decision made on these basic guidelines will, to a certain extent, determine the manufacturing of the panel: what materials should be used, what detailing is necessary, etc.

Construction material for interpretive panels can vary according to the requirements of the manager. Research has shown (Lindesay and Dagnall, op. cit.) that the most popular materials are melamine laminates, glass reinforced polyester, silk screen printing on acrylic or polycarbonates, self-adhesive letter, printing on rigid PVC, routed wood and cast metal. Each of these methods has its own advantages and disadvantages, based mostly upon the product's cost, durability and maintenance. Routed wood is relatively cheap for example, while melamine products can be expensive as too can glass reinforced polyester. The maintenance requirements of each are different; for example, routed wood requires regular inspections and, once it has been vandalized, it is difficult if not impossible to repair.

Materials also have implications for design and vice versa, with detail drawings and lengthy text being impossible to reproduce on wooden surfaces. Where such technical detail is required, the choice of materials is therefore limited. This clearly dictates that the manager must become acquainted with the construction techniques of interpretive panels, or alternatively delegate this task to someone else. Should the latter course be taken, the manager must, as always, be prepared to accept the interpreters knowledge of the subject and allow the responsibility for interpretation to rest firmly with the interpreter.

9.3.2 Leaflets

Many of the basic guidelines above are equally applicable to the process of producing leaflets: the acceptability of a leaflet, the design of leaflet with the users in mind, the content of the leaflet, and so on. A leaflet, or guide, does however have many qualities which sets it apart from other interpretive media and which need to be understood by the manager.

First and foremost is the target audience. The group for whom any publication is intended will determine the publication's layout, script, illustrations – indeed, the whole production of the leaflet or guide. This can be learned most graphically from the various formats and language used by newspapers; their approach to any news article is geared to the newspaper editor's knowledge of his or her target readership. The interpreter must also have a good working knowledge of the target audience but the production of the finished publication will be tempered by other objectives and/or constraints such as the technicalities of the subject to be interpreted or the financial constraints of an interpretive budget.

The other objectives and constraints are discussed in *Environmental Interpretation* (December, 1985 issue). For example, a leaflet is a one-way medium, which must therefore prejudge any questions that the visitor might ask as a result of a visit to the site or feature. Similarly, reading a leaflet requires some effort on the part of the visitor, so any publication must be attractive, interesting but, above all, readable. The attention span of most people to an issue with which they are not familiar is measured in seconds not minutes, so if the casual visitor is expected to read the leaflet it cannot afford to be technical. Alternatively, if the target audience is not the casual or lay visitor but a more technical or environmentally aware group (such as other leaflet producers!), the production of a guide could be advantageous because it can be taken off site and read comprehensively. The production of a publication, therefore, has a wider context within which it is placed. The manager and the interpreter must be aware of this context.

There is a large amount of technical information which needs to be understood by the manager or the interpreter before a leaflet can be produced. Knowledge of the target audience has been mentioned but equally important is an understanding of the subject matter – the countryside or some elements of it. Whether or not a leaflet is to be produced in-house or by external contract designers/printers, the manager or one of his or her staff must be able to understand precisely what is going to be said to whom. Preparing a brief for external contract designers is a sure way of identifying whether these basic prerequisites have been understood.

Once those basic facts have been established, all other issues can be seen as parts of the process of meeting these objectives or constraints to the process.

The planning process for interpretive publications involves several specific stages, namely: establishing the cost of leaflets/budgets available, deciding upon the format, designing the leaflet, printing and distributing. It is suggested above that the countryside manager may not have detailed knowledge about the technical processes of the designing and printing stages of leaflet production. What will be needed by the manager is sufficient knowledge about his or her own objectives and constraints in order to prepare a detailed brief for designers.

The design brief should be undertaken in discussion with the designer.

The manager should not have fixed ideas about the finished article – the designer is the expert in his or her own field. However, the manager should have some idea about the final size of the required leaflet, how many are required, the number of pages, colours, finish (matt, gloss, mixture), delivery dates and the number required in the future (a 'run on' for the leaflet).

Close contact is needed between the manager and the designer throughout the whole process once the brief has been established. The designer will produce for the manager typescripts (or copy) of a text prepared by the manager, illustrations, arrange these into a pre-agreed format for a 'mock up' (or paste up). The mock up can be changed and altered into a final format (agreed text size, juxtaposition of illustrations, and so on). The final paste up should be clearly checked for mistakes. Once the paste up has been cleared (and the manager will usually have to sign off this particular stage to accept responsibility for any spelling mistakes or other errors) it will go for printing. Again the designer should ensure that colour and reproduction are acceptable, if it has been included as part of the brief. In truth, most designers would wish to see their work through the printing stage, rather than allow someone else to handle their work and thus risk 'mistakes' in quality.

In planning a series of leaflets and other printed material, the manager must accept that a house-style or continuity of appearance of posters/leaflets/fly-sheets and other related publications is valuable. Pennyfather (1975) suggests that leaflets and related materials are cost effective and efficient for relating to visitor groups and good at linking with surroundings with as much effort as the visitor wishes to exert. However, Pennyfather also suggests that leaflets have poor impact and poor flexibility. This serves to re-emphasize the contention that the leaflet is one of the most commonplace interpretive media, yet requires careful planning if it is not to fall into the problems identified by Pennyfather.

9.3.3 Audio visual techniques

The impact of audio visual media on the public is well known. Advertising on television, for example, has an enormous impact upon the viewing public. As the Countryside Commission (1980b) states: 'There is no doubt that it works', but the Commission continues 'but when is it appropriate, to apply these techniques in countryside interpretation?' In answer to this question, the Commission suggests that there are two areas within which audio visual techniques are particularly powerful:

1. when their use provides the best means of interpretation or the means which is likely to reach the wider audience having due regard to all constraints, e.g. availability, practicability and cost;

2. when canvassing the sympathy, support or even just the attention of the uncommitted.

Pennyfather (1975) lists most of the audio visual media under 'Gadgets', however, only five years later, the Countryside Commission produced a booklet devoted to the subject of audio visual techniques in countryside interpretation. This reflects that what was once seen as unusual or gimmicky is now accepted as main stream. Present ownership levels of televisions in Britain are around 95–98% and the ownership levels of video recorders are approaching equally high levels. In short, people are used to technology and are used to absorbing the messages transmitted through such technology. For this reason alone, audio visual techniques are becoming an integral part of the countryside manager's interpretive repertoire.

The Countryside Commission (1979) identifies some four methods of audio techniques, four visual interpretive techniques and some nine combined audio visual techniques (Table 9.1). All of these techniques fit into the continuum of interpretive techniques, covering 'blind spots' that other techniques have and introducing advantages that other techniques do not possess. The advantages of audio visual techniques can be summarized as follows:

Table 9.1. *Audio-visual techniques used in countryside interpretation*

A) AUDIO SYSTEMS
    i The audio station
    ii The portable tape-player
    iii The inductive loop aerial system
    iv The listening post

B) VISUAL SYSTEMS
    i Pictures
    ii Models
    iii Closed circuit television
    iv Other visual devices

C) COMBINED AUDIO AND VISUAL SYSTEMS
    i Cine film
    ii Video
    iii Son et lumière
    iv Slide-tape
    v Single projector slide-tape
    vi Twin projector slide-tape
    vii Multi-image slide-tape
    viii Multi media
    ix Tape recorders for audio-visual use

Source: Countryside Commission (1980b).

1. They fill a place between personal and purely written techniques.
2. They offer a medium commonly experienced by the public, giving an opportunity to reach almost all of the visiting public.
3. Drama, timing, and special effects can all be introduced through the numerous techniques.
4. Most audio visual techniques do not require full-time attendance from staff.
5. A high standard of presentation can be assured almost continually, presenting the public with the quality that they are used to from television, videos or similar techniques.

Clearly, too, audio visual techniques carry with them disadvantages which are mostly a result of the sophistication of the media. This level of sophistication not only puts the actual management of the media outside the scope of all but the most expert individuals, but the media also usually require special locations for them to have their best effect. Sophistication too does not come cheaply and such items as video films and integrated slide shows are expensive.

The risk involved with committing such relatively large amounts of money can be minimized with careful planning. Firstly, the manager must be aware of all the basic elements of interpretive planning: the objectives, target audience, the issues to be interpreted, and so on. If these are fully understood, the sophistication of the techniques adopted by the manager will survive better and will not eclipse the actual message to be interpreted. Furthermore, the manager will also need an understanding of (or, in some circumstances, a detailed working knowledge of) the technicalities of the media. While there is no room here to devote space to analysing the technical detail of running an audio visual programme, the Countryside Commission (1980b) offers a checklist for providing an efficient audio visual display.

Pennyfather's assertion that 'the media in this group (audio visual) may be regarded as substitutes for use where a more dynamic, direct approach is impracticable' is now clearly out of date. The public almost expect the modern 'gadgets' to be used in interpretive programmes. For his or her part, however, the manager must accept that audio visual media form only part of a wider and more diverse portfolio of interpretive techniques, and are not always the most appropriate media from that portfolio.

9.3.4 Live arts

Interpretation through live preformances is a wide area of expertise in its own right. Live art can cover anything from mock battles by the

Sealed Knot or similar organizations to environmental theatre groups. It might also cover working museums, with staff in period costumes, or indeed any 'live' activity which helps in the interpretive process. For the countryside manager, therefore, it represents one available means for interpreting a site in a wider repertoire. Early examples of 'live' interpretation concentrated upon the interpretation of the historic perspective of sites – Pennyfather (1975), for example, suggests that live interpretation is restricted to 'costumed guides, period play enactment and period musical performances'. Furthermore, his analysis of the techniques was not too flattering, with only costumed guides having anything above a 'fair' impact upon visitors, for example. This historical aspect to live interpretation has remained an integral part of live performances (*Environmental Interpretation*, 1987, for example). However, the live, dynamic approach to interpretation is one of the more innovative areas of interpretation. Public involvement is becoming important for interpretation not only in Britain but also in Europe and the United States of America. This relatively recent exploration of more dynamic interpretive media results partly from the large number of urban-based people using the countryside for a variety of reasons. For the same reasons that modern technologically advanced media are now an integral part of the countryside manager's range of options, so too are live media; many of the urban-based population not only expect or like to see live performance, but can only understand or begin to accept media with which they are familiar. Therefore, in order to begin the interpretive process at all, the interest and the attention of the visitor has to be caught. Interpreters must 'start where the learner is, not where you are' (Van Matre, 1974).

9.4 MANAGING THE INTERPRETIVE PROCESS

The interpretive process needs managing in much the same way that the manager needs to control other aspects of countryside work. This, therefore, involves the stages of planning, designing, implementing and monitoring. It also involves funding any proposals for interpretation. The planning, designing and implementation functions have all been dealt with; the management of the system that concerns us here is therefore the monitoring and financing of the interpretation.

9.4.1 Monitoring

Interpretation is increasingly becoming not only an educative and/or informative process, but it is also becoming increasingly enjoyable. For many people multi-media shows of live 'battles' are more exciting to watch or participate in than a guided walk on a wet afternoon. It is therefore tempting for the manager to measure success in terms of the number of people attending an interpretive event (or activity, which interpretation is increasingly becoming) or the number of leaflets that are distributed or sold within a financial year. This is clearly missing the basic *raison d'être* of interpretation. The success lies not simply in the number of people attending or participating in events or activities but in the knowledge and understanding of countryside issues (be they ecology, landscape, rural sociology or history) that individuals take with them after the interpretive activity has stopped. The Countryside Commission (1987) identify targets for awareness and understanding not in terms of numbers of people but in terms of 'better awareness by the occasional visitor of the opportunities for enjoying the countryside' and 'people wishing to explore the countryside should be aware of their basic rights and responsibilities'. The countryside manager must therefore ensure that a monitoring procedure is in place that records the effectiveness of chosen interpretive media.

First and foremost within this process is an understanding of the aims of interpretation. Several aims have been explained earlier in this chapter, but for each manager, however, there will be specific objectives which relate to target groups and the levels of understanding which the manager wishes to see absorbed by the target groups.

There are several ways of establishing the effectiveness of the interpretive medium, once the objectives have been explained in a way that can easily be monitored. The commonest methods for monitoring interpretation are:

Questionnaires A questionnaire which is designed to ask target groups about their ability to absorb interpretive messages is one of the simplest and most effective ways of getting directly to the individuals concerned. As with all questionnaire surveys, the correct methodology must be followed (TRRU, 1977) and care must be taken to ensure that the interpretive process itself does not become compromised by the questionnaire, or that the questionnaire does not reduce the actual enjoyment of the interpretive activity. Notwithstanding these factors, regular use of questionnaire surveys provides a good picture of the effectiveness of interpretation.

Observation Simply observing individuals absorbing interpretive activities or information gives a good indication of the impact that a particular technique is having. Observation, for example, will reveal any particular weak spots in an exhibition where visitors simply fail to stop and look. Similarly, observation will reveal whether hour-long visitors are

House Style: A corporate style for information boards lets visitors know at a glance whether they are welcome on site, and what they can expect.

willing to observe a display or watch a video. Standard data do exist for parameters such as these but detailed site specific data are still valuable.

Research Research data already cover a wide range of topics that can increase the manager's understanding of the criteria which influence an individual's ability to absorb information. Such research includes information on the reading age at which leaflets should be written to allow access by the majority of the population (in fact it is at about the reading age of 8 or 9 – quite a surprise to most people). Data might also include surveys on the popularity of two different media giving the same message or their relative effectiveness. Most managers do not have the resources to undertake all the necessary research to fully understand the interpretive process. For this reason, much research is undertaken either by academic or research institutes or, alternatively, by consultants employed by managers to identify and provide information to cover gaps in the manager's knowledge.

The monitoring process also covers the ongoing study of the impact that interpretation has on the resources that the manager controls. A visitor centre, for example, will undoubtedly increase visitor numbers and have a major impact on the flow of visitors in and around the site. This in turn will have an impact upon vegetation, footpath surfaces and congestion for example. The manager must therefore be aware of all of these potential impacts and, where necessary, monitor them as the interpretation proceeds.

9.4.2 Finances

The financial implication of an interpretation programme are identical to all aspects of management. The finances require planning, controlling and monitoring. The budgets required to implement interpretation form an integral part of the manager's overall budgets and therefore are subject to the same rules and principles. It is important to stress, however, that budgets to support interpretation are not afterthoughts or gestures. In the same way that interpretation is a key element of countryside management, so too do the budgets form a vital part of the funding process. As the Centre for Environmental Interpretation (1989) has suggested, the funding of many interpretive facilities is woefully underestimated. This leads to an ineffective programme which, in turn, leads to a lack of faith in the ability of interpretation to influence visitors or provide a good return on money.

While interpretation must clearly be budgeted for from within core funds, the manager is able to use the various media to generate additional income, which in turn supports the overall work of the manager or, more specifically, allows a greater financial commitment to interpretation. In short, the methods that the manager might use to generate additional income are:

Sponsorship Many interpretive media are ideal vehicles for organizations to offer sponsorship to the manager. Leaflets, for example, can be paid for by local businesses or sympathetic organizations. Many national and local companies offer sponsorship for leaflets, videos and even live display interpretation, particularly in the voluntary sector.

Advertising Closely allied to sponsorship is the additional money generated through advertising. Again, many organizations see the target groups for interpretation programmes as being similar to their own target groups – schools, families or ethnic groups. Many smaller interpretive ventures can be self-financed through advertising alone.

Charging policy As interpretation is often an enjoyable experience as well as an educational experience, it is often viable for the manager to charge for the activities. Farm open days, live displays and large audio visual displays are all entertaining as well as enjoyable. As core funding becomes more difficult to secure within many countryside organizations it is increasingly necessary to generate funds from a wider variety of sources. Thus, many organizations now charge for guided walks and ranger services.

Grants The subject of grant is dealt with more exhaustively in Chapter 10. However, many grant-aiding organizations are willing to sponsor interpretation. This grant aid falls into one of two categories: capital in which the grant aid for interpretation forms part of a large practical project and revenue where the grant aid is directed exclusively towards interpretation.

Each of these additional means of generating income adds work to the financial management of the organization. Cash flow, staffing, security, stocking and sales, for example, are all elements of interpretation which require managing once the process is in operation.

9.4.3 Other management

While the monitoring and financial aspect of interpretation are of most immediate importance to the manager, other aspects also require management. These are summarized by the Countryside Commission (1979) as:

1. Control of visitors
2. Site management

3. Maintenance and repair
4. Emergency planning
5. Staffing
6. Publicity
7. Relations with other organizations.

While this list is comprehensive each manager will be faced with a unique situation which demands that some elements of the interpretation pro-gramme will require closer management than others. That decision lies with the manager.

9.5 NEW INITIATIVES

Interpretation is a continually developing science, which interacts closely with many other activities, such as education, recreation, science, art and threatre to name just a few. As a result, the manager is often hard pressed to keep abreast of new development as well as undertake his or her other duties. For this reason, if for no other, it is often important that the manager, if possible, delegates responsibility for interpretation. This allows an individual (or group of individuals) the time and resources not only to keep aware of new developments in interpretation but also to mould these new techniques for their own site specific purposes. Of course, not all managers will be in a position to delegate and in this position the manager must take a careful look at his or her priorities, but in any event high within these must be interpretation.

Several new approaches to interpretation have developed since Tilden first tried to define the process. These have come from a variety of sources which confirms that the number of spheres of human activity with which interpretation has contact is greater than for any other function of the countryside manager. The following analysis draws out some of the more important strands of the new initiatives.

9.5.1 Acclimatization

One of the strongest modern trends in British interpretive techniques arose, as did many movements within countryside management, in the United States. The pioneer of the approach of acclimatization is Steve Van Matre. In 1972 the first book appeared, and this was expanded upon two years later in 1974. The approach is geared to total sensory immersion in the environment using initially the basic senses. Thus phrases such as 'Listen to natural voices, everything has its own sound. Go sit and listen', 'Touch with your hand but feel with your body',

'Trace the smells around you', and 'Pay attention to your feelings' are almost designed to give your some notion of how the individual should, through acclimatization, begin to relate to his or her environment. It is not enough to simply look at things or even touch them in a cursory way. The essence of acclimatization is to replace what many feel to be the lost contact between humans and the natural environment. Acclimatization is therefore not a specific technique which is comparable to, say, a slide tape display but is more of an approach to the process of interpretation. This is summarized by Van Matre (1974) through his own belief in the environmental qualities that he wishes to interpret: 'I am concerned about essential concepts of beauty. I believe natural resources are not things but communities, I believe that self-awareness follows natural awareness and . . . good teachers do not teach; they create exciting learning situations.'

This approach to interpretation gives rise to several specific characteristics of acclimatization. Firstly, it requires more concentrated and lengthy contact with individuals. Children respond particularly well to some of the techniques, but even they may feel some confusion about the things required of them. Because of the time required to re-awaken people's awareness of the natural environment to such a detailed extent, only a relatively small number of people can be effectively dealt with in an acclimatization programme. Perhaps, for these reasons, children tend to be targeted through such programmes. Furthermore, it is likely that children have lost less of their natural awareness than their adult counterparts. Pretending to be an insect will raise an infinite number of hang-ups in most adults.

The techniques used in acclimatization also tend to be characteristics. They revolve around the individual's relationship with the environment and the group relationships of people and their combined relationship to that environment. Therefore, at an individual level, participants must 'let the natural world engulf them and examine things from varying view points . . . it is not possible to describe the feeling of wholeness . . . go out and experience it for yourself' (Van Matre, 1974). The teacher must lead in all exercises through introducing techniques, such as pretending to be a movie camera, looking for negative space, echoing and looking for natural friends.

The process of acclimatization is therefore concerned not only with an approach to relationships within the natural world, but also with specific techniques geared towards awakening awareness of these relationships. This is all based upon an underlying assumption that 'Urban life militates against natural awareness. There are just too many obstacles.' It is therefore impossible to indicate briefly how a successful acclimatization programme might be assembled because, in part, the programme would aim at counterbalancing the desensitizing process of urbanization. This puts many of the issues relevant to acclimatization closer to green politics and environmental morality, than to an interpretive programme. (These aspects are discussed in the final chapter.) For the countryside manager, however, acclimatization represents a new approach to environmental interpretation which may or may not have a place within a wider interpretation programme. Acclimatization is an integral part of the overall process of interpretation and, at its final conclusion, provides a unique framework for environmental awareness in its own right. As a self-confessed aphorist, Van Matre makes use of phrases to summarize entire trains of thought. In his own words: 'Acclimatization was like six hours of preparation before playing the game . . . acclimatization is the game.'

9.5.2 Urban interpretation

Urban and rural interpretation are coming closer together often with similar aims. Urban interpretation is aimed at increasing participant awareness of the urban environment, often as a lead in to other, wider objectives. It is therefore relevant to look at some of the initiatives arising in urban interpretation and their relationship to countryside management.

In one sense, acclimatization as a concept has been introduced into the urban environment and is used on many urban fringe or urban sites. The 'Countrywings Training Programme' is based on the belief that 'acclimatization techniques are as demanding and educational in an urban setting as they are in the countryside' (Vasey, 1989). Thus the excitement and discovery available within the urban environment needs interpreting and new techniques are needed not only to gain the participants' enthusiasm but also to cross possible gaps between the manager's attitudes and those of the participants. The concept of camping out in the 'urban jungle' or 'rock climbing' on building sites may therefore appear strange to many people, but techniques such as these are used to develop individual confidence (Vangelder, 1986). This is, however, more 'natural' than going on a guided walk within a country park, or reading a leaflet for people raised in urban areas. Whether or not the individuals concerned ever see the countryside is, in many respects, irrelevant. What is important is that the participants become aware of their environment and can come to terms with it through physical contact. In this respect, Countrywings is intrinsically bound up with community initiatives, guided play, facilitators and directed group work and a host of community-based activities, rather than the traditional countryside approach of resource-based activities.

Other urban initiatives are similarly valuable because of the emphasis that is placed upon attempts to influence and encourage target groups and individuals that have, in the past, not been attracted by more familiar countryside interpretation. Operation Gateway (see Case Study, Chapter 4), for example, represents an attempt to give ethnic groups the confidence to use the countryside for recreational and other uses. This mainly involves working with target groups initially in their own familiar predominantly urban environment. In this and other cases the ultimate objective is to introduce other reticent groups to the attractions, value and beauty of the countryside.

It is irrelevant here that some initiatives do not have this countryside objective as their final goal: the important issue is that the urban environment is producing many innovative techniques and approaches to interpretation. This innovation can be seen in the media used for the interpretation and in the targeting of groups that, until relatively recently, have not been influenced by countryside interpretation. In any event, the intermix of urban and rural interpretation techniques has opened up new roles for countryside managers, and countryside rangers in particular.

9.5.3   Future trends

The future of interpretation will undoubtedly be one of change: change in order to maintain the interest of existing markets and, more particularly, to introduce more people to the process of interpretation. The basic question which, in many senses, is as yet unanswered is: 'How can we reach individuals who, to date, have not shown a great degree of interest in the rural environment?' In a purely economic sense, this move towards new target groups represents a risk because of the uncertainty of success in an unknown area. Furthermore, there is also a great degree of constraint on the interpreter in that the product (in this case, the countryside) is a predetermined entity. While its many attractions can be promoted to various groups, or a variety of events can be staged to attract visitors, any major attempt to change the countryside will undermine the very subject of the interpretation. In this sense the countryside cannot be changed too greatly in order to attract people who, from all external signs, are ambivalent to the countryside.

This is the paradox that lives at the heart of countryside interpretation: should any attempt be made to interest people in the countryside who do not appear to want to be interested in the countryside!

Notwithstanding this apparent dilemma, the Countryside Commission is committed to 'experiments which improve awareness' (Countryside Commission, 1987). The underlying promise of this desire to seek new techniques is that awareness will lead to interest, which in turn will lead to desire to increase knowledge about the countryside. This will finally give individuals a greater appreciation of the countryside, and will enable them to both enjoy and protect that resource for the future. For this reason, experiments are vital. To this end, the Countryside Commission suggest several areas of attention for countryside managers and interpreters. These include:

- a new countryside presence in large towns and cities;
- creating neighbourhood and local countryside information packs;
- testing the potential of new media, and outlets for interpretation including radio, newspapers, pubs, shops, garages and estate agents.

Underlying these new proposals is the objective of increasing knowledge of the countryside in a wider proportion of the general public than at present. Clearly, however, each individual manager needs to determine whether existing target groups should form future targets or whether new areas of activity are needed to interest and influence other groups. Whatever the answer to this particular question, the manager will not only need to keep the underlying principles firmly in view, but also accept that change will be inevitable in order to provide even a minimal interpretive service interesting and informative to that public.

9.6 SUMMARY

Interpretation is a process; it is not static. It therefore needs close management if it is to succeed in meeting objectives. This clearly means that interpretation requires planning, implementing and monitoring and, just as importantly, needs to be integrated fully with other elements of countryside management. Interpretation is not simply the leaflet that appears at the end of the development of a country park, or the video that accompanies a nature reserve. Interpretation needs to form part of the core management process, and within that four basic questions need to be asked: why provide interpretation?; what might be interpreted?; for whom is interpretation intended?; and how might the interpretation be undertaken?

The techniques and objectives of interpretation are constantly developing. For this reason the manager must pay particular attention and remain aware of these changes. While the countryside resource may change only relatively slowly, the methods available to the manager to interpret that resource change rapidly. An innovative interpretation programme therefore lives centrally in the countryside manager's workload.

9.7   CASE STUDIES

Interpretation covers a vast array of techniques and media, as well as a wide variety of emphasis of objectives (education, enjoyment, information and promotion to name just four). Any analysis of specific techniques must be seen as an attempt to fit underlying principles to case studies. The two case studies presented here represent two different approaches to interpretation. The first is farm open days, which are within themselves a varied category. Farm open days are, however, a technique (albeit in a very broad sense) used to interpret a very amorphous resource: the farmed countryside. They therefore give us an opportunity to assess an approach to interpreting a non-specific type of environment. By way of contrast, the Tatton Park Interpretive Study (United States National Park Service, 1975) is a site specific plan for a countryside facility in Cheshire. Furthermore, the Tatton Park Study is interesting in that it was prepared by the United States National Park Service and is therefore a link between the initial work undertaken within the United States and the adoption and subsequent adaption of these techniques and attitudes within Great Britain.

Farm open days and the Tatton Park Study are therefore both very specific issues, yet at the same time are examples of wider interpretive concern.

9.7.1   Farm open days

Farm open days fulfil several objectives. They provide an enjoyable experience for the visitors, with a variety of activities, demonstrations and 'live exhibits' being available: they can provide a focal point for a day out in the countryside; they can give the farmer some extra income if visitors are charged for car parking, entry onto the farm, farm produce that is sold to the visitors; and the farm open day can provide a useful and relatively unique means of interpreting the farmed countryside. A farm which opens its gates to visitors still remains at heart a working farm – basically the real thing as opposed to, say, an urban farm or a working museum. Notwithstanding this fact, if the farm open day is to succeed in its interpretive objectives (and this is one aspect with which the countryside manager must be concerned) the basic rules must still be applied. Often, it is not the farmer himself who is in the best position to make sure that the interpretive process fits in with all of the other important issues, but the countryside manager, be it through a joint venture between the farmer and the local authority or through the manager being employed as a consultant by the farmer.

The farm open day has been seen as a viable means of interpreting the agricultural environment for many years. For example, the Countryside Commission (1974) ran a series of on-site studies into farm open days, suggesting that farm open days were valuable methods of:

(a) increasing the visitors' enjoyment of farmed countryside;
(b) increasing the public's understanding of farming and the countryside;
(c) reducing conflict between farmers and visitors.

This list of objectives was further expanded (Countryside Commission, 1980a) to include:

(d) to allow the agricultural community to understand the urban visitors' viewpoint of the countryside.

In addition, other benefits to the farmers were identified as: publicizing farm gate sales; contributing to village/town life through a regular event; experimenting in recreational provision before establishing a more commercially based recreation/ tourism concern.

Any farmer or countryside manager may wish to provide a farm open day for any one of the above reasons. It is vital, therefore, that the manager establishes where in a list of priorities the interpretive processes come. Having established this, the actual methods of interpretation can be determined. Prior to this, however, the manager must also be prepared to work with the farmer to establish target markets, not only to help determine the technical level of the information, but also to provide the necessary background for other decisions such as advertising, interpretive techniques, facilities, etc.

Studies show that over one-third of all visitors to farm open days are children under 14 (obviously for the most part with their parents). Most have no links with farming and most do not travel more than a 20-km round trip for the open day. Even these basic facts can begin to add some information to the manager's decision-making process. If the interpretive process is to be geared to the visitor's requirements, these facts are crucial.

For the farmer, there are clearly many other considerations that must be accommodated before an interpretive programme is developed. These include the nature of the farm itself, other features which could be interpreted (such as old buildings, archaeological remains or valuable habitat) and what damage might be sustained on the farm. The farmer must also be prepared to examine his own motives for wanting to run a farm open day – if finances are the main motivating force, it might be more appropriate to forego the interpretation and establish a more clear-cut commercial venture.

However, once it has been established that interpretation is one of the most important objectives for the farm open day, the methods of interpretation can be decided upon. These fall into the categories identified by Pennyfather (op. cit.) and might include guided walks, demonstrations, leaflets, panels, slide shows and special events. Matching the methods of interpretation with the target markets, the farmer's requirements and the constraints or opportunities offered by the farm is the role of the manager.

Survey work which supports the 1974 Countryside Commission report indicates

Open Farm: Popular with a wide cross-section of people, and can generate extra income for farmers.

that some 85% of farmers in the study used leaflets as a means of interpretation and a further 75% used guides; usually the farmer or a fellow agriculturalist. While these figures will change over the years, they do emphasize that matching the market (largely under 14 years old) with interpretive techniques (leaflets and untrained guides) require thought and attention. While a farmer would not perhaps feel at home running an acclimatization course on his farm, the manager should explore with the farmer innovative ways of meeting their mutual objectives. Most farmers in Britain are expert at producing food by one means or another; it is a little too much to expect them to be professional interpreters as well.

Farm open days represent a good example of an event that combines interpretation with an enjoyable and recreational experience. Furthermore, it allows an opportunity to use several different techniques in interpretation on one site. Finally, it represents a blend of private and public involvement coming together. All in all, farm open days represent a valuable means of interpreting the countryside, but only if the farmer's and the countryside manager's objectives are clearly established at the outset and expertise is brought to bear when necessary for effective interpretation.

9.7.2 Tatton Park study

Tatton Park is a property owned by the National Trust but managed by the Cheshire County Council's Countryside Service. It is a varied resource with an eighteenth-century hall, 60 or so acres of gardens, around 1000 acres of accessible parkland, an older hall, dating from Tudor times and a wide variety of other specific features such as lakes, woodland, farmland and additional buildings.

The Tatton Park interpretive Study (United States National Park Service, 1975) established a number of subjects for the interpretation of the resource, these being:

1. evolution of the estate from Tudor times to the present day;
2. the socio-political world of the house owners – the Egertons;
3. the life of the servants and others who worked on the estate;
4. the mediaeval socio-economic environment, based around the Old Hall;
5. cohesion of the internal (built) environment and the external (parkland) environment into an understandable whole;
6. participation in the experience of the historical context of the Hall and grounds;
7. environmental awareness and knowledge of the countryside forming part of the interpretive package;
8. interpretation of supporting management objectives;
9. not overburdening the surrounding countryside or communities as a result of the interpretive programme.

The proposed means of implementing these objectives may, today, appear commonplace, but the strategic overview when produced was innovative.

The formula involved extended opening hours (both daily and seasonally) to spread visitor pressures and the introduction of fees to visit the house to finance, among other things, the development of the interpretive process. The actual techniques suggested involved standard procedures such as adequate signs, interpretation boards, guided walks and a series of visitor centre orientation points. These orientation points were suggested for the courtyard area (mainly to interpret the Hall and the household) and the Old Hall (to interpret the mediaeval context of the parkland). In themselves, these orientation points were proposed to contain a range of interpretive features including audio visual displays, costumed performances and static but changing display panels.

The report also identifies the need for the interpretive process to develop in conjunction with the physical fabric of the overall site. For example, 'Consideration at some future date should also be accorded to returning the courtyard to its appearance in the days of the Egertons. This is long-range indeed, but the proposals would do much to enhance the Tatton atmosphere.'

The priorities identified by the study relate directly to the objectives, including 'Prepare self-guide trail on a theme consistent with overall interpretive proposals for Tatton Park, to replace the existing Nature Trail' and 'Produce free general guide to facilities, services and opportunities available at Tatton.'

It is also interesting to note that later priorities concentrate upon specifically targeting children with the interpretive material and the provision of off-site interpretive services. These priorities now match those of the Countryside Commission in their proposals for the future, particularly the concept of 'off site' interpretation.

The Tatton Park study provides a good framework for developing a site-based interpretive programme and, indeed, it is more than likely that many similar sites will have similar objectives and have similar means of implementing them. The process of assessing the resource, setting objectives, identifying means of achieving objectives, prioritizing work and making judgements to guide future work is, even some time after the original study, a sound basis upon which to base interpretive studies.

BIBLIOGRAPHY

Aldridge, D. (1975) *Guide to Countryside Interpretation: Part One: Principles of Interpretation and Interpretive Planning* HMSO, Edinburgh.

Beechel, J. (1975) *Interpretation for Handicapped Persons*, National Parks Service, Seattle.

Binks, G. (1981) Acclimatization, *Environmental Interpretation*, CEI, Manchester, Vol. 17.

Centre for Environmental Interpretation (1987) Focus on living history, *Environmental Interpretation*, CEI, Manchester.

Centre for Environmental Interpretation (1989) Visitor centre, *Environmental Interpretation*, CEI, Manchester.

Countryside Commission (1974) *Farm and Open Days*, CCP77, Cheltenham.

Countryside Commission (1979) *Interpretive Planning*, Advisory Series No. 2, Cheltenham.

Countryside Commission (1980a) *The Public on the Farm*, Advisory Series No. 14, Cheltenham.

Countryside Commission (1980b) *Audio Visual media in Countryside Interpretive*, Advisory Series No. 12, Cheltenham.

Countryside Commission (1987) *Enjoying the Countryside*, CCP235, Cheltenham.

Department of the Environment (1978) *Recreation Management Training Committee* (Yates Committee), HMSO.

Dower, M. (1978) *Interpretation and Environmental Education*, National Parks Conference, Losehill Hall.

Environmental Interpretation (1987) *Focus on Interpretive Publication*, CEI, Manchester.

Goodey, B. (1971) *Perception of the Environment*, CURS Occasional Paper No. 17, University of Birmingham.

Hall, N. (ed.) (1984) *Writing and Designing Interpretive Material for Children*, Conference Report, CEI, Manchester.

Lindesay, W. and Dagnall, P. (1985) A review of outdoor interpretive panel materials, *Environmental Interpretation*, CEI, Manchester.

Matre, S. Van (1972) *Acclimatization: A Sensory and Conceptual Approach to Ecological Involvement*, American Camping Association, Indiana.

Matre, S. Van (1974) *Acclimatization*, American Camping Association, Indiana.

Matre, S. Van (1979) *Acclimatization*, Acclimatization Experience Center, Illinois.

Miles, C.W.N. and Seabrooke, W. (1977) *Recreational Land Management* (Chapter 10), E. & F.N. Spon, London.

Ministry and Agriculture, Fisheries and Food (1983) *Direct Farm Sales to the Public*, Socio-Economic Paper no. 8, Alnwick.

Parfit, A. (1985) Designing interpretive panels, *Environmental Interpretation*, CEI, Manchester.

Pennyfather, K. (1975) *Guide to Countryside Interpretation, Part Two: Interpretive Media and Facilities*, HMSO, Edinburgh.

Piersenne, A. (1985) Planning, scripting and siting panels, *Environmental Interpretation*, CEI, Manchester.

Robinson, T.W. (1979) *Exmoor National Park Interpretive Plan*, Countryside Commission, Cheltenham.

Swanwick, C. (1983) *Education and Interpretation for Conservation*, Conference Proceedings, Losehill Hall.

Tilden, F. (1967) *Interpreting our Heritage*, University of North Carolina Press, Chapel Hill.

Tourism and Recreation Research Unit (1977) *Information System for Recreation Planning*, TRRU, Edinburgh.

United States National Park Service (1975) *Tatton Park Interpretive Study*, Countryside Commission, Cheltenham.

Vangelder, L. (1986), Pushing the city limit, *New Age Journal*, June, pp. 33–37.

Vasey, T. (1989) Countrywings, *Environmental Interpretation* CEI, Manchester.

TEN

Finances and budgeting

Money is like muck – not good except it be spread.

Francis Bacon, On Seeming Wise *(1594)*

Having established just what is needed in order to meet objectives, the country-side manager must also be concerned with the financial implications of any proposals. This does not imply that the funding of a project or part of a project should only be considered at the end of the planning process or that the budgeting and monitoring of finances is of little importance. Financial considerations are of crucial importance to the success of any scheme and the countryside manager, like all other managers, needs an insight into budgetary processes. The management of the countryside is as much based on financial constraints as it is on other issues. Financial planning is an integral part of any management process. McAlpine (1976) identified this by suggesting 'the total planning concept generally embraces the following subdivisions: strategic long-term planning; operational planning; budgetary planning'.

The countryside manager is concerned with two concepts of financial management: fund raising or financing any proposals and controlling and monitoring budgets. The two issues are clearly related but can be considered separately. This chapter analyses these two issues and further sub-divides financial management by assessing not only the various means of directly funding work but also ways of attracting work in kind. Work in kind (or help in kind) is a main source of support for many voluntary organizations and indeed local authorities.

The 'art of budgeting' forms the basis of a profession in its own right. Accountants have their own techniques, processes and professional standards, and it is not possible to discuss these in any detail here. It is necessary for the manager to understand something of these processes so that budgetary considerations can be built into the manager's planning. Schemes which cannot be funded or financially monitored have a habit of not being started or of becoming completely unworkable. Having said this, the possibility of under-funding should not put a stop on the necessary policy or innovative scheme development which is the lifeblood of any long-term planning. It is sufficient to realize that all schemes, at some point, need to be funded and that this funding will need managing. This chapter outlines the basic rules for both parts of the process.

10.1 FINANCING SCHEMES

Much of the work of the countryside manager can be considered as trying to stop things happening: stop hedgerows being removed, stop important wildlife sites being built upon, or stop heritage landscapes from being destroyed. All of these carry with them some problems of compensation for the opportunity cost of development. This financial approach to stopping the destruction of the natural environment is at the heart of the 1981 Wildlife and Countryside Act and financial guidelines for operating the Act are given by the Department of the Environment (1983a). The problems of compensation and offsetting opportunity costs are enormous and managers should be aware that by trying to encourage landowners not to do certain things, they may be liable to pay or offer compensation.

Of greater importance to the countryside manager is the need to generate funds to undertake positive works – hedge planting, country park development, leaflet production, marketing, surveys, wages, etc. The need for funds will vary from one organization to another, as too will the mechanisms for generating funds. A professional consultancy firm may not, for example, need to raise funds to implement schemes, but will simply be concerned with project design. In this case, the consultancy's clients will need to raise the necessary finance. On the other hand, a voluntary organization, such as a country conservation trust, may be more concerned with raising funds to improve its reserves. The means available to these organizations (and others) to raise money or finance schemes vary considerably, but all of them must increasingly look to a variety of sources to fund design costs, management costs and scheme implementation costs.

10.1.1 Core funding

Core funding means various things to various individuals depending upon the organization within which they work. As is suggested elsewhere, most countryside managers presently work within the public or voluntary sectors. The concept of core funds to both these sectors is markedly different. To the local authority employee, core funding represents an allocation from the community charge resources administered by the authority, whereas for the Central Government employee, core funding comes from tax supported exchequer funding. To the voluntary sector employee, however, core funding represents a financial allocation from within the organization's central funds, mostly derived from membership fees. (Although, in the case of the National Trust, for example, the organizational resources are made up of donations and bequests.) In the private sector, core funding similarly represents an allocation from the central budget of the partnership, group or whatever organizational framework is used.

The countryside manager must therefore seek to identify the core funding that is necessary to undertake his or her work. (This core funding can be described as an allocation directly from the organization within which the manager operates.) There are some obvious 'fixed costs' which should ideally be met from within the organization – wages, salaries, rates or rent bills and other overheads. The financial resources for staff are critical for the countryside manager, because much of the work of the manager is dealing with people (farmers, the public, other professionals and the workforce) and much of the work of a countryside team requires a labour-intensive input, such as design, policy preparation and project supervision. In an ideal situation, therefore, core funding should at least seek to meet the necessary fixed costs to support the work of the countryside team.

The real life situation is usually, however, far from ideal, and many organizations are unable to identify from year to year what resources are available to meet fixed costs. This has always been the case with the voluntary sector, which relies totally on donations, membership or sponsorship, but it is increasingly the case with the public sector, where funding from community charge or national taxes is becoming less predictable. Notwithstanding these problems, it is crucial that the manager establishes, as part of the overall budgetary process, the resources that will be available to him or her on an annual basis. This will enable the manager to programme work for the following year. Equally, the countryside manager should be part of the budgetary process and should know what funding is required to run the countryside service. This will be broken down into its constituent elements, following the pattern identified within the previous chapters – rangers, interpretation, projects, policy development, production of management plans, etc. This will enable the manager to identify what resources are needed, and what core funding is required. It is unlikely, however, that all of the requirements of the manager will be met through core funding, so in addition to having an overview of costs, the manager must also be able to prioritize these requirements.

Table 10.1. *Sources of income for Oldham/Rochdale Groundwork Trust 1987–1988*

Source	Amount (£)
Oldham MB Council	22 500
Rochdale MB Council	22 500
North West Water Authority	8 000
Grandwork Foundation	25 000
Fee earning	23 000
Fund raising	10 000
Countryside Commission	20 000
Total	£131 000

Source: Smyth (1988).

The concept of core funding is becoming increasingly nebulous because of the uncertainty of continued income from any sources. An integral part of the work of any countryside manager is therefore in securing funding in order to enable his or her staff to carry out the necessary work. However, it is to be assumed that if an organization (be it a local authority, voluntary group or private practice) sees fit to employ a countryside manager, some core funds will be available.

One of the case studies at the end of this chapter looks at a unique method of core funding in the Lee Valley, London. Another interesting case is that of the Groundwork Trusts. Smyth (1988) has identified how the increasing number of Groundwork Trusts seek to cover fixed costs by establishing a core working budget. The Oldham and Rochdale Groundwork Trust, for example, like all such Trusts, prepares a business plan which projects the finances of the organization on a five-year rolling basis (a vital discipline for any countryside manager).

Table 10.1 shows the income for one year within such a programme. It is clear that all but two items (fees and fund raising) are fixed and from the public purse. These can therefore be seen as core funds to support the Groundwork Trust. This provides not only a good example of how one organization seeks to establish a core budget but also identifies that the public sector is still directly responsible for providing 75% of the funding for the Trust, despite the fact that the initial aim of Groundwork Trusts was that they would be self-financing. In this particular case the pump priming money has not been met by funding from the private sector, which means that the core funding will still need to come from the public sector. As a boost to this process, the Countryside Commission launched Operation Brightsite in 1988 with the aim of 'making practical and financial help available to companies to enable them to improve their environment to the best advantage at minimum cost'. While this is approaching a more traditional landscape design role, it is beginning to blur the edges between the rural and urban environments. The difficulty will still remain in persuading industry that a good environment is affordable: in 1987, for example, of a total Groundwork budget of £4 million only £300 000 was provided by private businesses which, as Smyth says, 'hardly suggests that business is as yet fully converted to an awareness of its civic responsibilities'.

10.1.2 Grant Aid

It is unusual if levels of core funding allow the countryside manager to undertake all that is required of the countryside service that he or she operates. Indeed, if policies and work programmes have been properly drawn up the amount of work that could be achieved will be plotted over a three or five year period. This suggests that some schemes could be brought forward to be implemented should funds be available. These 'moveable' schemes will usually be specific practical projects rather than, say, an increase in staff.

In short, core funding will allow a certain amount of work to be undertaken, so in order to achieve a greater workload, other sources of finance need to be explored and, as core funding reduces, these other sources of income become more important. This clearly makes the budgetary process less secure, but this is now an inevitable part of environmental work.

One of the commonest methods for raising extra resources to implement schemes is through grant aid. For the countryside manager, several sources of grant aid are available, and it is only possible here to make brief reference to some of the guidelines necessary to make a successful application. However the sources of grant aid have a number of elements in common.

1. The grant is only available for a fixed period of time, so is usually awarded for a specific project which has a clearly identifiable life span (or alternatively will be funded using other sources once the grant aid expires).
2. Grant aid will only be offered if the specific bid is made within a comprehensive policy statement, which will need to be agreed by the grant aiding body.
3. It is usually easier to raise 'capital' money through grant aid rather than 'revenue'. This means that practical projects, rather than the people to run the projects, are easier to finance. This is largely be-

cause a capital scheme can more easily be given a finite life – it only takes so long to build a car park or plant a shelter belt but a ranger service could run and run!

4. Few, if any of the grant aiding organizations will give money towards the upkeep of existing schemes, or the future maintenance for projects supported by grant aid. Thus, the maintenance implications of any projects need to be firmly established before the development work goes ahead.

5. All grant awarding bodies have their own internal rules which must be followed. Similarly, they too have their own policies, which they are trying to get the recipients of the grants to help implement. Any awards will therefore be a result of careful wording of applications, negotiations and, in some cases, a compromise of ideals. Where the countryside manager feels that too many strings are being attached to a grant aid then some hard decisions will need to be made.

6. Most grant aid is retrospective, and the manager must first find the necessary resources to implement the scheme and then claim grant on work done. Similarly, most grants only cover a percentage of the overall cost, so some source of extra funding is still required. Grants do not totally substitute all other funds but just help existing funds to go further.

7. Some grants are only available to public and voluntary sector schemes, but an increasing number are becoming available to the private sector. Thus an important role of the countryside manager is helping the private sector to identify the available grants which will help them to achieve their objectives.

The sources of grant aid most often available for countryside work are:

(a)   *Countryside Commissions (England, Wales and Scotland)*

Funded from Central Government through the Department of the Environment or the Scottish Office. Funds are allocated to each of eight regions to support work in a number of policy areas (see various annual reports). In 1987/88 the total allocation came to £14389 million, £9958 million of which went to the public sector. In Scotland, the grants are administered by the Countryside Commission for Scotland. Grants to cover the individual policy areas are administered in different ways and can vary in size, up to a discretionary level of 50% of the cost of a scheme (Countryside Commission, 1984a,b and 1986b,c). Because of the large amount of policy and information produced by the two Commissions, a large emphasis is placed on the policy framework for any grant bids (Countryside Commission, 1988a).

(b)   *Nature Conservancy Council*

The Nature Conservancy Council is funded from Central Government, and its principal responsibility to the Government is to provide advice and designate the natural history sites across the country. For these reasons, their grant aiding capacity is limited by and large to research and to work on sites of special, natural history importance (e.g. Nature Conservancy Council, 1984). Increasingly, however, the Nature Conservancy Council has been active in urban areas in promoting work on greening the cities. Accordingly, grants have been made available for urban/pioneering projects and research. Limits to support are not restricted to any particular percentage level, but 50% is a working figure which is worth bearing in mind. In 1987/88, the Nature Conservancy Council awarded some £1 million worth of grant. However, monies were also paid to the lessees of nature reserves or landowners managing wildlife sites. While not strictly grant aid, these monies represent payment to support work (Nature Conservancy Council, 1988).

(c)   *Forestry Commission*

The Forestry Commission was created in 1919 to restock British forests and lift the total area of woodland within Britain towards self-sufficiency. To this end, the Forestry Commission has since 1919 planted its own woodlands and through grant aid encouraged private landowners to do the same. In the early 1980s the Commission received a large amount of criticism for encouraging block planting of alien conifers. Since 1988, therefore, Forestry Commission Grant Aid has been to encourage broadleaved woodlands and farm diversification into forestry. The main method of encouraging individuals or organizations is through the Woodland Grant Scheme (Forestry Commission, 1988) and the Farm Woodland Scheme (Ministry for Agriculture, Fisheries and Food, 1988). The rates of grant support vary for land over 0.25 ha, with preferential rates for broadleaved species. Again, woodland management plans are a prerequisite for grant aid. The Farm Woodland Scheme is an extra incentive to farmers to take land out of agricultural production and to increase the British stock of trees by some 36 000 ha. The grant regime offers some incentives for sustained management by offering management/maintenance grants over forty years. Given the fluidity of the forestry policy within Britain it is inevitable that grant criteria will vary from one decade to another, so countryside managers who need to keep their funding options open need to keep abreast of changes to the Forestry Commission (and other) rules of grant aid.

Joint funding of project: Most work in the countryside needs to be funded from many sources; this project has four on the board.

(d) Department of the Environment

The Department of the Environment (and corresponding Central Government departments in Scotland) offer grant aid to private, public and voluntary organizations to undertake projects which help to fulfil government policy. It is administered under various programmes, including the Rural Development Programme (through the Development Commission, formerly the Council for Small Industries in Rural Areas) the Urban Programme (to help alleviate social, environmental, housing and economic problems in inner-city areas) the Derelict Land Programme (to reclaim derelict and degraded lands) and the Urban Development Corporation/Government quangos (established to 'rejuvenate' the inner cities). All of these programmes seek, above all else, to increase employment opportunities, but some monies are available for environmental works which might be available to the countryside manager as a source of project-based funding. Guidelines and criteria for grant aid are available from local authorities or the relevant government department.

(e) Sports Council

The Sports Council is another Central Government funded organization which seeks, through grant aid, to encourage its partners to implement schemes which meet policies approved by the Council. For the countryside manager, schemes which promote recreation in the countryside, be it on footpaths, canal banks, on water bodies or through hang-gliding facilities. The main concern of the Sports Council is, however, with more obvious sports provision, in private, public or voluntary organizations.

(f) Ministry of Agriculture, Fisheries and Food

While mainly dealing with mainstream agricultural issues, MAFF (and the corresponding Department in the Scottish Office) do offer grants for work of a non-productive nature. This includes hedgerow management, tree planting, some habitat management. The Ministry's advisory service ADAS (Agricultural Development Advisory Service) offer advice and other services to farmers and some grants for work. Changes to the grant regimes (Ministry of Agriculture, Fisheries and Food, 1989) mean that financial support is available for landowners for non-agricultural work in most areas of Britain up to 40% of the total cost.

(g) English Heritage

English Heritage (and the Welsh and Scottish Offices) are responsible for managing sites of archaeological and/or architectural importance. As many sites that are managed by countryside managers are based around such features, a comprehensive plan for a site may include proposed works to the buildings or archaeological remains. To this end, grant aid might be available through English Heritage or, alternatively, English Heritage may undertake the work itself if the site is in its ownership.

(h)   Others

There are a wide range of government agencies and departments which offer grant aid to either local government or private agencies. Indeed, increasingly Central Government is controlling local and regional finances. While this means that localized sources of grant aid are becoming fewer, there are some corresponding available sources within Exchequer resources, usually through quasi-government organizations. These include the Arts Council, Tourist Boards, Rural Development Agencies or assisted areas sources.

10.1.3   Sponsorship

The concept of sponsorship for countryside schemes is becoming more important as the environment itself becomes a more saleable item. The money made available to many private trusts and, in some circumstances, public organizations is increasingly vital to the success of either individual schemes or the whole organization.

Sponsorship takes several forms and can be used in a variety of ways. In order to make initial contacts for sponsorship, however, several key points must be considered. Firstly, it is worth pointing out the value of environmental projects – they are usually easy to see and are popular – and therefore represent a good means of a company or industry allocating its scarce resources. Secondly, local contacts with companies are far better than 'cold' letters from unknown organizations. Thirdly, all companies wish to be associated with quality so the organization concerned must have a high-quality reputation. Finally, some companies have a programme of sponsorship for environmental work rather than deal with individual projects. The Better Britain Campaign Guide (Shell, 1986) gives a list of the possibilities for raising funds.

Most companies which become involved in sponsorship will be most willing to attach their name and funds to schemes which bear some significance to their own operations. This has two consequences for the environmental groups seeking support. Firstly, the type of sponsorship should be targeted to suitable prospective sponsors and, secondly, the sponsors may well wish to provide sponsorship through materials or work in kind.

Groundwork Trusts have been established with the explicit objective of raising money through sponsorship. The number of different sources of support often leads to complex financial deals: for example, Menzies (1988) has identified how an interpretive centre of the Macclesfield Groundwork Trust 'A complex financial packaging and funding effort including more than 17 sources of cash and goods in kind enabled the Trust to save and rehabilitate the building.'

As more obvious and predictable sources of finance become more difficult to identify for many organizations, it will become important for these groups to develop fund-raising skills in order to fund both schemes and the core work of the organization. The British Trust for Conservation Volunteers, for example, survives because several of their key staff in many regions are sponsored by companies either through assisting in wages or by providing back-up support.

This introduces a more recent development in sponsorship, that of companies offering facilities such as printing, computer time, or in some cases, the time of professional staff to help the environmental organization function. Several Groundwork Trusts, for example, have accounts prepared by staff working for sponsoring organizations who, temporarily, work on the Trusts' affairs.

These offers of technical and professional help do undoubtedly assist in the progress made by some environmental groups by providing a professional edge to some facets of their operations. It is fair to say, however, that the hand-to-mouth situation generated by over-reliance upon short-term sponsorship can lead to the energies of the countryside manager being spent on fund raising rather than on implementing environmental tasks. This is clearly unacceptable in a professional sense as it keeps the process of countryside management on a purely voluntary footing, and, as we have seen, good countryside management depends largely upon a balance between public, private and voluntary initiatives.

Occasionally a sponsor may be prepared to fund a medium-term project, and to provide a large amount of money to support the work of the project. One of the case studies at the end of this chapter explores such a scheme.

10.1.4 Charging policies

Many environmental organizations, in one way or another, charge for the provision of their services. Indeed, on the assumption that 'nothing is free' all countryside managers charge their customers in one way or another for the countryside service that they provide. Local authorities, for example, are supported through rate allocations or poll tax revenue.

Whether or not any of this allocation finds its way to the countryside manager's budgets by way of core funding is a different matter. Private companies or providers or countryside facilities charge entry fees to sites, as indeed do many managers operating within the public sector. Consultants also charge professional fees for their advisory or other services. Similarly, voluntary groups such as the National Trust or local county conservation trusts not only charge for some sites but also charge for membership; indeed, the money generated through membership fees is crucial to the survival of most voluntary organizations.

Increasingly, however, countryside managers in the public, private and voluntary sectors are using charging policies either to support other sources of finance which may be dwindling or to provide core funding which may not be available from elsewhere.

Pricing policies, however they are implemented, are dependent upon several factors:

1. *How much revenue is required?*   This will depend upon other sources of income that are available to the manager, e.g. the required levels of profit as identified in the business plan and the opportunities available elsewhere on site for generating money other than through initial charging. (The National Trust, for example, run shops on most of their sites, sales from which support site operations. Similarly, many local authorities and private sector managers also run shops on countryside sites.)

2. *What is the target customer?*   The target market for the countryside service will greatly influence the pricing policy. School children, for example, will be less able to afford entrance fees for membership fees to sites or organizations yet they form one of the key target groups for many countryside managers. Similarly, many political pressures can come to play for publicly based countryside managers to provide 'free delivery' of countryside services, thereby not alienating the poorer ratepayers from access to the countryside.

3. *Market conditions.*   These depend not only on the groups and individuals that are being targeted but also on the number of comparable facilities or services, their relative pricing policies and the physical location of sites. The ability to assess the pricing policy of sites within the competitive sphere is clearly crucial to their success. Many stately homes and their attendant parklands are open to the public and pricing for these is based not only on comparable prices for other such resources, but also other perhaps different leisure facilities nearby. Whereas the process of charging for countryside sites may have been haphazard in the past, pricing is now an integral part of the marketing process and, as McKenzie (1986) suggests: 'The

image is changing as people demand high quality in their leisure time environment, and become increasingly concerned with health, activity, holidays and opportunities to learn and explore.'

Without doubt the ability of some managers to raise money through pricing policies in various ways gives them greater opportunity to deliver finances to the protection and improvement of the countryside. A farmer who charges the public to visit his farm, for example, is arguably more likely to replace or protect hedgerows on his farm because the public like to see a varied landscape. The requirement of the countryside manager is to find a balance between pricing policies and other wider socio-environmental considerations.

10.2   WORK IN KIND

The countryside manager who works for a private or a voluntary organization must seek ways of financing their work through the methods identified in the previous section. For the manager working within a local authority, however, direct financing is not always necessary and it is often possible for the countryside manager to meet his or her objectives by encouraging or agreeing with other landowners for work to be done in kind. There exist a number of powers available to the local authority to help facilitate this process. Whittaker (1979) and Countryside Commission (1988b) explore several of these powers but three particularly are of great importance to the countryside manager and are usually referred to by their section number and relevant Act title. The three powers which enable local authorities to enter into agreement with other parties to have countryside (or other work) undertaken are available under Section 39 of the Wildlife and Countryside (1981) Act, Section 52 of the Town and Country Planning (1971) Act and Section 22 of the Town and Country Planning Minerals (1981) Act. Other powers are clearly available under the Acts and guidelines identified in Chapter 3, and Clamp (1989) has explored the restrictive powers which control countryside activities (such as tree preservation orders, development control, and so on). Clearly these are of vital importance to anyone working professionally in the countryside, and this includes the countryside manager, but the Section 39, 52 and 22 powers enable the manager to implement positive schemes through other agencies to help fulfil his own objectives.

10.2.1   Section 39 agreements

A Section 39 agreement is, above all, an agreement. It cannot therefore be entered into or imposed unwillingly on either party, but once it has

Private Sponsorship: Partnership between public, voluntary and private organizations is both necessary and welcome.

been signed and finalized it is a legally binding agreement which, if broken by any party, will result in legal action being taken. Furthermore, a Section 39 agreement passes from one landowner to the next or, more unusually, if one local authority is replaced by another. In other words a Section 39 agreement will, unless the wording of the agreement says otherwise, be legally binding in perpetuity.

Appendix 4 gives a model format for a management agreement under Section 39. It can be entered into by a local authority and a landowner or the occupier of the land, and because the agreement passes with the titles of the land, it is the land that is the beneficiary, not either of the parties involved.

The agreement can be entered into 'for the purposes of conserving or enhancing the natural beauty of any land . . . or promoting its enjoyment by the public'. It is clear how the framework of a Section 39 agreement fits closely to the work of the countryside manager. More specifically, Section 39 agreements may concentrate upon a number of issues, which are as follows.

1. Imposing upon the person having an interest in the land restrictions relating to the method of cultivating the land, its use for agricultural purposes or the exercise of rights over the land, and may impose obligations on such a person to carry out works or agricultural forestry operations or to do other things on the land.
2. Conferring on the relevant authority power to carry out works for the purpose of performing their functions under the National Parks and Access to the Countryside (1949) Act and the Countryside (1968) Act.
3. Containing such incidental and consequential provisions (including provisions for the making of payments by either party to the other) as appear to the relevant authority to be necessary or expedient for the purposes of the agreement.

A Section 39 agreement can therefore be used to protect interest in land in a number of ways. Landowners may wish voluntarily to protect features on their land, and many also wish to protect these features in perpetuity – landscape features, for example. A Section 39 agreement could be used not only to protect the feature but also to allow the local authority and/or the owner to manage it for its protection. Similarly, a Section 39 agreement would allow a local authority to manage private land as a public resource, either with or without financial assistance from the private landowner. The private land can be used or managed as a country park, a picnic site or simply a landscape feature or natural history resource. The future of the management arrangement can be safeguarded through a Section 39 agreement.

While not all management agreements contain financial elements other than identifying which party will actually undertake the work, guidelines for the financial implications of management agreements have been issued by the Department of the Environment (1983a). The guidelines seek to create a framework which avoids large payments of money being made to landowners in order to protect features on their land. A Section 39 agreement was not proposed to act as a means of giving landowners financial assistance for *not* removing valuable landscape features; it was designed to be a much more positive tool than this.

A similar type of agreement to the Section 39 agreement is the access agreement which can again be entered into by landowners and local authorities, this time under Section 64 of the National Parks and Access to the Countryside Act. Appendix 5 gives a standard format for such an access agreement.

As with a Section 39 agreement, certain conditions can be placed upon access agreements which restrict types of access or allow it only at certain times of the year. However, once the agreement is in place, it does restrict the landowner in the operations that he or she may carry out which might restrict either the access or the area to which access is being permitted.

The countryside manager needs to decide whether only access to an area of land is required or whether the land in question needs to be managed – perhaps with public access explicity excluded. In any event, there exist mechanisms for entering into voluntary legal agreements with landowners to meet both of these objectives.

10.2.2   Section 52 agreements

All developments which are subject to the machinery put in place by the Town and Country Planning Acts 1977 (Section 22) can and often do have specific planning conditions placed upon them; the development can only proceed providing certain specific conditions imposed by the planning authority are met. (A specific example of this is explored in the next section.) However, a Section 52 agreement, from the 1971 Town and Country Planning Act, allows local authorities and the developers (or other person interested in the site or adjacent sites) to enter into agreements 'for the purposes of restricting or regulating the development or use of the land'. Thus a Section 52 agreement can be used, for example, to agree with a developer to create a wildlife area or a major landscape feature as part of or as a spin off of the development process. This type of arrangement is conveniently termed 'planning gain'.

At first glance, it is tempting to see planning gain as a trade off between development and a price that needs to be 'paid' to the local authority. However, the Department of the Environment (1983) has indicated strongly that 'a wholly unacceptable development should not of course be permitted just because of extraneous benefits offered by the developer'.

A Section 52 agreement can, however, be of asistance to the countryside manager in several ways, and indeed, of assistance to the developer. For example, a built development which contains within the site boundaries a site of either landscape or ecological merit could be designated in such a way as to protect and possibly enhance the important site. Such an arrangement could be accommodated under a Section 52 agreement, as too could the transfer of the site of importance to either a local authority or a local wildlife trust for sympathetic management.

Similarly, open space which forms part of a development can be enhanced as part of a Section 52 agreement and the developer under such an agreement can also make with the local authority arrangements for financial or other considerations to help with the future management of the site. A further possible way in which a Section 52 agreement might be of value to the manager is through arrangements to be made for a visitor centre or other built facility to be provided as part of a larger development. In the overall context of, say, a residential development, one 'extra' building is relatively inconsequential in terms of cost.

The most important points about the Section 52 agreement are therefore that first and foremost it is an *agreement* to be entered into willingly by both parties. Secondly, it is not a lever to convince local authorities of the validity of an otherwise dubious development, and finally the gain sought should be 'fairly and reasonably related in case and kind to the proposed development' (Department of the Environment, 1983).

10.2.3 Section 22 conditions

Section 22 of the Town and Country Planning (Minerals) Act 1981 is an example of the types of planning conditions that local authorities can impose upon developers; in this case mineral extractors. Aftercare conditions can be imposed upon the developers; these deal with the treatment of the land subject to extraction after the restoration has been completed. Restoration is itself a further prerequisite for planning approval being given for mineral extraction. This package enables planning authorities power to enforce 'reasonable' conditions before the mineral extraction begins so that an agreed afteruse is planned for and aftercare provided.

Until the early to mid-1980s the usual afteruse for such schemes was for agriculture, but with the agricultural industry being faced with problems of over-production and an inability, on its own, to support a viable countryside this has changed. Increasingly, afteruse is a balance between agricultural, natural history, access and other considerations. Clearly, in order to be 'reasonable' the local authority cannot impose the conditions on the developer to create a country park. What would in some cases be reasonable would be for a developer to create the necessary land forms and provide some of the initial planting necessary for such a park. This process has, indeed, produced many first-class resources be they as a result of gravel extractors in the south of England or coal extraction in South Yorkshire or Scotland.

The pros and cons of agricultural or forestry afteruse of reclaimed sites are given in Forestry Commission (1988), wherein the planning and legal processes of restoration are discussed, as too are some of the technical details. The planning and legal issues are similar to those which surround any development as defined in the Town and Country Planning legislation. The central issues are that the conditions are 'necessary, relevant enforceable, precise and reasonable' (Department of the Environment, 1985).

10.2.4   Other powers

Planning and other related legislation contains many powers which relate to the countryside. It is safe to say, however, that these powers are less positive than those available to the urban planner, except perhaps in some specially designated areas. These powers include the power to place conditions on development in the countryside, place tree preservation orders, be consulted on forestry proposals by the Forestry Commission and acquire and dispose of land. As has been argued elsewhere in this book, however, it is partly because of the gaps within traditional planning mechanisms that the role of the countryside manager has developed. Notwithstanding these gaps, the countryside manager who works within the public or voluntary sector can work with the Local Authority Planning Department in order to achieve certain landuse objectives. It is clearly necessary, therefore, for the manager to have an overview of these objectives so that he or she is not simply responding to individual planning cases.

10.2.5   Summary

The significance of any of these powers either to impose conditions or, more appropriate, to enter into agreements with developers or others interested in land, is that they are legitimate and invaluable mechanisms for achieving both balanced development and some of the objectives of

the manager without direct payment of implementation by the manager
or his or her staff. It is, of course, necessary for the manager or the planners to monitor the restoration conditions or the agreement which is
finalized. Therefore, it is increasingly necessary for countryside managers to have knowledge of environmentally sensitive management
not only so that managers can implement schemes through their own
resources but also so that they can monitor work undertaken on their
behalf by other groups and parties.

10.3 BUDGETING

The process of budgeting is an integral part of the management functions; indeed, the control of budgets is one of the key components of
management, as it is difficult to imagine how managers can function if
they do not have control of budgets with which to implement proposals
and meet objectives.

Budgeting is not to be confused with accountancy, audit, forecasting or profit and loss accounts. These detailed issues of organizational
finances are specialisms in their own right, but the manager also needs
to understand how his or her actions affect the wider financial objectives of the organization. For this reason all managers should work with
their colleagues to prepare their own budgets which, in turn, collate
into an overall master budget.

Depending upon the size of the organization, the master budget could
be 'synonymous' with the countryside budget. In a larger organization,
the countryside budget will be only one component of the overall budget. In any event, the countryside manager should construct (or at
least be party to the construction of) his or her own budgets.

Budgeting involves three crucial stages: constructing, co-ordinating
and controlling. Increasingly, countryside managers are having to operate within the budgetary framework not only on a project by project/site
by site basis, but in a broader business environment. Conservation
trusts, community groups, private practices and local authorities all
operate within the competitive world and must respond accordingly.
While each operation will use different detailed methods to raise finance,
control working capital or construct and assemble budgets, the three
underlying principles remain the same (Hemingway, 1984).

10.3.1 Constructing budgets

The advantages of constructing budgets carefully are many and varied:
the organization's objectives are clearly defined in financial terms; measures of performance are easily identified; an overview of an organiza-

tion's priorities can be constructed in a common language; and budgets provide a means of identifying problems before they occur (Young, 1986).

The advantages indicate that the manager should construct his or her budgets carefully. In simple terms, the careful allocation of resources to key areas of responsibility ensures that these areas of work are successfully covered in the manager's plan. Should budgets not be constructed carefully, the logical and clearly unacceptable end point would be that the manager would simply have one pot of money into which everyone within the manager's organization had access. By constructing budgets in close co-operation with colleagues and subordinates the manager can ensure that each area of work is sufficiently well identified. Furthermore, budget construction is part of the process of delegation, whereby the various managers responsible for certain elements of work are not only allocated resources but also allocated responsibility for achieving objectives, including the management of the budgets.

In constructing a budget the countryside manager must identify all sources of income and expenditure against each budget head. Most of the main areas of income were covered in the previous section and levels of expenditure vary between organizations, but the principles remain the same. Firstly, there are definitely unknown or unclear areas in income and expenditure and these should be identified during the budgeting process. (For example, grant allocations may not be finalized until the national budgets that grant aid to organizations are determined by central government. On the expenditure side, some projects may be unclear – if a private landowner needs to be convinced of the benefits of a proposed scheme.)

This uncertainty introduced a further principle of budget construction: that the standards set, including the resources allocated and the expectation of full expenditure, should be attainable. A ranger service that is suddenly allocated a larger proportion of a manager's overall budget without the necessary co-ordination or discussion will inevitably fail. Similarly, a new countryside project which is allocated too few or too many resources will also fail to perform.

10.3.2 Co-ordinating budgets

The co-ordination of countryside budgets will depend upon the range of responsibilities of the countryside manager. At its most basic level, a countryside budget should contain income and expenditure identified for all of the central elements of the managers work. This may include practical operations, a ranger service, interpretation and perhaps a specialist project. How the budgets are constructed and co-ordinated will depend upon the objectives and operational requirements of the manager.

One option may be to split budgets and co-ordinate them on a site-based basis with each site having its own overall budget, similarly segmented by the site manager. Alternatively, the countryside manager may segment the overall budget to cover the key areas as separate elements managed by, for example, a head ranger, a site manager and a project officer.

In all budgeting programmes the first stage of co-ordinating budget heads is that of identifying the limiting factor. This factor must be budgeted for first; with private or commercial operations it will usually be 'how much money can we generate?'.

The ability to raise money in the various ways identified previously represents the long-term survival of the relevant operations be they private companies or voluntary organizations. In the public sector, the level of available money is still the main limiting factor, although this money is clearly raised in a different way.

Having identified the limiting factors, the manager needs to co-ordinate the budgets in order to accommodate the limiting factor. For example, a large programme of project implementation without the necessary co-ordination and appropriate levels of funding for a ranger service or interpretation will lead to problems of site misuse or under-use. Where a countryside manager is only responsible for one element of a budget – for example, as a private consultant brought in to undertake a specialist project – it is still professionally necessary to identify shortcomings of the type mentioned here.

Co-ordination also indicates a level of commitment and co-operation between lower levels of management. Should a site manager attract extra financial support for a project, an extra work programme could throw the ranger service or the workforce into confusion.

10.3.3 Controlling budgets

There are three stages in the control of budgets, the first of which is to review the budgetary expenditure. Having identified what needs to be undertaken within each area of work and how it is to be financed, it is necessary during each financial year to monitor expenditure against each budget. The frequency of the review will depend upon the nature of the work and the level of the manager requiring the information. Budget reports should be clearly understood, up to date, accurate, varied for different levels of management and discussed by relevant managers (Parker, 1982).

The review process is only as good as the budget construction process. It is not possible to spot variances between projected costs and actual costs without well-constructed budgets. However, budgeting for environmental work can be difficult because so much depends upon the environment itself. Projects can be put back or postponed due to bad weather, or income at a visitor centre or shop is conversely dependent upon having high visitor numbers. Notwithstanding these problems, a review of budget expenditure is necessary – be it as part of running a contract or through day to day revenue management – in order to undertake the second stage of controlling budgets, namely reacting to potential problems.

Variance between budgets and actual levels of expenditure needs to be addressed and reacted to. Whether this is simply through closer monitoring for a period of time or more positively by bringing about amendments to work programmes which will bring about a change within the budgets – by finding other sources of finance for a project, or by implementing schemes quickly where, for example, a group of volunteers seems unable to provide a consistent workforce. However, a great degree of variance identifies problems not only in implementation but also in the budget construction stage. Variance in budgets is therefore not simply a reflection of failure on the part of a manager. As stressed at the beginning of this section, budgeting is a tool to allow managers to undertake their tasks more effectively. Reacting to variances in budgets is therefore part of this process.

The final stage of controlling budgets is the budget revision following the reaction from the manager to the variation between projects costs or spend and actual spend. These variations may arise for a variety of reasons in countryside projects. In commercial concerns, for example, visitor numbers may be down (or up) on projected levels or per capita spend may vary from projected levels. At a project-based level, grant aid may be refused on some projects; bad weather may have postponed planting or other practical works; or any number of problems may delay progress for the manager. While the manager can plan for some contingencies (by having penalty clauses in contracts, for example, or by identifying areas where money can be transferred should some schemes not materialize) it is inevitable that the budget review process will reveal variations. Reaction to these variations is part of the responsibility of the manager.

The size of variance is one of the factors determining what should be done. A small variation in, say, spend on a practical project could perhaps be accommodated within contingencies identified at the beginning of the budgeting process. Alternatively, levels of income may fall at the turnstile following a particularly bad period of weather only to pick up later as weather improves. More significant variations may require measures more drastic than sitting and watching. For example, should alternative arrangements be made, or should advertising be stepped up?

Budget revision is therefore a continuous process and nothing is ever written in tablets of stone.

10.3.4 The business plan

Financial planning or budgeting is a central part of the process of producing a business plan. Increasingly, as countryside managers find themselves subject to many more variables (sponsorship, visitor numbers, grant aid, changes in legislation and so on), it is clear that most countryside managers should prepare a business plan, be they based in a local authority, a voluntary sector or a private practice. McKenzie (1986), in *Putting the Funding Together*, has identified eight key components of a business plan as:

1. the objectives of the organization and the role of the countryside manager's team;
2. the management team – their individual roles and the way in which their work is co-ordinated and organized;
3. the market which the team serves, how it is to reach these markets and what competition, if any, is faced;
4. the marketing policy of the team – product, place, price and promotion;
5. the resources of the team, be they fixed assets, advantages held by the team or particular levels of expertise;
6. financial forecasts including grant aid, core funding, sales, visitor numbers and, importantly, the key assumptions of these forecasts;
7. the main risks faced by the team and how these risks can be avoided or, at worst, have their impact lessened;
8. timescale – over how long a period the business plan will operate.

A scaled down version of the business plan is the manager's work programme (Table 11.1) which represents a working document for the manager.

10.4 CASE STUDIES

The two case studies presented here offer examples of different approaches to raising the necessary finances in order to implement countryside management objectives. One is a relatively unique situation – The Lee Valley Regional Park in North London – and the other represents a major example of joint working between the private sector and the public sector. At this stage, the details of financing a purely private sector countryside site have not been given. This is because, on the one hand, at a 'pay as you enter site' the single most important issue is getting people onto the site which raises many issues outside the direct remit of this book, while, on the other hand, the two examples given here represent innovative approaches to the problems of funding work which would not otherwise be financially viable.

10.4.1   The Lee Valley Regional Park

Lee Valley Regional Park was established under a specific act of Parliament (the Lee Valley Regional Park Act) in 1966. Its conception, however, goes back to before the Second World War when the concept of a green wedge moving into north London was first considered. The actual site of this 'people's playground' was identified in the Greater London Plan of 1944. The idea again became becalmed until in 1961 the Civic Trust was commissioned to prepare a report to study the potential of the Lee Valley to become a Regional Park.

After the Park became a reality its first plans identified a 38 km stretch of land running from the northern banks of the Thames at Limehouse to Stanstead Abbots and Ware in Hertfordshire. Its width varies from 2.5 km in some places in the north to no more than the width of a track or a towpath (Sherry, 1988).

The original remit of the authority established to manage the Park concentrated upon intensive leisure facilities for formal and organized sports. It was only in the early 1980s that part of the emphasis of the authority became countryside access and nature conservation. The resultant 1986 version of the Regional Park Plan is as much concerned with footpath networks and the ranger service as with the construction of leisure, centres and roadways. Furthermore, the 1986 Plan also emphasizes the need for careful management of the Sites of Special Scientific Interest in the Park and also the need to identify and protect other sites of natural history importance.

The Park authority, therefore, has now a countryside management service in position which covers the whole spectrum of countryside management works.

The specific element of the Park with which we are concerned here is, however, the funding mechanism. The mechanism identified and put into place by the 1966 Act is, in British terms, unique. The Regional Park authority can set a rate precept againt all thirty-three of the London authorities and Essex and Hertfordshire. The amount that could be precepted is 0.42p. If all of this was collected, it would raise in the order of £10.5 million. The Park authority settles for approximately half of this figure. This core funding is augmented with admission charges and normal methods of borrowing.

Collectively these incomes establish a capital programme of works which runs at approximately £2.5 million per annum, much of it on 'environmental' projects. A fifteen-year programme of works is identified within the 1986 Plan, taking the Lee Valley Regional Park up to the year 2001. Thus the unique funding mechanisms allows a detailed work programme to be developed, central to which, since the preparation of the 1986 Plan, is an integrated countryside service.

The Lee Valley Regional Park Authority is not without its critics; for example, Turner (1988) suggests that 'the Authority suffers from on antiquated view of park planning. They see the Lee Valley as a "green lung extending right into the city" . . . It may have been true when Pitt the elder made his famous speech but no more.' However, there are others who believe, given the continuation of the method of funding provided in the 1966 Act, that by the year 2001 '. . . Abercrombie's green wedge will finally have come to pass' (Sherry, op. cit.).

10.4.2   Stocksbridge Steel Valley Project

From a swift appraisal, the Stocksbridge Steel Valley Project in Stocksbridge to the north of Sheffield, South Yorkshire, is similar to many other countryside projects. The type of work with which the project officer becomes involved is on a par with many urban fringe projects – tree planting, community action, events programmes, landscape design and management, and so on. What makes the scheme different is the mechanism for funding.

The leading impetus for the project came from Stocksbridge Engineering Steels, a private company where connections with the area go back for many generations. The company's genuine concern for their (and the local community's) landscape first found voice in a landscape plan, prepared for the Stocksbridge Steel by a private landscape consultant. The purely private venture to develop a landscape and recreational plan for land predominantly in the ownership of the steel company took a step further when the company, again at its own instigation, went into partnership with the Countryside Commission, the local community, Stocksbridge Town Council, Sheffield City Council and the landscape consultant. Core funds are provided largely by the steel company for a five-year project with other groups contributing towards elements of the master plan.

It has been suggested that, 'initiatives of this scale are rare enough in Britain and exceptional in South Yorkshire. The scheme is quite unique in having originated from private industry' (Anon, 1988). The scale of the commitment, which ranges from employing landscape contractors, developing a 'Steel Valley Walk', and employing a community woodland officer (effectively, a project officer), is indeed a unique means of funding a countryside initiative.

BIBLIOGRAPHY

Anon (1988) Stocksbridge Steel Valley Project, *Landscaping*, July/August, pp. 10–11.

Bradley, S. (1988) Designer's analysis of the Lee Valley Regional Park, *Landscape*

Design, April, pp. 29–31.

Clamp, H. (1989) *The Professional Landscape Practice*, E. & F.N. Spon, London.

Countryside Commission (1984a) *Conservation Grants for Farmers and Landowners*, CCP171, Cheltenham.

Countryside Commission (1984b) *Conservation Grants for Local Authorities, Public Bodies and Voluntary Organizations*, CCP172, Cheltenham.

Countryside Commission (1986a) *Heritage Landscape Management Plans*, CCP205, Cheltenham.

Countryside Commission (1986b) *Grants for Countryside Conservation and Recreation*, CCP211, Cheltenham.

Countryside Commission (1986c) *Countryside Grants for Voluntary Organizations*, CCP219, Cheltenham.

Countryside Commission (1988a) *Enjoying the Countryside Recreation 2000*, CCP223, Cheltenham.

Countryside Commission (1988b) *Planning Tools*, CCP227, Cheltenham.

Department of the Environment (1983a) *Wildlife and Countryside Act: Financial Guidelines for Management Agreements*, Circular 4/83, HMSO, London.

Department of the Environment (1983b) *Planning Gain: Obligations and Benefits which extend beyond the development for which planning permission has been sought*, Circular 22/83, HMSO, London.

Department of the Environment (1985) *The Use of Conditions in Planning Permissions*, Circular 1/85, HMSO, London.

Forestry Commission (1988) *Woodland Grant Scheme*, HSMO, Edinburgh.

Hemingway, J. (1984) *Budgeting*, Video Arts, London.

HMSO (1981) *Town and Country Planning (Minerals) Act*, HMSO, London.

McAlpine, T.S. (1976) *The Basic Art of Budgeting*, Business Books Ltd, London.

McKenzie, S. (1986) Putting the funding together, *Interpretation*, Centre for Environmental Interpretation, pp. 2–3.

Menzies, W. (1988) Running a small visitor centre, *Interpretation*, Centre for Environment Interpretation, pp. 8–9.

Ministry for Agriculture, Fisheries and Food (1988) *Farm Woodland Scheme*, HMSO, London.

Ministry for Agriculture, Fisheries and Food (1989) *Farm and Conservation Grant Scheme*, HMSO, London.

Nature Conservancy Council (1984) *Nature Conservation in Great Britain*, NCC, Peterborough.

Nature Conservancy Council (1988) *Annual Report 1987/8*, NCC, Peterborough.

Parker, R.H. (1982) *Understanding Company Financial Statements*, Penguin Books, Harmondsworth.

Shell UK (1986) *Raising Money for Environmental Improvements*, Macclesfield Groundwork Trust, Macclesfield.

Sherry, J.F. (1988) The Lee Valley Regional Park – Origins, *Landscape Design*, April, pp. 23–29.

Smyth, R. (1988) The affordable environment, *Environment Now*, June, pp. 15–16.

Turner, T. (1988) The Lee Valley Assessment, *Landscape Design*, April, pp. 33–35.

Whittaker, J. (1979) *Handbook of Environmental Powers*, Architectural Press, London.

Young, A. (1986) *The Manager's Handbook*, Sphere Books, London.

ELEVEN

Putting it all together

For what a many sided pleasure there is in looking at a view anywhere, not simply as a sundrenched whole, . . . but in recognising
everyone of its details by name . . . and in knowing how the various
patterns and parts fit together to make the whole. One may like the
countryside to a symphony

W.G. Hoskins, The Making of the English Landscape.

*Given the wide range of ingredients, it is not surprising that the practicalities
of countryside management vary considerably across the country. This is no
bad thing. While a common approach to, say, letting a landscape contract or a
building contract may be appropriate, the countryside manager is concerned
with far more than satisfying a client's brief. Social, cultural, economic, community and educational pressures all come to bear in the manager's decision-
making process. The case studies given throughout this text attempt to explore
briefly some examples of managers' approaches to specific issues. This chapter
looks in depth at two theoretical case studies and elaborates upon the key management issues as identified within this text: how should projects be funded?; what
type of managerial/organizational system should be used?; should rangers be
employed and, if so, on what basis?; and how will the community be involved?
While these questions can only be answered in very specific contexts, in keeping
with individual managers objectives, the examples presented here identify some
of the key decisions to be made, and provide some solutions.*

*The two case studies chosen reflect two of the many initiatives with which a
countryside manager may become involved – a countryside project area and the
management of a site.*

11.1 PROJECT AREA MANAGEMENT

Countryside projects can exist wherever the manager feels it appropriate
that a special initiative is needed to overcome a particular problem or

even a group of problems. Thus countryside projects have been established in National Parks, Areas of Outstanding Natural Beauty, National Scenic Areas in Scotland, the urban fringe around many of Britain's towns and cities and in farmed landscapes from Cornwall to Caithness.

The first decision that confronts the manager is, therefore: Why is there a need for a countryside project and what should it achieve?

11.1.1 The Nature of the problem

The decision about a project area may arise out of an array of constraints, parameters and influences. Political pressure upon local government officers to 'do something' is often matched, at a private level, by the ability of some individuals or organizations to afford to run a project, rather than the underlying requirements of the countryside.

The manager must be able (and prepared) to identify the environmental priorities and debate these alongside other issues. National patterns and priorities will clearly play a part in identifying a project area – nationally rare habitats or landscapes, for example, or nationally treasured areas are all candidates for countryside management projects.

The second consideration is whether, having identified this special area, it is felt by the manager that a countryside project is the most appropriate means of managing an area of land. It might be, for example, that an increased ranger service would overcome many problems found in some areas or, alternatively, an education programme may be a better means of contacting some individuals or groups. At another extreme it took a major shift in grant regimes and legislation for forest planting of some of Scotland's most valuable habitats to be arrested. A countryside project is therefore only one method of tackling the problems associated with an area of land.

Once the manager has identified a priority area, has established precisely what problems are to be overcome and finally, in the light of this decision-making process, has decided that a management project is the optimal way of overcoming the problems, he or she can begin to draw up the terms of reference for the project; i.e. identify what is to be done, who is to do it and how it should be achieved.

In order to examine the problems that existing or past management projects have attempted to overcome, it is best to examine the reports prepared by project officers attached to the schemes. One of the first, the Lake District Upland Management Experiment (Countryside Commission, 1976a), for example, identified that 'key features of the upland landscape were disinteresting or being replaced by newer, cheaper and less acceptable alternatives' or the Bollin Valley Management Project (Countryside Commission, 1976b) identified that 'the urban fringe is

Pressure in the Countryside: Most of Britain's countryside is accessible, at least to the private car. Where management is not active, problems can and do arise.

a rural zone where . . . uncertainty . . . has deleterious effects on traditional users of the countryside. Where vandalism, trespass or dumping
are at a maximum but also that the urban fringe is often the nearest real
countryside in which to walk the dog, picnic, ramble or bird watch.'

A clear definition of the problems will therefore give a firm base for
the proposed project by helping to refine the boundaries of the project
area, establishing clear objectives and helping to frame the job descriptions for proposed staff.

11.1.2   Establishing the project

Funding   Establishing a countryside project is a somewhat circular process. Within this context, it is useful to use the concept of 'the limiting
factor' as discussed in Chapter 10. The limiting factor will determine the
scale, scope and nature of the project. It is more than likely that the
limiting factor will be the amount of money that can be provided to fund
a special project, so one of the most important tasks for the countryside
manager is putting the financial support for the project into an appropriate package. This usually includes at least three or four sponsoring
organizations but can include upwards of ten or twelve. While it is true
that more partners in a project will probably mean more money to run
the project, it could also be counterproductive in that ten or more partners could also mean that ten or more organizations will want a say in
how a project should be managed.

The countryside manager must therefore be prepared to balance the
financial requirements with the problems of efficient management. A
brief look at the Annual Reports prepared by any of the many countryside projects which operate across the country will give some indication
of the usual number of sponsors and budgets for countryside projects.
Core funds are inevitably provided by Local Authorities, the Countryside Commission, Central Government (usually through Government
Employment measures) and less often local voluntary organizations.
Other sources for funding tend to be brought in on an individual basis –
for site-based work, for leaflets or for sponsoring training.

Lifespan   By definition a countryside project is a solution to a specific
problem or set of problems. It follows, therefore, that a project should
have as its ultimate goal its own demise – the problems having been
solved. Most environmental problems are the result of many years of
misunderstanding, decline or landscape neglect and are not going
to be 'solved' by a short-term measure. However, a countryside project
can act as a catalyst or a flagship to help bring about a change by begin-

ning to show others how things can be achieved. Countryside projects therefore usually operate for a limited period of time, often three to five years. The lifespan is determined by the scale of the problem, the size of the probject area and, perhaps more influential, the willingness of the sponsors to support (and fund) the project beyond a few years.

A finite lifespan becomes a limiting factor by putting parameters upon objectives. In order to be realistic and achievable, objectives must relate directly to the time available within which they must be accomplished, as well as the problems being addressed and the funds available.

Project management   The management of the countryside project will be determined by several factors, but should aim at providing, on the one hand, clear policies and objectives for the project while, on the other, giving the project staff the freedom to respond to the needs of the project area and to establish their own work methods. It has been suggested (Countryside Commission, 1978) that a Project Steering Group be established with representatives of the sponsoring organizations and possibly other interested and relevant groups such as the Nature Conservancy Council, the Ministry of Agriculture, Fisheries and Food (or its equivalent in Scotland) or the representatives of local landowners, private or public. While this larger group could make the steering of the project unwieldly it could also establish better links between the project and the relevant organizations. Again, the countryside manager must be prepared to weigh the options and help to decide the best course of action.

The steering group need meet no more than three or possibly four times a year, provided that the objectives, priorities and monitoring procedure for the project have been agreed. The project staff will be directly accountable to the Steering Group to whom written reports should be presented at each meeting.

At a day-to-day level, project staff will need to be responsible to a manager within one of the sponsoring organizations, and will therefore be employed by one of these organizations. The project must, however, have a clear, separate identity and not be seen as a part of any one of the individual sponsors, even the direct employer of the staff. While a separate identity may be difficult to achieve, it is vital to the success of a new, possibly experimental, project.

The countryside manager who is responsible for the day-to-day management of the project staff should establish his or her own methods for managing the project and should fill in the gaps left by the Steering Group; if outside bodies are not on the steering group, should they be invited to comment on the project?; what contacts will project staff need to make?; and how will the project fit into existing organizational and

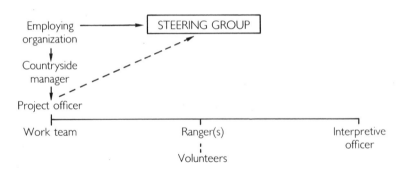

Figure 11.1 *Countryside project: possible management structure.*

management systems? A lot of work must be done by the manager before any project staff are employed.

Staffing the project   The number of staff appointed to run a countryside project depends upon the main limiting factor which, as we have seen, tends to be money. It is more usual for projects to be run by a single project officer than by a team. However, before this common model is adopted, the countryside manager must examine the optimal staffing level for the project and be prepared to look for extra resources to staff the project accordingly.

Projects were able, until 1988, to employ extra staff through the then Government Sponsored Special Employment Measure – Community Programme. This meant that work teams, rangers and other staff could be employed by the project, through the employing organization, at no extra cost to the sponsors on the steering group. Since this particular measure was removed, however, such an option is not available and this overreliance upon Community Programme has ended. This means that as staff have to be appointed from core funds, either more money needs to be provided or staff levels are reduced accordingly. Figure 11.1 shows a generalized staff structure of a countryside project of an unspecific location. Emphases could change should objectives demand it. Appendix 3 gives a model job description for a project officer for an urban fringe project which aims to address the community problems associated with countryside access as much as addressing the land-based problems.

11.1.3   Running the project

Having established the project by appointing staff and building a management structure, the countryside manager is (it is to be hoped) to be allowed the freedom to manage the project with the project officer and the other staff. Before the practicalities of project management are analysed it is necessary to discuss the nature of management of countryside projects. To quote the Countryside Commission (1978): 'The essence of a countryside management project is simplicity. It is not concerned with long, drawn out complex or abstract planning, but is designed to identify and resolve conflicts of interest through direct practical works.' This has two implications for management systems. Firstly, if the required level of practical work is to be realistic, project staff need to be given the freedom to operate as quickly as necessary to meet perceived needs. This not only implies a flexible response budget to be spent within predetermined limits by the project officer, but it also implies a relatively high degree of delegated authority. As we saw in Chapter 2, delegated authority does not negate the manager's overall responsibility but requires trust and mutual understanding between the manager and the project officer.

The second implication is that the countryside project has clearly defined objectives and its staff have clearly define roles. As a result, the project staff form a (usually) small team which needs clear and effective team management. In this context, particularly, the countryside manager's role is not to issue orders and direct instructions, but more to encourage a team performance within the pre-agreed objectives. As many countryside projects are short-term measures, it is even more crucial that an effective team is created as soon as possible by the countryside manager.

While the concepts of delegation and team efficiency are difficult styles for some managers to adopt, they are absolutely crucial in managing a countryside project, and indeed many countryside services outside the project framework.

Given these underlying principles of management, there are four areas with which the countryside manager must operate in order for the project to the efficient, namely: the work programme, project budgeting, identifying suitable tasks and finally monitoring the project.

Project work programme The process of devising a project work programme is the most important initial step for the project officer. It marks the first stage in translating the policies and objectives of the project into practical schemes. While it is an important step, however, it should not be rushed. The project officer must be prepared, along with his or her manager, to develop contacts and opinions within the project area. A work programme that is too hastily produced will inevitably contain schemes that were handed on to the project officer by outside groups or individuals, usually those on the Steering Group. While it is legitimate for the interested parties to have their own opinions, it is not legitimate to expect the project officer to implement these 'pet projects'. The project officer needs to be allowed time to develop the priorities of the project, in consultation with the countryside manager and the Steering Group. This is not a waste of time, but an inevitable part of the planning process that even a short-term project requires. Clearly, if the countryside manager can pre-empt some of this consultation work before the project officer is appointed, some of the responsibility will be taken off the project officer and more time can be devoted to scheme implementation, which is usually why a project was started in the first place.

The work programme should relate directly to the project objectives and the job description of the project officer. If the project has a range of staff, elements of the work programme will be given greater detail in the work programmes of individual staff. However, the main thrust of the project should be identified within the work programme, with the project officer being responsible for determining individual work priorities for other project staff. (In this context, the project officer is a manager, subject to the same guidelines identified for the countryside manager.)

The manager should work closely with the project officer to develop a work programme. This should form the basis of planning, practical work and monitoring. A work programme should also be capable of projecting into the years after the project. This is vital if the impetus of the project is not to be lost after the project disappears. Furthermore, a work programme will never be rigid and will inevitably be subject to many outside influences; it should therefore identify external factors which may affect the projects or which need to be addressed before a project can proceed.

Table 11.1 shows a model work programme for a countryside project. For the sake of continuity it is assumed that the project works on an urban fringe area where community consultation and community action is seen as a priority. In this respect it links closely with the job description given in Appendix 3. The table cannot identify the full range of issues for a wide range of countryside projects or, indeed, one specific project. The comments/constraints, for example, will change from month to month. Similarly, where work on private land is involved, the whims of the landowners will dictate the progress of schemes and the priorities of the project may develop as community consultation progresses. This will have implications of budgetary and time management. However, the principles involved are general and a similar exercise, required for all projects, will form the basis of subsequent management meetings. This programme will need to be agreed by the Steering Group, and 'work areas' will clearly change from project to project.

Budgetary control   Every organization has its own system for controlling the flow of money into and out of that organization. The principles of

Table 11.1. *Work programme: urban fringe countryside project (1987–1990)*

Work area	Project	Year 1 (£)	Year 2 (£)	Year 3 (£)	Comments
Community liaison	Public meetings Lectures Discussion groups	1 000	1 000	500	Hire of hall, fees, refreshments etc. Minutes of meetings Community led?
Community open-space	Housing areas Footpaths/rural landscape	5 000 1 500	7 500 2 000	9 000 3 000	Materials only Housing sites on council land. Landscape on private land – see landowners
Interpretation	Leaflets Activity days/events	1 200 500	1 200 500	1 200 500	1 leaflet per year. Check sponsorship. Community based – theatre, arts, etc.
Voluntary rangers	Advertising Support Training	750 250 200	250 200 500	— 100 200	Delegate to project ranger. Train to local authority standard Become part of authority scheme
Maintenance (years 4, 5+)					Community groups to 'adopt' sites Establish Trusts (?) Pass schemes on to local authority?

managing countryside project finances can therefore only cover the general issues, with each manager having the responsibility of understanding his or her internal systems.

Other than the basic principles of budgeting identified in Chapter 10, there are three principles that are of particular importance within countryside projects: autonomy, phasing and the type of projects.

(a) *Autonomy* One of the main advantages of a specialist project is that it can be seen to act and react independently of existing organizations. It is vital, therefore, that the project be afforded with some financial independence to match its practical independence. This is usually established initially by agreeing the work programme which the countryside manager and the project officer should then be allowed to implement. Furthermore, within each individual scheme of the programme the project officer should be able to respond quickly to problems if they arise. This will mean that the project officer will need ready access to money (obviously within previously agreed limits) without going through normal ordering, delivery and invoicing procedures. The ability of a project officer to respond quickly to, say, a broken stile or a damaged hedge could mark the difference between perceived success and failure in the eyes of the public. Similarly, if the project officer cannot buy a few packets of balloons or a tin of beans for an environmental party his or her credibility will soon drop!

(b) *Phasing* However much work has been undertaken before the project officer takes up post, it is inevitable that a process of familiarization will be needed. This suggests that, in the first year of a project, practical schemes may be more difficult to generate. While this is disappointing for some of the project sponsors, it is a necessary part of the process and should be planned for and accommodated by the countryside manager.

One of the most important implications of this is on the financial phasing of a project. Funds should be weighted towards the end of a project, or in years 2, 3 and beyond in a long-term project. This removes the pressure on the project officer to spend money too quickly. Having access to resources is important, but having access to properly planned and phased resources is vital. Table 11.1 shows the financial phasing of a hypothetical project while Table 11.2 shows an actual example, taken from the Upland Management Experiment (Countryside Commission, 1976a), undertaken between 1973 and 1976. While the levels of funding are now clearly out of date, the implications are still relevant.

Table 11.2. *Project costs for Upland Management Experiment; years 1–3 (1973–1976)*

Year	Project officer's salary, office and associated expenses	Project payments	Total	Countryside Commission grant paid
1973–74				
First quarter	1 075	169	1 244	933
Second quarter ⎱	1 853	4 000	5 853	4 390
Third quarter ⎰				
Fourth quarter	1 266	2 356	3 622	2 716
Total	4 194	6 525	10 719	8 039
1974–75				
First quarter	963	5 922	6 885	5 164
Second quarter	998	2 979	3 977	2 983
Third quarter	1 265	3 341	4 606	3 455
Fourth quarter	1 238	3 336	4 574	3 430
Total	4 464	15 578	20 042	15 032
1975–76				
First quarter	1 244	5 956	7 200	5 400
Second quarter	1 334	4 426	5 760	4 126
Third quarter	1 392	3 672	5 064	3 992
Fourth quarter	1 359	3 557	4 916	3 687
Total	5 329	17 611	22 940	17 205
Grand Total	13 987	39 714	53 701	40 276

Source: Countryside Commission (1976a).

(c) *Suitable tasks*   While special projects are established to solve specific problems or address special issues, there often exists, in those not immediately connected with the project, a belief that the project will solve a wide range of problems. This misinformation can be overcome when objectives and priorities are set, but throughout the life of the project it is necessary to set achievable objectives and not to raise false hopes. This also applies equally as well to the individual elements of the project. A small project team can often do no more than identify solutions to problems and then pass on those solutions to the appropriate agencies, private landowners, local authorities or government bodies. The project itself can only hope to achieve projects in line with its own resources. The Countryside Commission (1978) identify a range of tasks suitable for a countryside project. The list is relatively limited, and with the increased funding being made available by many sponsors for such projects, the range of tasks could well increase. As a starting point, the Commission suggest

1. clearance of eyesores;
2. landscape improvements – tree planting, small landscape projects, treatment of eyesores;
3. maintenance of landscape features – rehabilitating woods or ponds, repairing landscape features such as dry stone walls, fences, etc.;
4. improving access – footpaths, way marks, providing picnic sites;
5. traffic management – providing facilities for all sorts of transport;
6. repair of visitor-induced damage;
7. information and interpretation – for example, guided walks, notice boards, community festivals or school talks.

While this list is not exhaustive it provides a guide to the level of involvement that can be expected from a countryside project. The scale of projects, be they practical or interpretive, needs to consider the resources and time available to the project.

(d) *Monitoring* Monitoring a countryside project is necessary for several reasons. Firstly, managers need to monitor all aspects of their work in order to plot progress and confront problems. Secondly, projects tend to have an experimental nature to them, so monitoring is vital to ensure that lessons are learned from new ideas. Finally, monitoring allows projects to develop from one problem area to another, either by becoming a new project, following issues identified from previous work, or by turning the project into a mainstream programme.

Monitoring follows logically on from the process of setting objectives and work programming and relates directly to the individual elements of the project's activity areas. It is evident, however, that parts of a countryside project are easier to monitor than others. Tree-planting programmes, for example, can be monitored by the number of trees planted or recordable landscape changes, but it is more difficult to record attitude changes within a community or to record public involvement in projects. These types of human changes are long term and can only realistically be monitored over years, not months. In some parts of Britain, it may well take two or three generations for attitudes to the environment to change. In this context, the impact that a single project can have will be relatively small, but is nonetheless vital.

Notwithstanding the difficulties of monitoring certain aspects of a countryside project, it is necessary to take a measure of how objectives are or are not being achieved. The rate of feedback of this information will depend upon the manager's involvement with the project. The project officer, who is a manager in his or her own right, may require monitoring data weekly or even daily in some circumstances. The countryside manager, on the other hand, may only wish to receive the information monthly. The steering group will monitor the project quarterly or perhaps only twice yearly.

11.1.4 Summary

A countryside project represents a specific response to a specific problem or opportunity. For this reason, it requires special management. This may often be different from existing management patterns within an organization, but the countryside manager must ensure that the project does not suffer as a result of this.

Notwithstanding the originality of the project, the basic management principles of planning, allocating resources, co-ordinating and monitoring still apply. In this respect, all of the individual elements of countryside management must be brought to bear on the project and its relationship with other aspects of the manager's responsibility. For this reason, a countryside project officer should, as a matter of priority, prepare a business plan for the project and, upon the completion of the project, prepare a report summarizing the progress and management of the scheme. Only in this way can lessons be learned through countryside projects.

11.2 SITE MANAGEMENT

The management of a site is, in practice, different from the management of a project area. Whereas a site has clearly defined boundaries and allows careful and tight control within those boundaries, a project area is broader and project objectives are less easily defined. Despite the differences, however, the underlying principles of site management are similar to those of project or other management.

The overall aim of site management is inevitably to generate the optimum use of the site commensurate with the various objectives of the management. These objectives can range from reaching a predetermined level of income by charging visitors to protecting the natural history integrity of the site and avoiding habitat damage. In these cases, the former objective will be achieved by matching visitor numbers with a charging policy so as to achieve financial targets. This will not, however, necessarily lead to the overall destruction of the site, thus removing the 'countryside feel' of a site; this in turn will lead to a reduction in numbers. Many country estates are faced with the dilemma of balancing the visitor numbers with protecting the landscape and natural integrity of the site.

The second example above could well involve almost total exclusion of visitors except under tight supervision, and may well apply to a local nature reserve or a site of special scientific interest. In most cases, the balance to be struck will lie somewhere between the two ends of the continuum identified here. However, at the heart of all examples of site management lies the balance between use, conservation, interpretation and the objectives of the managers.

This section therefore covers the main topics of site management, namely: setting objectives, management planning, site control and the provision of services.

11.2.1 Setting objectives

It is paradoxical that the most crucial decisions about any site are often made before the manager of that site, who may be able to add valuable input, has been appointed. Miles and Seabrooke (1977) suggest that 'ideally such decisions should be come to in consultation with the management organization, if it is yet in existence'.

Paradoxical as it may be, setting objectives for a countryside site is absolutely vital. Site objectives will vary according to the priorities of the site developers. A conservation trust or the Royal Society for the Protection of Birds will not be necessarily interested in maximizing visitor numbers on all of their sites, whereas a private sector enterprise or a commercially run public sector enterprise will, initially at least, seek to increase visitor numbers in order to increase site revenue.

Whatever the objectives, they should be clear and concise and capable of measurement. The benefits of clarity can be identified simply as the ability to refer to the objectives as the management process operates and ask simply 'What is it we are actually trying to achieve?' If the answer is clear and unambiguous the manager can make better decisions than if the answer is vague and woolly.

Once the initial decision to develop and manage a countryside site has been taken, therefore, the site specific objectives will need to be defined quickly before any on-site work is undertaken. Management objectives will be made easier if a site layout is designed with these objectives in mind. A site catering for over 100 000 visitors a year, for example, will need to consider the implications of car parking, visitor flow, on-site entertainment and interpretation points. On the other hand, a nature reserve – the primary objective of which is to conserve a particular habitat – will clearly need different design considerations. Time and again, therefore, the countryside manager will ask 'What am I actually try to achieve on this site?'

Finally, the objectives of a site may change for a number of reasons; change of ownership, changes on site or changes in management. While objectives that change too often bring confusion, some change is inevitable and is to be welcomed. As long as it is clear that objectives are changing and all staff concerned are involved as far as possible in the process, living with change is an integral part of management which can successfully be accommodated in the management system.

All site management plans and reports should contain the management objectives for the site. Only in this way can the contents of the report, and hence the actual management of the site, be effectively underpinned. As the site is developed and as more information becomes available, these objectives may become more specific: 'Protect 10 breeding pairs of small Bitterns' for example, or 'Attract 150 000 visitors per year to the site'. However, these objectives will progress naturally from previous objectives and will therefore still be in keeping with the overall aims of the manager.

The process of setting objectives and planning the management of the site accordingly is best exemplified by the management plan, which, in itself, forms part of the process of management.

11.2.2 Management planning

Having established site objectives, the manager must plan for the allocation of resources to meet these objectives. In its simplest form this is the planning process for site management. While there will inevitably be differences between the objectives of a commercially run site and one that is run for non-commercial reasons, the process of allocating resources will still be necessary. Privately and publicly operated sites will therefore require similar processes of management, and it is these that are important rather than the differences between sites and management.

More often than not, the site manager has no choice in the location of his or her venture. This clearly has many implications on the potential for increasing visitor numbers, the quality of the habitats to be protected or the amount of material on site capable of being interpreted. For the manager this means that, as part of the planning process, he or she will need to survey not only their own site but also the wider physical and economic environment. Any planning process must begin with a review of available resources, and this includes not only available finances, manpower and 'ideas' but also the physical resources on site and this position relative to the wider environment; a site manager may have to work harder to attract greater visitor numbers (or indeed, greater numbers of migratory birds!) if a more appealing site is located nearby.

The manager must therefore survey the viable resources, and at a practical level this will involve habitat surveys, landscape surveys and

Table 11.3. National Park expenditure.

National Park authority	Conservation			Town and country planning			Interpretation and information			Recreation		
	1986/87	1987/88	1988/89	1986/87	1987/88	1988/89	1986/87	1987/88	1988/89	1986/87	1987/88	1988/89
Brecon Beacons	110.1	169.5	207.0	42.5	63.5	65.4	213.1	219.2	277.7	117.9	135.1	163.7
Dartmoor	341.7	401.3	516.4	47.3	55.1	68.9	129.2	158.7	182.1	264.7	309.3	343.7
Exmoor	247.3	313.5	414.9	55.0	59.5	68.0	146.5	185.5	270.6	179.3	191.7	217.9
Lake District	385.0	444.9	523.7	300.4	341.7	352.2	445.6	377.2	437.5	380.8	429.2	508.9
Northumberland	110.2	129.5	164.9	8.2	8.7	9.1	155.8	171.1	321.2	96.2	132.0	140.8
North York Moors	343.2	350.4	457.9	56.8	73.2	77.1	126.6	203.6	157.7	204.5	277.3	332.0
Peak District	816.8	1010.0	1237.4	187.9	215.7	264.9	360.5	369.7	407.6	624.2	677.6	806.5
Pembrokeshire Coast	205.9	157.7	245.5	93.5	99.2	119.5	299.4	178.5	196.3	118.5	387.4	326.6
Snowdonia	193.0	234.0	351.0	79.0	108.0	124.0	223.0	240.0	284.0	333.0	394.0	453.0
Yorkshire Dales	252.5	310.2	461.3	86.8	92.4	139.6	144.9	238.6	200.1	263.7	323.2	372.8
Total	3005.7	3521.0	4580.0	957.4	1117.0	1288.7	2244.6	2342.1	2736.8	2582.8	3256.8	3665.9

National Park authority	Support to local community			Management and administration			Total		
	1986/87	1987/88	1988/89	1986/87	1987/88	1988/89	1986/87	1987/88	1988/89
Brecon Beacons	12.4	20.7	31.1	224.9	248.0	269.4	720.9	856.0	1014.3
Dartmoor	33.4	51.4	67.0	332.4	345.9	379.9	1148.7	1321.7	1558.0
Exmoor	32.7	24.3	30.6	207.6	186.5	198.8	868.4	961.0	1200.8
Lake District	(−264.0)	46.7	68.6	447.0	385.7	429.1	1694.8	1957.7[1]	2213.0[6]
Northumberland	—	—	—	152.7	165.5	176.1	523.1	606.8	677.1[7]
North York Moors	5.1	6.9	9.2	357.1	365.0	362.0	1093.3	1179.0[2]	1395.9
Peak District	71.5	83.7	123.6	464.0	493.4	541.3	2524.9	2830.0[3]	3381.3
Pembrokeshire Coast	11.3	12.4	23.4	281.0	334.8	362.1	1009.6	1170.0	1275.4
Snowdonia	10.0	11.0	11.0	397.0	403.0	586.0	1235.0	1390.0	1809.0
Yorkshire Dales	3.5	10.7	15.5	371.6	400.7	395.2	1123.0	1184.0[4]	1559.5[8]
	(−84.1)	267.8	380.0	3235.3	3328.5	3699.9	11941.7	13456.2[5]	16084.3[9]

Note: Figures for 86/87 represent actual expenditure; those for 87/88 represent forecast expenditure; those for 88/89 represent bid figures.

Total less extra finance from reserves, etc:

[1]67.7 [2]97.4 [3]20.1 [4]191.8 [5]377 [6]107.0 [7]135.0 [8]25.0 [9]267.0

Source: Countryside Commission (1988)

visitor surveys. Furthermore, should cash flow or the availability be seen as a major constraint (and it usually is) it may be necessary to prepare a separate business or financial plan to identify how these financial constraints may be overcome.

The survey and review process should ideally take place as the site is developed, so that any relevant information can be used to influence site design and so that managers can operate within a purpose-built environment. Unfortunately this is rarely the case and countryside managers are more often appointed at the end of the site development process and must therefore begin to collect relevant information and assess the relative value of available resources after some of the most critical decisions have been made.

Having gathered the relevant information and matched against site objectives, the manager can begin to allocate the necessary resources. A review of financial statements usually gives a good indication of how managers prioritize their objectives. Table 11.3 shows expenditure by the ten National Park authorities in England and Wales on their priority areas of concern: conservation; town and country planning; interpretation and informatin; recreation; support to local communities; and management.

Each of these areas of concern will be given further detail by the manager and more likely by specialist staff, so that work programmes can be developed for each area of work. However, if we remind ourselves of the original aims of the National Parks as established under the 1949 Act, we can see how this financial profile fits into the objectives. The 1949 Act States that the purpose of National Park designation is to 'preserve and enhance the natural beauty of the areas . . . and to promote their enjoyment by the public' (Section 5). Further, priority in the Act concentrates upon the local communities (particularly the need to have due regard to agricultural and forestry interests), the powers of local planning authorities and the provision of recreational facilities (Sections 8–13). These objectives, vague as they are in the 1949 Act, provide the framework for management. The managers of the National Parks will inevitably have used the political objectives within the Act to develop tighter management objectives, but the financial profile in Table 11.3 still follows the original priorities very closely.

For smaller sites, the process of resource allocation will be similar, with broad aims comparable to the statements in the 1949 Act being refined into objectives for management.

11.2.3 Site control

Site control covers the wide range of activities which go under the general heading of day-to-day management. Miles and Seabrooke (1977)

Blending in: Managers need to pay careful attention to detail. Sympathetic materials, plant species and siting can lessen the impact of even a car park.

suggest that there are three areas of concern for the manager: firstly, to display the site and ensure that visitors approach and use the site as is intended by the manager; secondly, to prevent wear and tear by overuse; and, thirdly, to exclude or discourage visitors from using certain areas, either permanently or temporarily.

The ability of the manager to influence use of the site will be expressed in any one of a number of ways. The signing of the site from nearby roads, and the orientation of maps, for example, will lead the majority of visitors to approach the site in predictable ways. Similarly, the provision of paths, waymarks and strategically placed planting will influence visitor flows within the site. In practice, site control is a balance between pro-active planning and reactive repair and maintenance. While the former is clearly preferable, the latter is inevitable.

The key elements in site control whether it is pro-active or reactive is that the manager must stay in control of the use of the site. Once misuse of a site becomes well established (either through intent or ignorance) it is very difficult to remove. Thus fences need to be replaced, walls rebuilt, planting re-established and notice boards well maintained. As well as helping in the management of the site this also gives the visitors the welcoming, managed and semi-natural environment that they seek. Surveys regularly show that this is the single most influential factor in encouraging people to visit the countryside and, just as importantly, revisit the countryside (Countryside Commission, 1985).

Control of site use implies that monitoring processes need to be built into the management process. Therefore, as well as the site and its wear and tear, visitor satisfaction, habitat loss/creation, landscape improvements and interpretive programmes all require routine checking.

11.2.4 Provision of services

The services provided on site will vary according to the manager's priorities. The service may be no more than a permissive right-of-way across a nature reserve. On the other hand, the services may include a visitor centre, a ranger service, an interpretation/activity programme of recreational attractions or specialist activities for target groups.

Because of this variety the following section concentrates upon four elements of on-site provision which may or may not be present on countryside sites. Many of the services can be included within the original site design (such as footpaths or buildings) while others can only be developed after site works have been completed (such as a ranger service or a programme of activities). However, all parts of the on-site countryside service need constant and continual management and cannot simply be 'designed away' by building tougher paths or more robust notice boards.

(a)   Visitor centres

'Visitor centre' is a catch-all phrase for a building that can fulfil a variety of functions. Information centres, orientation centres, interpretation centres, heritage/history centres or a combination of all of these can be considered as a visitor centre (Barrow, 1988). It will therefore come as no surprise that the building (its design, layout, contents and management) will depend upon the managerial requirements of the building. In short, what will the centre offer to the visitor? A building which is designed to offer office accommodation to a group of rangers and site managers will be a poor centre in which to lay out interpretive exhibitions. The reason for having a visitor centre will therefore need to be established before the first brick is laid. This context will come from either the site management plan, the site interpretation plan or possibly, a wider policy of which covers a number of sites – for example, in the Broads, wherein the Broads authority have established a chain of interpretation/information centres across the area.

The reason for a visitor centre should be recorded and its objectives stated clearly; only in this way can the centre hope to succeed, especially if managerial or political circumstances change. A number of reasons could lie behind the provision of a visitor centre: to offer visitor facilities such as toilets or refreshments, to provide a shop to house interpretive displays, to act as a lecture theatre, to house staff and rangers, to provide work space for estate workers to repair small signs, or simply to find a use for a redundant building.

As a major capital and revenue commitment to a site, a visitor centre will require detailed planning and management in its own right. Barrow (op. cit.) gives a checklist for visitor centre management (cf. Figure 11.2 and Table 11.4).

(b)   Ranger service

A ranger service which is provided on site will have to fulfil a number of functions, and the management of the ranger service will vary accordingly. On a site that is important for its natural history, and on which visitor numbers are to be kept low, the ranger service may be expected to survey and patrol the site more than, say, provide educational activities. In this case, an efficient report system and thorough site knowledge is invaluable. A base for the rangers may also need to be no more than a building in which to store reports and tools for practical work.

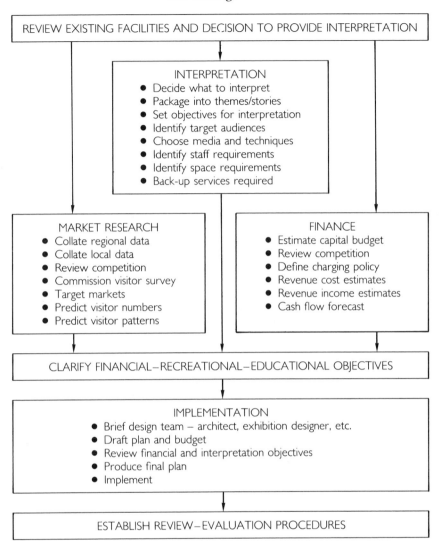

Figure 11.2 *Checklist for developing a countryside visitor centre.* (Source: *Barrow, 1988.*)

On the other hand, a ranger service on an urban fringe country park may be expected to perform and undertake a different set of duties. This may mean that community-based activities and contact with local schools are seen by the manager as being more important than, say, practical conservation work. It may also suggest that an on-site building

Table 11.4. *Usual vs preferable costs for establishing and running a visitor centre (1988 prices)*

CAPITAL BUDGET

	The norm	A better option
Interpretive plan for site*	Nil	£5 000
Architects fees*	£10 000	£6 000
Interpretive planner fees*	Nil	£8 000
Interior design fees*	£10 000	£6 000
Capital cost of building	£150 000	£130 000
Capital cost of interior exhibitions/displays	£10 000	£50 000
Capital cost of external interpretation services	Nil	£10 000
Total Capital	**£180 000**	**£215 000**

ANNUAL REVENUE BUDGET

	The norm	A better option
COSTS		
Staff	£15 000	£35 000
Temporary exhibitions	Nil	£3 000
Building maintenance	£5 000	£5 000
Services	£10 000	£10 000
Travel and training for staff	Nil	£2 000
Teaching/a/v material	Nil	£2 500
Events budget	Nil	£3 000
Marketing/promotion	£500	£5 000
Publications	Nil	£2 000
Depreciation on exhibitions	Nil	£5 000
Security, cleaning, etc.	£2 500	£3 000
Total Cost	**£33 000**	**£75 000**
INCOME		
Admissions/donations	£15 000	£25 000
Shop	£5 000	£25 000
Guided walks	Nil	£2 000
Events	Nil	£5 000
Publications	£1 000	£3 000
Refreshments (net profit)	£5 000	£5 000
	(deficit)	
Total Income	**£16 000***	**£65 000**

* Fees are approximately 10–15% of capital costs in each case. These costs are assuming an outside consultant is used.

* The poor performance of the centre is due to poor planning, limited staff, and bad layout, meaning that financially the performance is poor

† Most visitor centres do not make a profit on running costs

Source: Barrow (1988).

will need to accommodate more than the rangers themselves, and an interpretive centre may be required. This in turn suggests that some financial expertise may be required for the senior ranger at least.

Whatever the objectives of the ranger service, the countryside manager will need to ensure that the rangers operate as a team and that the service is integrated. Where a senior ranger exists, this task can be delegated, 'but the preparation of rotas, collection of site reports and so on will need to be undertaken by one of the site-based staff'. If the on-site ranger service is part of a larger ranger service, this co-ordination will have to be extended outside the immediate confines of the site.

(c) *Events and activities*

Events and activities fulfil several roles. They can provide an educational experience, a recreational experience or they can be interpretive or simply thought provoking. A site-based events programme will be dictated by several factors:

(a) *Management objectives* Some activities may not accord with the manager's objectives, and may thus not be appropriate. Similarly, other activities may bring with them new problems and opportunities for the manager.

(b) *Visitor profiles* The visitors to a site will enjoy, appreciate or understand certain types of activity more than others. This will be a result of a complex mix of their own individual and collective socio-economic profiles. The manager should therefore be aware of these visitor profiles (numbers of return visitors; number of family units/ individual visitors; ages of visitors, and so on). The manager should also be aware of the visitors' reaction to activity programmes, and this reaction should be monitored and recorded through questionnaires, observation and, if necessary, discussion with the visitors.

(c) *The site* The site may lend itself to certain types of activity because of its age, its topography or its location. Furthermore, the sensitivity of the site's wildlife will also, to a greater or lesser extent, determine the proposed activity or events programme.

(d) *Interpretation*

The first question that a manager should ask is whether interpretation is needed at all. Having determined this, an interpretive plan of the site can be prepared. Ideally, the interpretive process should start with site design, but more often than not, interpretation follows after most of

Table 11.5. *Profiles of visitors to two country parks*

	Sherwood 318 %	Rufford 306 %
Sex of respondent		
Male	66	48
Female	30	49
Age of respondent		
16–24	7	10
25–44	53	52
45–59	24	18
60+	15	17
Employment status of head of household		
Full-time employment (30+ hours)	80	75
Part-time employment (under 30 hours)	2	2
Unemployed, seeking work	3	1
Wholly retired	14	18
Non-working housewife	2	3
Full-time student	*	1
Other	*	1
Socioeconomic group of head of household		
Professional	11	8
Employers and managers	18	20
Intermediate and junior non-manual	32	30
Skilled manual and own-account workers	28	26
Semi-skilled manual workers	4	7
Unskilled manual	1	—
Unclassified/Armed Forces	3	4
First time/repeat visitors to the Park		
First visit	30	32
Repeat visit	70	68
First time/repeat visitors to the visitor centre/craft centre		
First visit	53	55
Repeat visit	47	45
Frequency of taking day or half-day trips into the country or to places of interest round about		
More frequently than once a week	12	10
Once a week	26	38
Two/three times a month	22	18
Once a month	21	19
Several times a year but less frequently than once a month	14	15
Once a year or less frequently	3	*

* Less than 0.5%

Source: Social and Community Planning Research (1983).

Contentment: At the end of the day, most people simply require the opportunity to walk, sit or spend some time in a quiet, natural environment.

the design and implementation of site works have been completed. The techniques used in interpretation will be determined by the factors identified above, namely: management objectives, visitor profiles, and the site itself. This ties in with the concepts of marketing identified earlier in the book. All managers need the base data on visitor profiles to establish interpretive programmes. Nottinghamshire County Council undertook a large visitor survey of two country parks in 1982 (Social and Community Planning Research, 1983) and established profiles of visitors (Table 11.5) with the explicit aims of increasing visitor awareness of facilities on offer, and to promote special events/interpretive displays; the research information sought to identify target markets.

11.2.5 Summary

Site management is perhaps the most easily recognizable part of countryside management, although throughout the book it has been stressed that it forms only a part of the overall process. Sites do, however, form a focus for many of the ideas, techniques and visitor management with which most countryside staff are concerned. The range of countryside sites is enormous; from large, relatively wild areas in single ownership (such as the tracts of open land owned by the National Trust in the Peak District or the Cornish Coast, or the large privately owned estates which are open to the public) to small sites (such as local nature reserves or community-managed pocket parks).

All of these sites have in common the features identified in this chapter and are therefore similar in that they all need managing. The intensity and mechanics of this management will vary, but management will always be present.

BIBLIOGRAPHY

Barrow, G. (1988) *Visitor Centres: An introduction* in *Environmental Interpretation*, October, pp. 3–5.
Countryside Commission (1976a) *The Lake District Upland Management Experiment*, CCP93, Cheltenham.
Countryside Commission (1976b) *The Bollin Valley*, CCP97, Cheltenham.
Countryside Commission (1978) *Local Authority Countryside Management Projects*, Advisory Series No. 10, Cheltenham.
Countryside Commission (1985) *National Countryside Recreation Survey: 1984*, CCP201, Cheltenham.
Countryside Commission (1987) *National Parks: Our Manifest for the Next Five Years*, CCP237, Cheltenham.
Miles, C.W.N. and Seabrooke, W. (1977) *Recreational Land Management*, E. & F.N. Spon, London.
Social and Community Planning Research (1983) *Visitor Surveys at Sherwood Forest and Rufford Park*, SCPR, London.

TWELVE

Wider Issues

To see a World in a Grain of Sand,
And a heaven in a Wild Flower,
Hold infinity in the palm of your hand,
And Eternity in an hour.

William Blake, Auguries of Innocence (1803)

Any environmentalist or earth scientist will know that no organism exists in isolation from other organisms or in isolation from its habitat. Similarly, all managers accept that their work exists within a much wider environment. This environment has physical, social, economic and political parameters, all of which impose constraints or conditions on the work of the manager. The work of the countryside manager is therefore linked to a wide spectrum of issues which both influence and are influenced by the manager's operations. This wider spectrum of issues is clearly of relevance to the countryside manager for several reasons. Firstly, political or social changes will have a direct bearing upon the work of the manager – political attitudes to afforestation or farm surpluses, for example, will in turn bring changes in public attitude (or indeed, vice-versa!) and, in the longer term, changes in the grant regimes available to fund countryside work. Secondly, the countryside manager is often interested in the wider environmental issues at a personal level: a commitment that is often deeply rooted and, therefore, tends to blur the edges of the managerial responsibilities and areas that the manager feels he or she might like to influence. While this is understandable in managerial terms it could be dangerous because it could lead to vague and unachievable objectives being set. Many countryside managers will have some sympathy for the plight of the tropical rain forests of South America and else-where; however, it is beyond the scope of most countryside managers to greatly influence such global issues through their managerial work! The problems and opportunities that exist for many managers are similar not only throughout Britain but also across the world – a situation that is summed up by the adage 'think globally, act locally'. While the manager may be operating in a small area,

the implications on that work could well be of importance nationally or glob-
ally. The links, connections and momentum built up by a number of relatively
localized initiatives are important agents in bringing about change which, in
turn, helps the manager achieve some of his or her local objectives.

The wider issues with which the countryside manager should have some
contact are almost limitless. The environment is a concept that is literally all
embracing. There are, however, some very fundamental links which lie at the
heart of countryside management, namely the relationship between countryside
management and the community, landuse reform, rural sociology and politics.
This final chapter, therefore, takes the discussion away from the detailed pre-
requisite of countryside management into the broader sphere of environmenta-
lism and some of the ways that the links may develop in the future.

In this respect this chapter acts both as a summary of the professional work of
the countryside manager and as a forecast for future trends and opportunities.

12.1 COMMUNITY ACTION

The involvement of the community in countryside management is central to the work of the countryside manager. This involvement can take
many forms – as volunteer rangers, as participants in practical schemes
or through active involvement in scheme design. Increasingly, though,
the community (however it is defined) is showing a greater desire to
be involved in protecting and managing its own local, personal area of
natural environment. The concept of community woodland, for example,
is an entirely different model than the more commonplace one of a
picnic site or a nature reserve. Community woodland is in a real sense
adopted by the community which lives near the wood and manages to
meet their objectives, not necessarily those of the manager. While it has
been stressed throughout this book that contact and consultation with
the public is vital to successful management, the concept of community
action involves much more than consultation. In many respects the
manager in such a situation will become the agent of the community
rather than his or her employer.

Many existing projects do seek to generate community involvement
(Roome, 1988, for example) but, for many reasons, can only do so at a
relatively superficial level. Firstly, until recently mechanisms for direct
community involvement have not been in position so opportunities for
community action have not been available. Secondly, and partly as a
result of this, the 'community spirit' has not been directed towards
environmental work. Thirdly, as an extension of this, communities
in many urban areas have lost much of their confidence, and even if
mechanisms for community involvement are put in place (through a

countryside project or a community-based ranger service, for example) the response can, for managers, be somewhat disheartening. This can be interpreted as a lack of concern on the part of the public but it is more probably the result of many decades of alienation both from the environment and, indeed, from the real process of decision making and direct action.

'Making community involvement work' is therefore near the top of the agenda for countryside managers for the end of the twentieth century and the beginning of the twenty-first. Other efforts and projects designed to give real involvement to communities in shaping their own environment are therefore of interest to the countryside manager; the extent to which this interest is expressed in a professional sense will depend very much on how important the manager perceives his or her own commitment to community action. Two initiatives are worthy of note for their explicit preoccupation with linking community action to the environment.

The Parish Maps Project is intended 'to help people discover more about . . . what they themselves value in their own locality' (Clifford, 1987). The discovery is translated into the creation of a map, which can be of any form – either a map in the accepted sense of any other record of the community's feelings towards its local environment.

Similarly, several new initiatives are dedicated to promoting the link between community and environment. *Holding your Ground* (King and Clifford, 1985) provides a framework for local action and conservation and *Practical Conservation* (Tait *et al.*, 1988) is a guide to nature and landscape conservation based on the management plan approach. The underlying principle behind these and other studies is that the community could and should become involved in shaping its own natural (and built) environment.

All of this assumes that the community feels motivated towards that evironment. In many areas, particularly urban areas, this motivation is lacking at the community and the environmental levels. Any attempts at raising awareness, motivation and ultimate action can be seen as closely connected to the work of the countryside manager. The chocolate box or coffee table view of the countryside may well raise awareness, but the image of peace, tranquillity or changelessness it evokes is false. Interpretation seeks to bridge the gap between awareness and motivation, as too does art. The relationship between art and nature has always been close in Britain – landscape painters' and the British novelists' 'sense of place' has been strong throughout history. Modern links between art and nature are, however, becoming more direct. Martin (1988) suggests that art in or about the environment can 'develop a deeper personal environmental awareness . . . and develop an enriched personal relationship with the environment'. Sculpture, theatre, poetry and a whole host of artistic media can serve to heighten awareness. Where the dividing line between interpretation and art falls is open to debate, but 'heightened awareness by stressing the aesthetic spiritual and cultural importance of trees and woods (the environment) leads to a broadening of popular concern and practical caring' (Clifford, op. cit.). This could be a definition of both countryside interpretation or environmental art.

The thread which links all of these apparently disparate ideas is that of community: the place that people occupy with the environment and ultimately the influence they wish to have on that environment, and it on them.

The most clearly identifiable manifestation of popular concern is political pressure. Here, too, we find several strong connections between the work of the countryside manager and political environment.

12.2 GREEN POLITICS

The politics of the environment has always been a controversial area; public-rights-of-way system and the National Parks system are just two examples of this. In the last quarter of the twentieth century, however, the concept of green politics has taken on a new face. Not only are some environmental issues dealt with at the political level, as has always been the case, but political parties themselves are now becoming increasingly concerned with their own 'green image'. Conversely, as the public become more and more informed about the problems facing the environment, they in turn are more willing to put direct political pressure on governments and local authorities to bring about changes in policy and legislation. Within the whole machinery of government and the relationship between people and politicians, the environment is moving steadily into the pivotal position. Memberships of 'conservation' organizations (such as the Wildlife Trusts, the National Trust, the Royal Society for the Protection of Birds, and so on) have been increasing steadily for many years as, too, has the membership of environmental lobby groups such as Friends of the Earth and Greenpeace. Indeed, the divisions between the public, the voluntary groups, political pressure groups and political parties have become increasingly indistinct, if they were ever clear cut in the first place.

This increased political profile for the environment will have two effects. Firstly, political parties will begin to debate and examine their own policies on the environment, and, secondly, the debate and increased pressure could bring about changes in the legislation that controls the work of the countryside manager and could also help to realign the ministerial framework that implements Central Government policy.

The internal debate about environmental policies is exemplified, at one end of the spectrum, by the Green Party, the policies of which are based upon a 'sustainable planet'. The assertion by leading political figures within the Green Party that 'the old system is bankrupt and only the wisdom of ecology will show us how to create a new economic order' (Porritt, 1984) has not gone unchallenged by more established political parties but it has helped to concentrate and fuel the debate. From the Left, for example, we hear that 'no one can lightly dismiss the struggles and figures of the generations who have fought in the labour movement for an ideal of economic and social justice . . . which in short bears a very strong resemblance to that of the greens themselves' (Pender, 1985) and also 'without working for a form of socialism we are unlikely to attain an ecologically conscious and harmonious society' (Pepper, 1986). From the Right, we learn that 'The Conservative Party has always felt that it understood and protected the countryside better than any other party' (Carlisle, 1984).

The debate will continue for a long time!

The implications of this renewed interest in the environment on the work of the countryside manager are twofold, as has been suggested: legislative and organizational.

Political movement inevitably leads to legislative change. This, in turn, leads to a different legal environment within which the countryside manager operates. The increased awareness of political parties with the environment could be viewed with a certain amount of cynicism, but there is no doubt that it should be welcomed. Just where it will lead in terms of new legislation is unclear. What is clear is that historical precedent has been towards voluntary arrangements between those who wish to manage the countryside and those who actually own it. Another historical feature of legislation is the division that is made between the various issues, such as nature conservation, landscape conservation or public rights-of-way. This has been partly a result of the voluntary sector pressure put on pre- and post-Second World War governments (Lowe and Goyder, 1983) which came from specialist interest groups, but it is also partly a result of the British reticence to integrate overall landuse issues. In other countries this is not the case, and some European partners have a more co-ordinated approach to the issues of countryside management.

Perhaps the most wide-ranging political movement which seeks to co-ordinate an approach not only to countryside issues, but to all environmental, social and, ultimately, economic issues is the Green Party. While the Green Party is a relatively young political movement, it is an increasingly popular one across the whole of Europe and beyond.

In Britain, its impact is greatest at a local level. However, as national concern for global warming, the destruction of the ozone layer and toxic dumping, for example, increases it is likely that political debate will begin to shift further towards the presently isolated stance of 'the Greens'. For the countryside manager, this could mean that many of the areas with which he or she is professionally concerned become popularized and politicized.

Part of this politicization will inevitably be reflected in a more integrated approach to rural landuse and land management. Whether such integration will come in a piecemeal fashion, with existing Central and Local Government agencies taking separate initiatives, or whether Central or Local Government will attempt to formulate comprehensive legislation and/or strategies will only emerge with time. Whatever the political outcome, the countryside manager will need to work within the legal framework provided to meet the objectives identified throughout this book. The links between political and managerial concerns will therefore undoubtedly intermesh further towards the year 2000 and beyond. This has, to a certain extent, begun with the need for Environmental Impact Assessments, now necessary on certain large developments (Department of the Environment, 1988). The Environmental Assessment is a politically demanded environment analysis of all of the implications of development. While restricted to large, predominantly power-based, projects it still marks a move towards including the environmental impact of projects into the overall cost equation.

The Department of the Environment circular was issued in direct response to a directive issued by the European Community in 1985. In this context, it marks a move towards common European standards for environmental management being developed. This will clearly have repercussions on countryside managers. The legal framework within which they and other land-based professionals operate will increasingly take on a European dimension. Similarly, the quality of the service provided by countryside managers will also become standardized across Europe. Moves towards this can be identified in BSI 5750: Part I, which in turn relates specifically to European and international standards. The process of countryside management is at various stages of development across Europe and indeed the world, as too are the types of legislative framework within which people operate. However, the British process of countryside management is a model that is transferable into a wide variety of legal systems.

The move towards a more co-ordinated European Perspective can be traced in many ways. Lee (1989), for example, examines the European (and worldwide) implications of Environmental Impact Assessment. Lee (1989) examines the changing agricultural landscapes of Europe and the Organization for Economic Co-operation and Development (1989) assess changes in overall rural policy making in the European Community and the United States.

At a domestic level, political changes is inevitable. This will affect the immediate working framework of the countryside manager. For example, it has long been suggested by some political commentators that the Nature Conservancy Council and the Countryside Commission should merge. In July 1989, the Secretary of State for the Environment announced that this process should begin despite the protestations of both organizations. As and when this process is completed the working environment of the countryside manager and his or her policy framework will have altered dramatically. For managers of the countryside these are continually 'interesting times' in the words of the Chinese proverb.

12.3   RURAL LANDUSE

Despite the growing interest in and concern for the countryside, Britain is still predominantly an agricultural country, at least in terms of land use. Running a very poor second in area is forestry, which covers some 10% of the country, as opposed to approximately 80% under agricultural use of one kind or another.

The complex cross-hatching of private land, agricultural use, specialist designation (such as National Parks, Scottish National Scenic Areas, Sites of Special Scientific Interest, and so on) and the demands for recreational access suggests that in the vast proportion of the land that is not controlled through designation, a fully integrated landuse policy is needed. This is the basis of the report by the Countryside Policy Review Panel (Countryside Commission, 1987). Addressing the issues of agriculture, forestry/woodlands, recreation and access and nature conservation separately, the report defines the need for 'the retention of the whole fabric of the British Countryside, but the enhancement of its rich diversity of landscape, wildlife and human interest'.

For many countryside managers, such an integrated approach can only be welcomed. At its most basic level, it is difficult to see how managers can prepare landscape (or other) strategies if that landscape is outside their immediate control and, in many respects, other pressures are pushing the landscape in the opposite direction to that desired by the manager.

As a means of achieving the aims of 'retention and enhancement' the Policy Review Panel suggest numerous recommendations, aimed at central and local authorities, private individuals and what are termed 'general' recommendations. These cover a wide range of points, such as 'there should be a shift in landuse away from food production' and 'public enjoyment of the countryside should rank in importance as a landuse with food and timber production' to more specific recommendations such as 'local authorities should assist in providing more countryside interpretation facilities' and 'Central Government should extend the scheme for Environmentally Sensitive Areas'.

However far Central and Local Government and private individuals wish to take to heart the call for greater integration of landuse objectives, it is clear that at all levels it will be countryside managers who deliver the service, as indeed, they are presently doing in localized areas. It has been estimated that landuse integration at the level proposed by the Panel would cost in the order of £320 million per annum at 1987 prices (as against a £2 500 million budget expenditure on agriculture, for example). This, suggests the Panel, 'would be a small price to pay for the retention of a beautiful countryside and the revitalization of the rural community'.

12.4 RURAL COMMUNITIES

Rural communities and economies have always been dynamic entities and it is wrong to suggest that the rural scene is changeless and idyllic. As Newby (1979) states, this idyllic scene is located 'only in the minds of those engaged in searching for it . . . and in the wholly misleading paintings of John Constable'.

In Scotland, for example, the Highland Clearances of the eighteenth and nineteenth centuries cannot be described as indicative of a quiet rural existence (Prebble, 1963). Similarly, in England the enclosure movement around the same time as the Highland Clearances led to wide upheaval in rural economies and communities and led John Clare the poet to remark:

Inclosure, thou'rt a curse upon the land,
And tasteless was the wretch who thy existence planned.

It is clear, therefore, that actions on the physical fabric of the countryside have an influence on and/or are influenced by social changes in the countryside. It has been argued (for example, Pahl, 1965) that incomers to rural villages are likely to have a perception of life in a rural community that is markedly different from that of the local, resident population. This new population may, therefore, have a greater desire to see local landscapes conserved than have new industrial estates or new farm enterprises. Conversely, agricultural workers who become unemployed because of the intensification of agricultural productivity may see their job prospects increase if more and better farm land can be brought into production, possibly at the expense of the landscape or natural history.

These are simplistic views, but are central to the dilemma faced by the countryside manager; as well as the physical environment, he or she operates within a cultural and social environment. As part of the basic role of a countryside manager, this cultural and social environment needs to be acknowledged and some efforts are needed to accommodate it within the decision-making process. It has been argued that the provision of countryside recreational opportunities is inherently a social process, allowing access to the countryside for some groups, but not for others. 'No piece of ground used for leisure is merely a physical place: it is always a social entity too – the filters are always there' (Emmett, 1974). This theme has been extended to cover the whole of the countryside by Shoard (1980) who argues that socio-political powers threaten not just recreational access but the landscape, the natural history and 'a very part of our national identity'.

The countryside manager seeks actively to balance many issues often within just one area of land, but he or she is part of a complex web of physical, social, political and economic changes. The activities of the manager have a two-way relationship with other processes and the spheres of influence are never clear. However, the countryside manager has a most immediate responsibility to meet the localized objectives that, hopefully, he or she has helped to formulate. At a wider level, though, the impact of other pressures can never be ignored.

12.5 SUMMARY

This chapter attempts to do no more that blur the edges of the total environment within which the countryside manager operates. This is not done to confuse, but to put the work of the manager in true perspective. Planting a small woodland, for example, can and does have an impact on a huge range of issues: local communities may be divided about its desirability; adjacent landowners may consider it to be detrimental to their crop-growing operations; local habitats may be changed; access may be jeopardized. However, if all of these potential pitfalls are allowed to overwhelm the manager, nothing would be started at all; and it has been stressed throughout that the manager is responsible for taking ideas and policies and converting them into actual programmes for implementation.

The concept of managing the countryside is still relatively new in Britain, although in effect the countryside has always been managed since man first began clearing forests and planting corn for food. It is the pressures that now prevail upon the countryside that have increased the need for more active and identifiable management, and these pressures are unlikely to disappear, even in the long term.

The countryside manager has therefore a responsibility, alongside other professionals, to address the problems and take the opportunities that emerge in modern Britain. The legislative framework may change, but there will always be a need to protect the countryside to ensure (1) that its landscape and natural history are enhanced, (2) that access to its beauty is available and (3) that people understand and appreciate its workings. Achieving this balance is at the core of the countryside manager's work. Then, perhaps, we can all greet the environment with the wonderment felt by Laurie Lee in *Cider with Rosie*:

> The June grass, amongst which I stood, was taller than I and I wept. I had never been so close to grass before. It towered above me and all around me, each blade tattooed with tiger skins of sunlight. It was knife edged, dark and a wicked green, thick as a forest and alive with grass hoppers that chirped and chattered and leapt through the air like monkeys . . . snow clouds, elder blossom banked in the sky. High overhead ran frenzied larks, screaming, as though the sky were tearing apart.

BIBLIOGRAPHY

British Standards Institute (1989) *Management Quality*, BS5750, BSI, Milton Keynes.

Carlisle, K. (1984) *Conserving the Countryside: A Tory View*, Conservative Political Centre, London.

Clifford, S. (1987) Common Ground: Where art and nature meet, *ECOS*, **8**, No. 1.

Countryside Commission (1987) *New Opportunities for the Countryside*, CCP224, Cheltenham.

Department of the Environment (1988) *Environmental Assessment*, Circular No. 15/88, HMSO, London.

Emmett, I. (1974) The social filter in the leisure field, *Recreation News Supplement*, July.

King, A. and Clifford, S. (1985) *Holding your Ground*, Temple Smith, London.

Lee, N. (1989) *Environmental Impact Assessment*, Occasional Paper No. 18, University of Manchester.

Lowe, P. and Goyder, J. (1983) *Environmental Groups in Politics*, Allen and Unwin, London.

Martin, P. (1988) Arts and environmental understanding, *ECOS*, **8**, No. 1.

Newby, H. (1979) *Green and Pleasant Land?* Pelican Books, Harmondsworth.

Organization for Economic Co-operation and Development (1989) *New Trends in Rural Policy Making*, OECD, Paris.

Pahl, R. (1965) *Urbs in Rure*, Weidenfeld and Nicolson, London.

Pender, P. (1985) Reds and Greens in Europe, *New Ground*, **6**.

Pepper, D. (1986) Radical environmentalism and the Labour movement, in *Red and Green: The New Politics of the Environment* (ed. J. Weston).

Porritt, J. (1984) *Seeing Green*, Basil Blackwell, Oxford.

Prebble, J. (1963) *The Highland Clearances*, Penguin Books, Harmondsworth.

Roome, N. (1988) Take care, *Landscape Design*, No. 174.

Shoard, M. (1980) *The Theft of the Countryside*, Temple Smith, London.

Tait, J., Lane, A. and Carr, S. (1988) *Practical Conservation*, Open University, Milton Keynes.

Weston, J. (ed.) (1986) *Red and Green: The New Politics of the Environment*, Pluto Press, London.

Site ranger –
possible job description

Main Duties   To assist in the management of countryside sites by providing visitor services and interpretive, educational and recreational information. Some practical management will be required, and an input to the management planning process will be important.

Responsible to   Head ranger/countryside manager.

Responsibilities   To provide information and interpretation to the visitors to the site and enhance the visitors' enjoyment of the site through guided walks, talks and other media.

To patrol the site to ensure visitor safety and compliance with bye-laws and the country code.

To visit schools, community groups and other bodies to promote the recreational and educational potential offered by the site.

To assist in the management of the physical fabric of the site, including waymarks, interpretation boards, fences, habitats, displays and visitor facilities.

To supervise volunteer and part time rangers when necessary.

To attempt to remove any eyesores/problems of misuse as they arise; such as litter, trespass and motorcycle use.

To survey and record information on site for inclusion in the updated site management plan.

Area ranger –
possible job description

Main Duties   To act as a point of contact for all landowners and visitors to the area, and to establish good contacts and relationships with them. To provide an interpretive and educational service to visitors and landowners and provide information for the successful management of the area.

Responsible to   Head ranger/countryside manager.

Responsibilities   To represent the employer in all dealings with visitors and local communities within the area, and foster good relationships between them.

To prepare an interpretive programme for the area aimed at promoting enjoyment and good use of the countryside.

To oversee the public-rights-of-way network and access agreements, and assist in some practical management of the paths.

To patrol the area to ensure protection for the public and restrict misuse, such as trespass, vandalism and the use of motorcycles where not allowed.

To maintain close liaison with other agencies including the National Farmers Union, the Nature Conservancy Council, the Forestry Commission, the Water Authority and local landowners.

Project officer – Possible job description (Urban fringe with many community problems)

Main Duties   To establish, through working with the community in the project area, the needs and requirements of that community and to implement environmental/access projects to meet those needs. 'Community' includes farmers, landowners and members of the general public.

Responsible to   Countryside manager/Steering Group.

Responsibilities   To establish contact with community groups and individuals to assess their countryside and recreational requirements.

To establish a work programme of schemes which will meet the communities various needs and ultimately prepare a management plan for the project area.

To lead a small workforce which will be responsible for undertaking part of the work programme.

To supervise the work of two community rangers, in conjunction with whom the project officer will seek to interpret the countryside for the benefit of the community. This will involve practical and educational work.

To supervise volunteers whenever they are involved on practical projects.

To report three times yearly, in writing, to the Steering Group and prepare an annual report of the success of the project.

To liaise with outside agencies, including the Nature Conservancy Council, the Local Conservation Trust, the National Farmers Union and the Farming and Wildlife Advisory Group.

To monitor the progress of the project.

Any other work which, from time to time, will be in the interests of the project.

Requirements　　The project officer will have a qualification and/or experience in practical countryside management and have experience of working with communities and volunteers. As the project officer will be expected to manage a project budget, the appointee will also have experience of budgetary control.

Model format for management agreement

MANAGEMENT AGREEMENT made the   day of 198   BETWEEN
(hereinafter called 'the authority') of
the first part and AB of

of the second part CD of

of the third part EF of

of the fourth part and GH of

of the fifth part (the parties of the second third fourth and fifth parts together being here-inafter referred to as 'the other parties').

WHEREAS:

1. Section 39 of the Wildlife and Countryside Act 1981 (hereinafter referred to as 'the 1981 Act') provides for the making of agreements between persons with an interest in land and a planning authority for the purpose of conserving or enhancing the natural beauty or amenity of land in the countryside or promoting its enjoyment by the public.

2. The authority is a planning authority for the area in which the land comprised in this agreement (hereinafter referred to as 'the managed land') is situated.

3. The other parties have the following interest(s) in the managed land –

   (a) the said AB is the estate owner in fee simple free from incumbrances of the managed land

   (b) the said CD is the agricultural/woodland [specify] tenant of [part of] the managed land

   (c) the said EF is entitled to [part of] the following sporting/fishing right(s) in the managed land that is to say EF has the right to [specify] on or over [that part of] the managed land

   (d) the said GH is interested in the managed land as [specify].

NOW THEREFORE it is agreed between the authority and the other parties to this agreement as follows:—

1. ANY of the other parties whose interest in the managed land is changed terminated or disposed of shall within one month thereafter give notice in writing to the authority of such change termination or disposal.

2. THE managed land is the area of land described in Part A and the extent of the interests of the other parties is described in Part B of the First Schedule hereto.

3. THE authority and the other parties undertake to use their best endeavours to [conserve] [and] [enhance] [the appearance of the managed land] [and to] [promote the enjoyment of the countryside by the public over the managed land] In particular it is agreed that [here specify – see footnote 1] To these ends the authority undertakes to carry out at its own expense the works specified in Part A and the other parties undertake to carry out [at their own expense] [at the expense of the authority] the works specified in Part B and to adopt and maintain the land-use practices specified in Part C of the Second Schedule hereto In addition the other parties undertake to allow public access to the managed land on the conditions specified in Part D of that Schedule.

4. (1) SUBJECT to sub-clauses (2) and (3) of this clause the authority shall pay to the other parties on the date of this agreement [and on the   day of   in each succeeding year] the sum of £   in   consideration of the making of this agreement provided that if any of the other parties shall terminate or dispose of his interest in the managed land or if his interest as aforesaid is terminated he shall if so required by the authority repay to the authority such proportion of any payment made to him under this clause as represents the proportion of the period after the termination or disposal of his interest as aforesaid.

(2) Any sum payable under sub-clause (1) hereof shall be apportioned by the authority between the other parties in such manner as may from time to time be agreed in writing between the other parties and [and in default of such notification in such manner as may be determined by the authority] notified in writing to the authority by the other parties.

(3) The amount payable by the authority under sub-clause (1) hereof may be reviewed and if the parties so agree varied with effect from the dates [e.g. five, ten and fifteen years respectively] from [day of] [the date hereof] having regard to any change since the date hereof or the last review date as the case may be in the effect of this agreement on the value of the interests of the other parties in the managed land or the expenditure incurred by them for the purpose of complying with their obligations hereunder. The party requiring such a review shall give notice in writing to that effect to the other parties (including the authority if not itself serving the notice) not more than twelve months nor less than six months before the dates from which any variation is to have effect as specified above [time to be of the essence of this clause].

5. (1) SUBJECT to the provisions of this clause this agreement shall subsist for a period of [e.g. twenty] years from [day of] [the date hereof].

(2) This agreement may be terminated –

    (a) by the authority by giving to each of the other parties

or (b) by any of the other parties by giving to the authority and to the remaining other parties

twelve months' notice in writing to expire at the end of a period of [e.g. six, eleven or sixteen years] as the case may be from the said [day of] [date hereof].

(3) This agreement may be terminated as it affects the whole or any part of the managed land at any time by the authority giving notice in writing to all the other parties in the event of a breach by any of the other parties of any of the undertakings on their

part contained in this agreement In the event of partial termination the amount payable under sub-clause 4(1) hereof may be reviewed with effect from the date of termination in accordance with sub-clause 4(3) excluding the provision relating to the service of a prior notice requiring a review.

(4) Termination under sub-clauses (2) or (3) hereof shall be without prejudice to any rights of the authority or of the other parties which may have accrued up to the date of termination.

6. IN this agreement the expressions 'interest' and 'land' shall have the meanings assigned to them by Section 114(1) of the National Parks and Access to the Countryside Act 1949 and references to the conservation of the natural beauty of land shall be construed in accordance with Section 52(3) of the 1981 Act.

7. THE authority shall pay to the other parties reasonable expenses [specify if appropriate] of and incidental to the preparation and granting of this agreement and any duplicate copy thereof and any stamp duty payable thereon.

8. ANY dispute arising under this agreement between the authority and the other parties (or between the other parties) shall be referred to and determined by a single arbitrator to be agreed between the parties to the dispute or in default of agreement to be appointed on the request of [any of] the party(ies) by the President for the time being of the Royal Institution of Chartered Surveyors and in accordance with the provisions of the Arbitration Act 1950 or any statutory modification or re-enactment thereof for the time being in force.

IN WITNESS whereof

FIRST SCHEDULE

Description of the Managed Land

Clause 2

Part A   All that [here insert a description of the managed land and identify it by reference to a plan to be attached].

Part B   ... [here specify the extent of the interests of the several other parties and identify them by reference to a plan to be attached].

SECOND SCHEDULE

Operation and Management of the Managed Land

Clause 3

Part A   The authority undertakes to carry out the following specified works at its own expense – [see footnote 2].

Part B   CD undertakes to carry out [at his own expense] the works shown against his interest – [see footnote 3].

Part C   The other parties undertake for their respective interests to use the managed land in the following specified ways – [see footnote 4].

Part D   The other parties undertake to allow the public to have access to the managed land as follows [specify means of access, routes, times and any other conditions agreed].

Footnote 1   E.g. the appearance of the managed land would be enhanced by reducing grazing and browsing of the semi-natural woodlands by deer or other wild animals and by farm stock in order to allow natural regeneration of these woodlands providing always that growth of the woodlands thus protected does not interfere with the enjoyment of scenery as viewed from specified vantage points.

Footnote 2   E.g. the construction of a deer- and stock-proof fence to exclude deer, rabbits, hares and other grazing or browsing wild animals from the land lying between the public road A1234 and the upper limit of the natural tree-line on the hill and to maintain the same for the duration of this agreement.

Footnote 3   E.g. the construction of internal stock-proof fences to sub-divide that part of the managed land within the deer fence so as to contain parcels of woodland where farm stock may be excluded and to maintain the same for the duration of this agreement.

Footnote 4   E.g. farm stock shall be excluded from the fenced parcels of the managed land for the first ten years of this agreement in order to encourage natural regeneration of the woodlands and may be permitted to under-graze up to half of these areas thereafter by agreement with the authority. Deer and other wild animals shall at all times be excluded from these areas.

Model clauses for access agreement

THIS AGREEMENT is made the   day of 198   BETWEEN
                                            (hereinafter called 'the authority') of
the first part and ABC of

of the second part DEF of

of the third part GHJ of

of the fourth part (the parties of the second third and fourth parts being hereinafter referred to jointly as 'the grantors')

WHEREAS:

1. Part V of the National Parks and Access to the Countryside Act 1949 (hereinafter called 'the 1949 Act') as amended and extended by the Countryside Act 1968 (hereinafter called 'the 1968 Act') makes provision for enabling the public to have access for open-air recreation to open country to which the provisions of Section 60 of the 1949 Act are applied by an access agreement made under that Act.

2. By virtue of Section 64(1) of the 1949 Act as amended by Schedule 8 of the Local Government Act 1974 a local planning authority may make an access agreement with any person having an interest in land being open country in the area of the authority whereby the provisions in that behalf of Part V of the 1949 Act shall apply to that land.

3. The authority is the local planning authority for the area [of the   national park/outstanding natural beauty] in which the land comprised in this agreement is situated such land being open country and being hereinafter called 'the access land'.

4. The grantors named as parties to this agreement have the following interest in the access land –

    (a) the said ABC is the [owner in fee simple] of the access land

    (b) the said DEF is the [tenant] of the access land

    (c) the said GHJ is the [tenant of the sporting rights/owner of a right to [   ]] on the access land

[5. The access land being in the   national park the authority has consulted with the Countryside Commission as respects the making of this agreement].

[5. The access land being land outside a national park which comprises [all or any part of or of land adjacent to] [a river] [an expanse of water through which a river or some part of the flow of a river runs] [a canal] the authority has consulted with and obtained the consent of   the authority having functions relating to the [river] [canal] to the making of this agreement].

NOW THIS DEED WITNESSETH as follows—

1. (1) Any undertaking or agreement contained herein shall be deemed to have been given or made by or with each of the grantors jointly and severally.

   (2) Any of the grantors whose interest in the access land is changed or terminated shall within one month thereafter give notice in writing to the authority of such change or termination.

2. (1) The provisions of Section 60 of the 1949 Act as amended and extended by the provisions of the 1968 Act shall apply to the access land.

   (2) Subject to the provisions of part V of the 1949 Act and of the second schedule thereto (general restrictions to be observed by persons having access to open country or waterways by virtue of part V of the 1949 Act) and subject to the provisions of this agreement any member of the public who enters upon the access land for the purpose of open-air recreation without breaking or damaging any wall, fence, hedge or gate or who is on such land for that purpose after having so entered thereon shall not be treated as a trespasser on that land or incur any other liability by reason only of so entering or being on that land.

3. The access land is the land described in the first schedule hereto and delineated on the plan annexed to this agreement but excluding any land which for the time being is 'excepted land'.

4. (1) The means whereby members of the public may obtain entry to access land shall be as [specified in part A of the second schedule hereto and] shown [   ] on the plan annexed to this agreement or as subsequently amended by agreement between the grantors and the authority.

   (2) For the purpose of securing that sufficient means of access will be available for the public the [authority/grantors] shall undertake the carrying out of the works specified in part B of the second schedule hereto with regard to the following matters:

   (a) the improvement or repair of any means of access to the access land in existence at the date of this agreement

   (b) the construction of new means of access to the access land and

   (c) the maintenance of any such means of access to the access land as are mentioned in sub-paragraphs (a) and (b) hereof.

5. (1) The authority shall at its own expense provide and maintain –

   (a) 'Boundary of open country' notices

   (b) 'Footpath to open country' notices and

   (c) suitable and sufficient notices informing persons of the restrictions upon public access at the places listed in part C of the second schedule hereto and at such other places as may be agreed in writing between the authority and the grantors.

(2) The authority may if it thinks fit provide and maintain –

(a) a map or maps showing the area of the access land and

(b) warning notices informing persons of dangers to public safety at such places as may be agreed in writing between the authority and the grantors.

6. (1) Subject to paragraphs (2) and (3) hereof the authority shall pay to the grantors on the completion of this agreement and on the   day of [and   day of   ] in each succeeding year the sum of £ in consideration of the making of this agreement. Provided that if any of the grantors shall terminate his interest in the access land he shall if so required by the authority repay to the authority such proprotion of any payment under this clause as represents the period after the termination of his interest.

(2) Any sum payable under paragraph (1) hereof shall be apportioned between the grantors in such manner as may from time to time be agreed in writing between the grantors and any such apportionment shall be notified in writing to the authority [and in default of agreement in such manner as may be determined by the authority].

(3) The amount payable by the authority under paragraph (1) hereof may be varied –

(a) with effect from the dates 5, 10 and 15 years respectively from the [day of   19 /   date hereof] and

(b) at any time in the event of any part of the access land becoming excepted land

such variation to be agreed between the grantors and the authority or in default of agreement to be determined by the Lands Tribunal. Provided that there shall be no variation under sub-paragraph (a) unless any of the grantors who desires such a variation shall have given to the authority and the other grantors notice in writing of his desire not more than 12 months nor less than 6 months before the relevant date specified in sub-paragraph (a).

[(4) In addition to any sums payable under paragraph (1) hereof the authority shall [pay the total cost/contribute a proportión not exceeding £   towards the cost] of any works carried out by the grantors in accordance with clause 4(2) hereof].

7. (1) The grantors hereby undertake that they will not do or suffer or permit to be done any work on the access land whereby the area to which the public are able to have access by virtue of this agreement is substantially reduced.

(2) The grantors hereby undertake that they or any of them will not [without the consent in writing of the authority] plough or fence or apply chemicals (other than fertilisers [lime and basic slag]) to or do or suffer or permit to be done any thing on the access land whereby any part of the access land becomes excepted land. [Provided that the authority shall permit the grantors or any of them to plough or fence or apply chemicals (other than fertilisers [lime and basic slag]) to or do or suffer or permit to be done anything as aforesaid on any part or parts of the access land not exceeding   acres in aggregate at any one time.]

(3) The grantors hereby undertake that they or any of them will not destroy remove alter or stop up any means of access to the access land or do or suffer or permit to be done anything whereby the use of any such means of access by the public would be impeded.

(4) The grantors hereby undertake that they or any of them will not provide or maintain or suffer or permit on the access land any misleading notice or [keep on the access land any animal known to have a mischievous propensity or] do or suffer or permit to be done any other thing which is likely to deter the public from exercising their right of access.

(5) If the grantors or any of them fail to comply with the provisions of paragraphs (3) or (4) hereof the authority may on giving the grantors reasonable notification in writing enter on the access land for the purpose of removing any obstruction or any misleading notice or of preventing the grantors or any of them from doing or continuing to do any other thing which may deter the public from exercising their right of access and the authority may recover from the grantors or any of them any expenditure which the authority may reasonably incur in such removal or prevention.

8. (1) The restrictions to be observed by persons having access to the access land are

   (a) The general restrictions contained in the second schedule to the 1949 Act (a copy whereof is set out in part A of the third schedule hereto)

   (b) The special restrictions set out in part B of the third schedule hereto and

   (c) Such other restrictions as may from time to time be agreed in writing between the authority and the grantors.

   (2) If the county planning authority makes a direction under Section 69 of the 1949 Act as amended by Section 1 and Schedule 3 of Local Government (Planning and Land) Act 1980 (Suspension of Public Access to avoid exceptional risk of fire) that Section 60(1) of the 1949 Act shall not have effect in relation to the access land or any part thereof the right of persons under this agreement or otherwise to enter and be on the access land or such part thereof and to use means of access thereto shall be suspended during the period specified in that direction.

9. It is hereby declared that the bye-laws made by the authority under Section 90 of the 1949 Act (as amended by the Act of 1968) and confirmed by the Secretary of State (which said bye-laws are specified in part C of the third schedule hereto) shall apply to the access land [and to the means of access thereto] [and the authority shall consult with the grantors and the Countryside Commission on any proposals to amend the said bye-laws in so far as they relate to the access land] [or means of access thereto].

10. In accordance with the provisions of Section 92 of the 1949 Act (as amended by the 1968 Act) the authority shall appoint such number of persons as appear to the authority to be necessary or expedient to act as wardens as respects land (including the access land [and the means of access thereto]) in relation to which bye-laws made by the authority are in force and shall consult the grantors as to the provision and operation of the warden service on the access land.

11. (1) Subject to the following paragraphs hereof this agreement shall have effect for a period of 20 years from the [day of   19   /date hereof].

   (2) This agreement may be terminated –

   (a) by the authority by giving to the grantors or
   (b) by any of the grantors by giving to the authority and the other grantors

   12 months' notice in writing to expire at the end of a period of 6, 11 or 16 years from the said [day of   19   /date hereof].

(3) This agreement may be terminated forthwith by the authority giving notice in writing to all the grantors in the event of a breach by any of the grantors of any of the undertakings on their part contained in this agreement.

(4) Termination under paragraphs (2) or (3) hereof shall be without prejudice to any rights of the authority or the grantors which may have accrued up to the date of the termination

12. For the purposes of this agreement –
'excepted land' means land which for the time being is of any of the following descriptions that is to say –

(a) agricultural land other than such land which is agricultural land by reason only that it affords rough grazing for livestock and excluding any strip of land adjacent to a river canal or expanse of water and land affording access from a highway to such strip of land

(b) land comprised in a declaration for the time being in force by the Nature Conservancy Council that the land which is subject to an agreement for the establishment of a nature reserve or is held by the said Council is being managed as a nature reserve or land comprised in a declaration for the time being in force by a local authority in accordance with Section 21 of the 1949 Act that the land is being managed as a nature reserve

(c) land covered by buildings or the curtilage of such land

(d) land used for the purpose of a park garden or pleasure ground being land which was so used at the date of this agreement

(e) land used for the getting of minerals by surface working (including quarrying) land used for the purpose of a railway (including a light railway) or tramway or land used for the purposes of a golf course race course or aerodrome

(f) land (not falling within the foregoing sub-paragraphs) covered by works used for the purposes of a statutory undertaking or the curtilage of such land

(g) land as respects which development is in course of being carried out which will result in the land becoming such land as is specified in sub-paragraphs (c), (e) or (f) hereof.

(h) land to which Section 193 of the Law of Property Act 1925 applies

Provided that land shall not become excepted land by reason of any development carried out thereon or any change of use made thereof if the development or change of use is one for which planning permission is required and either that permission has not been granted or any condition subject to which it was granted has been contravened or has not been complied with

'means of access' means any opening in a wall fence or hedge bounding the access land or any part thereof with or without a gate stile or other works for regulating passage through the opening any stairs or steps for enabling persons to enter on the access land or any part thereof or any bridge stepping-stone or other works for crossing a watercourse ditch or bog on the access land or adjoining the boundary thereof

'open-air recreation' does not include organised games

'open country' means any area appearing to the authority to consist wholly or predominantly of mountain moor heath down cliff or foreshore (including any bank barrier dune beach flat or other land adjacent to the foreshore) and includes any woodlands and any river or canal any expanse of water through which a river or some part of the flow of a river runs (other than a reservoir owned or managed by statutory undertakers or by a river authority or a canal or part of a canal owned or managed by the British Waterways Board which is for the time being a commercial waterway or cruising water-way within the meaning of Section 104 of the Transport Act 1968) and a strip of the adjacent land on both sides of any river or canal or of any such expanse of water of reasonable width and where a highway crosses or comes close to the river canal or other water so much of any land connecting the highway with the strip of land as would if included together with the strip afford access from the highway to some convenient launching place for small boats.

13. The authority shall pay the reasonable expenses incurred by any of the grantors them-selves and their reasonable legal costs of and incidental to the preparation and comple-tion of this Agreement and any duplicate copy thereof and any stamp duty payable thereon.

IN WITNESS whereof the   [County Council] have caused their Common Seal to be hereunto affixed and the grantors have hereunto set their respective hands and seals the day and year first above written.

FIRST SCHEDULE – Access land   [Clause 3]

SECOND SCHEDULE
[Part A   Means of Access]   [Clause 4(1)]

Part B   Access works to be undertaken by the authority/grantors   [Clause 4(2)]

Part C   Notices   [Clause 5(1)]

THIRD SCHEDULE
Part A   Restrictions contained in the Second   [Clause 8(1)]
         Schedule to the 1949 Act

Part B   Special restrictions   [Clause 8(1)]

         Including

         1. There shall be no right of access for members of the public during the period
            from   to   in any year.

         2. Members of the public shall not be permitted to bring dogs on to the access
            land unless the dogs are [kept under proper control/held on a lead] at all times.

         3. Members of the public shall not be permitted to bring or ride horses on the
            access land except with the consent of the occupier.

         4. Members of the public shall not interfere with any animal pen shed implement
            stack or other thing on the access land.

Part C   Bye-laws   [Clause 9]

Index